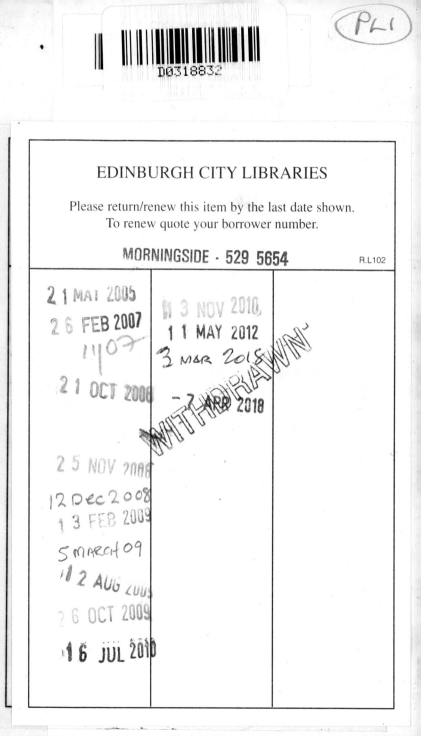

Ben A'an and Loch Katrine
(The old name of the hill is Am Binnein)

Highways and Byways
in the
CENTRAL HIGHLANDS

Highways and Byways

in the

CENTRAL HIGHLANDS

Seton Gordon

Introduction by
Raymond Eagle

Illustrations by
Sir D. Y. Cameron, R.A.

*Foreword and a glossary of place-name elements
with aids to pronunciation by*
W. J. Watson

This paperback edition published in 1995
by Birlinn Ltd,
13 Roseneath Street,
Edinburgh

First published in 1935 by MacMillan and Co., Limited.

ISBN: 1 874744 33 5

British Library Cataloguing-in-Publication Data
A Catalogue record for this book is available
from the British Library.

Cover photograph of *Loch Pityoulish*
by Colin Baxter

Designed by Gourlay Graphics Glasgow

Printed and bound in Great Britain
by Cromwell Press Limited

INTRODUCTION

In writing of the Central Highlands it has not been easy to decide on appropriate boundaries : to the west it has been easier than to the south and east, for in this direction I have taken the reader as far as the ground covered in my preceding volume, *Highways and Byways in the West Highlands*. The area covered is so great that in a single book it would be impossible to write exhaustively of it all. I have devoted considerable space to the Cairngorm area, for that area I know well and also many people visit it.

Many friends — and in writing the book I have made new friends — have helped me with the work. To name them all were impossible, but I should like to offer my special thanks to Professor W. J. Watson, a distinguished authority on Celtic place-names who, besides giving me invaluable help, has read the proofs of the book. Sir Stewart MacPherson, K.C.I.E., has given me much help in the Badenoch district and Major Stewart of Ardvorlich and Major W. Joynson of the Glassart, Aberfoyle, have given me valuable notes on their areas, as also has the late Dr. Barbour of Bonskeid who recently gifted the Falls of Tummel to the National Trust. During many of the walks in the area my companion has been Mr. F. Cameron-Head of Inverailort, whose interest in Gaelic lore and whose companionship during many days of good and bad weather have been an encouragement to me. I should like also to record my indebtedness to the late Mr. J. Mathieson, Librarian of the Royal Scottish Geographical Society, and to Mr. Walker its Secretary, in loaning me volumes to consult. The illustrations are from etchings done specially for the book by that brilliant Landscape artist, the late

Sir D. Y. Cameron, R.A., and I feel honoured that both *Highways and Byways in the West Highlands* and the present volume should have had their value heightened by his genius. His sudden passing is an irreparable loss to Scottish art. I have also to thank the Rev. William A. Gillies, D.D., of Kenmore, author of *In Famed Breadalbane*, for valuable help.

SETON GORDON

ISLE OF SKYE, *January* 1947

FOREWORD

By Professor WILLIAM J. WATSON, D.Litt. (Celt), LL.D., Hon. F.E.I.S. Formerly Professor of Celtic Languages, Edinburgh University

GOOD wine needs no bush, but since I have been asked to write a short Foreword to Mr. Seton Gordon's latest book, *Highways and Byways in the Central Highlands*, I do so with pleasure and in fact regard it as a privilege.

This valuable work is a companion volume to Mr. Gordon's *Highways and Byways in the West Highlands*, published in 1935. The author is to be congratulated on having produced a book of lasting merit, which will be widely and deservedly welcomed. It comes at a suitable time, and will be found invaluable both to natives and to visitors. Mr. Gordon has spared no pains in making himself thoroughly acquainted with the physical features of the districts which he describes, and his wide experience and great knowledge give him unusual qualifications to deal alike with topographical features, and the habits and characteristics of their fauna—birds and wild animals, as also the trees and plants, etc., found in them. In addition he gives their historical associations and the native traditions. The wealth of the latter is unfortunately diminishing rapidly with the decline of Gaelic, as also owing to the critical times in which we now are. Mr. Gordon has done much to preserve these traditions, and for that he deserves our gratitude.

Most of the place-names mentioned are, of course, Celtic, mainly Gaelic, with some instances of pre-Gaelic adopted into Gaelic, *e.g.* Kincardine (Welsh Pen-cardden, Copse-end). For these the author uses sometimes the anglicised forms, but often the native Gaelic. In the latter he deserves praise for correctness of spelling, evidently the result of care. Too often Gaelic words and phrases are mishandled, as would be the case with no other language. Unlike English, Gaelic spelling and pronunciation are mutually consistent : we have nothing like English *cough, tough, hough, though,* etc. etc. As regards Gaelic spelling, the book may be taken as a standard example.

Every chapter of the book will convince the reader of the author's thoroughness both on low ground and on the high hills. Instances are unnecessary, but special mention may be made of the treatment of the Cairngorms, mountains with which Mr. Gordon is familiar from base to summit.

A specially valuable part is that which deals with the church, *e.g.* the Girth of Dull (in Gaelic still known as *an Teagarmachd*, the Shelter). The churches of every district are carefully mentioned.

Mr. Gordon's book will live, and be the more appreciated the better it is known. Let us hope for further volumes on the same lines, to cover the rest of the Highlands.

CONTENTS

CHAPTER VIII

CHAPTER IX

CHAPTER X

CHAPTER XI

CHAPTER XII

CHAPTER XIII

CHAPTER XIV

CHAPTER XV

CHAPTER XVI

CHAPTER XVII

CHAPTER XXIX

ILLUSTRATIONS

INTRODUCTION

THE POPULAR *Highways and Byways* series, with their familiar blue covers and gold lettering, embraced Scotland, England and Wales. Most were of individual counties while others, particularly for Scotland, covered larger geographic regions.

In selecting Seton Gordon to write two of the major titles, on the West and Central Highlands, the Publisher made a wise choice. A trained field naturalist and foremost authority on the golden eagle, he had lived in both areas; his early days on Deeside where he spent many hours in all seasons exploring the Cairngorms or neighbouring Speyside. Later he moved to the Isle of Skye from where he regularly spent days or weeks in various locations from Kintyre to the Outer Hebrides. These two volumes are enhanced by the pen and ink drawings of artist Sir David Young (D.Y.) Cameron who, in 1930 was appointed King's Painter and Limner in Scotland.

Seton Gordon published twenty-five books and hundreds of articles on the Highlands and Islands. He was unique in many ways, not the least that he wore the kilt as his everyday dress, summer and winter. The uniqueness of his writing lay in his ability to transport the reader so that they saw the world through his all-discerning eyes; eyes that were still strong and unaided when he died aged ninety-one in 1977.

This volume on the Central Highlands was originally planned to be published in 1939 but the war intervened and it was not until 1948 that it was released. In the meantime Seton Gordon was not idle. He continued to write nature articles for several magazines and newspapers, produced two more books for other publishers and, despite wartime travel restrictions, he spent as much time as possible adding to his already prodigious knowledge of Highland history. One unusual wartime request came from the Royal Air Force Coastal command and the Royal Navy to give lectures oncoastal birdlife. To become adept at identifying seabirds added some interest to men stationed on remote airfields or at sea.

In his early life Seton Gordon spent a great deal of time exploring the easter fringe of the Central Highlands, especially the Cairngorms. These hills do not have peaked summits, instead their tops are a series of plateaus where a variety of alpine flora can be found. It was on these tops that he learned natural history well enough to graduate with honours in the subject from Exeter College, Oxford in 1913. There is a pass through the Cairngorms known as the Lairig Ghru and Seton Gordon knew it well from constantly traversing it during his long life. He sometimes walked it at night for an unusual reason; he had a great knowledge of Highland bagpipe music and often judged at piping competitions. During August and September when the Highland Gatherings took place he regularly judged at the Aboyne and Braemar Gatherings and would then walk over the pass to Speyside to be there to judge the next day. He was seldom successful in persuading other piping judges to join his nocturnal walk!

The City of Stirling is known as the Gateway to the Highlands and northward from here the visitor becomes more aware of the changing landscape. Stirling Castle, which sits high above the town was made famous by the film "Tunes of Glory" and there is a panoramic view from the castle ramparts. The southern section of the Central Highlands includes Loch Lomond and the Trossachs. A fitting historical figure mentioned by Seton Gordon early in this volume is Rob Roy MacGregor, whose exploits took place largely in this area. He was a living, breathing Highland hero, though it is doubtful if many would have agreed during his lifetime. He was an outlaw, as were many of his clan. Rob Roy's grave is in the Braes of Balquhider west of Lochearn. The drive from here to Perth via Lochearnhead is through some of the finest glens in the region.

The eastern boundary of the Central Highlands is at Dinnett in the Dee valley, but still included is the village of Braemar, where the world famous Braemar Highland Gathering takes place. Many locals fondly recall Seton Gordon leaning forward intently to catch each piper's notes through his hearing aid.

Close to Dinnett is Aboyne where he spent much of his childhood and began to study the birds that inhabit the rolling farmland surrounding the town. His father, William, commuted daily to Aberdeen, where he was the longest-serving town clerk, dying in office in 1923 at the age of eighty-five.

The estates to which Seton Gordon refers in his historical accounts are owned by the same families today. Because he grew up in the area he knew, in some cases, up to three generations over the years. The estate of Rothiemurchus, near Aviemore in the Spey Valley has been in the Grant family since the 16th Century and in the days of inter-clan rivalry their lands were not immune from attack by neighbouring clans. Rothiemurchus is in a wonderful setting, with the Cairngorms rising to the east and much of land covered by Scots pine forests, with their red bark and irregular shaped tops.

Public access is provided to Loch an Eilein which has a visitor's centre and a nature path to be enjoyed along the banks. The osprey was for many years extinct in the region but has now make a strong comeback and is nesting once again. In the middle of the loch is a picturesque ancient fortress which has featured in the Grants of Rothiemurchus history.

The Central Highlands is a region to be enjoyed and many places will make the visitor want to linger. Tarry awhile because there is much to learn through the pages of this book and its companion on the West Highlands.

RAYMOND EAGLE, *F.S.A. Scot.*,
West Vancouver, B.C., Canada, 1995

Lake of Menteith

CHAPTER I

AT THE GATEWAY

Across the Lake of Menteith, guarding the southern gateway to the Central Highlands, the west wind blew softly over waters dark beneath a winter's sky. Deeply snow-clad were the noble cone of Ben Lomond and the more broken slopes of Ben Venue, where drifting snow, caught up on the wind, showed soot-grey like a cloud of smoke against the steel-green and stormy heavens. We rowed out, my friend and I, across the waters of the lake to the small, hallowed isle of Inchmahome, and at once were in the friendly keeping of the Spirit of the Past.

No other sheet of Scottish water has so romantic a history as the Lake of Menteith. Is it not strange that this loch should be the only " lake " in all Scotland ? Can it be that its placidity and its immediate surroundings, which are Lowland rather than Highland, have caused the word " lake " to be substituted for the earlier term " loch " ? A more likely explanation is that " lake " is the translation of the word *lacus* occurring in some

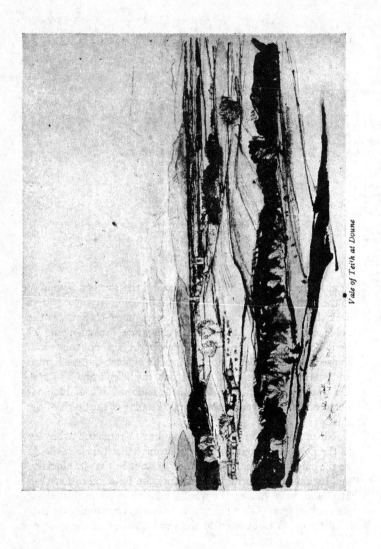

Vale of Teith at Doune

Latin manuscript, or charter of the monks. Sir Walter Scott wrote of the *Loch* of Menteith, but even that name is comparatively recent, for Graham of Duchray was, in the year 1724, the first writer to name it so. Before that, the name of the Lake of Menteith was the Loch of Inchmahome. Professor W. J. Watson tells me that Inchmahome was in early Gaelic Innis mo Cholmaig, the Isle of my Colmoc, and that the day

Inchmahome, Menteith

of St. Colmoc of Inchmahome was June 7. In Timothy Pont's map of the Province of Lennox, published in 1654, the name appears as Loch Inche Mahumo, and in the rental of the feu-duties of Inchmahome in 1646 the name is written as the Loch of Inchemahummoe.

Slowly (for the wind was adverse) we approached the sombre, wooded isle of Inchmahome, with its Gothic priory church, its ancient recumbent grave-stones and its scarcely less venerable guardian trees. The traveller, on setting foot upon this low isle, feels the ancient sanctity of the place ; he is on the instant transported from the present to a past age. The trees whisper to him old tunes of hospitality. He sees ancient grave-stones which bear record of an art long since lost. Some of these stones have been brought recently under cover by the Ancient Monuments experts of the Office of Works. A remarkable stone commemorates the first Stewart Earl of Menteith and his Countess Mary, who died near the close of the thirteenth century. The Countess is clad in a beautifully sculptured flowing garment, and her left arm lovingly encircles the neck of the Earl. His right arm is across her shoulder, and his left is laid across her waist. He wears a suit of armour covered with a surcoat, and his legs are crossed below the knee, showing that he was a Crusader. On his left shoulder he bears a large triangular shield, charged with his coat of arms.

Near this stone lies another of the same period. It was found buried in the ground, where it may have been contemptuously hurled long ago, and the figure on the stone, lying face-downwards through the centuries, has been preserved in a remarkable manner. This figure is believed to represent the Stewart who changed his name to Sir John Menteith (1392) and who was perhaps the False Menteith who betrayed Wallace. The sword-blade carried by this figure carved on the stone is missing : it is known to have been of metal, and the base of the sword-hilt of lead. The shield is finely portrayed, and the arms upon it are clearly shown, as are also the buckle and strap above the surcoat.

Within the choir lie two ancient grave-stones, one to the memory of Sir John Drummond, who died about the year 1300 and who, according to tradition, gifted the lands of Cardross to the Priory of Inchmahome. Here, too, is seen the recumbent stone to the memory of that romantic figure, Robert Bontine Cunninghame Graham, author and connoisseur of art. The lettering and the appearance of this stone are in perfect taste. Cunninghame Graham lies beside the site of the old sycamore tree within the priory, where, in the early days of his boyhood, the osprey had her home. At that time ospreys nested on Loch Lomond also, but now there is not a single osprey's nest in all Scotland.

The old trees of Inchmahome add grandeur to the isle. Splendid Spanish chestnut and walnut trees many centuries old show the beauty, the dignity and the poetry of age in their gnarled trunks and wide-spreading branches. They may have been saplings when Robert the Bruce visited the isle : they were certainly grown trees when Queen Mary, then a little girl less than five years old, lived for three weeks on the island in the charge of the monks, and planted the old boxwood tree that is still, almost four hundred years later, in full vigour of growth. Other memorials of the young Queen's visit are her garden and her bower — the latter by the shore of Inchmahome, over against the sister isle of Inchtalla, which throws back the human voice. In this small bower, looking out on to the hills, the young child Queen played happily, and the monks were no doubt exceedingly proud to have her among them, and loved her for the charm of her personality, even at that early age apparent to all who saw her. The monks fed her on the choicest morsels of the fish of the lake. It would be interesting to know whether the practice of fishing with geese was known in the time of the monks. A graphic account of this fishing was published in the year 1797 :

The manner of catching this fish [pike] is somewhat novel and diverting. On the islands a number of geese are collected from the farmers who occupy the surrounding banks of the lake. After baited lines of two or three feet in length are attached to the legs of these animals, they are driven into the water. Steering naturally homeward, in different directions, the bait is soon swallowed. A violent and often tedious struggle ensues ; in which, however, the geese at length prevail, though often much exhausted before they reach the shore.

It is believed, however, that this account is an exaggerated one ; that it was never actually a practice, but that occasionally a fish hunt of this kind was organised as a day's sport.

Inchtalla was the residence of the Earls of Menteith, and on a small island near, it is said that the Earls were in the habit of keeping their hounds, hence the name Inchcuan (Innis nan Con), Dogs' Island.

There is a story that one of the Earls of Menteith was entertaining a company in the hall of his island fortress when it was discovered with dismay that the supply of liquor was running low. The butler in trepidation conveyed the news to the Earl, who ordered him to set off at once for Stirling for a fresh supply. The butler, taking an empty cask, rowed himself to the shore, wondering how it might be possible for him to make the journey to Stirling, obtain more drink, and return with it before the feast was over. As he neared the margin of the loch, the butler saw two witches among the reeds. As he watched them, each cut a reed for herself and, mounted on the rushes, rose into the air. The butler, having overheard the words they used before setting forth, himself cut a reed, and grasping it firmly in the appropriate attitude and shouting the magic words " Hae wi' ye ! " found himself also in the air, and steering a similar course to the witches, whom he saw some distance ahead of him. They all reached the palace of the King of France, and the butler, having kept hold of the empty cask during his flight, at once replenished it with the best of the royal wine. Lest his story of his flight should be doubted by his master, the butler stole the King of France's own drinking-cup of silver, and then, holding the replenished cask in one hand and the cup in the other, he got once again astride of his reed, called out " Hae wi' ye ! " and before he knew it was back again in the servants' hall in Inchtalla.

When winter comes and the Lake of Menteith is deserted, except for the wild swans and the waterfowl which visit it, Inchmahome withdraws within herself and steeps herself in memories of the past, fragrant and peaceful. On these memories of saintly, gifted men she meditates and dreams through the short twilit days and the dark stormy nights when the west wind, rising to the strength of a gale, roars through the leafless branches of her immemorial trees, and sends hurrying waves to break with music upon her low shores. Thus she dreams and ponders until the warmth and sunshine of another summer recalls her to her task of welcoming pilgrims to her sacred shores, and of sending them back refreshed, with peace in their hearts, to their tasks in the world.

Menteith and road to the Trossachs

CHAPTER II

IN THE TROSSACHS : BEALACH NAM BÓ

NEAR the east end of Loch Katrine, where the river leaves the loch, there is an old track leading along the south shore. This track climbs deviously to a rock-strewn shoulder of the hillside. The pass, where the track crosses the shoulder of the hill, is known as Bealach nam Bó, the Pass of the Cattle, and through it, if the tradition of the country is believed, Rob Roy drove the cattle he had " lifted " from the Lowlands to his Highland home.

On the winter's afternoon when I climbed to Bealach nam Bó the scenery called to mind the land of the Cuillin hills in the Isle of Skye. Sleet and snow were falling heavily when my friend and I crossed the hill separating Aberfoyle from the Trossachs. We travelled by way of the fine new road which climbs steeply from Aberfoyle beside the waters of the Forth, and at its summit, 800 feet above the sea, a satisfying view of

8

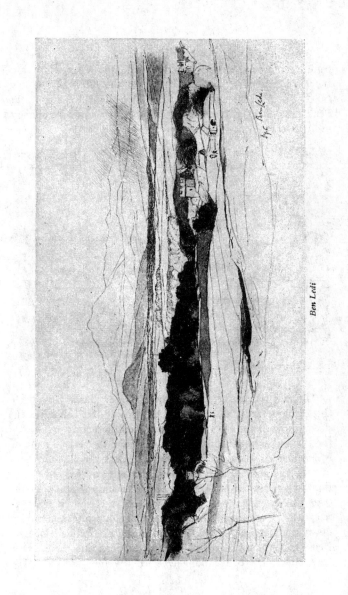

Ben Ledi

the surrounding hills can be had on a fine day. A transient
thinning of the cloud showed Ben Ledi, spotlessly white, and
the lesser summit, dark and rocky, of the hill which is now
called Ben A'n (the old Gaelic name, Am Binnein or the Rocky
Peak, was changed by Sir Walter Scott, perhaps for euphony,
in his celebrated novel to the modern form Ben A'n).

Loch Achray and Loch Vennachar

The rain was heavy as we descended, past Easan Gruamach,
the Gloomy Waterfalls, to Loch Achray and left behind us the
sleety snow of the heights. At the Pass of Achray we parked
the car and set out along the old hill track to Bealach nam Bó
which loomed, dark and forbidding, against the skyline ahead
of us. The ground, as we climbed, became covered with snow
that was saturated with rain. Our feet slipped and slithered
over this wretched surface and walking was slowed down to
a crawl. Each small hill stream foamed, white and milky,
down the steep hill face. Above us the precipitous slopes of
Ben Venue, haunt of the raven and the peregrine, were lost in
the clouds. There are wild goats on Ben Venue, and more than

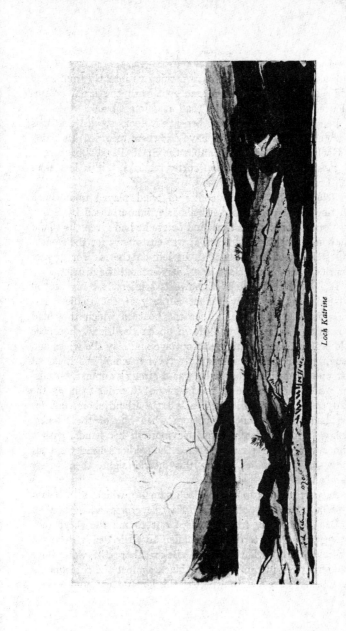

Loch Katrine

once we caught sight of a goat watching us intently from some
giddy ledge of rock. Near one goat with the usual cream-
coloured hair we saw another that was almost black.

Ben Venue, to one passing beneath it, looks so vast that it is
strange to realise that (as I have elsewhere recorded) its name
in Gaelic is A' Bheinn Mheanbh, the Small Peak, " because ",
as the old *Statistical Account* curtly remarks, " it is less than
Ben Ledi ".

Below us flurries and eddies of wind played upon Loch
Katrine, from which rose Ellen's Isle, immortalised by Scott.
But long before Scott's time, and before he had given the island
the name which it now bears, it was customary for the women
and children of the district to be left on the isle for greater
security when hostile clans or soldiers entered the district.

It is said that one of Cromwell's soldiers lost his life on
this island. The story is that a party of the soldiers saw
the women on the isle. Since the boat in which they had
crossed to that retreat was drawn up on the island shore, the
soldiers, who were planning to outrage and slay the wives and
daughters of their foes, saw no way of reaching the isle. At
last one of their number, who was a strong swimmer, entered
the water and swam over to the island, in order to bring the
boat to the mainland. He reached the island shore, but his
feet had scarcely touched bottom when one of the women,
rushing into the water with a claymore in her hands, with a
wild sweep of her weapon severed the soldier's head from his
body. His comrades, seeing this horrid sight, then wisely
made all haste to leave the place.

As we climbed towards Bealach nam Bó, which, at a height
of perhaps 1,000 feet above Loch Katrine, crosses a low shoulder
of Ben Venue, my friend pointed out to me the sheer rock
where two of his terriers had fallen to their death during a
fox-hunt the previous spring. Below that cliff were huge
boulders, piled in confusion and black against the surrounding
snow : they gave a stern aspect to this lonely scene, and seemed

to bring the past near to us, so that it was not difficult to visualise cattle, snorting and breathless, being driven up the *bealach* by sturdy, kilted figures who had brought their *creach* from the fertile lowland grazings to the east under cover of night.

The track led beyond this country of boulders out on to a broad grassy ridge. Here we found shelter behind a large

Ben Ledi and Menteith

upright boulder, from which water, dripping in a miniature cascade, served to dilute the strong *uisge beatha* my friend produced from a large well-used flask.

As we ate our lunch, a pack of grouse suddenly appeared close to us. They had flown through the defile of the *bealach*, and as they rocked in fast, swerving flight the whitish undersides of the wings of the old cocks showed silvery against the snow and served to bring into greater relief the dark body plumage. The grouse were agitated, and it seemed that they must be flying from their old enemy the golden eagle. We hoped to see the pursuer appear, for had he done so he must have passed very near us. But we watched in vain, and gradually the grouse, which had settled near us, flew more leisurely back again across the hill whence they had come. That sudden onrush of birds amid surroundings so wild was a remarkable and inspiring sight.

The rain ceased, and a thin blue opening in the cloud brought into greater relief the austerity of the scene. Across the loch rose many hills, all of them deeply snow-covered. The wind, from which we were now sheltered, was lifting the snow from these hills and was hurrying it along in clouds of spindrift, so that the higher peaks showed ice plumes, like miniature Everests. So deep was the snowy covering that no rock nor stone rose above it, and the waters of Loch Katrine were the more dark in comparison with the snowy heights beyond it. Beneath us was a rock-strewn corrie that is named Coire nan Uruisgean, the Goblins' Corrie. The whole district must indeed have been thought haunted in olden times, for the Gaelic name of Loch Katrine, according to that eminent Gaelic scholar Professor W. J. Watson, is Loch Ceiteirein, the Loch of the Furies or Fiends. He tells me that this is from the Welsh word *cethern*, furies, that the appearance of Welsh in Gaelic place-names is fairly common, and that the Welsh words often become Gaelicised. Professor Watson in his letter to me on the subject writes: " The form Loch Ketyerne is found in 1463. The Gaelic *t* for Welsh *th* is quite regular, for example Welsh Peth, Gaelic Peit. The Welsh *th* here arose from an older *tt*: the name was taken over into Gaelic at an early stage."

We made our way, slipping and slithering on the half-liquid snow, down the hillside through birch trees fringing a hill torrent to Coire nan Uruisgean. Tradition, as recorded by Graham in his *Highlands of Perthshire*, makes this corrie the solemn meeting-place of all the Uruisks in Scotland, who gathered for converse in the deep, boulder-scarred hollow which has so long borne their name, but it is said that they came here from an earlier

haunt on the shore of Loch Ard. Their day was doubtless
before that of Rob Roy, whose exploit of capturing Graham of
Killearn, the Duke of Montrose's kinsman and factor, and of

In the Trossachs

carrying him, and his servants, to a small isle near the west
end of Loch Katrine (afterwards known as Rob Roy's Prison)
is still spoken of by old people of the district. On the island
Rob Roy entertained the factor, as the representative of a
Duke, in his best manner. He had courteously relieved him
of the rents which he had been collecting (this seems to have

been a habit of Rob Roy's !), but demanded, in addition, a ransom of 3,400 merks from the Duke. After a few days, having apparently despaired of receiving this ransom, he rowed Graham back to the mainland shore and there allowed his prisoner to depart, having given him a receipt in full for the money of which he had relieved him.

Dorothy Wordsworth in her *Tour in Scotland* writes charmingly of the scene we beheld that winter's afternoon in the failing light :

We now came to steeps that rose directly from the lake and passed by a place called in the Gaelic the Den of the Ghosts, which reminded us of Lodore ; it is a rock, or mass of rock, with a stream of large black stones like the naked or dried-up bed of a torrent down the side of it ; birch trees start out of the rock in every direction, and cover the hill above, further than we could see. The water of the lake below was very deep, black and calm. Our delight increased as we advanced, till we came in view of the termination of the lake, seeing where the river issues out of it through a narrow chasm between the hills. Here I ought to rest, as we rested, and attempt to give utterance to our pleasure : but indeed I can impart but little of what we felt. We were still on the same side of the water, and being immediately under the hill, within a considerable bending of the shore, we were enclosed by hills all round, as if we had been upon a smaller lake of which the whole was visible. It was an entire solitude ; and all that we beheld was the perfection of loveliness and beauty.

We had been through many solitary places since we came into Scotland, but this place differed as much from any we had seen before, as if there had been nothing in common between them ; no thought of dreariness or desolation found entrance here ; yet nothing was to be seen but water, wood, rocks, and heather, and bare mountains above. We saw the mountains by glimpses as the clouds passed by them, and were not disposed to regret, with our boatman, that it was not a fine day, for the near objects were not concealed from us, but softened by being seen through the mists. The lake is not very wide here, but appeared to be much narrower than it really is, owing to the many promontories, which are pushed so far into it that they are much more like islands than promontories.

They crossed the loch and —

Just as we came in sight of two huts, which have been built by Lady Perth as a shelter for those who visit the Trossachs, Coleridge hailed us with a shout of triumph from the door of one of them, exulting in the glory of Scotland. . . .

After we had landed we walked along the road to the uppermost of the huts, where Coleridge was standing. From the door of this hut we saw Ben Venue opposite to us — a high mountain, but clouds concealed its top; its side, rising directly from the lake, is covered with birch trees to a great height, and seamed with innumerable channels of torrents; but now there was no water in them, nothing to break in upon the stillness and repose of the scene; nor do I recollect hearing the sound of water from any side, the wind having fallen and the lake perfectly still; the place was all eye, and completely satisfied the sense and the heart.

We descended almost to Loch Katrine, but the snow was so treacherous that we were obliged to climb the steep slope again, to find easier footholds. In the ebbing daylight of the short winter afternoon we could see the loch's pleasure steamer lying at her winter's anchorage and not far from her a white buoy which in the uncertain light seemed like a lonely swan. That buoy marks the site of an island now submerged by the loch (the level of the loch has been considerably raised to add to the City of Glasgow's water supply) and called locally Jonathan's Island. On this island goat's milk and whisky of doubtful origin were formerly sold to visitors, who were rowed across by a boatman named Peter MacGregor, a man with much knowledge of old lore. It was said that this island whisky was unusually strong, and its origin may have been connected with the Gaugers' Pass, a pass about a mile west from Bealach nam Bó.

Dusk was falling as we left Loch Katrine. We thought of the water bull which had its home in the loch, and remembered that old Parlan MacFarlane of the Brig o' Turk once told Professor Watson, " Tha tarbh-uisge air Loch Ceiteirein : chan fhaca mise an tarbh, ach chunnaic mi an laogh " (" There is a water-bull on Loch Katrine : I myself have not seen the bull, but I have seen the calf "). Can it be that Loch Katrine, like Loch Ness and, if tradition is believed, other Highland lochs, harbours a large creature unknown to science ? The two names, Loch Katrine (Loch Ceiteirein), Loch of the Furies, and Coire nan Uruisgean, Corrie of the Demons, seem to show that the district in early times was the haunt of the supernatural : both place-names convey the same idea of spirit forces.

c

CHAPTER III

'TWIXT LOCH ARD AND LOCH KATRINE

FOR innumerable nature-lovers in those cities it is a fortunate thing that one of the most beautiful districts in the Highlands lies within an hour's motor run from Glasgow and little more from Edinburgh. Yet much of this district, despite its accessibility, remains unspoilt, and retains its associations with olden days. In the depths of Loch Katrine the supernatural water bull may still have his home and, as I have recorded in the last chapter, a wild corrie near the loch commemorates the gathering-place of a clan of demons.

As I rowed up Loch Katrine from Stronachlachair to the head of the loch on a soft, windless morning of early summer I realised that the district is now indeed more lonely than in the days when MacGregor of Glengyle called out his men to follow Prince Charlie and Rob Roy kept the Duke of Montrose's factor prisoner for a week on Eilean Dubh, a small island near the west end of the loch.

It was perhaps upon such a day of dappled sky and calm, restful beauty that Wordsworth, when in the neighbourhood of Loch Katrine, composed his immortal verses :

> Behold her single in the field,
> Yon solitary Highland Lass,
> Reaping and singing by herself —
> Stop here, or gently pass.
> Alone she cuts and binds the grain,
> And sings a melancholy strain.
> Oh ! listen, for the Vale profound
> Is overflowing with the sound.

No nightingale did ever chaunt
So sweetly to reposing bands
Of travellers in some shady haunt
Among Arabian sands ;
No sweeter voice was ever heard
In spring-time from the cuckoo-bird
Breaking the silence of the seas
Among the farthest Hebrides.

Will no one tell me what she sings ?
Perhaps the plaintive numbers flow
For old unhappy far-off things,
And battles long ago ; —
Or is it some more humble lay —
Familiar matter of to-day —
Some natural sorrow, loss, or pain
That has been, and may be again ?

What'er the theme, the Maiden sung
As if her song could have no ending ;
I saw her singing at her work,
And o'er the sickle bending ;
I listened till I had my fill,
And as I mounted up the hill
The music in my heart I bore
Long after it was heard no more.

As I looked back down the loch, which lay dark and silent below motionless clouds, I saw with pleasure the graceful cone of Ben Venue rise against the horizon. Scott has immortalised Ben Venue, but we have to go back beyond Scott's time to discover the original name of the hill. We find — as I have mentioned in the last chapter — that in the old *Statistical Account* it is named A' Bheinn Mheanbh, the Small Peak. This name persists among the Gaelic-speaking natives of Perthshire.

At the head of Loch Katrine is the house of Glengyle, standing amid stately trees, the birth-place of Rob Roy. As I landed here many sand-martins, and a few house-martins, distinguished by their darker plumage and white rumps, were hawking insects above the calm waters of the loch, on which trout were idly rising. Above the doorway of Glengyle house are to be seen cut in the stone the initials of two of the Glengyle

lairds and the ladies they married. Under date 1704 are the
initials J. M. G. and what (these initials are difficult to decipher)
may be J. B. The other initials are under the date 1728. They

Ben Venue, Trossachs

are G. Mc G. and M. H. "G. Mc G." would appear to stand
for Grigor MacGregor, he who was termed Black-knee and was
" out " with Prince Charlie in 1745. Behind the house is the
old MacGregor burial-ground (there is another old burial-place
of the clan on the north shore of the loch, opposite Stronachlachair), and old recumbent stones show the fir tree, emblem
of the clan, and the royal crown which proclaims their descent

from early Scottish kings. I liked the description on one of the more modern stones, that he who is here commemorated " has done his best for the old name " : it seemed to me that this description was dignified, restrained and singularly attractive.

As I walked up Glen Gyle heavy clouds gathered in the sky and the sombre heavens and oppressive air seemed in keeping with this dark and rather gloomy glen where grey crows make harsh music and gnarled birches cling to black rocks. Except on the crowns of a few great boulders, most of them split by the action of the frost, I did not see heather in Glen Gyle, and the ground, even after a long dry spell, was spongy and water-logged in many places. The old track up the glen has been almost obliterated by winter storm and summer growth, yet it must have been well trodden in the days when Rob Roy often passed that way. The ancient ruined summer shielings which I saw below Bealach nan Corp may then have been inhabited. Bealach nan Corp, the Pass of the Dead Bodies, may have associations with Sithean a' Chatha, the Knoll of the Fight, which is near it, but I have somewhere read that the MacGregors carried their dead by this pass across the hills to the saintly isle of Loch Lomond for burial.

The MacGregors have gone from Glen Gyle and an air of sorrow pervades the place. But over the ridge to the south, down by Loch Con and Loch Ard, I found a more cheerful country. Indeed, in early summer, I can imagine few more lovely districts. In the quiet waters of Loch Con and Loch Ard the delicate greens of the birches and the bronze foliage of the oaks are faithfully reflected. South-west, sentinel-like and aloof, stands the noble cone of Ben Lomond, where golden shafts of light mystically play at sunset. Sandpipers raise their wings in courtship on the green banks of Loch Ard, swifts and swallows fly above its waters, and the dipper gathers food for her grow-ing brood. To the north Ben Venue and Beinn Bhreac, the Speckled Hill, ward off the cold winds of spring, but on the day when Fear na Glasaird led me up to the airy summit of

Ben Venue there was little wind stirring. We climbed from the old farm of Ledard, where, it is said, Sir Walter Scott once stayed, past the Falls of Ledard, then out through the oak wood (here wild hyacinths were opening blue flowers) to the hillside beyond. Scott thus describes the scene in *Rob Roy* as the meeting-place of Francis Osbaldistone (with whom were Bailie Nicol Jarvie and Rob Roy) and Rob's wife Helen :

> We ascended about two hundred yards from the shores of the lake, guided by a brawling brook, and left on the right hand four or five Highland huts, with patches of arable land around them so small as to show that they must have been worked with the spade rather than the plough, cut as it were out of the surrounding copsewood, and waving with crops of barley and oats. Above this limited space the hill became more steep, and on its edge we descried the glittering arms and waving drapery of about fifty of MacGregor's followers. They were stationed on a spot, the recollection of which yet strikes me with admiration. The brook, hurling its waters downwards from the mountain, had in this spot encountered a barrier rock, over which it had made its way by two distinct leaps. The first fall, across which a magnificent old oak, slanting out from the farther bank, partly extended itself, as if to shroud the dusky stream of the cascade, might be about twelve feet high ; the broken waters were received in a beautiful stone basin almost as regular as if hewn by a sculptor, and after wheeling around its flinty margin, they made a second precipitous dash, through a dark and narrow chasm at least fifty feet in depth, and from thence, in a hurried, but comparatively a more gentle course, escaped to join the lake.

The wood sorrel and wood anemone flowered not only below the trees but far up the hill also. We climbed by the course of the Ledard burn, where birches scented the air, and before we had reached the head of the glen saw the outline of Goat Fell in Arran rise on the south-west horizon. As we passed the *bealach* between Beinn Bhreac and Ben Venue I was shown a small rock where the golden eagle at one time nested, and I pictured her hunting the hares of Ben Venue.

Far up on the rocky side of Beinn Bhreac a fox lay asleep outside her den (which, the old keeper of the ground told me, had been untenanted for almost fifty years) and on heathery knolls red grouse sunned themselves. Crowberry plants, on which lay ptarmigan feathers, scented the sun-warmed slopes of Ben Venue, and from the hill-top (2,393 feet above the sea)

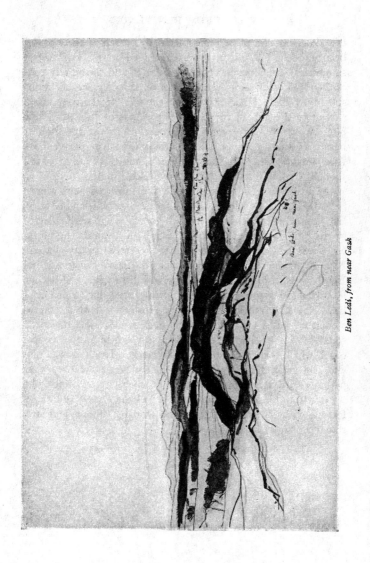

Ben Ledi, from near Gask

the view was one to be remembered by reason of the singular beauty of the hill ranges toward the north-west. The austere summit of Stob Inneoin above Crianlarich and the stately cone of Ben Lui, still under snow, were outstanding among many splendid peaks. I had hoped that the view to the west might extend to the hills of the Hebridean islands of Jura and Mull, but the intervening ground behind Arrochar was too high to permit of these being visible. Distant Cruachan, above Loch Awe, was dappled with sun and shade, and to the right of it I thought I could distinguish the top of Ben Dòrain.

As my friend and I sat beside the cairn we saw, almost beneath us, Ellen's Isle on Loch Katrine, a small island of fairy-like beauty where delicate greens of young foliage were reflected in the quiet waters of the loch. Ben Ledi, towards the north-east, was less imposing than I had expected, partly perhaps because all the sky in that direction was heavily overcast, but Ben Lawers, rising above Loch Tay, was distinctive, and beyond it I could distinguish a distant mist-capped hill which may have been Ben Vrackie in eastern Perthshire. A white-painted steamship sailed up Loch Katrine and, so clear was the air, I could see in the field of my telescope a rich-plumaged copper beech which stands beside Glengyle house. The loch was blue and the grass green beside that lonely house, as they were perhaps on that summer day of 1745 when Grigor Glùn Dubh set out from his home beside the Loch of the Furies, to link his fortune with that Royal Prince who brought sadness, and later romance, to the land of the Gael.

CHAPTER IV

THERE is a journey undertaken by many persons — for the
road is good and the distance from Edinburgh and Glasgow is
not great — from Aberfoyle, by way of Loch Ard and Loch
Con, to Loch Arklet and then west to Inversnaid on Loch
Lomond, where the road ends. If a detour of half a mile is
not grudged, the west end of Loch Katrine at Stronachlachair
may be visited also.

In spring and early summer, when oak, birch and elder
are in young leaf and the lochs reflect and intensify the
deep blue of the sky, this hill-encircled land is one of great
charm. On the winter day when I visited it the low sun shone
on snowy hills, golden bracken and leafless plum-coloured
birches above which flocks of slate-grey fieldfares uncertainly
flew.

Aberfoyle, with its Bailie Nicol Jarvie inn, still holds strong
associations with Scott's historical novel *Rob Roy*, and with a
scarcely less remarkable person, the Rev. Robert Kirk, seventh
son of the minister of Aberfoyle, who himself at a later date
was minister of the same parish. In or about the year 1691
Robert Kirk wrote a remarkable book, *The Secret Commonwealth
of Elves, Faunes and Fairies*, with which he was strangely
familiar. It was implicitly believed by many people of this time
that Kirk (I spell his name in the modern form, but I understand
that he himself signed his name Kirke) did not die, but was taken
by the fairies, whose ways he knew so well. In the words of

his son, " He has gone to his own herd ", and there, some say,
he remains to this day.[1]

In *Sketches of Perthshire,* written by Patrick Grahame,
minister of Aberfoyle (p. 63), is a curious record of the supposed
ending of Robert Kirk's mortal life :

> Mr. Kirk was the near relation of Graham of Duchray, the ancestor
> of the present General Graham Stirling. Shortly after his funeral, he
> appeared, in the dress in which he had sunk down,[1] to a medical relation
> of his own and of Duchray. " Go," said he to him, " to my cousin Duchray,
> and tell him that I am not dead. I fell down in a swoon, and was carried
> into fairyland, where I now am. Tell him that when he and my friends
> are assembled at the baptism of my child (for he had left his wife pregnant),
> I will appear in the room, and that if he throws the knife which he holds
> in his hand over my head, I will be released, and restored to human
> society." The man, it seems, neglected, for some time, to deliver the
> message. Mr. Kirk appeared to him a second time, threatening to haunt
> him night and day till he executed his commission, which at length he
> did. The time of the baptism arrived. They were seated at table ; the
> figure of Mr. Kirk entered, but the Laird of Duchray, by some unaccount-
> able fatality, neglected to perform the prescribed ceremony. Mr. Kirk
> retired by another door, and was seen no more. It is firmly believed that
> he is, at this day, in fairyland.

I am told that a part of the present manse of Aberfoyle is
the original building in which Robert Kirk lived.

The ancient name of Aberfoyle, as noted in *Celtic Place-Names
of Scotland,* pp. 225, 370, was Eperpuill. It is recorded in the
Irish *Life of St. Berach* that the saint came to the fort of Aedan
and that Aedan offered up the fort to Berach, " even Eperpuill,
which is Berach's monastery in Alba ".

The October market formerly held at Aberfoyle was known
as Féill Barachan, after St. Berach.

Aberfoyle is near the head-waters of the River Forth, and
some distance above Loch Ard (where, near the shore, is a
cave in which it is traditionally believed Rob Roy passed a
night on his way to lift cattle in the Lowlands) a large stone
stands beside the young river. It is the Big Stane of Couli-
gartan, and of it Rob MacPharic predicted that the waters of the

[1] He was walking upon a small eminence to the west of the present
manse of Aberfoyle when he sank to the ground, apparently lifeless.

Forth would flow round the Big Stane when the Great War of 1914 came. The stone when the prophecy was made was well clear of the river, but I am informed by Captain Joynson of the Glassert that in, or about, the year 1914 the river did indeed change its course here, and begin to flow round the stone. When in November 1938 I was taken by Captain Joynson to see the place, a narrow but rather deep channel of water was flowing between the bank of the river and the Big Stane.

Other prophecies of Rob MacPharic were that Loch Ard should be surrounded by the English and that no Grahams should in course of time be left in the parish. The first of these two prophecies was considered to be fulfilled when the Joynsons acquired the estate of Glassert, and although there were at one time six families of the name of Graham between the Glassert and Frenish, not one of them now remains.

West of Loch Ard, on the right-hand side of the road going towards Inversnaid, is the Tea-Pot inn. The inn is said to have received its name in the days when illicit whisky was served in tea-pots, and no doubt the strength of the whisky more than compensated for the unorthodox method of serving it! You entered the inn, asked for a pot of tea, and knew (if you were in the secret) what to expect.

Near the inn are old workings of a gold mine which was abandoned because it was unprofitable: it is said locally that the Duchess of Montrose of that day was presented with a gold ring from this unsuccessful mine.

The Crimean War is commemorated in an area of moderately level ground on the hillside above Loch Con. This piece of ground still goes by the name of Sevastopol, because at the time of the siege of Sevastopol men working at the City of Glasgow's water reservoirs camped here. Beyond Loch Con (Loch of Dogs) lies Loch Arklet. Professor Watson tells me that Loch Arklet is in Gaelic Loch Arcleid, the Loch of Difficulty-slope: the name apparently refers to the steepness of a part of the slope on the

Loch Con in Menteith

north side of the loch. The level of Loch Arklet has now been raised in order to supply more water to Glasgow, and the loch covers a considerably larger area than formerly.

At the west end of Loch Arklet are the ruins of a fort named the Garrison, with old graves where rest the mortal remains of the non-commissioned officers and men of the 2nd, 3rd, 4th, 12th, 13th, 14th, 15th, 16th, 17th, 19th, 20th, 21st, 23rd, 31st and 43rd Regiments, who died on duty here between the years 1721 and 1796.

The Garrison was built and manned because of Rob Roy's raids in the district. Rob Roy was traditionally the poor man's friend, and the following story, one of many which are told of him, bears this out :

In the year 1716, when on his way from Inversnaid on Loch Lomond to Aberfoyle, Rob was told of a widow of the name of MacGregor who was the tenant of a small farm on the Duke of Montrose's estate. She was behind with her rent and that very day the Duke's factor was to sell her belongings over her head. Rob Roy called on the widow and advanced her the money which she owed the Duke as her landlord, telling her that when the factor came, and she paid him the rent that was due, she must be careful to obtain from him a receipt. There was a small inn near, and Rob Roy, knowing that the factor was in the habit of calling there for refreshment, concealed himself and his men about the inn. The factor soon arrived, with the £20 of rent he had obtained from the widow, and Rob Roy firmly yet politely relieved him of the cash and got his own money back ! Since the widow was able to show the receipt for the money she had paid the factor, he was unable to ask her for further rent that year.

It was the year before this episode that the MacGregors seized the boats on Loch Lomond, during the rising of 1715, and in them made a warlike foray to the lowland shores of the loch, near its estuary. A punitive force was organised against the MacGregors, and one hundred seamen from war vessels lying in the Clyde, supported by volunteers from Paisley and Dumbarton, were marched up to Loch Lomond. Several men-of-war's boats were towed by horses up the River Leven, for it was decided to attack by water the MacGregor stronghold at Inversnaid.

That night the expedition encamped at Luss, where it was joined by Sir Humphray Colquhoun. Next day the boats crossed the loch to Inversnaid, and the sailors searched the hills, but no traces of the MacGregors could be found, although some of the stolen boats were recovered.

A farm-house and its outbuildings now conceal the ruinous Garrison from the road. The walls, of great strength, persist, and the loopholes from which the soldiers fired upon the turbulent MacGregors can be seen. Despite its strength the Garrison, soon after it had been manned, was captured and destroyed by Rob Roy and his men. It was re-built and re-garrisoned, but in 1745 was again taken and burnt, this time by Rob Roy's son Seumas Mór (Big James) who had with him no more than twelve men. James was acting under the orders of MacGregor of Glengyle, he who was known in Gaelic as Grigor Glùn Dubh (Gregor Black-knee) because of a black mark on one knee. Grigor had supported the cause of Prince Charles Stuart, and in a contemporary account it is recorded that he and his men, to the number of two hundred, passed through Aberfoyle on a Sunday. The chieftain and his followers halted on the green, where the young ladies of the district adoringly presented white cockades to officers and men. On their way to join Prince Charlie the party surprised and captured forty men of General Campbell's regiment, who were at work road-mending. It is worth recording that in *The Lyon in Mourning* MacGregor of Glengyle is named " Graham of Glengyle " presumably because the name " MacGregor " had been proscribed.

After its second burning in 1745 the Garrison was again re-built, and continued to be manned until the year 1792,

when a single veteran was in charge. In his Introduction to
Rob Roy Sir Walter Scott mentions that when he passed that
way " the venerable warder was reaping his barley croft in
all peace and tranquillity ; and when we asked admittance to
repose ourselves, he told us we would find the key of the Fort
under the door ".

It is interesting to recall that after its third re-building the
Garrison was commanded by General Wolfe (of Quebec fame)
when a young man.

Seumas Mór, one of Rob Roy's sons — he who with his
little band of twelve men daringly captured the Garrison in
1745 — must have inherited his mother's love of pipe music.
It is not, I think, recorded that the lady herself actually played
the pipe, although she may well have done so, but she is
credited with being the composer of at least one pipe tune,
" Rob Roy's Lament ", which has now been lost to us. Only
a few weeks before his death in France a destitute and heart-
broken man, Seumas Mór, wrote a sorrowful letter to Bohaldie,
his chief. A part of this letter is quoted by Scott in his Introduction to *Rob Roy*. The postscript to the letter is as follows :

> If you'd send your pipes by the bearer, and all the other little trinkims
> belonging to it, I would put them in order, and play some melancholy
> tunes, which I may now with safety, and in real truth. Forgive my not
> going directly to you, for if I could have borne the seeing of yourself, I
> could not choose to be seen by my friends in my wretchedness, nor by
> any of my acquaintance.

As a piper I feel it is unfortunate that practically nothing
is known of the piping, nor of the pipers, in the Prince's campaign. Pipers of repute there must have been in plenty,
although the great MacCrimmon, much against his will, was
compelled by his chief, MacLeod, to oppose the Prince. That
Prince Charles Edward himself was a piper is not generally
known : perhaps his hearing of good piping during his campaign
may have inspired him to try his hand at that grand old Highland instrument. There is, I think, no record of his playing
during the stirring times of the '45, nor during his subsequent

wanderings when a fugitive, but there is an interesting record (*Tales of the Century*, by John Sobieski and Charles Edward Stuart, 1847, p. 102) that during the last years of his exile the Prince was accustomed to recall sad memories of the Highlands by playing on the pipe, using, it is said, " the small chanter ". It is also recorded that the drones of his pipe were silver-mounted and that the bag was covered in " velvet tartan ".

But let us return to present times. A short distance west of the ruined Garrison the road descends abruptly and steeply to Loch Lomond at the hotel of Inversnaid where a splendid waterfall foams into the loch. Were a motor-car ferry to ply across the loch from Inversnaid it would, I am convinced, prove a gold mine. By this ferry, which would cross Loch Lomond to join the main road from Glasgow to Fort William and Inverness, motorists would be able to complete a very pleasant circular tour from Glasgow, or would be able, after visiting the district of the Trossachs, to continue their journey towards the north or west. There was indeed a ferry here in the year 1803, and Wordsworth and Coleridge crossed the loch by it during their tour in Scotland. From Inversnaid they walked over the hill to Loch Katrine, and were then rowed down the loch to the Trossachs. Dorothy Wordsworth, the poet's sister, in her *Recollections of a Tour in Scotland*, gives a vivid description of the district as it then was, and of the hospitality of the inhabitants. Her book should be read by all who wish to know the conditions obtaining in this part of the Highlands over 130 years ago. After visiting the Trossachs the Wordsworth party returned to the Inversnaid ferry on a Sunday, and as the ferry-boat was absent — it had taken people to church farther down the loch — Wordsworth, his sister and Coleridge were most hospitably entertained at the ferry house.

Dorothy Wordsworth's description of the return of the church party is worth reprinting, for it very clearly shows that the black, funereal clothes of a Highland Sunday are comparatively modern. She writes :

We hastened to get ourselves ready as soon as we saw the party (who were returning from church) approach. As they drew near we could distinguish men in tartan plaids, women in scarlet cloaks, and green umbrellas by the half dozen. The landing was as pretty a sight as I ever saw. The bay, which had been so quiet two days before, was all in motion with small waves, while the swollen waterfall roared in our ears. The boat came steadily up, being pressed almost to the water's edge by the weight of its cargo; perhaps 20 people landed, one after another. It did not rain much, but the women held up their umbrellas; they were dressed in all the colours of the rainbow, and, with their scarlet cardinals, the tartan plaids of the men, and Scotch bonnets, made a gay appearance. There was a joyous bustle surrounding the boat, which even imparted something of the same character to the waterfall in its tumult, and the restless grey waves; the young men laughed and shouted, the lasses laughed, and the elder folks seemed to be in a bustle to get away.

On the winter day when I visited Inversnaid the waterfall, eager and impetuous as on that far-off Sunday so clearly described by Dorothy Wordsworth, was singing a subdued and solemn song. I looked across the loch and saw a view of great beauty. The snow-clad heights of Beinn Bhàn and Ben Ime rose to the quiet sky, and shafts of sunlight threw into yet stronger relief the shadowed country beside them. Above the clouds appeared for a few brief moments the dark cone of Ben Vorlich, where, unseen in the deep hollow below the hill, was Loch Sloy, of old a MacFarlane loch.

Rather less than a mile up Loch Lomond from Inversnaid is a deep cave, or rather a deep recess among great boulders, where, according to tradition, Rob Roy and his amazon wife, Helen, concealed themselves for a time after the burning of their house by Government troops. A path winds along the shore of the loch to the cave, and the hill slope it crosses is pleasantly wooded. The tumbled mass of boulders is easy to find, but the cave itself is elusive. It is a hole, perhaps fifteen feet deep, among the boulders: after much searching the hole was located, and my friend who was with me with praise-worthy determination descended to its dark depths. The last part of the descent is a sheer drop, but an ancient crumbling wooden ladder set against the rock permits of the floor of the cave being reached by a person of moderate agility. In winter, at all events, matches or a torch are essential here to light the explorer.

If Rob Roy MacGregor did indeed hide in this gloomy recess he must have had some of his men always near to warn him of danger. The MacFarlanes across the loch were doubtless on friendly terms with him and would have found some way of communicating news of importance.

CHAPTER V

IN MACFARLANE COUNTRY: AN OLD RIGHT-OF-WAY FROM GLEN
KINGLAS IN ARGYLL TO LOCH LOMOND BY WAY OF LOCH SLOY

IT was a winter's morning when my friend and I drove
eastward from Inveraray along the road which leads from
Argyll, by way of the Rest-and-Be-Thankful hill, to Arrochar,
and thence to Glasgow. A few miles short of Rest-and-Be-Thankful we halted the car at the stream known as the Water of
Kinglas and prepared to walk, by way of an old hill track, to
Loch Sloy and then to Loch Lomond beyond it. My friend's
car was in the meantime to go round by Arrochar to meet us.

It was not a cheerful scene that we saw as we left the comparative warmth of the car. A drizzle of rain, accompanied
by mist, was replacing the moderately fair weather of the earlier
morning. Glen Kinglas under these conditions seemed a gloomy
place, and the only comfort we could take was that the wind
during our long walk through the hill would be favourable.

Our main object of the walk, which had been long planned,
was to see Loch Sloy. This loch is in the heart of the hills, and
immediately below the steep rocky slopes of Beinn Bhàn. It
is indeed in the midst of a very rugged territory and it was fit
that the MacFarlanes, who had their strong fortress on Eilean a'
Bhùth on Loch Lomond, should have taken "Loch Sloy!"
as the war-cry they shouted as they rushed into the heart of
the fight. Clan Parlan, as the MacFarlanes were named, was
a turbulent clan, and its members were often in trouble. It is
not without significance that their *Pìobaireachd* or Gathering
Pipe Tune was *Togail nam Bó*, the Lifting of the Cattle. Among

35

the people of the lowlands, who suffered from these cattle "liftings", the moon was known as MacFarlane's Lantern, and on moonlit nights a close watch was kept on lowland herds. In the year 1624 many of the Clan Parlan were removed, as a punishment for some cattle raid or clan fight, to the uplands of Aberdeenshire, and to Strath A'an in Banffshire : like their neighbours the MacGregors, they were no longer permitted to bear the surname MacFarlane. In the eastern Highlands the descendants of these exiled men are found at the present day. In the Braemar district, and in Strath Don, their surname to-day is Allan or MacAllan, and it is said that they are still distinguished by their Highland courtesy.

Walter MacFarlane, twentieth chief of his clan, was eminent because of his researches into the genealogies of the Highland clans — genealogies which have been published in book form by the Scottish History Society in three volumes. No Highland library should be without this work, which is entitled *MacFarlane's Geographical Collections*. MacFarlane's day was from 1716 to 1760 — he died at the comparatively early age of forty-four — and he was succeeded as chief by his brother, Dr. William MacFarlane, the twenty-first laird of Arrochar, who sold the estate in March 1784, after it had been in the family for the long period of 559 years. " When a black swan shall appear among the herd of white swans on Loch Lomond, MacFarlane's lands shall go from him " was an old saying, and the black swan did indeed appear shortly before the estate was sold.

Knowing a little of the romantic associations of Loch Sloy and its rugged district, and the unusual beauty of the country, we prayed, as we began our walk, that the weather might improve. Glen Kinglas in its upper reaches is a lonely glen, and there is but one house, and that a ruined one, to be seen. It is curious that the old house should be named Abyssinia. It received its name because its owner, Iain Mór or Big John, had visited Abyssinia, and when he went of an evening to his neighbours down the glen to *céilidh* he spoke so much of this distant country that in course of time he, and then his house, came to be named Abyssinia !

As we made our way up the glen, heavy rain showers swept across from the west and the hillside ran water. Dreary was the prospect, and the hill pass, Bealach a' Mhargaidh, the Pass of the Market, at the head of Allt Uaine, the Green Burn, was invisible in mist. The *bealach* received its name because at one time a market was held here in summer and cattle were driven up to this high pass, and were sold on it, from the counties of Argyll, Dumbarton, Stirling and Perth. At such times the scene on the *bealach* must have been a remarkable one as the cattle lowed and snorted, the dogs barked, the drovers shouted Gaelic injunctions and the hill mists eddied and swayed through the pass.

At the county march at the head of Glen Kinglas we left Argyll and entered the county of Dumbarton. Here we saw four grouse crouching uncomfortably in the short heather and hill grass. On the misty hill-top to the north of us a shepherd stood. He seemed of immense stature, like one of the Fèinne or Fingalians, and his oilskin coat bellied and stood out stiffly as the squalls of wind struck him. We looked again : his phantom-like figure had disappeared, nor did we see it again. Ahead of us Ben Vorlich from time to time showed faintly her snowy slopes. Ben Vorlich of the Loch Lomond country is 3,055 feet high, and is thus 200 feet lower than her comparatively near neighbour which rises from Loch Earn.

Somewhere ahead of us — we knew that it could not be far — lay Loch Sloy, as yet invisible. We were walking through a country that was very lonely and spoke strongly of past times ; we might have been pioneers exploring an uncharted land.

The rain continued to drive in relentlessly from the west ; each burn flowed bank-high and the ground was sodden. We reached Glen Sloy, and near its head, beside a ruined house, were obliged to wade across an ice-cold burn. Three short-eared owls here rose ahead of us and drifted rather than flew down-wind out of our sight. Then at last the clouds lifted to the west and the sky showed blue. The rain slackened and ceased and a golden eagle flew overhead and for a time sailed low over the stony slopes of Ben Vorlich, then rose grandly until he was half hidden in the clouds.

The country until now had been dreary, but as we floundered forward over the uncertain path it became grand and inspiring — a fit land for the gathering-place of the MacFarlanes. The burn draining the glen no longer flowed placidly and gently: it leaped from pool to pool past great rocks which sought to hold it back, and then at last we saw before us a long and narrow loch, set deep amid the hills — Loch Sloy.

Almost sheer from the clear water of this hill loch Ben Vorlich rose to the clouds that eddied and drifted past its higher slopes. Here a pair of kestrels played, rising and falling like dancing gnats above that giddy abyss. On the farther side of the loch the dark slopes of Beinn Dhubh, the Black Hill, were the birth-places of hill streams that dropped, white as snow, to Loch Sloy. Storm clouds added mystery to the place.

There were times when the loch was almost quiet; then came the rush of the hill wind, driving white waves across the sombre waters where a dipper was feeding and playing. A spirit of mystery brooded over the scene, and one's thoughts went back to the time when the MacFarlanes gathered secretly here before a foray, and to that day, centuries ago, when the clan got the better of the MacDougalls from Lorne. Beside the track, as it winds along and beyond the shore of Loch Sloy, are two great rocks with a narrow opening between them: this place is called Sabhal Mhic Pharlain, MacFarlane's Barn. The story goes that the chief of the MacFarlanes during that fight stood at the opening between the rocks and with his claymore sliced off the heads of the MacDougalls as they appeared, and threw them from him with disdain until a considerable heap arose.

The MacFarlanes have gone, but their loch remains and surely no more beautiful hill loch exists in Scotland, although it is not far, as the eagle or raven flies, from the Lowland country. From Loch Sloy the Water of Inveruglas flows in a milk-white torrent into and through Glen Sloy. Rarely is seen a hill stream of such energy ; the very glen and its surrounding hills seem to quiver with the force of these short waterfalls as they churn the pools beneath them into yeasty foam. Birches and aspens, storm-harried all of them, grow here, clinging with gnarled roots to the rocks. On the horizon toward the south Ben Lomond stands, but of Loch Lomond and the low country beyond it there is no sign, and the scene is completely wild and uncivilised.

As we reached the lower part of Glen Sloy, where a shepherd's house nestles beneath dark Coire Grogan, we looked back. The clouds had partly lifted from Beinn Bhàn, Ben Vorlich and Ben Ime, and the scene was of a grandeur which could not have been exceeded even in Glen Coe. But when, descending through broken woods of birch, hazel and alder, we reached Loch Lomond, the Loch Sloy country had become invisible, although in reality it was so close. We were still in old Mac-Farlane territory, and now looked down on to two ancient MacFarlane island strongholds — Eilean Uglas and, higher up the loch, Eilean a' Bhùth. Later on, as dusk was falling, we were rowed over to the latter isle. It is said that Eilean Uglas was the earlier MacFarlane stronghold, but that the castle on this island was burnt by Cromwell and the MacFarlanes then moved up the loch to Eilean a' Bhùth — the name, it is said, was given this island because, at one time, a man had his shop here, for better security in those lawless days.

As we approached Eilean a' Bhùth in the failing light of a winter's afternoon the old yew trees which grow on the island near the water's edge rose sombre as night and almost hid the ruined stronghold, from which in earlier days the shrill notes of " MacFarlanes' Gathering " must often have sounded across waters where the silvery powan[1] now play undisturbed and of a summer evening salmon and sea trout leap. It was from the wood of the yew that the Highland bow was fashioned and this may explain the presence of yew trees beside old Highland dwellings.

The dungeon on Eilean a' Bhùth is still strong and intact, but trees now grow in niches in the castle walls : gone are the rooms in which revelry and dancing celebrated some successful foray. As we stood within the walls of this roofless ruin and saw soft rain fall on the branches of the trees there came a distant rumble, followed by a shrill whistle, as the Mallaig express, Glasgow-bound, thundered above the shore of Loch Lomond. Had MacFarlane heard that sound he would doubtless have thought that the Evil One himself was raiding his country, but the old chief sleeps quietly in an island grave and the old days in which he lived, with their romance, their ruthlessness and their chivalry, are gone.

The origin of the Macfarlanes is lost in the mist of antiquity. In Stewart's *Sketches* and in Browne's *History of the Highlands* it is recorded that the chief of the MacFarlanes, and so presumably the clan also, fought on Bruce's side at the battle of Bannockburn, and thus the following tradition which I shall relate is not altogether improbable.

At Firkin, some miles farther down Loch Lomond from the island which I have just described, stands what is obviously a very old yew tree, and the tradition of the country is that Bruce and some of his men sheltered below that tree before the battle of Bannockburn. It is said that his army were being ferried across Loch Lomond (presumably by their friends the Mac-Farlanes) in a small and leaky boat, and to while away the time the Bruce told the story of his adventures as a fugitive to an audience of admiring and respectful followers. In another

[1] Powan is a fish, of the herring family, and possibly a land-locked herring, which goes in shoals in Loch Lomond.

chapter I have described the old yew of Fortingall, which is reputed to be at least 3,000 years old, and as yews are proverbially long-lived trees the tradition may be founded on truth. This particular tree, which is well known in the Loch Lomond district, grows in a rock at a little distance above the loch and close to the railway. It is remarkable for the girth of its trunk, and even more remarkable for its roots, which, gnarled and massive, creep serpent-like across the rock, as though capable of supporting the tree against the storms of eternity.

This old yew, shaken by the hail squalls of a winter day when I saw it, looked out on to turbulent Loch Lomond, whitened by clouds of spindrift caught up from its waters by the gale. But the old tree was undismayed by this fierce winter storm, for had it not seen the coming and the going of Clan Parlan, and had not St. Columba himself perhaps passed by its branches on one of his journeys into the interior of Scotland ?

On the authority of Skene, the MacFarlanes are descended from Gilchrist, a younger brother of Malduin, Earl of Lennox. A son of Gilchrist, Duncan by name, obtained a charter of his lands from the Earl of Lennox, in which the Earl ratifies and confirms " donationem illam quam Malduinus Avus meus comes de Lennox fecit Gilchristo fratri suo de terris superioris Arrochar de Luss ". From Parlan, grandson of Duncan, the clan took their name of MacFarlane.

Duncan MacFarlane of that ilk was slain, with a number of his clan, at the battle of Pinkie in 1547, and it is recorded of his son Andrew that, at the battle of Langside, " the valliancie of ane Highland gentleman named MacFarlane stood the Regent's part in great stead, for in the hottest brunte of the fight he came in with three hundred of his friends and countrymen, and so manfully gave in upon the flank of the queen's people, that he was a great cause of disordering of them ". The MacFarlanes boast of having taken at this battle three of Queen

Mary's standards, which were for long preserved in the families of successive chiefs.

Walter MacFarlane of that ilk was on two occasions besieged by Cromwell, and his castle of Inveruglas was (as I have mentioned earlier in this chapter) burnt to the ground. The badge of the MacFarlanes is the cloudberry ; their crest is a savage, and their war-cry " Loch Sloy ! "

There is a rock on Loch Lomond where MacFarlane is traditionally said to have hung the " savage " figured on the clan's crest, and the rock is still known to the man who gave me the story of the event. MacFarlane's lady (he said) gave birth to a child in the castle on Eilean a' Bhùth and died. At the time one of the ancient inhabitants of the country (perhaps a Pict) was living with his wife on the side of Ben Vorlich. Now it happened that this man's wife, too, had just given birth to a baby, and MacFarlane had the woman seized and brought over to his castle to suckle his own infant. The " savage ", who was absent when his wife was abducted, when he returned and learned how matters stood, decided to be revenged on Mac-Farlane. The chief's cattle were pastured on the mainland, and this man knew that at a certain hour the dairymaid from the castle would come to the mainland shore to milk the cows. He therefore hid himself near, and when the dairymaid appeared he seized her and cut off her breasts.

MacFarlane after that caught the " savage " and hung him from a yew tree growing from the rock, and thereafter the MacFarlanes had as their crest a " savage " holding in his hand a sheaf of arrows. But the crown, and the motto " This I'll defend ", were added by the Regent after the battle of Langside, in recognition of the bravery the chief and his men there displayed.

Hills 'twixt Braco and Comrie

CHAPTER VI

THE COUNTRY OF BEN VORLICH AND LOCH EARN

It is interesting that there should be two hills at no great distance from one another as the eagle flies, each bearing the name Ben Vorlich. Professor W. J. Watson, in his standard work *History of the Celtic Place-Names of Scotland*, writes that the Ben Vorlich of Loch Earn and the Ben Vorlich of Loch Lomond both received their names from small bays in the lochs which lie beneath them. *Mur-Bhalg* is a " sea bag " or " sea bay ", and the place-name has, he thinks, worked its way inland, perhaps through the agency of those who, as the Gaelic puts it, have " followed the sea ".

The " Ardvorlich " on the shore of Loch Earn (from which Ben Vorlich takes its name) is, says the Professor, in Gaelic Ard Mhurlaig, Promontory of the Sea-bag or Sea-bay. This country is the home of the Stewarts of Ardvorlich, an old Highland family who have held their lands for 350 years.

In the house of Ardvorlich is preserved the family talisman, the celebrated Clach Dhearg (the Red Stone) which was held to have miraculous properties. If the stone were dipped in a pail of water and moved thrice, *deiseil* or sun-wise, round the pail, the water would then have healing powers in the illnesses of cattle. So renowned was this crystal that people walked great distances to carry back to their ailing cattle water in which Clach Dhearg,

Edinample, Loch Earn

no doubt with appropriate incantations, had been dipped.

In this crystal, as in the great crystal of the Brooch of Lorn, a hidden fire seems to glow. The tradition in the family of the Stewarts of Ardvorlich is that the stone was brought back by an ancestor in the fourteenth century after a crusade.[1]

[1] Cf. the Lee Penny.

A smaller heirloom, the Glenbuckie Stone, is also carefully preserved by the same family. It has — or had — miraculous properties when dipped in water by the lady of the house. The water in which this stone had been dipped, and perhaps moved thrice *deiseil* round the vessel, was then handed to the guest, who drank the water and silently wished a wish. No doubt the runes recited during these solemn ceremonies were of great importance, but, so far as I am aware, all record of them has been lost.

The district of Loch Earn is in a part of the Central Highlands which has a most interesting history. In the early centuries of the Christian era the district between the central ridge of Scotland (now sometimes called the Grampians) and the River Forth was occupied by a tribe called Verturiones. That tribe spoke as their language Celtic not of the Irish but the British type — a type represented at the present day by Welsh, Cornish and Breton. Under the Irish influence, which began to be felt during the Roman occupation, or even earlier, this wide district was called Fortriu (genitive Fortrenn), meaning the Verturian country, and as the Irish occupation increased, the north part of the district was known as Ath Fhodhla [1] or New Ireland, now Atholl. To the south or south-west of Ath Fhodhla were Srath Eireann (Strathearn) or Ireland's Strath, and Loch Eireann (Loch Earn). Professor Watson believes that here was a district called Eire or Ireland, and he writes that early Irish immigrants were in the habit of naming their new home Ireland, and that the districts of the new settlement were usually named after Irish districts. In the district of Upper Strathearn, besides the place-name Loch Eireann, is found that of Drummond Eireannach : Drummond of Drummond Eireannach was the King's Forester in the Royal Forest of Glen Artney.

The west wind was shaking the leaves in russet showers

[1] Fodla (of which Fhodhla is genitive) was one of the three pagan queens of Ireland (W. J. Watson, " Some Sutherland Names of Places ", *Celtic Review*, vol. ii), and from her arose the poetic name for Ireland — Fodla.

from the stately old trees which surround the house of Ardvorlich and was raising white-capped waves on Loch Earn that
autumn morning when first I climbed Ben Vorlich. I had last
looked upon the hill in clear April weather, when at its heart it
had held a snowfield, white and ethereal as a cloud. The first
of the sun-fire, after a night of strong frost, had then rested
upon its crest while yet the lands of Ardvorlich beside the loch
were in shade and in the grip of the frost, and as this hill of
lovely curves rose to the unclouded blue of the sky at sunrise
it formed a picture so rare and inspiring that I hoped some day
to set foot on its summit. But when actually I did achieve my
ambition the weather was dark and boisterous, with a rugged
wind that sought out and whistled through the most sheltered
corries with cold, clammy breath.

At first as my friend and I walked up Glen Vorlich there was
shelter from the west wind, and we watched sun and shade
rapidly pass across the hill, and the mists rise and fall on the
cone of Ben Vorlich, which bounded the horizon ahead of us.
On the sheltered slope above the glen a stag and a few hinds
were feeding, the stag — for it was the rutting season — anxious
and restless. The bloom on the heather was past its best, but
here and there a small yellow tormentil flower caught the eye,
and beside clear hill streams pink blossom-heads of the lousewort
showed that summer had not entirely gone. We climbed by
way of an old *bealach* or hill pass across which cattle from the
Highlands had been driven for centuries to the Falkirk markets.
We passed a nameless stone that marks the last resting-place
of the body of an unknown traveller who long ago lost his life
here during a winter blizzard. Near the watershed between
Ardvorlich and Glen Artney we saw two old cock grouse chasing
one another so furiously and flying at so great a height that it
was difficult to recognise them as red grouse.

Far below us, down in Glen Artney, was a lonely house — a
shepherd's cottage named on the maps as Arivurochardich,
a corruption of Airigh Mhuircheartaich, Muircheartach's Shiel.

Strathearn, Perthshire

Muircheartach was a good old Gaelic name meaning (according to Professor Watson) Sea Director or Expert Navigator. It survives in the surname O Muircheartaigh or Moriarty. The *Annals of Ulster* record at A.D. 534 " the drowning of Muirchertach Mac Erca, *i.e.* Muirchertach, son of Eoghan, son of Niall Nine-hostages, in a vat full of wine in the fort of Cletech, over the Boyne ". The fact that the place-name of the shieling commemorates a Gaelic name having associations with Irish rather than of Scottish Gaelic seems to be another link in the Irish place-name chain of this district.

We were now in a wild storm-swept country, and watched a pair of ravens fly high overhead and a buzzard rock as the wind-gusts struck him. Through the *bealach* the wind swept with the strength of a gale, and made us realise the conditions which were likely to be experienced on the hill-top, 1,300 feet above the pass. We watched, perhaps a couple of miles to the east, the gusts of wind sweep down upon a small loch, dark and lonely beneath the stormy autumn sky. The name of that wind-vexed tarn is Lochan na Mnà, the Woman's Loch, and the strange story of the naming of the loch was told me by the descendant of the woman of the tragic tale, as the rough wind tore past us on the steep slopes of Ben Vorlich, and clouds and a haze from the far-off Atlantic obscured all distant view. The story is somewhat as follows :

The first Stewart of Ardvorlich married, towards the close of the sixteenth century, the daughter of Drummond of Drummond Eireannach, or Drummondernoch, the King's Keeper of the Royal Forest of Glen Artney and Steward of Strathearn. A party of MacGregors on their way home from the Lowlands took the opportunity of killing some deer in the royal forest as they passed through it. They were caught and, instead of being hauled before the sheriff (as they would have been at the present day), their ears were cut off and they were sent home gory and muttering threats of vengeance which may have raised anxiety in the minds of those who heard them. The MacGregors brooded on this insult. They made their plans for revenge and set out to capture the King's Forester when hunting alone in Glen Artney.

Glen Ogle

With hatred in their hearts they surrounded and slew him without mercy and, carrying his head wrapped in a plaid, they crossed the *bealach*, made their way down Glen Vorlich, and, heading for Balquhidder, chanced to hear that Stewart of Ard-

E

vorlich was away from home, so knocked at the door of his house and asked for food and drink. The lady of Ardvorlich saw the rough, travel-stained men at her door, and from their tartan she no doubt recognised them as MacGregors. She must have been well aware of the feud between that clan and her father, yet the law of Highland hospitality was binding, and she called them in, placed bread and cheese and oaten cakes on the table before them, and then left the room. When she returned she saw, set upright on the centre of the table, and with a piece of bread and cheese in its mouth, the blood-stained head of her father.

The rough taunts of the MacGregors were drowned in the volume of that piercing shriek of anguish uttered by her who was Stewart of Ardvorlich's wife and the King's Forester's daughter. Shrieking, she fled demented from that house of horror : as she made her way wildly up the glen where now blackcock display and red deer feed peacefully, the tumult of her wailing became softened by distance and then was no more heard. We may imagine that even in the hatred-soured hearts of the MacGregors there was remorse for their deed as they then made the best of their way towards the Braes of Balquhidder.

Ardvorlich himself returned home soon afterwards, and he and his people searched the glen and the hills beyond it for his missing wife, with no success. But some days later, those who at the time were living in the summer shielings at the head of Glen Vorlich — the ruins of these shiels can be seen at the present day — became aware that their cows were giving little milk. Some suspected the fairies, but a watch was kept at night, and a woman was seen milking the cows. She was quietly followed, and was discovered sheltering near the shore of the tarn which has ever since been named Lochan na Mnà, the Woman's Loch. Moaning pitifully and temporarily bereft of her reason, the poor lady was borne down the glen to her home. Soon after she gave birth to a son, James, who throughout his life bore the stamp of the terrible experience which had befallen his mother. It was this James Stewart of Ardvorlich who, growing into a strange and moody youth, murdered Lord Kilpont in a brawl in Montrose's camp before the battle of Inverlochy and, in escaping to Argyll's camp, killed one of Montrose's sentries also.

The MacGregors who had committed the murder were from Balquhidder, of the outlawed race known as the Children of the Mist. They carried the gory head along the wooded shore of Loch Earn, and when they had reached Balquhidder, sought out their chief, Alasdair of Glenstrae, then a young man of twenty-one, and flung themselves on his protection. Glenstrae took their side. He summoned the clan, and in the old church of Balquhidder a grim scene was enacted on a dark summer day when perhaps from the grey mist-cap which hid the hills white torrents leaped to the sombre glens. The head of the King's Forester was placed upon the high altar, and the chief, walking forward, laid his hands upon it and swore that he would defend with his life those who had done the deed. His clansmen followed his example, and the hearts of the murderers were lightened as they saw that they would not go friendless.

The wrath of the Government in Edinburgh was roused. On February 3, 1590, "the Lords of Secret Council, being credibly informed of the cruel and mischievous proceedings of the wicked Clan Gregor, so long continuing in blood, slaughters, herships, manifest reifs and stouths", outlawed and condemned to death the whole clan. John, Lord Drummond, was one of those who were granted letters of fire and sword against the MacGregors. Drummond was joined by Stewart of Ardvorlich, and these two, with their followers, proceeded into the Braes of Balquhidder where, in a field below Invernenty, they slew twelve men of the name MacGregor.

Ardvorlich beside its quiet loch is associated with another tragedy of long ago, perhaps not unrelated to the feud I have described above. On a stone, itself more than a century old, which stands on the shore of Loch Earn, is the following inscription: " NEAR THIS SPOT WERE INTERRED THE BODIES OF

7 MACDONALDS OF GLENCO, KILLED WHEN ATTEMPTING TO HARRY ARDVORLICH ANNO DOMINI 1620 ".

We mused on these days of desperate vengeance as we sat in shelter from the October wind. For some time Ben Vorlich had been clear of mist, but the clouds, moving in from the west at the speed of an express train, reached the hill-top before us. Mist and gloom enveloped the summit when at length we gained it. Across the narrow ridge the west wind rushed furiously. In gusts its speed must have reached a full ninety miles an hour, and its power was hard to withstand. Twilight brooded on that tempest-swept summit and the cold was intense. We sought a way out of the cloud and my friend, with his local knowledge, found the correct slope of descent on the farther side of the hill. Jostled and shaken by the wind, we ran before it and soon reached the heathery slope that is known as Sgiath nan Tarmachan, the Ptarmigan's Wing.[1] We now emerged below the cloud-cap and saw that the slope, or spur of the hill, had been well named, for a covey of ptarmigan which had risen unseen from the ground now swept past us down-wind at a speed of at least one hundred miles an hour. They remained in our view only a few seconds, but their snow-white wings against a background of gloomy rocks were singularly beautiful. Into the dark east-facing corrie of Ben Vorlich the ptarmigan sped : as they alighted and folded their white wings they became at once invisible.

It was strange to peer into that deep corrie and to pass in a moment beyond the power of the wind. As I looked down on to rocks several hundred feet below I saw a creature resembling a wild cat prowling here, perhaps stalking one of the ptarmigan.

That day, even below the mist, Ben Vorlich gave no view, but six months later my friend and I again climbed the hill at sunrise on a May morning and, although the Lowlands were then hidden in haze, the view west and south-west was clear, and extended as far as the peak of Goat Fell in Arran. On that

[1] The word *sgiath*, a wing or hill spur, is not a usual one in the Highlands.

still spring morning of fine weather blackcock were sparring at
their fighting-ground in the glen below, ptarmigan were courting
in the high corries, and a wheatear had made its territory on the
screes almost at the hill-top. At seven o'clock in the morning,
we had then sat in comfort and warmth on the dry grass a few
feet on the leeward side of the summit ridge, but on this autumn
day it was necessary to hurry down the hill at our best speed
in order to bring warmth again to our numbed hands. We saw
grouse and ptarmigan rise together near the middle slopes of
the hill, and at an elevation of 2,200 feet above the sea passed
the burrows of a mole. I cannot recall having elsewhere seen
mole-heaps on ground so elevated.

Down in Glen Vorlich we escaped the bitter wind, and that
evening when the fire burned cheerfully on the hearth in the
old house of Ardvorlich and the moon showed fitfully through
the storm wrack, the piper tuned his pipe and played a *pio-*
baireachd of the past, telling of days when broken men haunted
these hills, and when human life may have been of little account
but Highland hospitality was strong. As he played, the piper
thought perhaps of that nameless piper of long ago, he who is
commemorated in two place-names of Ben Vorlich — Sgiath a'
Phìobaire, the Piper's Wing or Slope, and Uaimh a' Phìobaire,
the Piper's Cave.

Although Loch Earn is at least 40 miles from the sea it is
no more than 317 feet above sea level, for the River Earn, which
drains it, flows through fertile and comparatively level country.
At the east end of the loch is St. Fillans, named after a St.
Fillan who would appear to be a different person from the Fillan
who is commemorated in the Healing Pool near Tyndrum. This
Fillan of Loch Earn gave his name to Dùn Fhaolain, which rises
at the east end of the loch. Near this ancient dùn is a healing
well of miraculous properties, described in the old *Statistical
Account*.[1] There was a pilgrimage to the well each year on
May 1 and August 1, and the writer mentions that in 1791

[1] Vol. xi, p. 181.

(he wrote in 1792) no fewer than seventy persons visited the well. The following is the account :

The invalids, whether men, women or children walk, or are carried, round the well, three times, in a direction Deishal, that is from E. to W. according to the course of the Sun. They also drink of the water, and bathe in it. These operations are accounted a certain remedy for various diseases. They are particularly efficacious for curing barrenness ; on which account it is frequently visited by those who are very desirous of offspring. All the invalids throw a white stone on the Saint's cairn, and leave behind, as tokens of their confidence and gratitude, some rags of linen or woollen cloth. The rock on the summit of the hill, formed, of itself, a chair for the Saint, which still remains. Those who complain of rheumatism in the back, must ascend the hill, sit in this chair, then lie down on their back, and be pulled by the legs to the bottom of the hill. This operation is still performed and reckoned very efficacious. At the foot of the hill, there is a basin, made by the Saint, on the top of a large stone, which seldom wants water even in the greatest drought : and all who are distressed with sore eyes must wash them three times with this water.

Near the lower end of Loch Earn is a small wooded island, the Neishes' Isle, with a history that is sinister and dates back to the time of clan warfare in the Highlands. This I describe in the chapter which follows.

The village and old chapel of St. Fillans are not far from Neishes' Island. In the burial-ground beside the chapel is an ancient grave-stone. It may be recalled that, after the Rout of Glen Fruin, the name MacGregor was proscribed, and the Drummond whom this stone commemorates was apparently a MacGregor. To show his true race to those who could understand the sign, there is incised on the back of the grave-stone the MacGregor coat of arms — a fir tree crossed saltire-wise with a naked sword, the point of which supports a royal crown. The crown brings to memory the MacGregors' boast, " Royal is my Race ".

Above the old graveyard rises Dùn Fhaolain, built on a hill. This old *dùn* is a large one, with considerable outer fortifications. In the days when it was in use the hill on which the fort stood was probably an island on Loch Earn, the level of which is believed to have been considerably higher before the country was drained.

Loch Earn

CHAPTER VII

THE TRAGEDY OF THE NEISHES' ISLE : A LOCH EARN
FORAY OF LONG AGO

NEAR the east end of Loch Earn, and scarcely two hundred
yards from the shore, is a small wooded island, Eilean nan
Naoiseach ; in English, the Neishes' Isle. There are old ruins
on the island and, could they speak, they might tell of a grim
deed that was done here long ago, when bloody vengeance was
wrought by the MacNabs upon their hereditary foes the Neishes.

More than a hundred years before the event of which I write
a grim fight had been fought in Gleann Bualtachan (Glen
Boltachan), in the Loch Earn district, between the MacNabs
and the Neishes. In this conflict the chief of the Neishes had
been slain, and his clan had been almost wiped out. It is possible
that the survivors then decided to retire, for greater security,
to the island of Loch Earn. Here we find them one day towards
the festive season of Christmas, in the reign of King James V.

The MacNabs, who lived over the watershed to the north, at the head of Loch Tay, had need of wine and delicacies for that Christmas season. They sent their servants across the old hill track to Loch Earn, thence to make their way to Crieff, or perhaps to Perth, to make their purchases. The Neishes from their island saw them pass, and a few days later, when they returned heavy-laden, they were set upon and despoiled of the Christmas cheer they were carrying to the great MacNab in his fastness over the hill. When MacNab was told of the deed he became, in the quaint phrasing of the old tale, " of an unsocial humour ". He called to him his twelve sons, recited the unpardonable wrong which had been done to their house, and ended his tale with the Gaelic words, which have since become historic in the Highlands, " 'S i an oidhche an oidhche, nam b'iad na gillean na gillean (" To-night is the night if the lads were the lads "). The chief who spoke these words was old ; his sons were quick to take the hint. Hurriedly arming themselves with pistol, dirk and claymore, they launched their boat upon Loch Tay. The present house of Kinnell, where the MacNabs latterly lived, is some little distance from the loch, but the chief's residence at that time (scarcely a trace of it now remains) was at Ellanryne, near the north-west shore of the loch. It was, perhaps, fine winter weather. Beneath the frosty stars Loch Tay lay dark and still. High above the snowy cone of Ben Lawers the North Star shone ; in the south-east Arcturus scintillated with pale-violet light, throwing its reflection on the loch. With lusty strokes of the oars the Mac-Nabs swiftly rowed down Loch Tay, and in little more than an hour had drawn up the boat on the shore at Ardeonaig, a place which, it is said, takes its name from St. Adamnan, Abbot of Iona and chronicler of St. Columba's life. From Ardeonaig an old and well-worn cattle track leads across the broad watershed to Loch Earn, and no doubt at that time cattle drovers from the West Highlands were accustomed to take their herds to the markets of the south by this track, which, it may be inferred, was then more clearly marked than at present. On the autumn day when I crossed from Ardeonaig by this old track I visualised the twelve sons of MacNab striding eagerly up the glen, relays of them taking it in turn to shoulder the heavy boat. In the darkness of a winter night it could not have been easy to have kept to the track near the watershed, where the hill country is a maze of peat haggs and black lochans : snow may have lain thick on the ground, and instead of sinking knee-deep in peat the MacNabs may have sunk thigh-deep in snow. On the map there are apparently two ways of descent from the watershed to Loch Earn — by Gleann Tarcain (Glen Tarken) or by Glen Beich. Before I actually saw the country here I imagined that the descent to Loch Earn was made by Glen Tarken, but the broad watershed is separated by rough and uneven country from the head of that glen, and I have now no doubt that the boat was carried down to the loch by way of Glen Beich. Even at the present day the country here is a very lonely one. Looking back from the watershed one sees Ben Lawers and other great hills of its massif ; south Ben Vorlich and Ben Ledi rise on the horizon, but north or south, east or west, no house is seen. There may indeed have been, at the time of the foray of the MacNabs, summer shielings in the high glens, but these, on that dark winter night, must have been cold and deserted.

Even those twelve stalwart sons must have been weary when they at length reached Loch Earn, and their stealthy row of four miles down the loch must have seemed pleasant in comparison with the arduous walk with a heavy boat on their shoulders. All was dark on the island stronghold of Neish. Cautiously the boat was grounded, and the eldest son, he who was known as Iain Min Mac an Aba, Smooth John MacNab, thundered at the stout door. It is said that old Neish, dozing beside the open fire of wood and peat, was aroused by the tumult without. " Có tha sin ? " (" Who is there ? ") he called in a quavering voice. " Who is it you would like least to be there ? " came the menacing reply from the gloom without.

Neish, with icy fear at his heart, after a moment's thought replied, " Iain Min Mac an Aba." " If he has hitherto been Smooth," came the same fateful voice, " you will find him rough enough for this one night." The door was forced open, and the MacNabs rushed into the darkened room with claymores drawn. They saw the old chief swaying helpless before them, and his family and retainers lying in a drunken stupor, for they had tasted too freely of the " choice wines " of which they had despoiled MacNab's servants.

A horrible struggle then took place, for the MacNabs gave no quarter, and the sight of those sodden with their rightful wine did but inflame their passion. All they saw they slew, so that the water which lapped the isle became tinged with crimson. Old Neish's head they cut off, wrapped it carefully in a plaid, and once more embarked in their boat, thinking that they had left none alive to tell the story of that night of horror. Yet, unknown to them, a young boy, a grandson of old Neish, had hidden himself away, and lived to remember deeds which must have influenced him throughout his life.

And what of the murderers ? Carrying their grisly trophy with them they rowed back along the shore of the loch. The laggard December morning had perhaps dawned ere they once again shouldered the well-tried boat and climbed the long slopes of Glen Beich. Near the watershed a great weariness overtook them, and in that wild hill country they left their boat and, thus lightened, made their way across the shoulder of the hills to their home. Old MacNab eagerly awaited their coming. They entered the house and silently unwrapped the plaid, exposing to their father's view the head of their hated enemy. MacNab looked long upon it, then, turning to his sons, he said, " The night *was* the night, and the lads *were* the lads."

I must now narrate an interesting sequel to this old tale. Miss Isabel MacDougall tells me that her grand-uncle, who was tenant of Dall in 1854, had seen the remains of the MacNabs' boat lying, deep-embedded in peat and heather, on the watershed 'twixt Earn and Tay. She believes that, even as late as 1894–5, the winter of the severe and prolonged snowstorm, a few stays of the boat still remained there.

To add insult to injury, the MacNabs, after the beheading of Neish, took his head for their crest — as I saw when I visited, a few weeks later, the house of Kinnell and saw there MacNab possessions on which was the grotesquely carved head of Neish, to recall to all who saw it that last deadly revenge wreaked by one chief upon another.

Iain Mìn later distinguished himself as a soldier and was killed in 1651 at the battle of Worcester; he had been a great supporter of Montrose and had commanded Montrose's castle of Kincardine.

The name Neish is itself interesting. In Gaelic it is Naoiseach, and there is reason to believe that the " Naois " is a dialectic form of Aonghus or Angus. It may be recalled that in the old Celtic tale (known as one of the " Three Sorrows of Story-telling ") of Deirdre, fairest of women, she and her lover Naoise fled from Eire to escape the wrath of the High King, and made their home awhile on Loch Etive. There is a tradition which makes Loch Ness take its name from Naoise and it is interesting that the Neishes should have lived beside Loch Earn, for it is believed that the district was long ago peopled with the men of Eire, and, as I have mentioned in Chapter VI, Loch Earn is in its original form Loch Eireann, and takes its name directly from Eire. There is therefore a possibility, faint though it may be, that Naoise was the illustrious ancestor of the Neishes who came to so unworthy an end on their island home.

When, on a calm day of autumn, I was rowed out to the Neishes' Isle, I saw there a white swan floating proudly on the still water. The old ruins are built over the entire isle, for it is but an islet, and it is evident must have been used only as a retreat, and that the fields and cattle of the clan must have been on the mainland.

When the mist drops low on Ben Vorlich and the south wind

sends white waves across Loch Earn, the trees on the isle sing a song of sorrow for the old days — days in which many dark deeds, now cloaked in romance, were done, and when the sword was all-powerful in the " Land of the Hills and the Glens and the Heroes ".

Balquhidder

CHAPTER VIII

ON THE BRAES OF BALQUHIDDER, AND A CLIMB
ON STOB INNEOIN

THE Braes of Balquhidder are sometimes known as the Country
of Broken Men, for these rocky fastnesses in earlier days served
as good hiding-places for men who had incurred the displeasure
of the law. In this district many legends persist of Rob Roy,
that Prince of Broken Men, renowned for the strength of his
sword arm. It was so long that it is said its owner was able
to "garter his tartan hose without stooping", and a part
of the Highlands so far removed from Balquhidder as Rothiemurchus was to feel the protective strength of that sword
arm.

It was a cloudless May morning when my friend and I passed
the old church of Balquhidder, where school children played
on the young green grass beside the recumbent stone which
marks Rob Roy's grave. This stone is very old, and from the
Celtic tracery on it — the roughly engraved sword and the
curious, primitive human figure — it is evident that it belongs
to a period much earlier than that of Rob Roy. It must there-

fore have been moved from a more ancient grave to where it
now lies. The practice of removing old grave-stones was not
unknown in the Highlands. There is, for example, in the
churchyard of Kilmuir in Trotternish, in the Island of Skye, a
very old stone said to have been brought from Iona by Angus
of the Wind, the first of the family of Martin, who now greatly
prize that stone and call it their own, as indeed it has become
through long custom.

The stone which rests on the grave of Rob Roy's wife, Helen,
also appears very ancient : there is no inscription nor tracery on
it but only the rough incision of a sword. Wordsworth, after
viewing Rob Roy's grave, wrote of Rob those oft-quoted lines :

> For why ? — because the good old rule
> Sufficeth them, the simple plan,
> That they should take, who have the power,
> And they should keep who can.

In the church of Balquhidder are preserved two old bells.
The larger and less ancient of the two bells is of unusual interest,
since it was gifted to the old church (the ruins of which can still
be seen beside the modern building) by that renowned personage,
the Rev. Robert Kirk, minister of Balquhidder until 1685. Of
Robert Kirk, a seventh son and deeply learned in fairy lore,
I have written in a previous chapter. It may have been of
Kirk's successor — whose name was Robison — at Balquhidder
that the following anecdote is related by Sir Walter Scott.
Robison was anxious that his stipend should be increased.
Rob Roy, knowing that the additional burden must fall on
the people of the district, dissuaded the minister from his
project, and to compensate him presented him each year
with a cow and a fat sheep, which the minister thankfully
accepted without enquiring too closely as to the origin of these
gifts.

Within the present church of Balquhidder is an old stone,
set upright. This is Clach Aonghuis, sometimes called Leac
Aonghuis, Angus's Stone, on which is incised the figure of an

Ben More and Stob Inneoin, near Crianlarich

ecclesiastic, robed and holding a chalice. Angus was patron saint of Balquhidder, and on his stone, which used to be recumbent in front of the pulpit of the old church, marriages and baptisms were solemnised. Little is known of Angus, but the place where he preached is still pointed out, and is always referred to by old people as Beannachd Aonghuis, Angus's Blessing. Féill Aonghuis, Angus's Fair, was held in Balquhidder on the first Wednesday after the second Tuesday of August.

In one of the walls (still standing) of the old church of Balquhidder is a stone which was placed there by David Stewart of Glenbuckie as a memorial to his father. David Stewart of Glenbuckie sheltered in his house Lochiel's brother, Dr. Archibald

Approach to the High Tops

Cameron, when the fugitive returned from France some years after the '45. Dr. Archibald was anxious to ascertain the feeling which prevailed a few years after Culloden on the chances of success of another armed rising : he mixed quietly

with the people of the west at the cattle markets at Falkirk,
and received valuable news. Becoming suspect, he was obliged
to fly for his life, and sought refuge in Glenbuckie's house.
While he was hiding there Glenbuckie one day saw a party of

Rob Roy's Country

armed men approaching the house. He realised that they had
come to search for Lochiel's brother, and was able to warn
Dr. Archibald in time for him to make his escape. But a little
later the fugitive was captured in the woods, and although, as
a doctor who had given his services freely to foe as well as to
friend throughout the '45 campaign, he deserved lenient treatment, this man, greatly loved throughout the Highlands because
of the kindness of his heart and the integrity of his character,
was sent without mercy to his death.

But the Braes of Balquhidder had thrown off the sorrows
of the past this radiant May morning. Beyond sheltering oaks
and birches, resplendent in their first delicate foliage, Loch Voil
reflected the cloudless sky : its waters were of a blue so ethereal
and altogether lovely as to delight, and fill with admiration, the
human traveller. Beyond Loch Voil is Loch Doine, and at the
head of that loch a lesser glen leads away into the hills
towards the north. This is Glen Charnaig, where it is said Rob

F

Roy at one time lived. Glen Charnaig ascends to the high
corries and is a good starting-off ground for the bare and wind-
swept summit of Stob Inneoin, the Anvil Hill, so named because of its resemblance to a huge anvil when viewed from the
south. This hill rises to a height of 3,821 feet above sea level,
and stands at the heart of the high country which separates
Loch Voil in Balquhidder from Loch Dochart beside Crianlarich.

Loch Doine in Balquhidder

As we climbed the slopes of Glen Charnaig we looked back
upon the neighbouring glen of Invernenty, and recalled the old
affair of the slaying of MacLaren of Invernenty by Robin Òg,
Rob Roy's youngest son, because of a quarrel regarding land
tenure. Stewart of Appin was proprietor of Invernenty hill
farm, the MacGregors after an armed dispute having agreed to
surrender the farm to Appin, who settled the MacLarens here
as his tenants. But Robin Òg, with his father's gun, shot and
mortally wounded MacLaren as he was ploughing. Robin Òg,
according to a Government notice calling for his apprehension,
was " a tall lad, aged about 20, thin, pale coloured, squint eyes,
brown hair, pock-pitted, ill-legged, in-kneed and broad-footed ".
Despite this close and unflattering description Robin for the

time being escaped, served in the 42nd Regiment, was wounded at the battle of Fontenoy, obtained his discharge and married a˙ daughter of Graham of Drunkie. Seventeen years later he was hanged at the Grassmarket of Edinburgh for his abduction of a young widow, at his execution (according to a contemporary account) " behaving with decency, and very genteelly dressed ".

High up in Glen Charnaig we saw a shepherd searching for young lambs (in the hill country the lambing season is late) and noticed him kindle a belt of old withered grass : a thin blue smoke-cloud rose from the fire and drifted slowly up the glen on the sun-heated air. A raven rose heavily from a dead sheep, and in the distance a herd of hinds and young " knobber " stags lay on the warm sun-dried grass. Near the burn, high up, we passed the ruins of two summer shielings ; close to them was a large stone, flat-topped, symmetrical and with rounded sides. It was said by an authority on the subject that when he came upon old summer shielings he invariably looked first for a well of clear water, and secondly for a flat churning-stone (*leac na muidhe*) close to them. As we climbed the view became more extensive, and we now could see to the east the cone of Ben Vorlich, tall and graceful.

Towards noon we reached the head of Glen Charnaig, and came at once in sight of a vast country of hills, glens and lochs, all of them sunlit. Ben Lawers, Ben Dòrain, Ben Nevis and its attendant peaks — each one was distinct. In early May the high tops usually hold much snow, but after that exceptionally mild spring of 1938 there was scarcely a snow wreath to be seen on any hill, far or near. We heard the croaking of ptarmigan and the " chacking " of a wheatear as we crossed the stony slopes of the spur of Stob Inneoin known as Stob Coire an Lochain. At the very summit of this spur lies a shallow peaty lochan, little more than a pool : its sun-warmed waters re-flected the blue of the sky as we lunched beside it. Close to the lochan was a small field of peat-stained snow, hard as ice, and at the edge of this snowfield club moss was growing. High overhead a raven sailed, the sun glinting on his dark plumage as he dived joyously from a giddy height. The smoke of hill fires rose from the slopes near Loch Lomond, the waters of which were silvered by the sun.

When we reached the summit of Stob Inneoin the air was windless and the sun warm, but of a sudden a furious blast of icy wind rushed across the hill-top, lifting dust, grit and moss from the ground and hurling them against us, so that for a moment we were half blinded. As suddenly as it had come, the whirlwind left us, and we sat again in warm air and bright sunshine, my friend's faithful collie dog stretched in dreamless sleep at our feet. Plant life is scarce on the upper slopes and summit of Stob Inneoin, but *Salix herbacea*, the tiny alpine willow, had begun to unroll its small leaves, close-pressed for shelter against the parched ground.

The upper slopes of Stob Inneoin gave the impression of being unusually wind-swept, and except for a wheatear we saw no bird life here. But more than 3,000 feet below us, beyond the neighbouring peak of Ben More, a stalking-glass brought the waters of Loch Maragan so near that seagulls could be seen wheeling on white wings above its sunlit waters.

We descended to Bealach eadar Dhà Bheinn, the Pass between the Two Hills, then made our way toward Glen Dochart, far below us, by the burn that is named Allt Coire Chaorach. At the head of Coire Caorach we were glad to quench our thirst at a spring of ice-cold water where plants of *Saxifraga stellaris* and *Thalictrum alpinum* were growing. Here we saw a huge boulder tilted on end and resting so precariously that a strong push would have sent it bounding into the glen below. We reached a burn with a rough and rugged bed fringed with old birches. As we neared those birches we saw that, old trees as they were, they had renewed their youth in a radiant covering of delicate green leaves, and the breeze that drifted across to us from them was charged with that most delightful and characteristic of Highland scents — the perfume of young birch foliage, drawn from the leaves not by rain but by the sun's rays. Beside the birches wood anemones flowered, and the young fronds of the bracken were uncurling.

Throughout a long day on the hill we had seen no human being except a shepherd, nor had we been in sight of any house. Now, toward evening, we reached Glen Dochart near Luib, and saw there the pungent smoke of a moorland fire that had been kindled by a passing train.

In Glen Dochart, perhaps three miles up the glen from Luib, are two lochs, Loch Iubhair, the Loch of the Yew Tree, and Loch Dochart. Both lochs are close to the main road, and the ruins of an old castle on an island on Loch Dochart can be seen. This is the remains of a MacGregor stronghold, and mention is made of the castle in a poem dedicated to MacGregor, chief of the clan, in the *Book of the Dean of Lismore*.

The old traditions of Glen Dochart are fast disappearing but Professor W. J. Watson has preserved a tale of Fionn or Fingal, who was the leader of the band of heroes commemorated both in Eire and in the Scottish Highlands. The legend is as follows :

On the island of Loch Iubhair lived a man named Taileachd whose sweetheart was one of the Sìdhe, or fairy race. Fionn met this fairy lady, and he, too, fell in love with her. When Taileachd came to find out how matters stood there was a stormy meeting between him and Fionn, and it seemed as though a fight to the death would ensue. The fairy woman then placed herself before the two rivals and spoke as follows : " Let your anger fall from you, and hear my words. He of you who gains the victory in a leap will I follow with pleasure." The island of Loch Iubhair is a considerable distance into the loch, but Taileachd leaped from the isle to the mainland shore, and Fionn had no difficulty in making the same jump. Taileachd then said that they must carry out the leap backwards, and this he did successfully, but when it came to Fionn's turn he just failed to reach the mainland shore and sank into the mud as high as his neck. Taileachd, before Fionn could move, struck off his

head with his sword. Being then in fear of the vengeance of
the other members of the Fingalian band, he fled, carrying
Fionn's head, until he had reached the head of Loch Laidon in
Rannoch. There, weary of his burden, he placed the head upon
a pole, and set up the pole on a knoll beside the river Bà where it
flows into Loch Laidon. The Fingalians in time found the head.
They then put a finger under Fionn's " tooth of knowledge "
which revealed all things, and from it learned that Taileachd
was in hiding in a cave in Ben Alder. They found him there,
and after striking off his right hand and his left hand, and
burning out his eyes with boiling beer, they drove their spears
through his heart.

In this chapter a brief account of the places of interest which
are passed on the main road between Crianlarich and Callander
may be of interest.

It may indeed be better to begin our itinerary still farther
west, at the county march between Perth and Argyll, where
the wide district of Breadalbane is bounded by the great hill
range, running roughly north and south, that was named by
Adamnan " Dorsum Britanniae ", the Dorsal Ridge of Britain.
Professor Watson has pointed out the interesting fact that
in Adamnan's time the name Alba, which is now Scotland,
denoted the whole of Britain, and that " Dorsum Britanniae "
is therefore a translation of the Gaelic Druim Alban — Alba
being correctly translated as Britain and not Scotland. The
road from the west into Perthshire crosses one of the passes
through the range " Dorsum Britanniae " between Dalmally
and Tyndrum. Near the watershed, and easily seen from the
road and the railway, is a small loch where many trout rise in
fine summer weather. This loch is Lochan na Bì, the Tarn of
Pitch-pine. Celtic scholars believe (*Trans. Gaelic Soc. Inverness,*
vol. xxxiv, p. 261), that Lochan na Bì was the scene of the battle
fought in the year 729 between Nechtan, king of the Picts, and
Oengus, son of Fergus. In Chapter IX I have mentioned that
near Tyndrum (Tigh an Droma, the House of the Ridge) was

fought the battle of Dalrigh between Robert the Bruce and the men of Argyll.

Crianlarich, standing at the upper end of Glen Falloch and beneath the high slopes of Ben More, is in Gaelic Crithionn-laraich, the Larach or Site of the Aspen or Trembling Poplar. The accent of this place-name is, be it noted, on the *first* part of the compound. Beyond Luib, in English the Bend or Loop, with its small railway station, the road forks beside Killin

Ben More and Strathfillan

Junction station, one branch leading down to Loch Tay, the other continuing south. Opposite the road junction, on the farther side of the River Dochart, is Bovain, from the fourteenth century onward the seat of MacNab, chief of his clan.

After leaving Killin Junction, the road and railway cross Glen Ogle to Lochearnhead (where Loch Earn is seen stretching away to the east), pass near the Braes of Balquhidder, then skirt Loch Lùbnaig, the Crooked or Winding Loch. In the old *Statistical Account* (vol. xi, p. 583) the following interesting account of a rock beside Loch Lùbnaig is given :

About the middle of this lake, there is a tremendous rock, called Craig-na-co-Heilg, the Rock of the Joint Hunting, which is the boundary between

Loch Lùdraig

two estates, and a common name given in the Highlands to such places. Upon hunting days, the two chieftains met there, with their hounds and followers, hunted about the rock in common, and afterwards separated, each turning away to his own property.

Loch Lùbnaig lies in the shadow of Ben Ledi, which rises, vast and round-headed, to a height of almost 3,000 feet. This great hill is a prominent land-mark from the low country to the south, especially on fine winter days when it is snow-clad. The derivation of Ben Ledi is unknown. The name of the hill in present-day Gaelic is Beinn Lididh, stressed on first syllable. The picturesque derivation, Ben-le Dia, the Hill of God, mentioned in the old *Statistical Account*, does not find favour with the Celtic place-names authorities of the present day, but it may be of interest if I quote the account of that ancient derivation from the old *Statistical Account*:

By reason of the altitude of Ben Ledi, and of its beautiful conical figure, the people of the adjacent country, to a great distance, assembled annually on its top, about the time of the summer solstice, during the Druidical priesthood, to worship the Deity. This assembly seems to have been a provincial or synodical meeting, wherein all the different congregations within the bounds wished to get as near to heaven as they could, to pay their homage to the God of heaven. Tradition says that this devotional meeting continued three days. The summit of the mountain is smoothed and free of stones ; which seems to be the work of art. But no stones with inscriptions can be found within the vicinity of that place.

Near the top of Benledi there is a small lake, called Lochan-nan-Corp, the Small Lake of Dead Bodies, which got its name from a whole company attending a funeral having dropt through the ice, and being drowned, when passing from Glen-fin-glass to the Chapel of St. Bridget. The most numerous clan, in this devoted company, were the Kessanachs, who were formerly a considerable people in this country ; but since this disaster befel them, they have dwindled very much.

The River Leny leaves Loch Lùbnaig at the Pass of Leny, and its beautiful falls are close to the main road. At Callander the Leny joins the River Teith, which flows from Loch Vennachar to the west.

Two miles west of Callander stands Dùn Bochastle, an ancient *dùn* or fort, which must have been a strong fortress in early times. Tom mo Cheasaig, commemorating St. Cessoc, is mentioned in the old *Statistical Account* as being situated beside

Callander. " Here ", says the account, " the people upon
Sabbath evenings, exercised themselves with their bows and
arrows, according to an ancient Scotch law for that purpose."

There is a tradition that when the plague was ravaging
Scotland and had reached Dunblane from the Lowlands, the

Dunblane

people to the west of Dunblane prevented the murrain from
spreading into the Highlands by setting fire to a quantity of
juniper (which grew plentifully in that country) several times
each day. The juniper when burnt has an aromatic scent,
resembling incense, and it was attributed to the virtue of this
scented, pungent smoke that the plague reached no farther.

To the east of Callander, and strictly outside the scope of
this book, which deals with the Central Highlands, is Dunblane,
chiefly celebrated for its venerable cathedral. It is believed

that Dunblane was the chief monastery (*cathair*) of St. Blaan, he who was sometimes known as Blaan Buadach Bretan, Triumphant Blaan of the Britons. North-east of Dunblane is Sheriffmuir, where the Earl of Mar and the Hanoverian force under Argyll contended evenly in 1715.

Hills of the Fairies and Ben Lomond

CHAPTER IX

IN ST. FILLAN'S COUNTRY: WHERE ROB ROY LATER ROVED

It was on a fine winter's morning that my friend and I reached Tyndrum. We had seen the planet Venus gradually dimmed by the light of the rising sun as Ben Lomond, throwing off his nightcap of hurrying cloud, glowed rose-pink in those early rays. We had passed the sombre old pines of Glen Falloch in deep shade, and as we approached Tyndrum saw the sun shine on Lochan nan Arm, the Tarn of the Weapons, which lies a little way to the left of the main road as you travel towards Tyndrum from the east.

In the neighbourhood of this small loch, the battle of Dalrigh (pronounced Dalree) was fought in the year 1306 between Robert the Bruce and the MacDougalls of Lorne: in this fight Bruce and his men were repulsed after a hard struggle. When the fight was going badly for the King's side one of MacDougall's men seized the plaid which the King was wearing and attempted (he was a strong man) to drag him from his horse. The Bruce with his claymore struck down and killed his adversary, but the dying man tore the plaid, fastened with a costly brooch, from the King's person. That brooch, now renowned as the Brooch of Lorne, remains in the possession of the chief of the Mac-Dougalls, who lives beside his ancestral castle of Dunollie looking out over the Firth of Lorne to the hills of Mull. There is a tradition that when the Bruce, hard pressed, was in retreat, he threw his sword far into Lochan nan Arm, where it may remain to this day, deeply embedded in the soft peaty bottom.

From Lochan nan Arm we retraced our steps a little way down the valley, in order to visit St. Fillan's Healing Pool and St. Fillan's Priory. St. Fillan, or more correctly Faolan, was the son of Kentigerna, a princess of Ulster, whose death is recorded in the *Annals of Ulster* at A.D. 734. There is a legend that Kentigerna fled with Faolan and his uncle Comgan from Leinster to Loch Alsh over against Skye. Comgan was patron of the ancient church of Loch Alsh, and also of that early chapel which stood beside the salt waters of Loch Eiseord at Ord, in the Isle of Skye.

There were no fewer than sixteen saints named Faolan (which in old Irish means "Little Wolf"), but the Faolan who gave his name to Strath Fillan had his day, according to the *Aberdeen Breviary*, on January 9, Old Style. It is said that on one occasion when the saint was ploughing, a wolf attacked and killed one of the oxen of his team, but when the saint called upon Heaven the wolf, approaching him with meekness, allowed itself to be yoked to the plough in place of the ox it had slain.

In Strath Fillan — the strath begins at Tyndrum and, as you travel toward the east, continues a little way beyond Crianlarich — the River Dochart is called the Water of Fillan.

The saint who gave his name to Strath Fillan must have been a man of singular renown : for centuries the bones of his left arm were believed to have miraculous properties, and (according to Boece) were venerated by the Bruce on the night

before the battle of Bannockburn. Boece tells us that as the
King, weary and anxious, knelt in prayer before that sacred
relic, sometimes called the Mayne, he was startled by a clashing
sound and at that moment the custodian of the relic saw the
arm of St. Fillan of its own accord opening the case and passing
within it. Full of awe and fear he straightway confessed to the
Bruce that he had brought the reliquary empty to him, and had
kept the saint's arm in his own tent, since he had greatly feared
for its safety. On the morning of that battle the silver reliquary
containing the saint's bones was carried along the lines of the
kneeling Scottish army by the Abbot of Inchaffray.

Linne Fhaolain, St. Fillan's Pool, is a deep pool in the Water
of Fillan half a mile up the valley from the old ruined priory
that stands a little distance above the bank of the stream and
near the West Highland railway to Fort William. A few old
trees surround the priory, which can be seen from the road.

St. Fillan's Pool is nearer to the road than the priory, yet
it is invisible from the highway. On the far side of the pool
is a knoll where at one time a number of cairns stood, but when
the road was made through the district that part of the knoll
on which the cairns were built was used as a quarry, and when
the cairns were demolished a number of coins were found below
them — old thank-offerings left there for miraculous cures
wrought in the sacred pool.

To seek a cure from the Pool of St. Fillan was no matter to
be lightly undertaken. That person afflicted by a mental illness
was submerged deep in the icy waters of the pool, with appropriate rites, and was then left, securely bound, to lie all that
night in the old priory. The dipped person was instructed to
take three stones from the bottom of the pool, and to walk thrice
round each of three cairns on the bank, throwing a stone on to
each cairn during this ritual. Many wonderful cures are said
to have been wrought here, but there is a tradition that the
healing powers of the pool have been lost ever since the day
when a mad bull, pursued by dogs, plunged into it.

The low mid-winter sun shone on the pool, yet failed to light its depths, on the day when my friend and I looked on it, and away to the west Ben Lui in a mantle of purest snow rose to the soft sky. The current boiled and eddied, as the young river seemed to linger as it passed through this historic pool, and we could see, beneath the peat-stained waters, pale-yellow quartz stones of a colour similar to the Healing Stones of St. Fillan, now preserved in the mill at Killin. These Healing Stones have a fancied resemblance to different parts of the human body, and when applied to those parts brought miraculous relief. Even now no work is done at Killin mill on St. Fillan's Day, and a man who disregarded the old custom met with a severe accident which incapacitated him for the rest of his life. It is believed that St. Fillan built the first meal mill driven by water in Killin : the present mill, although an old building, dates from many centuries after the saint's time.

Nothing is now left of the old priory of St. Fillan except part of the walls, yet an atmosphere of saintliness remains here. It would indeed seem as though the kindliness of the place has its effect even upon the dogs of the farm beside the priory, for I noticed that, instead of barking at the approach of strangers, they ran to meet them with friendly gestures.

The relics of St. Fillan were entrusted to the keeping of several men in Glen Dochart, and this office was hereditary. The Crozier or Coigreach (a Gaelic word denoting a stranger) received its name because it was carried to distant places for the recovery of stolen property. The Deor (the Custodian or Keeper) of the Coigreach was given the sum of four pence, or a pair of shoes, and food for the first night of his journey when he set out with the miraculous crozier to recover cattle which had been stolen and driven off to some distant glen.

The Coigreach is the head of a pastoral staff, and stands nine inches high. The external casing of silver encloses an earlier ornamented crozier-head of bronze or copper. The external case consists of three parts — the crook proper, the bulb or socket, and an ornamented crest, to strengthen and bind together the parts of which the staff-head is composed.

The custodianship of the Coigreach, and of the saint's Bearnan or Bell, were offices of honour, and were hereditary. The custodian was known as the Deor, derived from the old Gaelic word *deòradh* which in its original meaning (so the Rev. William Gillies, author of that scholarly work *In Famed Breadalbane*, informs me) denotes a stranger or exile, since the relic was carried by him to strange and distant parts. The surname Dewar, so long associated with Breadalbane, is derived from Deor.

The Bearnan, the Little Gapped One, was the Bell of St. Fillan and the custodian of the bell was, by right of his office, named Deor a' Bhearnain ; because of that right he held of the Crown, rent-free, the croft of Suidhe (near where the railway station of Luib now is). At Suidhe, between the public road and the River Dochart, may still be seen, on the summit of a mound, a stone on which is carved a simple Latin cross, seemingly of great age and perhaps dating from the time of St. Fillan himself.

The Bearnan (*In Famed Breadalbane*, p. 74) was borne in the pageant of the Coronation of King James IV in 1488. For centuries it lay, exposed to the elements and unguarded, on a grave-stone near the priory, and was used in the rites of curing insane persons who had been dipped in the Sacred Pool of the River Dochart. The bell was impudently stolen by an English tourist, whose diary is quoted in the book above mentioned (p. 75). We are not told the man's name.

August 9th 1798. Arrived at Tyndrum by 4 o'clock. Rode after dinner with a guide to the Holy Pool of Strathfillan. Here again is abundant cause for talking of the superstition of the Highlanders. The tradition avers that St. Fillan, a human being, who was made a saint about the beginning of the eighth century by Robert de Bruce, consecrated this pool, and endued it with a power of healing all kinds of disease but more especially madness. This virtue it has retained ever since, and is resorted to by crowds of neighbouring peasantry, who either expect to be cured of real diseases, or suppose themselves cured of imaginary ones. This healing virtue is supposed to be most powerful towards the end of the first quarter of the moon, and I was told that if I had come there tomorrow night and the night after I should have seen hundreds of both sexes bathing in the pool. I met five or six who were just coming away from taking their dip and amongst them an unfortunate girl out of her mind, who came for thirty miles distance to receive the benefits of the waters, and had been there for several months together, but had never derived the smallest advantage, and indeed, she appeared so completely mad, that, whatever may be the virtue of St. Fillan's Pool, I am sure Willis would pronounce her a hopeless case.

A rocky point projects into the pool. This pool is by no means the mountain-head, for the water runs for a long way up the country, yet it is not supposed to receive its virtue till it comes to the very place, on the one side of which the men bathe, and on the other side the women. Strathfillan derives its name from the saint. Near Strathfillan a famous battle was fought between King Robert de Bruce and the MacDougalls, which the former gained owing to the assistance afforded by the prayers of St. Fillan.

Each person gathers up nine stones in the pool and after bathing walks to a hill near the water, where there are three cairns, round each of which he performs three turns, at each turn depositing a stone, and if it is for bodily pain, a fractured limb, or sore that they are bathing, they throw upon one of the cairns that part of their clothing which covered the part affected ; also if they have at home any beast that is diseased, they have only to bring some of the meal which it feeds upon, and make it into paste with these waters, and afterwards give it to him to eat, which will prove an infallible cure ; but they must likewise throw upon the cairn the rope or halter with which it was led. Consequently, the cairns are covered with old halters, gloves, shoes, bonnets, night-caps, rags of all sorts, kilts, petticoats, garters and smocks. Sometimes they go as far as to throw away their half-pence. Money has often been called the root of all evil, but for the disease of what part of the body these innocent half-pence are thus abused I could not learn. However, we may venture to suppose that they seldom remain there long without somebody catching the disorder again.

When mad people are bathed they throw them in with a rope tied about the middle, after which they are taken to St. Fillan's Church, about a mile distant, where there is a large stone with a nick carved in it just large enough to receive them. In this stone, which is in the open Church-yard, they are fastened down to a wooden frame-work, and there remain for the whole night with a covering of hay over them and St. Fillan's Bell is put upon their heads. If in the morning the unhappy patient is found loose, the saint is supposed to be very propitious. If, on the other hand, he continues in bonds, he is supposed to be contrary.

The Bell is of very curious shape, and has an iron tongue. St. Fillan caused it to fly to this Church, and a soldier seeing it in the air, fired at it, which brought it down and occasioned a crack in it, which is still to be seen. I was told that wherever this Bell was removed to it would always return to a particular place in the Churchyard next morning.

The Church had been formerly twice as large as it is now, as appears by the ruin of what has been pulled down, a striking proof of the desecration, either of the population, or religion in this country.

In order to ascertain the truth of St. Fillan's Bell I carried it off with me to England. An old woman who observed what I was about asked me what I wanted with the Bell, and I told her I had an unfortunate relation at home out of his mind, and that I wanted to have him cured. "Oh, but," she says, "you must bring him here to be cured, or it will be of no use." Upon which I told her he was too ill to be moved, and off I galloped with the Bell to Tyndrum Inn.

The historic bell was lost until the year 1869, but after many vicissitudes it rests, together with the Coigreach or crozier, in the Scottish National Museum of Antiquities at Edinburgh.

The English traveller who had the temerity to steal the bell gives us a valuable contemporary account (if his snatches of Sassenach sarcasm be excused) of the rites of St. Fillan's Pool. But he does not seem to have realised that, centuries before his time, the priory had lost its sacred associations. When King James IV, in the autumn of 1501, hunted in Balquhidder and Ben More he lived for a time in the priory, and was entertained by "Heland bardis", harpers and fiddlers. It is likely that by that time the lay abbots of Glen Dochart resided in the priory: they were persons of importance in olden days, and it is believed that the MacNab chiefs were descended from one of these lay abbots.

In early Christian days Glen Dochart was renowned because of St. Fillan: a thousand years later the glen welcomed a hero of a different kind — Rob Roy. Robert MacGregor Campbell (to give him his full name) was a younger son of MacGregor of Glengyle, whose wife was a daughter of Campbell of Glenlyon, sister of the commanding officer at the Massacre of Glencoe. As the name MacGregor was suppressed by Act of Parliament in 1622, individuals of the clan assumed the names of men of rank and power who could afford them protection. Rob Roy took the surname of his friend and protector, the Duke of Argyll.

At this period the younger sons of gentlemen often took up the trade of drovers of cattle, and Rob Roy, who chose this profession, was soon one of the most successful drovers in his district. By the year 1707 he had purchased from the Duke of Montrose the estate of Craig Rostan, on Loch Lomondside, and had relieved heavy debts on his nephew's estate of Glengyle. Then the Duke and Rob Roy fell out, and having been, as he considered, unjustly treated by His Grace, Rob lost no time in making himself unpleasant to him ; yet he was always the poor man's friend, and enjoyed remarkable popularity far and wide. Rob Roy indeed became a hero, and one of the incidents which earned him renown occurred not far from the Healing Pool and the old priory of which I have written.

News was brought to the Government troops stationed in the district that Rob Roy was at Tyndrum, and a party of chosen men, led by an officer, were sent to apprehend him. The party arrived at Tyndrum and were quartered at the inn. Rob Roy, being well aware of their movements, disguised himself as a beggar, walked into the kitchen of the inn, and sat down among the soldiers. The soldiers, seeing that this was apparently a simple fellow, began to play practical jokes on him, and after a time the beggar in seeming anger said excitedly that if they did not desist from their unkind pranks he would tell Rob Roy.

The name of Rob Roy electrified the soldiers. The beggar was instantly questioned as to his knowledge of the great man, and apparently greatly pleased by the interest he had aroused, replied that he knew Rob Roy well, and that he even knew where he was at that moment in hiding. The soldiers sent for their officer, who engaged the beggar in earnest and secret conversation. After apparent hesitation the beggar said that Rob Roy was at Crianlarich, three or four miles below Tyndrum, and that, further, Rob and his men were in one house and, as their arms were in another, they would be found defenceless. The beggar continued, " Rob Roy and I are on very friendly terms, and he sometimes even puts me myself at the head of his table." Persuaded (against his better judgment, so it seemed) by the promise of a great reward, the beggar said that he would there and then lead them to Rob Roy.

At Dalrigh, near the Healing Pool of St. Fillan, it was necessary for the party to cross the river, then in spate. The soldiers
were unwilling to ford the flooded stream, and asked the beggar,
who was guiding them, whether he would carry them over on
his back. This he consented to do, and carried across the whole
party (the small men he carried two at a time), receiving for his
trouble a penny from each soldier. When they had almost
reached Crianlarich, their guide told them that he would go
ahead, and that they were to follow him in half an hour. He
then gave them full directions how they should find the house
in which Rob Roy was concealed and ended his injunctions to
the officer as follows : " Place your men at the back of the
house, and you yourself, with the sergeant and two men, walk
in at the front door, calling out that all within are your prisoners.
And do not be surprised (he added) although you see me at the
head of the company."

The officer found the house, and after sending his men round
to guard the back, he, with his sergeant and two soldiers, rushed
in at the front door, shouting out, as he did so, that those within
must immediately surrender. They had only just time to see
the beggar standing at the head of the table when the door was
slammed behind them and they were skilfully pinioned, each
by two Highlanders who held pistols to their ears and whispered
that they were dead men if they uttered a sound. The beggar
then went out, and called to the soldiers who were guarding the
back of the house that two of them were wanted inside. When
the two men came in, they were made prisoners, and then two
more were called in : this went on until the whole party had
been made prisoners and had been disarmed. The beggar, of
course, was Rob Roy in disguise, and he placed the discomfited
men under a strong guard until the morning, then gave them
an excellent breakfast and released them on parole, ordering
them to return at once to their garrison. To make sure that
they were incapable of further mischief, he took their arms and
ammunition from them.

Rob Roy in the course of his adventurous life had many narrow escapes, and on one occasion was actually captured by a party sent out by his enemy the Duke of Montrose. He was made fast to a horse girth and set on a horse behind one of his captors, but pleaded so eloquently for his freedom that the man who rode with him was prevailed upon to slip the girth as they were traversing very rough ground or, as some say, while crossing a river, where the fugitive was able to make good his escape.

It is a striking tribute to Rob Roy's character that, except for the Duke of Montrose and his circle, he had no enemy. He was often helped in a tight corner by his friend the Duke of Argyll, and a relic of this friendship, Rob Roy's sporan, is to be seen in Inveraray Castle at the present day.

CHAPTER X

LOCH TAY and its lands lie at the heart of Breadalbane (Breadalbane is the Anglicised form of Bràghaid Alban, the Upland of Alba), a country of hill and glen, shaggy moor and fertile straths sheltered by high hills. It is a country of stirring traditions, and of ancient ruins which show the skill of hands long since turned to dust.

Loch Tay gives character to this fair country. Its waters sparkle with life, or are grey and sullen, according to the mood of the weather. The loch is 15 miles long and its greatest depth is 500 feet — that is 164 feet below the level of the distant ocean. Loch Tay has seen the coracles of the ancient Celts, and a century ago gave a Highland welcome to the revered Queen Victoria. The Queen was rowed up the loch in a boat steered by MacDougall of MacDougall, an officer of flag rank in the Royal Navy, who wore, with full Highland dress, the historic Brooch of Lorne, and during the passage up the loch she heard the singing of Gaelic songs by boatmen who plied the long oars — one of these oars is still preserved by a clanswoman of MacDougall at Kenmore.

The country at the head of Loch Tay is the ancestral home of the MacNabs (described in Chapter VII), an ancient family who claim descent from the lay abbots of Glen Dochart. Of one of the MacNabs, a fine figure of a man as commemorated in that celebrated portrait by Raeburn, it is traditionally said that when proposing to the lady of his choice, he offered her

Inchbuie, " the most beautiful burial-ground in the world ", in the hopes that this would cause her to look favourably upon him. Yet even this doubtful attraction failed to soften the heart of the lady, and MacNab never married. Nothing now remains of the old MacNab residence at Bovain, on the Dochart, nor of their stronghold of Ellanryne, on the haugh close by the Lochay, below the ruined castle of Finlarig on Loch Tay. After the destruction of Ellanryne by the English in or about the year 1654, General Monk gave over the lands of MacNab to the Laird of Glenurchy (the old spelling of Glen Orchy). After the loss of his castle of Ellanryne the MacNab chief built the house of Kinnell, where the family lived for several centuries ; it is now one of the seats of the Earl of Breadalbane.

Here is to be seen the magnificent Kinnell vine, which is said to be the finest specimen in Europe. The glass-house in which it grows has been frequently enlarged, and now covers an area of 171 by 25 feet, yet the vine still attempts to spread beyond its confines, and has to be pruned back to keep it within the house. This vine measures 54 feet in circumference at a height of 6 feet from the ground. As an example of its prolific-ness, in the year 1936 it bore no fewer than 5,429 bunches of grapes, of which 4,673 were removed as thinnings, leaving a crop of 756 bunches to reach maturity. Despite its great age (it was planted in 1832), the vine is still hale and hearty, and its leaves, on the September day when I saw them, were fresh and green as those of a sycamore in early May.

In the house of Kinnell, a pleasant house and simply built, old MacNab furniture is still to be seen — furniture which bears the MacNab crest, the head of the family's enemy, Neish, whom they slew on his island on Loch Earn (*vide* Chapter VII), and whose head they bore back in triumph to Kinnell.

Within the house of Kinnell, on the south walls of which heavy-laden pear trees were growing on the day when I saw it, are preserved other relics : Rob Roy's claymore, pistol and *cuach* or drinking-cup, the latter singularly small and delicately made.

Killin is at the head of Loch Tay. In Southey's day, the church of Killin had an eagle's claw as the handle for its bell-rope, and one of the celebrated Bedel's Bibles is still preserved here. Killin Church bell, still in use, has an old inscription on it : " Sir Coline Campbel of Glenurchy Knygth Barronet causid cast yis Bel 1632, R.H." The old bell cracked in 1931 but was welded and re-hung.

Through the heart of Killin the Dochart thunders, and in heavy water its spray bathes the MacNabs' ancestral burying-ground of Inch Buie. Inch Buie, the Yellow Island, which may have been an ancient stronghold, is densely shaded by veteran beeches and pines, and golden moss covers the ground. Here are to be seen old grave-stones of the MacNab chiefs and their relatives. A silence broods about this old-world and majestic burial-place of the MacNab dead, where

> A wall of crumbling stones doth keep
> Watch o'er long barrows where they sleep,
> Old chronicled grave-stones of its dead,
> On which oblivious mosses creep,
> And lichens grey as lead.

Near Killin stands the old ruin of Finlarig Castle, built on a small height overlooking Loch Tay. Finlarig, in English the White or Holy Pass, takes its name from a pass at Killin which perhaps has associations with St. Fillan of Glen Dochart. The castle was originally a Drummond stronghold, but as far back as 1503 was sold to Sir Duncan Campbell of Glenurchy. It was added to by his successor, the Black Laird of Glenurchy — he who built the castle on the island of Loch Dochart, not far from Crianlarich. The Black Laird, sometimes called Black Duncan of the Cowl, was a celebrated figure in the history of the Highlands, and was not without certain characteristics of his powerful clan. In the year 1609 it is recorded that he sent a pair of eagles to Prince Henry, who in return gifted him a stallion. It was perhaps through Black Duncan of the Cowl that King James VI heard of the renowned white hind of

Corricheba [1] in the Blackmount Forest : the King sent skilled
hunters all the way from England to capture her, but she
escaped their wiles.

Black Duncan insisted that his tenants and cottars should
plant each year a certain number of trees on their land, and
arranged for his gardeners to supply the trees " at twa pennies
the piece ". It would appear as though he were the pioneer of
afforestation in the Highlands.

Above the doorway on the south side of Finlarig Castle is a
stone bearing the royal arms, and the letters

I R

A R

1609

The initials are those of the King and his Queen, Anne of
Denmark. It is believed that the date commemorates the
building of the castle, and it has been suggested that Black
Duncan was appointed by the King to be Constable or Captain
of the castle, and that the royal arms are the badge of his loyalty
to, and authority under, the Crown, for it was customary in
early times to place the arms of the feudal superior above the
arms of the actual owner. It is known that in 1608 Black
Duncan was granted by King James VI a Commission or
Justiciary for the execution of the Acts against slaying fish and
deer and destroying greenwood within certain bounds.

A forbidding, nay, sinister atmosphere is felt in the vicinity
of Finlarig where, if tradition is believed, many dark deeds
were done. The laird sat in judgment on criminals, and on
his enemies, beneath a yew, and a tree of this species still grows,
dark and brooding, beside the ruins. Some say that the hanging
tree was a gnarled oak which still lives ; others, that the tree
was a sycamore which was uprooted by a fierce gale at the
beginning of the twentieth century.

Although the tree on which luckless captives were hanged

---

[1] The stress in this place-name is on the " ba ".

may have gone, the rusty chains with which they were manacled remain, and the heading block with its pit beneath it. The block is a stone with a cavity on which the head of the victim was laid. It was indeed considered a mark of honour to have one's head removed, for captives of more humble origin, whether genuine malefactors or those who had merely incurred the enmity of the laird, were hanged from a stout limb of the hanging tree.

It was a sombre evening when my friend and I visited the castle : the windless air seemed to press heavily upon the hoary ruins with their immensely thick moss-covered walls. Each leaf of the old trees was motionless : only in the air was there active life, for across the darkening sky flew many swallows, backwards and forwards, hawking for insects.

Next morning I found a very different atmosphere pervading another old ruin of the Loch Tay country — the ancient priory on Eilean nam Bannaomh,[1] Isle of the Female Saints, an island which, at the present day, is usually known as the Isle of Loch Tay. For our expedition to this island my friend and I had as our guide the learned minister of Kenmore,[2] whose book *In Famed Breadalbane* has quickly become a standard work on that district. In his well-tried boat we fought our way with the oars across the deep waters of the loch, on which a fresh breeze from the south was raising crested waves, to a small wooded isle near the northern shore. Once in shelter of the isle we entered a profound, fragrant calm. In the still air insects danced : the September sun turned to gold the leaves of the old trees. It is a tribute to the sanctity of those who lived long ago that they have succeeded in leaving behind them, as their memorial, an immortal essence of joy and peace which, centuries afterwards, still pervades their homes. Visit the Garvelloch Isles, lonely Oronsay, Inchmahome and other secluded isles where holy men and women long ago lived simple

[1] Stress on " Ban ".

[2] Kenmore — stress on " Ken " (G. An Ceannmhor).

and devout lives, and if you are receptive you will at once recapture the joy, serenity and repose which hallowed, and still hallow, the small isles of those early Christians. In *The Apology of Aristides* is a fine description of those who practised that faith :

When they rise in the morning and when they lie down to sleep they praise God.

Before they take their food, and afterwards, they praise God.

When one of them dies, and they carry him to burial, they praise God as though he were only removing to another room.

When a child is born they praise God ; and if he should die in infancy they praise God mightily, that he has passed to Heaven without having sinned.

In the year 1122, King Alexander I in a charter granted Eilean nam Bannaomh to the monks of Scone Abbey, in memory of his queen, Sybilla, who died on the island and was buried there in the early summer of that year, so that " a church of God be built there for me, and for the soul of the Queen there deceased ". It is evident that, even at this time, the island had strong religious associations, or the Queen would not have been buried there.

For some centuries a priory existed on the isle and was replaced by a nunnery. Each year, on July 26, the sisters emerged from their seclusion and attended a fair at Kenmore, known as Féill nam Bannaomh, Fair of the Female Saints. Here, it is said, they sold their work and helped to maintain themselves. Throughout that day also they ministered to the poor and infirm. When the Campbells of Glenurchy obtained possession of the district they used the convent as their castle, enlarging and fortifying it. But on Palm Sunday of the year 1509, during the absence of the family at church at Kenmore, the castle was mysteriously burnt. It was rebuilt, was besieged by Montrose and was considerably damaged by his cannon. A little later it was for a time held by General Monk, one of Cromwell's high officers : his soldiers, it is believed, first introduced tobacco into the district. Yet despite its vicissitudes the isle has preserved its sanctity, and the ruin its nobility, and now (1947) when two great wars have ravaged the earth, its message of hope is good to receive.

We left the secluded, sunlit isle and rowed out into the world. Yet within the church of Kenmore we again found evidences of olden times. We were shown the poor's-box, a strongly-made box of oak with two locks, which has been in continuous use since 1630. During the Civil War raiders broke into the church and stole the font, but the poor's-box escaped, and on January 12, 1645, the minister and elders distributed the sum of £3 from it among " poore people who had been spoyled and burned, and had nothing to live on ". We also saw here a Bedel's Bible (1685), the work of Dr. William Bedel, Bishop of Kilmore in Eire. In the bible, in the handwriting of the celebrated Rev. Robert Kirk (of whom I have written elsewhere), is the following inscription :

1688. The donation of ye Pious and learned Robert Boyle Esq. a principal member of the Royal Societie, Bestowed on the Church of Kenmor in Breadalbane. To continue there as a Church Bible for the use of the present Mini^r, and his Successors ministers of that parish.

The bible is printed in Erse lettering.

At this time there were no Gaelic bibles in Scotland and yet Gaelic was the language spoken by at least 200,000 persons. James Kirkwood, at one time chaplain to the first Earl of Breadalbane, happening to meet Boyle and telling him how matters stood, was presented by him with a few copies of a bible which had been printed for use in Ireland. There are, I understand, five copies of this early bible still preserved in the district — at Killin, Kenmore, Weem, Moulin and Blair Atholl.

Of the high hills which rise from Loch Tay, Ben Lawers is the highest and most imposing. This hill, of noble proportions, reaches a height of almost 4,000 feet, and in his book *In Famed Breadalbane* Mr. Gillies puts on record the interesting fact that Malcolm Ferguson, a native of the district, knowing that the summit of Ben Lawers was but 14 feet short of the 4,000-foot level, decided to pay for the erection of a high cairn of stones so that it might be said that Ben Lawers was 4,000 feet high. The cairn was built some fifty years ago, but there is now little left of it.

I had often looked across to Ben Lawers from the high tops of the Cairngorms on days of summer brilliance, when the horizon shimmered with heat haze and all the western summits rose ethereal and delicately pencilled to the blue sky; when the air was aromatic with the scent of crowberry, and great herds of red deer grazed on the high passes and tablelands. I had seen the snowfield in its north-east corrie quiver in the heat haze and the sunlit summit rise above that snowy corrie. But I waited for many years before climbing to that summit, and when, in the autumn of 1940, my friend and I made the ascent, mist hid all the hill ranges, both north and west.

The beaten track to the summit of Ben Lawers ascends from Lawers, but we climbed by way of the Carie Burn as far as the Carie Corrie, and then ascended the steep shoulder of the hill which rises to the right of the corrie. There is a very old winding track which leads up to the corrie. It is now scarcely used and is grass-grown, for it is a relic of the days when the people of the district took their carts up to the corrie, over 2,000 feet above the sea, to bring down the peats from it. In this corrie are the ruins of summer shielings. At the present day little remains of these humble dwellings, but the Rev. Hugh MacMillan in his book *Highland Tay*, published in 1901, mentions that in his time they were more easily seen. He writes :

The most interesting of all these relics of the past are the remains of the hoary shielings, scattered about the uplands in considerable numbers. There is one cluster especially that attracts one's notice on account of its large size and apparently great age. These shielings are in the corry of Ben Lawers, following up the old zigzag peat-track on the western bank of the Carie Burn till the first plateau, where the people used to make peats, is reached. Here is a curious assemblage of circular foundations made of stones and turf, looking wonderfully green in contrast with the dark bogs around them — an oasis in the wilderness. All tradition of these shielings has disappeared in the district, and several hundreds of years must therefore have elapsed since they were in active use.

The old tale of the origin of Loch Tay was, one cannot doubt, sometimes narrated by those who lived simple lives in these shielings, on summer evenings when the polled cattle had been milked and in the quiet, dew-drenched dusk men, women and bairns had gathered around the peat fires. The tale is as follows :

In Carie Corrie is a clear, strong spring which gushes from the earth to form the source of the attractive Carie Burn, where the water flows, strong and cold, even in times of summer drought. The spring was kept secure by a strong door, which each evening was locked after the dairymaid had watered the cows which fed on the sweet hill herbage. As the old rhyme has it :

> Three nines of hillocks :
> On each hillock three nines of stakes :
> To each stake three nines of polled, dun cows tied.

One evening the dairymaid was late in finishing her work. She may have been eager to meet her lover, or to *céilidh* with friends. Certainly she forgot to fasten and lock the door which imprisoned the spring during the magic night hours. All through the night, therefore, the spring flowed mightily, and when the people of the shielings rose in the morning they saw that a vast sheet of water — Loch Tay — had covered the fertile strath beneath them.

It is pleasant to wander by the Carie Burn when the autumn sun shines full on its white cascades, where ferns are bathed in spray, and warms the steep slopes where the ling still retains some of the fragrance it has lavished on the winds of August. As we climbed, the western sky was heavily overcast and a sun-suffused shower drifted slowly down Loch Tay. Ahead of us the cone of Ben Lawers remained hidden in white, fleecy cloud, but all the country east of the hill lay in bright sunshine.

From the mouth of Carie Corrie, a favourite haunt of ptarmigan, we ascended the steep shoulder of Ben Lawers, where the air was dark and mist raced across the ground, but as we approached the summit ridge the mist thinned and the sun shone brightly. Here, 3,900 feet above sea level, in a sheltered hollow we came upon many meadow pipits. A short time previously a sparrowhawk had passed us, flying fast towards the south and rocking in the strong wind, and it is possible that it had been preying upon these pipits. Meadow pipits rarely if ever make their summer home as high as the summit of Ben Lawers, and it is probable that the flock seen were migrants, resting awhile on their autumn journey towards the south, and feeding on the insects aroused by the sun's warmth.

Great boulders lie beside the summit ridge of Ben Lawers, and the scene here is wild and stern. Far below, the waves of Loch Tay caught the sunlight. Beyond it, on the southern horizon, Ben Vorlich and its neighbour Stuic a' Chròin rose clear, but all the western hills were obscured by Atlantic clouds.

As we traversed the airy ridge to the summit cairn we looked into a deep corrie to the north-east in which a dark loch nestled. This loch is named Loch a' Chait, Loch of the Cat, and perhaps commemorates some fabulous wild cat which had its home here. From Loch a' Chait a burn flows to the low ground, and in a cave behind a waterfall of the burn an out-lawed MacGregor—one of the family of the chief — is tradi-tionally said to have hid from his pursuers. He was tracked by a bloodhound, but shot the hound with an arrow and suc-ceeded in making his escape.

In the scant shelter of the summit cairn we sat awhile. From the west came at intervals driving showers, and each hill in that direction was mist-capped, yet through a gap in the hills we could see an island-studded loch which may have been Loch Bà in the Blackmount Forest, or the neighbouring Loch Laidon. Eastward, brilliant sunshine flooded the Lowlands, and the air was so clear that on the far eastern horizon the distant North Sea was visible beyond the Firth of Tay — where a high chimney-stack could be seen, perhaps at Lochee in Angus. Far below us, yet at no great distance to the north, were the green slopes of

Glen Lyon where St. Adamnan, when the world was young, stayed the advance of the plague with his staff.

The mist was close as we descended westward to the *col* above the Carie Corrie, and when we had entered the corrie and had passed beyond the wind and the mist it was pleasant to rest awhile behind a large boulder in the quiet sunlit air and to look across Loch Tay to Ardeonaig, that district of old chapels and saintly associations. Of the chapel of Cill Mo-Charmaig, commemorating St. Cormac, scarce a trace remains ; nor is there ought to tell how it came about that Ardeonaig commemorates St. Adamnan.

From Ardeonaig an old drove road leads across the hills to Loch Earn. Here cattle were driven to the markets of the south, and here the twelve MacNabs carried their boat when they raided and slew Neish on his island of Loch Earn (*vide* Chapter VII).

It was good to think, at a time when the monstrous shadow of war darkened the land and swift and sinister death hurtled almost nightly from the skies, that warfare is in reality a fleeting thing, and that the beauty of hill and glen, corrie and stream, remain unchanged throughout the ages, for Beauty is a thing of the spirit, and indestructible.

Glen Orchy

CHAPTER XI

THE GLEN LYON COUNTRY

THE first time that I saw Glen Lyon I crossed the hill pass from Bridge of Orchy, which leads through the hills to the head of the glen.

Bridge of Orchy and the Blackmount Forest beside it were the home of Donnchadh Bàn nan Oran, Fair-haired Duncan of the Songs — he who has been described as the best-loved poet of the Gael. His songs are simple and direct. He was a nature observer, a nature lover and a climber of the steep hills of his home: some of his descriptions of the birds and beasts of his native corries are very fine. Donnchadh Bàn was versed in the classical music of the Highland bagpipe, and one of his most celebrated poems, " Moladh Beinn Dòrain " (" In Praise of Ben Dòrain "), is written in the form of a *pìobaireachd* with *ùrlar* or ground, *siubhal* or swift movement, and finally the

H

rippling, crowning movement of the tune, the *crùnluadh*. It is possible that this poem may have been written in 1784, after the Highland Society's piping competition in Ceòl Mór, at which " Bard MacIntyre " recited his poems.

Donnchadh Bàn was born at Druimliart, in the Blackmount Forest not far from Loch Tulla. A short distance west of the inn at Inveroran a bare ridge can be seen on the moor. This is

Blackmount

Druimliart, and here stand the ruins of the home of the old Gaelic poet. Of his house little remains, but the byre, which stands near it, is in better preservation, and the walls (with rounded corners) after more than two hundred years are almost intact. Near the ruins of the house is a large stone, and here the poet may have sat when composing his verses. In his day there were other houses on the ridge, for the Highland glens were then thickly populated, and Donnchadh Bàn doubtless went from one house to another after dark to *céilidh* and to recite his poems.

From his house he had an inspiring view. To the south, Ben Dòrain and its neighbouring peaks rise steeply ; north are the steep slopes of Stob Gabhar, down which a white waterfall plunges after rain. In places the old road to the clachan on Druimliart is easy to follow, and it is strange to notice that heather grows on the old track, although the ground on either side is grassy.

Donnchadh Bàn gave his love to Mairi Bhàn Òg, whose father kept the old inn at Inveroran. She became his devoted wife, lovely in her youth, gentle and affectionate in her old age : in more than one of his poems he praises her endearing qualities. The old inn where she spent her childhood days can still be seen, although there is now little left of it. It is near a hump-backed bridge on the road from Bridge of Orchy to Inveroran. The old inn appears to have been built on both sides of the road. Toll-houses, in the Highlands, were sometimes built on either side of a road, and this old inn may at one time have been a toll-house.

Donnchadh Bàn, who was under arms in the rising of 1745, was unable to read English, but one day when he was handed a newspaper by a brother soldier he was too proud to confess his ignorance. After a time the soldier who had lent him the paper exclaimed, " Duncan ! it is the wrong end of the paper you have up ! " Duncan, who had been holding the paper upside-down, promptly replied : " It does not matter which end is up, to a good scholar." He was able to speak little English, and when a companion jokingly remarked to him, " A pity, Duncan, you had not the two tongues," he retorted, " The one tongue would do me, if I had the two languages in it ! "

In Fair-haired Duncan's country, a short distance south of Bridge of Orchy, is the River Conglais. The water of this small river is so clear that in early times it was described, because of its purity, as " one of the three waters of Alba " — Alba being the old name for Scotland, and a still earlier name for all Britain.

One of the hill burns which feed the river is named Allt na h-Annaide. An *annad* or *annat* was usually the church of a patron saint, or a church which contained the relics of the founder. " Wherever ", writes Professor W. J. Watson to me,

" there is marked on the map an *annat*, there are traces of an ancient chapel or cemetery, or both: very often the *annat* adjoins a well or clear stream." Allt na h-Annaide is a burn of clear, foaming water. It flows below the new highway and eagerly enters the river of Conglais.

I drank of the waters of Allt na h-Annaide, of which Donn-chadh Bàn wrote:

> Fìon uillt na h-Annaide
> Blas meala r'a h-òl air
>
> (The wine of the burn of the Annat
> Its taste was of honey to drink it),

and when I had drunk, I watched the burn gush in full vigour from a spring on the hillside, near where stags were grazing.

The last of the harebells were in flower beside the burn, where are the faint ruins of the old nameless chapel. The broad modern motor track from Glasgow to Fort William passes only a few yards from these ruins, yet I doubt whether one of the motorists who rush by at the speed of an express train knows of this healing stream, or of the ancient ruins of the saintly chapel beside it. Donnchadh Bàn knew the virtue of this burn, else he had not written

> That is the unfailing remedy.
> Good manifold was wont to be received from it without purchase.

As one stands, of an autumn morning, and surveys the grand country of Donnchadh Bàn, one sees perhaps the hills the poet knew and loved so well free themselves from the mists of dawn. The Herdsmen of Etive glow warmly in the sun's rays. Ben Dòrain is longer in emerging from the cloud, and about the steep rocky sides of Ben Lui the mists slowly drift and eddy, rise and fall.

There is a hill pass, well known to that old poet with his checked broad bonnet made from a fox's skin, which leads through the hills from Auch, four miles south of Bridge of Orchy,

to Glen Lyon.   On the autumn day when a companion and I
crossed the pass there was no wind and the clouds were high.
The track, centuries old, leads up the River Conglais, between
Ben Dòrain and Beinn a' Chaisteil.   It passes the deserted
shepherd's house of an t-Sìthein (where two gillies with their
ponies were awaiting the return of a stalking party from the
steep, grassy slopes of Ben Dòrain) where Donnchadh Bàn, when
in the employment of the Earl of Breadalbane as under forester,
for a time had his home.   Thence it climbs a gentle slope to
the watershed and the county march between Argyll and Perth,
where the clustered remains of four summer shielings tell mutely
of an earlier age, when the people of the Highlands went up into
the hill country to live during the months of summer.

I confess that I was disappointed with this walk from the
country of Bridge of Orchy across to the head of Glen Lyon.
The view was restricted throughout the nine miles and there
was little of interest to be seen.   Shepherds were finishing a
hay-stack beside the lonely, solitary home at Lùban, and there
were three friendly collie dogs outside a shepherd's house beside
the clear waters of Loch Lyon, where many rising trout, and a
few salmon, were rippling the still surface of the loch.   We had
almost reached the end of Loch Lyon when we passed two small
children walking wearily along the wet and boggy track from
school to their home at the head of the loch, and in a pleasant
house beside old trees I was surprised to receive a welcome from
a woman from the Isle of Mull.   This good lady's mother I
remembered well.   Like Donnchadh Bàn she had no tongue
but the Gaelic, and was the most expert maker of scones I
have ever met.   More than twenty years ago my wife and I
had often received her island hospitality, and it was strange to
come unexpectedly upon one of this good lady's daughters in a
central Highland glen.

It has been suggested that Captain Campbell led his troops
from Glen Lyon to the west before the Massacre of Glencoe,
but the old tradition is that he was serving in Argyll with

Argyll's regiment at the time, and thus journeyed to Glencoe
from Argyll and not from Glen Lyon : it is further traditionally
believed that the men of Argyll's regiment, although they were
Campbells, were not (except their commanding officer) Campbells
from Glen Lyon.

We had now reached the road which traverses Glen Lyon
from the east. For rather more than nine miles we had walked
over the track that for centuries must have been used by cattle
drovers and which, like most of these old paths, was broad and
straggling. Like other hill tracks, it maintains its character,
although nowadays it is little used.

The solemn quiet of early autumn lay over all the country
at the head of Glen Lyon — a glen which becomes more beautiful as its mid reaches are viewed and the charm of its clear
salmon river and the old pines which rise dark from the hillside
are seen. The sun that day was near his setting when at last he
broke through the clouds and shone upon the crown of Ben
Lawers with soft golden light seen on the hills only in autumn.
I thought of Donnchadh Bàn in his old age wandering through
this glen with his wife and sweetheart, Màiri Bhàn Òg.

> He travelled slowly [writes one who knew him in those days]. He was
> dressed in the Highland garb, with a checked bonnet over which a large
> bushy tail of a wild animal hung, a badger's skin fastened by a belt in
> front, a hanger by his side, and a soldier's wallet strapped to his shoulders.
> He had not been seen by any present before then, but he was immediately
> recognised. A forward young man asked him if it was he that made
> Ben Dòrain ? "No," replied the venerable old man, "God made Ben
> Dòrain, but I praised it."

It was again the season of autumn, and two years later, when
next I visited Glen Lyon. This time I came by car (I feel sure
that Fair-haired Duncan of the Songs would not have approved
of cars) and reached the glen from the east.

I had the privilege to have with me the *seanchaidh* of the
district, Alexander Stewart, whose book *A Highland Parish*
gives the most scholarly and accurate account that we have of
Glen Lyon and its traditions. It was a still, warm day after a

night of rain, and when we reached the old churchyard of Fortingall, not far from the birth-place of that celebrated scholar of olden times, the Dean of Lismore, we halted to see the famous old yew tree of Fortingall.

This yew is believed to be 3,000 years old and is perhaps the oldest tree in Europe. When Pennant saw it, in the summer of 1772, this great tree measured 56 feet in circumference. " The middle part," writes Pennant, " is now decayed to the ground, but within memory was united to a height of three feet ; Captain Campbell, of Glen-lion, having assured me that, when a boy, he has often climbed over, or rode on, the then connecting part."

It is possible that this yew may have been a sacred tribal tree hundreds of years before the time of Christ. Its wood has afforded material for innumerable bows : for centuries, perhaps thousands of years, the fires of Beltane were kindled beneath its spreading branches : shoemakers of many generations esteemed its wood for their awl handles.

This veteran yew is now protected by a wall, and although its great stem in places shows signs of disintegration, its needles and young shoots are as fresh and green as when Adamnan (or Eónan as he was locally named) a century after the death of Columba came to preach the Gospel in Glen Lyon, dwelling for some years in the glen and perhaps preaching beneath this yew, even at that time old. It was pleasant to look on this tree, beside which the oldest pine in the Caledonian forest is in age no more than a seedling. The sunlight glinted between the fresh green needles of its branches. The air was soft and heavy ; thundery clouds drifted idly overhead and rested upon the green summit of Ben Lawers which dominated the lesser hills. Schiehallion we had seen that morning and its top was also enveloped in the mist that had followed the rain : the River Lyon flowed peat-stained through its rocky bed.

Sir James MacGregor, whose home was at Fortingall, died in the year 1551. He was Vicar of Fortingall and Dean of

Lismore, and is remembered by the remarkable *Book of the Dean of Lismore*, in which many poems of the fourteenth, fifteenth and sixteenth centuries are collected. The poems are of course all in Gaelic (or Erse as it used to be called by old writers) and are the work of Scottish and Irish authors, " not only professional poets, but others, including members of the ruling family of Argyll and the chief of the MacNabs ".

Perhaps the Dean of Lismore sat beneath the old yew of Fortingall when compiling his historic book ; he must often have admired it, for he lived in sight of it, although even the ruins of his house have now disappeared.

At Fortingall the glen is comparatively wide, and is pastoral. Higher up, at the Pass of Lyon, it narrows, and here is to be seen MacGregor's Leap. Grigor MacGregor, of Glen Strae, chief of his clan, performed the remarkable feat of leaping across the Lyon from north to south, when pursued by his enemies with bloodhounds on his track. Grigor, a wild bold man, without fear, had married a daughter of Duncan the Hospitable, one of the Glen Lyon Campbells, and was always in peril after that midnight of June 11, 1565, when two members of his clan, Grigor MacGregor, son of the Dean of Lismore, and Robert MacConil or Gregor, were murdered by James MacGestalcar, son of a renowned archer, at the instigation of the Campbells of Glenurchy.

Grigor MacGregor, as chief of his clan, was in honour bound to avenge this murder, and that he did so is recorded in the *Chronicle of Fortingall*, which mentions that on July 27 of the same year " James MacGestalcar or Patrick was killed with his accomplices by Grigor MacGregor of Stronmelecon at Ardo-wenoc ". The *Chronicle* adds that the slain man was " a most wicked man and an oppressor of the poor ". But by avenging the murder of one of his clan Grigor MacGregor incurred the fierce enmity of the Campbells of Glenurchy, and it was when pursued by Campbell bloodhounds that he leaped the Lyon at the gorge which still bears his name. His daring leap saved his life for the time being, but he was later murdered by his relentless and powerful enemies.

Only one man since that day has sought to emulate Grigor MacGregor's feat. This was a showman, and he did indeed succeed in leaping the chasm, but lost his life in the attempt. A cairn of stones, known as Carn an Duine Ghointe, the Cairn of the Wounded Man, marked the place of his death leap until a road was made up Glen Lyon, when the cairn was pulled down.

Higher up Glen Lyon, at Craigianie, on the right-hand side of the road as you ascend, stands a rock on which is a curious hollow or imprint which recalls the old legend of the glen — that an *uruisg* or water demon once had his home here. If you climb to the top of the rock you will see this deep hoof-like imprint, which is known as Caslorg Pheallaidh, the Footprint of Peallaidh. Peallaidh, the Shaggy One, was a hairy being, king of the *uruisgean*, and Aberfeldy is named after him. This water demon haunted the swift rushes and deep pools of the Lyon, and the speed of his swimming was such that no salmon or otter could compete with him — and yet his foot, judging by the imprint in the rock, must have been a heavy one.

Perhaps the Stewarts of Garth caught a glimpse of Peallaidh on that day in the fifteenth century when they fought a hard fight with the MacIvors (who at that time held the greater part of Glen Lyon) on the grassy hollow which to this day is named Lagan a' Chatha, the Hollow of the Fight. Stewart of Garth in his *Sketches* mentions that before the fight MacIvor and Stewart stepped forward and held a parley in order, if possible, to settle the affair amicably. Stewart wore a plaid, one side of which was red and the other of a dark-coloured tartan. Before the parley, he told his men that if the result of the conference should be favourable the dark side of his plaid would remain outward, but if no agreement could be reached he would give the signal that they should attack, by turning his plaid and showing the red tartan. The two head men were in deep conference when suddenly MacIvor gave a loud whistle, and armed Highlanders started up from the neighbouring rocks and bushes. "Who are these?" asked Stewart. "These," replied MacIvor, "are a herd of my roes, frisking among the rocks." "Then," replied Stewart, "it were time for me to call my hounds." With a quick gesture he turned his plaid, and his men rushed forward to the attack. The fight was a long and hard one but at last the MacIvors were defeated. Before going into the fight each of Stewart of Garth's men removed his deer-skin sandals or *cuarain* and placed them on a flat rock, to this day named Leac nan Cuarain. After the fight each man returned for his *cuarain*, and by the number of sandals which then remained, the number of men who fell in fight could be told.

There is an old Gaelic saying that a man who wore *cuarain* had to bestir himself an hour earlier in the morning than a man who wore *brògan* or brogues, the inference being that *cuarain* took much longer to fasten. Stewart of Garth mentions that in the year 1816 a sword and battle-axe were dug up on the site of the fight, and that the sword was small and remarkable for its elegance.

My companion in Glen Lyon that day was (as I have mentioned earlier in this chapter) Alexander Stewart, a distinguished son of the glen. Although an old man, he was still in excellent health, and when we came in sight of cloud-capped Ben Lawers he told me that in the summer of 1887, the year of Queen Victoria's Jubilee, he had remained all night on the summit of this hill and had seen the sun, large and red, climb above the north-east horizon where stood the dark and distant summits of the Cairngorm Hills. He remembered, too, the still more distant Paps of Jura which had risen clear and delicately-pencilled far, far westward in the keen air of dawn.

He told me that when he was a young man Glen Lyon had a population of 700 but that, on the autumn day of 1938 when I met him, there was a resident population of no more than 200 in the glen. He also gave me an interesting account of Clach Bhuaidh, the Stone of Virtue, which was preserved in

Glen Lyon house. A man who was sprinkled by water in which the stone had been dipped was believed to be invulnerable in battle : it is said that all the Glen Lyon men before they set out to join the Prince in the 1745 campaign were sprinkled with this water, except one man, a tailor. He was killed at Culloden — the others came safely through the campaign.

Alexander Stewart told me also of the curious Glen Lyon tradition that in Dùn Geal, an old *dùn* not far from Fortingall, Pontius Pilate was born. Pontius Pilate's father, it is averred, had been sent on a mission of peace by the Emperor Caesar Augustus to Metellanus, King of Scotland, whose fortress at the time was Dùn Geal. There is preserved in Glen Lyon house a curious staff of Roman appearance which, it seems, Pennant must have seen, for he writes of a staff " iron cased in leather, five feet long, at the top a neat pair of extended wings like a Caducus, but on being shook, a poniard 2 feet nine inches darted out ". A visitor to the district, anxious to find the site of Dùn Geal, asked a native working on the road whether he could point out to him the birth-place of Pontius Pilate. " I have never heard of that man," was the answer. " But surely," protested the visitor, " surely you go to church ? " " Yes," came the reply, " but he does not go to my church ! "

The history of the Massacre of Glencoe is well known, and the behaviour of Campbell of Glenlyon, commanding officer of the Government regiment, towards MacDonald of Glencoe has had no defenders. But Campbell of Glenlyon had a bitter grudge against the men of Glencoe, because, a few years before the massacre, they had passed up Glen Lyon, when the Glen Lyon Highlanders were away on some war-like foray, and had " lifted " all the cattle and sheep in the glen. When the people returned the glen had been swept bare, and Campbell of Glenlyon found himself almost a ruined man. It was perhaps because of this that the Government ordered Argyll's regiment, of which Campbell of Glenlyon was commander, to carry out the massacre.

CHAPTER XII

PERTH : AN HISTORIC COMBAT

THE " Fair City of Perth ", which until 1437 was the chief city of Scotland, stands at the threshold of the Highlands : the tides of the North Sea almost reach it from the east, and to the west the hills of the Central Highlands rise to the horizon. Pennant records that the present Perth rose after the destruction of the old Perth or Bertha, which stood perhaps two miles farther up the Tay and was overwhelmed by a flood in the year 1210, in the time of William the Lion, who, with his family, with difficulty escaped in a small skiff. William re-built Perth and named it Saint John's Town, in honour of the saint. It was taken by Edward I, and later by Robert the Bruce in 1312. The city was seized by Montrose after the battle of Tibbermuir in 1644, and in 1651 Cromwell made himself master of it. Pennant also records the interesting fact that in his time no beggars were to be seen in the streets of Perth and that the city supported its indigent.

I cannot, within the scope of this book, do more than touch lightly upon the rich and varied history of Perth — that is admirably set forth in David Peacock's *Perth : its Annals and its Archives* — but no one who visits the place should fail to see its beautiful and ancient Church of St. John the Baptist, which dates from the twelfth century and was re-built in 1328 by command of Robert the Bruce ; nor its Salutation Hotel where Prince Charles Edward had his headquarters during the campaign of 1745 and where the room in which the Prince slept is still used.

But as those who fought in it were Highlanders from the

Central Highlands, I feel that I should give some account in this Central Highlands book of the historic combat known as the battle of the North Inch of Perth.

The accounts given by the early chroniclers of this remarkable combat vary. Skene believes (*Celtic Scotland*, vol. iii, p. 310) that the earliest account is given by Wyntoun, who wrote his *Chronicle* somewhere around the year 1420, and since the battle of the North Inch was fought in 1396 this may be said to be an almost contemporary account. Wyntoun describes the combat as taking place at " Saint Johnstoun " or Perth between sixty men (thirty against thirty) who had long been at variance in old feud. Wyntoun names the clans Clahynnhe (Clan) Qwhewyl and Clahiny (Clan) Ha, and their leaders Scha Ferqwhareisone and Christy Johnesone. He records that the opposing sides fought within barriers, that fifty or more of the combatants were slain, but that he could not say who had the best of the fight.

The next chronicler of the fight is Bower, who wrote twenty-five years after Wyntoun. Bower mentions that the " Clan Kay " and the " Clanquhele " agreed, at the representations of David de Lyndesay of Crawford and Thomas Earl of Moray, to settle their quarrel before the King at Perth, by a combat between thirty chosen men on either side, armed only with their swords, bows and arrows, and without their plaids. Bower records that the fight took place on the North Inch of Perth in the presence of the King, the governor and a great multitude, on the Monday before St. Michael's Day, when, of the sixty fighters, all of the Clan Kay except one man were slain, but that eleven survived from the " Clanquhele ". The chronicler adds that as the combatants were passing through the barrier one of them dashed into the river and escaped by swimming across, and that one of the spectators offered to take his place for half a mark, on condition that, if he survived, he was to be maintained during the rest of his life. This was agreed to, and the man entered the lists.

The next account of the battle of North Inch is given by

Maurice Buchanan (who wrote in 1461) in the *Book of Plus-carden*. He mentions that, a great contention having arisen among the " wild Scots ", the King, finding himself unable to restore peace, arranged, in a council of the magnates of the kingdom, that the two captains of the clans at variance, with their best and most valiant friends, amounting on each side to thirty men, should fight in an enclosed field after the manner of judicial combatants, armed only with swords and cross-bows having each no more than three arrows, and this before the King on a certain day on the North Inch of Perth. This, by the intervention of the Earl of Crawford and other nobles, was agreed upon. Buchanan states that in the fight five on the one side and two on the other escaped alive — and that of these two one escaped by swimming the Tay and the other was pardoned " though some say he was hung ". He mentions that before the fight one of the combatants could not be found, and that a spectator, who belonged to the same clan, and was hostile to the other party, agreed to take his place for 40 shillings, fought most valiantly, and escaped with his life.

Skene inclines to the belief that the fight was of the nature of a judicial wager of battle, to decide some question of right or privilege which both claimed, for had it been an ordinary feud, it is, he thinks, difficult to see how the fight could have restored peace between the contending parties.

MacPherson (*Glimpses of Church and Social Life in the Highlands in Olden Times*, p. 465) believes that the " Clanquhele " were Macintoshs [1] and the Clan Ha were MacPhersons. He

[1] Both Macintosh and Mackintosh are anglicised from the Gaelic Mac an Tòisich, Son of the Thane. Having dropped the final syllable (*-ich*) and shifted the stress from *tòis* to *mac* both are more or less incorrect. The *k* of Mackintosh is a further error, so on the whole Macintosh is to be preferred.

A number of names have *k* in the anglicised forms, *e.g.* Mackay for MacAoidh, Mackenzie for MacCoinnich, MacKechnie, MacKendrick, MacKillop and others. On the other hand the *k* is seldom (or never) found in MacAlpine, MacAndrew, MacArthur, MacAskill, or MacAulay.

It should be noted that the Chief has spelled his name " Mackintosh of Mackintosh " for at least 150 years.

mentions that in a MS. of 1450 the MacPhersons are stated to be descended from a son of Heth, and brother of Angus, Earl of Moray, and suggests that the word Heth is a corruption of the Gaelic name changed by the historian to Ha. He believes, therefore, that the Clan Heth was the ancient name of the MacPhersons. To strengthen this belief it would appear that the " Scha Ferqwhareisone " of Wyntoun was the Shaw who, according to the MS. of 1450, was chief of the MacPhersons, and the " Christy Johnesone " was the Gilchrist Mac Jan mentioned in the old MS. histories of the MacIntoshs of that period, and that the conflict was fought to decide the chiefship of the Clan Chattain. If this surmise be correct, the victors in the fight were the Macintoshs, for their chiefs seem afterwards to have assumed the chiefship of Clan Chattain and to have been called captains of that clan.

It is almost certain that the combatants of the battle of the North Inch had their pipers to cheer them, and there is a tradition that the Feadan Dubh, the Black Chanter, of the MacPhersons by its strains of immortal music encouraged the members of its clan.[1]

Although in the early accounts of the fight there is no mention of the identity of the spectator who took the place of the missing combatant, he is subsequently — and no doubt correctly — described as the Gobha Crom, the Bent or Stooping Smith. He appears to have been a man of great strength and stature, and in the fight, which he survived, he acquitted himself with much distinction. It seems that he must have taken the place of one of the Macintoshs who, for some unknown reason (not necessarily cowardice), had withdrawn before the fight opened. The descendants of this doughty smith came to be known as Sliochd a' Ghobha Chruim, the Race of the Bent Smith, and the Smiths are to this day a sept of the Clan Chattain.

[1] The chanter, it is said, was playing a sublime melody as it fell from heaven : on touching the ground it cracked and the crack is still to be seen on its smooth-worn, well-fingered surface.

The North Inch of Perth is, after more than five centuries, still open grassy land on which no building is permitted. On the winter day when I visited that old historic battlefield the Tay was frozen across, and against the piers of the bridge spanning the stream the ice had been pressed high by the current. In the open " lanes " of water a great assembly of waterfowl were feeding. The majority of the birds were mallard, but it was more unexpected to see handsome golden-eye drakes swimming and diving in full view of the citizens of Perth. Herring gulls were standing disconsolately on the ice, and black-headed gulls — small gulls with pointed, black-tipped wings — were flying restlessly to and fro and, like their relations of the London parks, were taking food from the hands of their human friends.

The North Inch is now set aside for the purpose of peaceful recreation, but I do not imagine that the character of its ground has greatly changed since 1396, when its level, grassy acres must have formed an ideal setting for the sanguinary conflict watched by the King and his nobles and the citizens of Perth.

A few miles up the river from Perth is the site of the historic Abbey of Scone, where the kings of Scotland were crowned. But the glory of Scone has long departed, for, even in the time of the writing of the old *Statistical Account*, " on the spot where our ancient kings were crowned there now grows a clump of trees ". At Scone the Coronation Stone or Stone of Destiny [1] was " reverently kept for the consecration of the kings of Alba " and, according to an old chronicler, " no king was ever wont to reign in Scotland unless he had first, on receiving the royal name, sat upon this stone at Scone, which by the kings of old had been appointed the capital of Alba ". The Stone of Destiny, now in Westminster Abbey, is an oblong block of red sandstone, some 26 inches long by 16 inches broad, and $10\frac{1}{2}$ inches deep : on the flat top of the stone are the marks of chiselling. Tradition affirms that it is the same stone which Jacob used as a pillow at Bethel and then set up as a pillar and anointed with oil : later,

[1] The Celtic name is Lia Fàil, hence Inis Fàil, Ireland.

according to Jewish tradition, it became the pedestal of the ark in the Temple. The stone was brought from Syria to Egypt by Gathelus, who in order to escape the plague, sailed, on the advice of Moses, from the Nile with his wife and the Stone of Destiny, and landed in Spain. Gathelus sent the stone to Eire when he had invaded that country, and it was later brought to Scotland where it remained in the Abbey of Scone until, in the year 1296, Edward I of England carried it off to Westminster Abbey.

An interesting tradition has been given me by the Earl of Mansfield, whose family have owned the lands of Scone for more than three hundred years. The tradition, which has been handed down through several generations, is that, somewhere around the dates 1795–1820, a farm lad had been wandering with a friend on Dunsinnan, the site of MacBeth's castle, soon after a violent storm. The torrential rain had caused a small landslide, and as the result of this a fissure, which seemed to penetrate deep into the hillside, was visible. The two men procured some form of light and explored the fissure. They came at last to the broken wall of a subterranean chamber. In one corner of the chamber was a stair which was blocked with debris, and in the centre of the chamber they saw a slab of stone covered with hieroglyphics and supported by four short stone " legs ". As there was no evidence of " treasure " in the subterranean apartment the two men did not realise the importance of their " find " and did not talk of what they had seen. Some years later one of the men first heard the local tradition, that on the approach of King Edward I the monks of Scone hurriedly removed the Stone of Destiny to a place of safe concealment and took from the Annety Burn a stone of similar size and shape, which the English king carried off in triumph. When he heard this legend, the man hurried back to Dunsinnan Hill, but whether his memory was at fault regarding the site of the landslide, or whether the passage of time, or a fresh slide of earth, had obliterated the cavity, the fact remains that he was unable to locate the opening in the hillside. It may be asked why the monks of Scone, after the English king had

I

returned to London, did not bring back to the abbey the original Stone of Destiny, but the tradition accounts for this by explaining that it was not considered safe at the time to allow the English to know that they had been tricked, and that when the days of possible retribution were past, the monks who had known the secret were dead. This tradition, it is held, explains why the Coronation Stone in Westminster Abbey resembles geologically the stone commonly found in the neighbourhood of Scone.

The Sma' Glen

CHAPTER XIII

THE SMA' GLEN

In this still place, remote from men
Sleeps Ossian, in the Narrow Glen.
WORDSWORTH

AN CAOL GHLEANN, the Narrow Glen (Sma' Glen is a comparatively modern name, and does not correctly translate the original
Gaelic), lies near the head-waters of the River Almond in Perthshire. It is a glen of remarkable beauty, and not the least of its
charms is that it is entirely different from the surrounding
country.

The Sma' Glen can be reached by car with ease, from Crieff
to the south, or from Dunkeld by way of Strath Bran. From
Aberfeldy it is rather less than twenty miles, and on the May
morning when my friend and I climbed the steep hill out of
Aberfeldy the weeping birches were drenching the warm, still air

with perfume. The road quickly reaches an elevation of 1,400 feet at Loch na Craige, and shortly before we arrived at the loch we had a glimpse, through a gap in the intervening hills, of one of the high Cairngorms — Cairntoul or Braeriach — deeply covered with snow and gleaming like a jewel on the far horizon. At the watershed near Loch na Craige the road begins to descend Glen Cochill, a glen of little character, and reaches Amulree beside the River Bran. At Amulree a small chapel, dedicated to St. Maolruba, formerly stood. The name Amulree itself commemorates the saint, for in its Gaelic form it is Ath Maol Ruibhe, Ford of St. Maolruba. The ford, which crosses the River Bran, is still known to old people of the district. The Amulree Market, which was held in May, was an event of even greater importance than the Falkirk Tryst. Amulree stands high, and summer is late in arriving at this upland strath. The last snowdrift had scarcely melted on the hill-slopes, for the winter had been one of unusual severity (1939–40) and for a month some of the pupils attending Amulree school had been imprisoned in their homes in the side glens. But now frost and snow were forgotten, and the sun shone joyously on a country where curlews, drifting on vibrating wings over the moors, made sweet plaintive music that mingled with the rollicking, cheerful cries of courting lapwings. The music of the whaup or curlew is esteemed highly by Scotsmen, and my friend told me that on one occasion, in the south of England, a discussion arose on a summer evening as to the identity of a sweet songster which had recently been heard. Some said that the singer was a nightingale ; others that the liquid music came from the throat of a garden warbler. An old Highland gardener, an exile from his native land, overhearing the discussion, gravely said : " I'm thinking the bird wi' the grand song ye have heard is neither warbler nor nightingale. I'm thinking that ye have heard the bird wi' the finest o' all songs — the whaup."

Even from Amulree the Sma' Glen is invisible, and as the road descends to it the restful beauty of the place is seen, and felt, with almost startling abruptness. The glen has affinity with the

Western Highlands rather than the Central Highlands and it is difficult to realise that the comparatively Lowland scenery of lower Strathearn is only a few miles to the south.

The hills which set bounds to the Sma' Glen rise abruptly on either side of the clear waters of the young Almond. On that day of early summer when I visited the glen the steep slopes, carpeted with blaeberry plants, were of a fresh green, tinged with bronze — a colour that is sometimes seen in the young foliage of oaks on a May day, rare and delightful. The slopes climbed steeply to high rocks where, I doubt not, the golden eagle formerly had her eyrie, and here and there, in striking contrast to the austerity of the scene, the feathery green, sweet-scented foliage of a sturdy larch caught the eye. Near the head of the glen, and standing between the high road and the river, is a huge ice-scarred boulder renowned as Clach Oisein, Ossian's Stone. There is a tradition that Ossian, immortal bard of the Gael, was buried here. It may be of interest to quote the *Ordnance Gazetteer*, which in turn quotes information supplied by Newte, who was in the glen in 1791, on what happened after the despoiling of the grave beneath the stone by Wade's soldiers :

> The people of the country, to the number of three or four score men, venerating the memory of the bard, rose with one consent, and carried away the bones with bagpipe playing and other funeral rites, and deposited them with much solemnity within a circle of large stones, on the lofty summit of a rock, sequestered and difficult of access . . . in the wild recesses of Glen Almond.

The event took place when General Wade's military road was being driven through Glen Almond. In one of Burt's *Letters from a Gentleman in the North of Scotland*, written in or about the year 1730, there is a full account of the moving of the boulder by Wade's road-making soldiers. Burt writes as follows :

> There happened to lie directly in the Way an exceedingly large Stone, and as it had been made a Rule from the Beginning to carry on the Roads in straight Lines, as far as the Way would permit, not only to give them a better Air, but to shorten the Passenger's Journey, it was resolved the Stone should be removed, if possible, though otherwise the Work might have been carried along on either Side of it.

The Soldiers, by vast Labour, with their Levers and Jacks, or Hand-screws, tumbled it over and over, till they got it quite out of the Way, although it was of such an enormous Size that it might be Matter of great Wonder how it could ever be removed by Human Strength and Art, especially to such as had never seen an Operation of that Kind : and, upon their digging a little Way into that Part of the Ground where the Centre of the Base had stood, there was found a small Cavity, about two Feet square, which was guarded from the outward Earth at the Bottom, Top, and Sides, by square flat Stones.

This Hollow contained some Ashes, Scraps of Bones, and half-burnt Ends of Stalks of Heath ; which last we concluded to be a small Remnant of a Funeral Pile.

· Upon the whole, I think there is no Room to doubt but it was the Urn of some considerable Roman Officer, and the best of the Kind that could be provided in their military Circumstances ; and that it was so seems plainly to appear from its vicinity to the Roman Camp,[1] the Engines that must have been employed to remove that vast Piece of Rock, and the Unlikeliness it should, or could, have ever been done by the Natives of the Country. But certainly the Design was to preserve those Remains from the injuries of Rains and melting Snows, and to prevent their being profaned by the sacrilegious Hands of those they call Barbarians, for that reproachful Name, you know, they gave to the People of almost all Nations but their own.

Give me leave to finish this Digression, which is grown already longer than I foresaw or intended.

As I returned the same Way from the Lowlands, I found the Officer, with his Party of working Soldiers, not far from the Stone, and asked him what was become of the Urn ?

To this he answered, that he had intended to preserve it in the Condition I left it, till the Commander-in-Chief had seen it, as a Curiosity, but that it was not in his Power so to do ; for soon after the Discovery was known to the Highlanders, they assembled from distant Parts, and having formed themselves into a Body they carefully gathered up the Relics, and marched with them, in solemn Procession, to a new Place of Burial, and there discharged their Fire-arms over the Grave, as supposing the Deceased had been a military Officer.

You will believe the Recital of all this Ceremony led me to ask the Reason of such Homage done to the Ashes of a Person supposed to have been dead almost two thousand Years. I did so ; and the Officer, who was himself a Native of the Hills, told me that they (the Highlanders) firmly believe that if a dead Body should be known to lie above Ground, or be disinterred by Malice, or the Accidents of Torrents of Water etc., and Care was not immediately taken to perform to it the proper Rites, then there would arise such Storms and Tempests as would destroy their Corn, blow away their Huts, and all Sorts of other Misfortunes would follow till that Duty was performed.

---

[1] The site of a Roman camp is to be seen near the south entrance to the glen.

From the above account it will be seen that Burt thought the human remains beneath the stone to be those of a great Roman officer. If he had heard the tradition that Ossian lay here, he does not mention it. Yet the veneration shown the bones by the Highlanders seems to be in favour of the veracity of that tradition, for it is unlikely that the men of the country would have shown so great respect for the bones of a Roman as for the ashes of a Fingalian hero, whose wingèd words still remained with them.

The high road at the present day traverses the Sma' Glen a short distance above General Wade's Road, the undeviating course of which can still be seen. Around the great boulder lie smaller stones which may well be those, mentioned in Burt's account, on which the boulder originally rested. In the immediate vicinity of the great stone are visible the remains of a grass-grown mound, rather low, and apparently of great age, forming a circle.

There brooded stillness and a sense of rest and tranquillity in the glen, as my friend and I sat awhile beside Clach Oisein. It seemed as if the poetry of Ossian — his immortal songs of heroism and love and fidelity — permeated the soft sunlit air on this afternoon of early summer. From a small alder tree which grew beside the limpid waters of the Almond a cuckoo called huskily. Oyster-catchers flew swiftly above the gleaming shingle-beds of the river, calling one to another with high-pitched whistling cries, and a pair of ring ousels, which had lost no time in nesting on their arrival from their winter quarters in Africa, scolded us roundly from a neighbouring tree.

CHAPTER XIV

THE COUNTRY OF DUNKELD

From Perth northward to the approaches to Dunkeld the valley of the Tay is broad, fertile and Lowland rather than Highland in character. But at Dunkeld the valley narrows, the hills approach and the scenery at once becomes truly Highland.

The Gaelic name for Dunkeld is Dùn Chailleann, Fort of the Caledonians, and in the *Annals of Ulster* (A.D. 873) the designation " princeps Dúin Chaillden " is found.

The history of Dunkeld may begin at an even earlier date than the burning of Iona in the year 802, for a MS. of the fourteenth century records that Columba was the first Bishop of Dunkeld, and there educated St. Cuthbert. To Iona " Pagans from the northern region came like stinging hornets . . . plundering, tearing and killing not only sheep and oxen, but priests and Levites, and choirs of monks and nuns. They . . . laid all waste with dreadful havoc, trod with unhallowed feet the holy places, dug up the altars, and carried off all the treasures of the holy church. Some of the brethren they killed, some they carried off in chains, many they cast out naked and loaded with insults, some they drowned in the sea." When, four years after the burning of Iona, the northern pirates again descended upon that small island, and put to the sword the whole community, consisting of 68 persons, it was resolved to move the chief seat of the Columban monasteries to a safer locality. This (says Skene) was not to be found in any of the Western Isles, and the respective claims of Scotland and Ireland were satisfied by the foundation in each country of a church which should be supreme

over the Columban monasteries of its own land. In Eire the
church of Kells was founded and was completed in 814: in
Scotland that supreme church was the church of Dunkeld. The

Tay at Stanley

relics of St. Columba, greatly venerated on Iona, were now
transferred partly to Kells and partly to Dunkeld. The church
of Dunkeld was treated with great honour by the Picts, and in
the year 865 the *Annals of Ulster* record that the Abbot of Dunkeld was placed at the head of the Pictish church. By the year

1000 or thereabouts he who bore the designation Abbot of Dunkeld was not an ecclesiastic but a great secular chief (like the lay abbots of Glen Dochart), and the eldest daughter of King Malcolm was about that time given in marriage to the " Abbot of Dunkeld ". This abbot, by name Crinan or Cronan, seems to have been in possession not only of the extensive lands pertaining to the church of Dunkeld, but also those of the monastery of Dull. The lands of Dull, which also had by this time been secularised, extended from Strath Tay to the boundary between Atholl and Argyll. The abbey of Dunkeld by now had apparently lost the position of pre-eminence which it formerly held, and the *Annals of Ulster* record that in the year 1027 it was entirely burnt. The abbey was later rebuilt, and Pennant mentions that about the year 1127 it was converted into a cathedral by " that pious prince David I ".

The present church, according to the same writer, was built by Robert Arden, the nineteenth bishop, about the year 1436. Even in Pennant's time, " except the choir, which serves as the parish church, the rest exhibits a fine ruin, amidst the solemn scene of rocks and woods ". Pennant also takes note of the Gothic arches and the two supporting rows of round pillars, with squared capitals, and puts on record that he looked in vain for the tomb of one Marjory Scot, whose epitaph thus addresses the reader :

> Stop Passenger, until my Life you read,
> The Living may get knowledge from the Dead.
> Five Times five Years I liv'd a virgin Life ;
> Five Times five Years I liv'd a happy Wife ;
> Ten Times five Years I liv'd a Widow chaste ;
> Now wearied of this mortal Life I rest.
> Betwixt my Cradle and my Grave were seen
> Eight mighty Kings of Scotland, and a Queen.
> Four Times five Years a Commonwealth I saw,
> Ten Times the Subjects rise against the Law ;
> Thrice did I see old Prelacy pull'd down,
> And thrice the Cloak was humbled by the Gown.
> An end of Stuart's Race I saw, nay more,
> I saw my Country sold for English Ore.
> Such Desolations in my Time have been ;
> I have an End of all Perfection seen.

According to Pennant, who was an accurate chronicler, Dunkeld Cathedral was demolished in 1559, and the monuments were destroyed in 1689 by the garrison that was placed there at this time.

The most interesting tomb in Dunkeld Cathedral is perhaps that of the third son of Robert II — he who, because of his cruelty and impiety, was justly styled Wolf of Badenoch and whose Gaelic title was Alasdair Mór Mac an Rìgh (Big Alexander the King's Son). The epitaph on this tomb is now, because of the breaks and gaps in the stone, difficult to read. The damage must have been done at least two hundred years ago, for Pennant writes : "   epitaph WHEN ENTIRE ran thus : ' Hic jacet bonae memoriae, Alexander Senescallus comes de Buchan et dominus (dus.) de Badenach, qui obiit 24 Novemb. 1394 ' ".

A more recent memorial within the cathedral is to

Lieutenant Colonel
WILLIAM CLELAND
The Cameronians
The Earl of Angus' Regiment
who fell at the Battle of Dunkeld on
21st August 1689.

An able poet, a devoted patriot,
A brave soldier, and a pious Christian.
Buried in the nave of this Cathedral.
Erected in 1903, by an old Cameronian.

It is believed that the cathedral of Dunkeld stands on the site of the ancient monastery which stood here even before the monks fled thither on the sack of Iona. This earliest Christian community was a Culdee brotherhood, and there is reason to suppose that Columba, accompanied by Kentigern, visited that community during his travels in the Highlands.[1] Of the relics of St. Columba, carried reverently from Iona by his followers, there is now no trace : they may have been lost when, on two separate occasions, the Danes, in 845 and 905, plundered and burnt the monastery

[1] Columba *ob.* 597 ; Kentigern *ob.* 612 (or possibly 608).

The architecture of Dunkeld Cathedral combines the Norman and the Pointed styles, for it was built at different periods by different founders. In 1127 King David I laid the foundation. The choir was built, in the First Pointed style, in 1318 by Bishop Sinclair, who was Robert the Bruce's own bishop. In or about 1406 Bishop Cardeny founded the nave, in the Second Pointed style, and it is said that the Bishop himself helped to carry the stones used in the building. In 1466 the great Tower, 96 feet

Dunkeld Bridge

high, and Chapter House were begun and completed by Bishop Laud in seven years.

Overshadowing the cathedral, but actually just outside its grounds, stands one of the historic larches of Scotland. It is one of a number brought from the Tyrol in 1738 by Menzies of Culdares. These seedlings were considered to be so precious that they were reared at first as greenhouse plants, and since they did not thrive under glass were thrown out on to a heap of refuse, where they revived and were then planted in various districts. Originally there were two great larches here, but the finest of the two was, I believe, struck and killed by lightning during the early

years of the twentieth century. Near the surviving larch grows
a splendid oak, one of the finest I have seen in the Scottish
Highlands.

At Dunkeld the Tay is crossed by a wide bridge, built in 1808

Tay, near Stanley

by the Duke of Atholl, its seven arches proudly spanning the
broad river. Rather less than half a mile below the bridge, on
the south bank of the Tay, are two very old trees — an oak and
a sycamore. Their height is not outstanding, and it was only
when I stood beneath them that I realised their great size and

the majesty of their leafless branches as they slept their winter sleep on the January day of frost when I admired them. The spread of their naked branches was truly majestic, yet even on this Arctic winter's day, when the ground was iron-hard and ice-floes slowly drifted down the Tay, the sycamore spoke of the coming of another spring — for its buds, tight-sealed against the frost, were fresh and green. The buds of the old oak besides it were small and brown, yet even they gave evidence of the young life that was hid deep within them. These two trees are believed to be 1,000 years old and to be a relic of the original Birnam wood of the time of MacBeth. I thought to myself, " Could these old trees speak, how stirring a tale could they unfold. They were veterans in the time of Dundee and Prince Charlie : they were perhaps saplings when the priory of Dunkeld was burnt by the Danes, and now, after the passing of centuries, in their old age they have seen the passing of yet another war, surely more menacing than any which has gone before it."

It was a strange thought to think that the trees may have been vigorous saplings when MacDuff, Thane of Fife, fulfilled the prophecy made to MacBeth, the Scottish King, that he should reign until " Birnam wood came against Dunsinnan ". MacDuff, and with him Prince Malcolm, son of the good and venerable King Duncan whom MacBeth had murdered, cut down many heavy branches from Birnam wood, and when MacDuff's men attacked the King's fortress these branches formed a green screen to hide their numbers. The watchman on MacBeth's tower came in excitement to the King's presence, to tell him that he saw a forest moving against them. MacBeth, hurrying to the look-out tower, saw that Birnam wood was indeed coming against Dunsinnan, and realised that the end of his reign had come. Shakespeare has immortalised this historic incident. His splendid lines may be recalled :

> MacBeth shall never vanquished be, until
> Great Birnam Wood to high Dunsinane Hill,
> Shall come against him. . . .

It has been suggested that the story of MacBeth was narrated to Shakespeare when he passed the district in 1601. He was then journeying with his company to perform comedies and stage-plays in Aberdeen, and it is likely that, hearing the story of MacBeth and seeing the romantic setting of that historical occurrence, he was inspired to write upon it.

The two old trees of which I have written are on the Birnam — that is to say the south — bank of the Tay, Dunkeld being across the bridge, on the north bank.

On the river-bank this winter day a considerable company of mallard were resting, and in a long, placid pool of the river two goosanders, swimming low on the water like miniature submarines, were threading their way among other waterfowl gathered there. In a stream of the river, a dipper was diving repeatedly as it searched the stones on the river-bed for its food. Each time it reappeared on the surface it was carried a short distance down-stream. After some half a dozen dives it had reached the end of its " beat ", and then rose from the water and flew perhaps one hundred yards up the river, there to go through its diving programme once more. Despite the extreme frost and the freezing temperature of the Tay, that dipper was the cheeriest bird I saw.

Away to the north-west, from either bank of the river, rose the two steep hills Craigie Barns and Craig Bhinnein. How trees were made to grow on these precipitous hill faces is a romance of comparatively modern times. The account of the sowing of these precipitous, rocky hills with the seeds of trees is given in *The Highland Tay* (Hugh MacMillan). He writes :

Originally these hills towered up to heaven bare and gaunt in their hoary nakedness; their sides being too precipitous to admit of being planted in the usual way. But Mr. Napier, the famous engineer, while on a visit to the Duke of Atholl, suggested that the cannon in front of his host's residence might be loaded with tin canisters, filled with seeds of pine and spruce and larch, and then fired at the Craigs. This was done, when the canisters, striking the rocks, burst like shells, and dispersed the seeds in the cracks and ledges, where they grew, and in course of time formed the vast billows of forest vegetation which have now submerged the highest points of the scenery.

On a knoll behind the town of Dunkeld is the King's Seat, the site of a Pictish fort. It received its present name because, when the whole of the district was a royal deer forest, it was a look-out station for deer. William the Lion hunted this great forest, and at a later time Queen Mary had a narrow escape here. Pennant quotes William Barclay in his treatise *Contra Monarchomachos* concerning this hunt :

In the year 1563, the Earl of Atholl, a prince of the royal blood, had, with much trouble and vast expence, a hunting-match for the entertainment of our most illustrious and most gracious Queen. Our people call this a Royal Hunting. I was then a young man, and was present on that occasion : two thousand highlanders, or wild Scotch, as you call them here, were employed to drive to the hunting ground all the deer from the woods and hills of Atholl, Badenoch Marr, Murray, and the countries about. As these highlanders use a light dress and are very swift of foot, they went up and down so nimbly, that in less than two months time they brought together two thousand red deer, besides roes and fallow deer. The Queen, the great men, and a number of others, were in a glen when all these deer were brought before them ; believe me, the whole body moved forward in something like battle order. This fight still strikes me, and ever will strike me : for they had a leader whom they followed close whenever he moved.

This leader was a very fine stag with a very high head, this sight delighted the Queen very much, but she soon had cause for fear ; upon the Earl's (who had been from his early days accustomed to such sights) addressing her thus : " Do you observe that stag who is foremost of the herd, there is danger from that stag, for if either fear or rage should force him from the ridge of that hill, let everyone look to himself, for none of us will be out of the way of harm ; for the rest will follow this one, and having thrown us under foot, they will open a passage to this hill behind us." What happen'd a moment after confirmed this opinion : for the Queen ordered one of the best dogs to be let loose on one of the deer ; this the dog pursues, the leading stag was frightened, he flies by the same way he had come there ; the rest rush after him and break out where the thickest body of the highlanders was ; they had nothing for it, but to throw themselves flat on the heath, and to allow the deer to pass over them. It was told the Queen that several of the highlanders has been wounded, and that two or three had been killed outright ; and the whole body had got off, had not the highlanders, by their skill in hunting, fallen upon a stratagem to cut off the rear from the main body. It was of those that had been separated that Queen's dogs and those of the Nobility made slaughter. There were killed that day 360 deer with 5 wolves, and some roes.

If the traveller, approaching Dunkeld along the main road from Perth, instead of turning to the right and crossing the Tay

by the bridge of seven arches, continues along the south bank
of the river, the road will take him across the River Bran, and he
will arrive at the old-world village of Inver, celebrated as the
home of Neil Gow, supreme among Highland fiddlers and the
composer of many strathspeys and reels. When the poet Burns
visited Dunkeld after composing his song " The Birks of Aberfeldy ", he stayed, in the late summer of 1787, with Dr. Stewart,
one of the Stewarts of Bonskeid and a direct ancestor of the
present owner of that property. The next morning Neil Gow
was invited to breakfast and is thus described by Burns :

> Friday. Breakfast with Dr. Stewart. Neil Gow plays : a short, stout-
> built honest Highland figure, with his greyish hair shed on his honest
> social brow ; an interesting face, marking strong sense, kind open-hearted-
> ness, mixed with an interesting simplicity.

Neil Gow was at that time in his sixtieth year ; Burns was twenty-
seven, and at the height of his fame. There is a portrait by
Raeburn of Neil Gow at Blair. The fiddler is seen in tartan
breeches with his fiddle beneath his chin. Elizabeth Grant of
Rothiemurchus describes in her *Memoirs* her meeting with Neil
Gow, and hearing him play. I imagine that his playing among
fiddlers held the same pre-eminence as the playing by John
MacDonald of Inverness of classical pipe music among pipers
during more recent years.

The Bran, this winter day, was frozen from bank to bank ;
the ice which held it was rough, yellow and of great thickness.
At Inver I left the road and, climbing a small hill, saw the old
cottage of Charles Macintosh, a celebrated Perthshire naturalist,
and, a few yards beyond it, Neil Gow's home, a long, low cottage
of which the walls are all that remain of the original building.
Beside the cottage gate is a large flat stone upon which Neil Gow
is said to have sat and played of a summer evening, and to have
charmed the senses of those who heard him. From that old stone
I was taken by a kindly guide by a rough path to the River Tay.
We walked up the river along its banks until we had arrived at an
ancient oak, beneath which, according to the tradition of the

K

district, Neil Gow sat when he composed. It is a quiet and restful place, even at the present day. Beside the old tree flowed the Tay, broad, deep and quiet, its margins held fast by the ice. No salmon ventured to leap into the frosty air, but on the river's surface were swimming golden-eyes and goosanders, and, a little farther down the river, a cormorant, regardless of the cold, stood with solemn dignity on a small ice-floe which had grounded on

Tay in Atholl

a shallow in mid-stream. Across the river were the tall and stately trees which surround Dunkeld house. Here Queen Anne stayed when, in 1703, she visited the first Duke of Atholl : her chamber is still known as Queen Anne's bedroom.

Life now moves at a faster pace than it did in Neil Gow's day, and because of this the Highlands are in some ways less attractive in summer than in fine winter weather, when the roads are empty of tourists, of buses, charabancs and cars, and when something of their early loneliness and primitiveness returns to the valleys and glens.

Rather more than eight miles above Dunkeld the Tay, at

Ballinluig, bends away to the west and is here joined by the River Tummel. There is a good road on either bank of the Tay, and in places, above the modern road on the north bank of the river, General Wade's road from Perth to Inverness can be seen.

Dalguise, on the south bank of the river, is the ancestral home of the Stewarts of Dalguise, an ancient Highland family who trace their origin to King Robert II. At Kennaird house, near it, is a holy well.

By following the Tummel the traveller arrives at Pitlochry and Killiecrankie. Thence the road ascends, by Dalnacardoch and Struan, over desolate Drumochter,[1] to Kingussie and Inverness: by following the Tay, Loch Tay, Killin and Crianlarich are reached.

There is a road up the Tummel, on its south bank, from Logierait to Loch Tummel, and this expedition is worth making to see the richly-sculptured block of sandstone at Dunfallandy. The carving on this stone is unusually delicate and evidently dates back to a very early time.

[1] Druim-uachdar, Ridge of the Upper Ground

Glen Lyon

CHAPTER XV

THE COUNTRY OF ABERFELDY

ABERFELDY takes its name from a celebrated *uruisg* (*anglice*, Uruisk) or water demon who had his home near the Upper Falls of Moness. The name of that sprite is Peallaidh (Shaggy One): he is a large and hairy being, and is the king of all the Uruisks. In the Isle of Lewis he is Piullaidh, the Devil himself. As I have described in Chapter XI, he has also associations with Glen Lyon. In his book *In Famed Breadalbane* the Rev. William A. Gillies mentions the Uruisks of Breadalbane, as described in an old Gaelic rhyme. The rhyme, as is fitting, begins with the chief Uruisk, Peallaidh an Spùit, Peallaidh of the Spout.

There is a particularly fine Wade's bridge of five graceful arches spanning the Tay at Aberfeldy. The bridge is built of the grey chlorite schist of the district, and its middle arch is of 60 feet span. On either side of this arch two tapering pillars stand, and the whole bridge is strikingly artistic. How unlike it is to the modern bridges which the Ministry of Transport is building at the present day throughout the Highlands !

This old bridge must have seen varied and stirring times. In the year 1745 Sir John Cope with his troops and artillery crossed it and encamped on the north side of the river, and the Duke of Cumberland sent a detachment of his army to guard the approaches of the bridge against Prince Charlie's Highlanders. On the bridge is the following interesting inscription :

AT THE COMMAND OF
HIS MAJTY KING GEORGE 2ND
THIS BRIDGE WAS ERECTED
IN THE YEAR 1733
THIS WITH THE ROADS AND OTHER
MILITARY WORKS FOR SECURING
A SAFE AND EASY COMMUNICATION
BETWEEN THE HIGH LANDS AND
THE TRADEING TOWNS IN THE LOW
COUNTRY WAS BY HIS MAJTY
COMMITTED TO THE CARE OF
LIEUT GENERAL GEORGE WADE
COMMANDER IN CHIEF OF THE FORCES
IN SCOTLAND WHO LAID THE FIRST
STONE OF THIS BRIDGE ON THE
23RD OF APRIL AND FINISHED THE
WORK IN THE SAME YEAR

Close to this old bridge, on the south side of the Tay, is a cairn raised to commemorate the first mustering of the Forty-Second Regiment or Black Watch (in Gaelic Am Freacadan Dubh). This celebrated regiment was named the Black Watch because of the dark-coloured tartan which its members wore, and their deeds of bravery since that time have caused them to be renowned throughout the world. The cairn is an attractive one, and on it stands the figure of a Highlander of distinguished bearing. In his bonnet he wears a single eagle's feather (in old days a chief was entitled to wear three eagle's feathers in his bonnet, a chieftain two feathers and a Highland gentleman one feather), his hair is worn long, in the old fashion, and he is shown in the act of drawing his sword. The figure is most striking. On the cairn are inscribed, in Gaelic and in English, the exploits of the Forty-Second in many lands.

As I stood, on a winter's morning, beside the Tay and looked upon this old memorial cairn, and the noble bridge which spans the stream, the ground was frozen iron-hard and the river flowed low and clear. Below the bridge I noticed a river watcher drag a dead kelt salmon from the shallows, and as he sought suitable ground in which to bury the fish — no easy task on the frost-bound banks — I talked to him on salmon lore and olden times. We agreed that Wade must have had a large body of skilled workers to have completed this wide bridge within eight months: the excellence of the work is apparent from the fact that, after more than two hundred years, the bridge is undamaged and as strong as ever. As we talked of the Tay fishing he told me that he had recently found and buried a considerable number of large male salmon kelts: the female kelt salmon, he said, were rarely found dead in the river, and presumably safely made their way back to the sea. Since the greater number of these female fish survived the spawning, we agreed that it was strange that so very few of them (the number is less than 2 per cent) returned to spawn a second time, and we wondered whether, once safely back in the sea, they might not perhaps remain there, in the depths of the Atlantic, for the rest of their lives.

I crossed Wade's bridge and walked west along the road with its avenue of stately Lombardy poplars, now dark and leafless, until I had reached the old ruined church of Weem, which has associations with St. Cudberct or Cuthbert and is dedicated to him. The Irish *Life of Saint Cudberct* records that

after the blessed youth Cudberct had arrived in Scottish land, he began to dwell in different parts of the country, and coming to a town called Dul forsook the world, and became a solitary. No more than a mile from it there is in the woods a high and steep mountain called by the inhabitants Doilweme, and on its summit he began to lead a solitary life. Here he brings from the hard rock a fountain of water which still exists. Here too he erects a large stone cross, builds an oratory of wood, and out of a single stone, not far from the cross, constructs a bath, in which he used to immerse himself and spend the night in prayer, which bath still exists on the summit of the mountain. Cudberct remains some time in the territory of the Picts leading a solitary life, till the daughter of the king of that province accuses him of having violated her ; but, at the prayer of the saint, the earth opened and swallowed her up at a place still called Corruen, and it was on this account that he never permitted a female to enter his church.

Doilweme is identified as the Dail or Valley of Weem. Weem, in its turn, is the anglicised form of the Gaelic word *uaimh*, a cave. That ancient cave still exists in a rock above the old church and village of Weem.

This venerable church, overshadowed by stately trees, is now the resting-place of two of the sanctuary crosses of the ancient monastery of Dull, some two miles farther up the Tay valley. How they come to be there I shall narrate later in this chapter.

A short distance up the valley from Weem stands Menzies Castle, the home for centuries of the chiefs of Clan Menzies. The castle was built in 1571, and one of the relics which it contained was the claymore said to have been wielded by the chief of Menzies at the battle of Bannockburn. The castle was pillaged by Montrose ; was garrisoned by Cromwell, and suffered at the hands of the Jacobites during the '45. It has now fallen upon evil days, and the proud Menzies supporters above the door look down upon a scene of neglect if not of desolation. Beneath the castle windows the Macintyres of Rannoch, hereditary pipers to the chiefs of Menzies, must often have played, and within the castle the chief's harper must have charmed his hearers with more gentle music. On days of great occasion the bard must have recited proudly the deeds of the chief and his ancestors. But there is silence now within the castle and the old trees which surround it dripped moisture from their leafless branches as I passed by it — for the frost was " lifting ", as they say, and a heavy shower of sleet had fallen. There was indeed an atmosphere of sadness about the place, an atmosphere heightened by the mist which hung low upon the hills on either side the valley. Could Mary of Scots — she who loved the castle and its shady walks and was commemorated in the finest sycamore which grew in the castle grounds — have seen the castle in its friendless old age her heart must have been filled with sorrow ; but the old family and its honoured friends are now gone, and new times and new faces have come to the district.

But higher up the valley, at Dull, sacred to the memory of Adamnan (or Eónan as he was usually named in the Scottish Highlands), he who was Abbot of Iona and recorded in Latin the life and miracles of St. Columba, I found a more cheerful atmosphere.

There is a tradition that Adamnan is buried at Dull. It was said that when the saint died he left instructions that his coffin was to be carried east from Glen Lyon until the withies which held it should break, and that there his body should be laid in the earth. At Dull the withies broke, and the saint was buried. But if indeed Adamnan were buried at Dull there is now no record of where his grave was. At Dull was one of the oldest religious establishments in the Highlands. The earlier ecclesiastical abbots of the monastery were in time superseded by powerful lay abbots. Crinan, Abbot of Dunkeld, who married the elder daughter of Malcolm II of Scotland and was the father of King Duncan, slain by MacBeth, was also Abbot of Dull, and held the extensive church lands in the district. Before the Reformation the college of Dull was moved to St. Andrews, and to the present day the minister of Dull receives part of his stipend from St. Andrews.

Like other ancient monasteries of the Highlands, Dull had its sanctuary, or girth, within which one fleeing for his life found sanctuary from his enemies.[1] There are known to have been three old crosses marking this sanctuary, but only one remains here. The story of how the other two came to be moved is a strange one. More than a hundred years ago the commissioner of the Menzies estates came to the conclusion that two of the sacred crosses would make excellent posts for his gate, and despite protests he

---

[1] The sanctuary is named in Gaelic " an Teagarmachd ", " the place of refuge ".

had them converted to this use. He was told that if he persisted in moving the crosses he would not long survive his deed, and shortly afterwards he did indeed meet with a violent death. The crosses, as I have mentioned earlier in this chapter, now rest within the old church of Weem. The third sanctuary cross stands near the modern church of Dull, beside the farm of Drumdian, which was formerly an inn. One arm of the cross has gone. It was broken when a runaway horse dashed against it the cart it was dragging, and the broken arm is said to be built into the wall of the farm building which stands beside it.

A few heaps of stones are all that remain to show where the monastery and college formerly stood, but St. Eónan's well still flows in the manse garden and, as MacMillan in his *Highland Tay* records, the miller at Milton Eónan up to the middle of the nineteenth century never thought of grinding corn on the day of the saint. Long after the time of the religious establishment the township of Dull was a prosperous one, and on the winter afternoon when I saw the place I could not but be impressed by the number of old ruined houses which told of a more prosperous era in the past — when people of the Highlands did not seek the artificiality and glamour of the cities, but were content to live simply, spinning and weaving, ploughing with the *cas chrom* and reaping with the sickle as they sang the old Gaelic songs which were formerly the accompaniment of pastoral labour in the Highlands.

The Garry

CHAPTER XVI

THE COUNTRY OF STRATH TUMMEL AND GARRY

Snow lay lightly and evenly on the ground as I looked out upon Pitlochry in the grey, lagging dawn of a mid-winter day. I had rested high on the hillside of Moulin, celebrated because of its old castle — the Black Castle of Moulin — which was broken down by artillery in order that those who were dead and dying of plague within it should in no possible way spread their infection to a terrified neighbourhood. In an old account it is mentioned that " the castell of Mowlin " was built " be David Cuming Earle of Athoill ". In this account the builder seems to be confused with Lord Walter Comyn, who met with a violent death at a ford over the River Tromie as he was hastening to Ruthven in Bade-noch in order to gratify his unholy desire of seeing the women of

Giant Steps at Pitlochry

that district go naked to the harvest (this occurrence I have described in *The Country of Badenoch*, chap. xxii, p. 8).

The historical associations of the country around Pitlochry are rich and varied, down to the time when, in 1881, Robert Louis Stevenson spent a part of the summer there and wrote *The Merry Men* and *Thrawn Janet*. In the year 1564 Queen Mary passed through Moulin — the old road in those days crossed the face of the hill, considerably above Pitlochry — on her way to Blair Castle to take part in a great deer drive, it is said in Glen Tilt. When the Queen reached the ferryman's house at the Pass of Killiecrankie she rested and, inspired by the beauty of the view, called for her harp on which to praise it. But the rough journey along the winding hill road had been disastrous for some of the harp strings, and the local harper was a proud man when he was sent for to repair the damage. From that incident the house where the royal harp was re-strung was named Tigh nan Teud, House of the Harp Strings. It still stands beside the main road, on the right-hand side as you travel north. It is recorded that Queen Mary afterwards presented the harp to Miss Robertson of Lude, as a queenly recognition of her sweet playing and her charming personality.

Before the beautiful old bridge spanning the Garry at the Pass of Killiecrankie was built in 1770 (this bridge carries the road which leads by Fincastle and the Tummel to Rannoch), the river was crossed by means of a ferry. It is said that the building of the bridge was hastened because of a disaster in which eighteen people lost their lives. As it was crossing the flooded river the ferry-boat overturned, and the only person saved was the boatman, whose wife caught him by a boat-hook.

There are historical associations with the country of the Pass of Killiecrankie which go back much further than the time of Queen Mary. On the west side of the pass, perhaps a mile beyond the bridge, on the estate of Bonskeid, is Coille Bhrochain, the Wood of Gruel. The old tradition is recorded on the gable of a house here, that Robert the Bruce rested at this spot after the

battle of Methven in 1306 and that in their dispirited and hungry
state the King and his weary men were given, by the people of
the place, a meal of *brochan* or gruel.[1] It is also recorded that,
in the year 1680, the last wolf in Perthshire was killed at or near
the pass by Sir Ewen Cameron of Lochiel.

The snow was falling thickly from a leaden sky as I traversed

Ben Vrackie, near Pitlochry

the Pass of Killiecrankie and thought of Viscount Dundee and
his Highland army who won a brilliant victory there. In that
fight Dundee fell, and his grave, and the inscription on it, may
be seen in the old burial-ground at the Church of St. Bride at Old
Blair. His death is commemorated in a mournful piece of classical
bagpipe music, the Lament for Viscount Dundee, which is sometimes set as a test piece in piping competitions at the present day.

John Grahame of Claverhouse, Viscount Dundie (to spell his

[1] The meanings of *brochan* are (1) gruel, (2) porridge; never
" brose ".

Pass of Killiecrankie

title in the original spelling), who commanded King James's forces at the battle of Killiecrankie, was, in the midst of the fight, mortally wounded through his breastplate (his helmet and breastplate may be seen at Blair Castle). As he fell heavily from his noble dun-coloured horse and lay upon the ground, his life ebbing fast, he asked, " How fares the fight ? " He was told, " The day goes well for the King, but I am sorry for your lordship." Dundee then whispered his last words, " It matters less for me, seeing that the day goes well for my master."

The stone beside which Dundee fell and died may be seen near the north entrance to the Pass of Killiecrankie, a little distance above the main road. With Dundee was the flower of Highland families. Clanranald and Glengarry were there. Lochiel and MacLean of Duart (then a lad of no more than eighteen years) were in the thick of the fight. The regiment of Sir Donald MacDonald of Sleat was commanded by his eldest son and fought most gallantly on that July day of 1689. Archibald MacDonald of Largie and his uncle, the Tutor of Largie, were killed, and the same fate overtook a brother of Alasdair Dubh, chief of Glengarry—he who, at the head of his men, mowed down two enemies at each sweep of his claymore. Lochiel was attended in the fight by the son of his foster-brother, who showed great devotion towards his chief and indeed gave his life for him. Shortly after the beginning of the fight Lochiel missed his companion in arms and, turning round to see what had become of him, saw him lying on his back, his breast pierced by an arrow. The dying man told Lochiel that, seeing one of the enemy aiming at him with bow and arrow from the rear, he had sprung behind him to shield him, and had received in his own body the arrow aimed at his chief.

The result of the battle of Killiecrankie is well known. The victory of the Highlanders over the force of William of Orange under the command of Major-General Hugh MacKay of Scourie was complete. No fewer than 2,000 of MacKay's men were killed and 500 made prisoners — a remarkable result when it is remembered that the Highlanders were outnumbered by two to one.

The fight was not fought actually in the Pass of Killiecrankie, but north of its northern entrance. MacKay's army indeed had marched through the pass in safety, with the loss of a single trooper who was shot by a local archer of renown, one Iain Beag MacRan. A well named Fuaran an Trùpaire, the Trooper's Well, is shown as the place where the horseman fell ; it is near the bridge which crosses the Garry. At the council of war, which was held at Blair before the fight, Dundee had, it is true, been urged to attack the enemy in the Pass of Killiecrankie, but had refused, partly because his chivalry forbad him to launch an assault under conditions so disadvantageous to his foe.

A few hundred yards below the bridge which spans the Garry at the Pass of Killiecrankie the river narrows. Here is the Soldier's Leap, and the history of the place is an interesting one. When MacKay with his army marched north through the Pass of Killiecrankie he left behind him a sentry to guard the pass. This man was out of sight of the contending armies, and his first inkling of the defeat of his own side was when he saw a body of Highlanders rushing towards him. It seemed as though he must be surrounded and killed, but he was an agile man, and with a tremendous leap launched himself across the Garry, which is some seventeen feet broad at this place.

Some three miles up the valley of the Garry from the Pass of Killiecrankie is Blair Atholl. The Tilt joins the Garry here, and there is a track up Glen Tilt across to Mar. Blair Castle, the ancestral home of the ducal family of Atholl, stands a little way back from the main road, from which glimpses of it may be had. The castle has been added to at several periods. The oldest part is the central tower, sometimes called Comyn's Tower, which is said to have been built by the Red Comyn about the year 1280. In the year 1644 the Great Montrose was here joined by a large body of Atholl Highlanders who were largely responsible for his subsequent victory at Tibbermuir. In the troubles of 1653 the place was taken by storm by one of Cromwell's officers.

During the Jacobite rising of 1745 Prince Charles Edward and his army were at Dalnacardoch, and hearing of this the Duke of Atholl (*The Lyon in Mourning*, vol. i, p. 208) sent a letter to Mrs. Robertson of Lude, a daughter of Nairn,

desiring her to repair to Blair Castle to put it in some order, and to do the honours of that house when the Prince should happen to come there, which he did the day following, August 31st.

When the Prince was at Blair he went into the garden, and taking a walk upon the bowling green, he said he had never seen a bowling green before. Upon which the above lady called for some bowls that he might see them ; but he told her that he had got a present of some bowls sent him as a curiosity to Rome from England.

On September 2nd he left Blair and went to the house of Lude (rather more than a mile down the valley), where he was very chearful and took his share in several dances, such as minuets, Highland reels — the first reel the Prince called for was " This is not mine ain house " — and a Strathspey minuet.

The following year the Prince was again at Blair Castle for two days or, as some said, for a whole week, in February. One of these days he spent hunting (*The Lyon in Mourning*, vol. ii, p. 134).

Among the varied and priceless relics in Blair Castle one which caught my imagination was the Prince's compass. Surely if that small pocket compass could speak it might unfold a breathless tale of Prince Charlie's wanderings after Culloden. It might speak of that wearisome ascent of Ben Alder to the cramped quarters of Cluny's Cage. It had perhaps been used by Donald MacLeod of Gualtragill in Skye, the Prince's pilot, on the perilous crossing of the Minch on a night of storm that sent angry seas racing in upon the small craft in which the fugitives sailed. It may have been shown to Flora MacDonald on that later night crossing of the Minch, from Uist to Skye, beneath the pale stars of summer twilight, and it no doubt guided its royal owner from the Central Highlands west to Loch nan Uamh, to embark on the French frigate which awaited him there. When the Prince stayed at Blair he doubtless had the compass with him, yet its value to him must have been greater at a later date.

Another relic of the '45 is seen in the set of bagpipes which

L

are preserved in Blair Castle. These pipes are believed to have been played during that Jacobite campaign by a MacGregor who was a piper in the Atholl Brigade and was known by his patronymic, Iain mac an Sgeulaiche (John, son of the Teller of Old Tales). The MacGregors were a celebrated piping family who had their home in Glen Lyon. They lived at Tigh Chunnairt, House of Danger — an appropriate name for the dwelling of a piper in old days. These MacGregor pipers were known as Clann an Sgeulaiche, perhaps because of their power by vivid narrative of bringing the great deeds of a past age before their hearers.

It would be instructive to know whether the John MacGregor whose pipes now lie in Blair Castle was the same John MacGregor who was piper to Colonel Campbell of Glenlyon in 1783. MacGregor was then a man of seventy-five, but at the Highland Society of London's competition of that year he played, as an exhibition *piobaireachd*, Clanranald's March. In Angus MacKay's book of pipe music it is recorded that one of John MacGregor's sons was for some time piper at Dunvegan, MacLeod's castle in the Isle of Skye.

It is interesting to recall, in these days when the playing of one *piobaireachd* or classical pipe composition is considered by some to take up too much time at a Highland Gathering, that at the Highland Society of London's competitions more than a century ago each piper was required to play no fewer than four of these pieces. This must have taken him the best part of an hour, yet he never failed to have a large and enthusiastic audience of Highland gentlemen and their ladies.

No longer do the MacGregor pipers awake the echoes in Glen Lyon: no longer do the Macintyres of Rannoch impart their lore of pipe music at their college of piping. Schiehallion, Fairy Hill of the Caledonians — she who has listened to much music of the past — veils herself in sorrow at evening for old things of joy and beauty which are now but a memory.

Fifty years after the Prince walked on the bowling-green at

Blair Castle, Mrs. Grant of Laggan writes one of her *Letters from the Mountains* from Blair in 1796:

> I have past three charming days here, during which I have been soothed by the novelty of ease and leisure ; so immersed in the luxury of embowering groves, flowery walks, solemn shades of dark larches with drooping branches, that seem to weep over the wanderers that muse or mourn beneath them or soft glades along the murmuring Tilt, where every vegetable beauty blooms in full luxuriance, safe from the nipping frost or chilling blast ; so lost, I say, in a dream of pensive musing, which I have enjoyed at full leisure, free from the restraints of form, and the disturbance of intrusion that, like other people given wholly up to pleasure, I seemed to forget my friends, my duty, and myself. Nay, I began to consider whether it was most eligible to turn hermitress, or hamadryad. When the fair form of the virgin huntress of the woods, which adorns one of these sweet walks, drew my attention I thought of sheltering in her haunts as a hamadryad : but when the opening of a long vista disclosed the Gothic form of the old church of St. Bridget, my intentions took a more orthodox turn, and I began to adjust the dimensions of my cell, and think of cold vigils, and midnight prayers. My head is now cooled ; my visions are vanished, and I am considering how I shall get home to make frocks and mend petticoats.

Blair Atholl has older historic associations than those with Prince Charles Edward. The King's Island, an island on the Garry about a mile below Blair, is said to have received its name because Robert the Bruce hid there, either after his defeat at Methven or on the occasion when, a few months later, he and his companions came by Glen Tilt from Mar on their way toward the west, before the battle of Dalrigh which was fought at Tyndrum, near the county march between Perth and Argyll (*vide* Chapter IX). It was on that journey, as Barbour records, that Lord James Douglas foraged in the woods and streams for delicate food for the Queen and her ladies. That old account narrates how Lord James " quhile he venesoon thaim brocht ; and with his handys quhile he wrocht gynnys [snares] to tak geddis [pike] and salmonys, trowtis, elys, and als menonys ".

I have mentioned that Montrose was at Blair in 1644 : from that place he began his two campaigns, Tibbermuir and the harrying of Argyll. Montrose's brother-in-law, Lord Napier, died at Fincastle, across the hill south of Blair, after Philiphaugh.

But even these events, distant as they are, are recent compared with the period in which Atholl received its name. As Professor Watson has pointed out in his *Celtic Place-Names of Scotland*, the name Atholl commemorates the ancient Celtic province of Fotla or Fodla, one of the early names of Eire. In the name Ath Fhodla (now Atholl) "ath" occurs in the sense of the Latin " re ", denoting repetition, and the word Ath Fhodla means New Ireland. It is known that the Gaels from Eire named the Highland districts which they colonised after their motherland. This (as I have pointed out in Chapter VI) is seen in Loch Earn (Loch Eireann, Ireland's Loch) and in other Highland place-names. The Irish influence began as early as the time of the Roman occupation, and the bond between Atholl and Eire must be old indeed. Almost as old was the Celtic earldom of Atholl, for, as Skene records (*Celtic Scotland*, vol. iii, p. 288), these earls were descended from a younger brother of Malcolm Ceannmór, and the last of that ancient line was Henry, Earl of Atholl, who died before 1215. At a rather later date the earldom of Atholl, which had become vested in the person of Robert, Steward of Scotland, was granted in a charter, about the year 1371, to Eugenius, thane of Glentilt, brother of Reginald of the Isles.

It may be that the moulding of the old bell which until recently was kept at Struan church some miles north of Blair was contemporaneous with the coming to the district of the early colonisers from Eire. The bell has been called the St. Fillan's Struan bell. Although it is associated with the name of St. Fillan it is doubtful whether this is the St. Fillan of Glen Dochart and Killin. This bell was named Am Buidhean. It is one of the five very old Celtic bells of Perthshire, three being those of Fortingall, Balnahanaid, and Strath Fillan, and the fourth St. Brennain's.

The Struan bell was removed to Lude, and there it remained until the summer of 1939 when the house and property of Lude were sold. The bell was then bought, and was gifted to Perth Museum.

CHAPTER XVII

BETWEEN the Tummel, where it emerges from the wood-fringed waters of Loch Tummel, and the River Garry four miles to the north is the hilly district of Fincastle and Bonskeid.

The Stewarts of Fincastle were an old Highland family whose descendant still owns the ancestral property. On the walls of the old house of Fincastle — a house in which lingers a restful atmosphere of olden times — are inscriptions which tell the history of the house and of the family who lived in it. Over a small window to the left of the door, facing south, is the following inscription :

1640   A G 7

BLISSIT AR THE MERCIFUL
FOR THEY SCHAL OBTAIN MERCE

THE FEIR OF THE LORD
ABHORETH WIKEDNES

I S   C M

Between I S and C M is inscribed a human heart.

I S (James Stewart) married Cecilia Mercer of Meikleour. They gave hospitality to the first Lord Napier and probably to Montrose (one of whose letters is still preserved at Fincastle) after the battle of Philiphaugh. In this house Lord Napier died : his heart, it is said, is buried beneath an old yew tree.

Over the door of the house are the initials

G S   .   I C   1702

Loch Tummel

commemorating Gilbert Stewart and Isobel Campbell his wife. On the wing of the house added in the year 1751, over the window to the left of the door, facing east, is the inscription

17 — H.S — 51

On the right of the door is to be read :

17   H S   C M   — 54

Between the letters H S and C M is incised a human heart.

Henry Stewart of Fincastle was out in the '45 as a lad of eighteen, but was permitted afterwards to retain his estate. He married Catherine Murchison, and appears to have died without issue. Colonel Robert Stewart, probably a younger brother, married Louise Graeme of Inchbrakie, a cousin of Lady Nairne, about the year 1792.

Henry Stewart's sister Elizabeth married John Stewart of Bonskeid, and they are the great-great-great-grandparents of G. F. Barbour of Bonskeid who now (1945) owns the property of Fincastle. Among the relics preserved at Fincastle house is the signet ring given by Prince Charlie to Laurence Oliphant, his aide-de-camp and the father of Lady Nairne, the song writer. Oliphant, who placed the laurel crown on the Prince's head at Holyrood, was great-great-grandfather of G. F. Barbour. On the ring are the Thistle, Rose and Harp, and also the Prince of Wales Feathers and the letters C.P.R.

Fincastle house stands 1,000 feet above sea level and looks south across lesser hills, on to Feargan, or Farragon, a hill of rather more than 2,500 feet high, and much thought of, and even worshipped, by Strath Tay folk in olden times.

The older form of the name Fincastle is Foncastle, in Gaelic Fonn a' Chaisteil, Land of the Castle. This information has been given me by Professor W. J. Watson, who points out that west of Fincastle is Achadh a' Chaisteil, the Field of the Castle.

Characteristic of the district of Fincastle are a number of Circular Forts. These forts are a feature of the territory of the Verturiones, who lived north of the wall between Forth and

Clyde, and whose name is derived from *vertera*, a fort, in Gaelic *forter*.

One of these old forts I had the privilege of inspecting with Professor Watson, on an autumn evening when the mist hung low on the hill, and the shadow of dusk was falling early on the old stones which had been laid one upon another by skilled hands long since crumbled unto dust.

One of these old forts is at Caisteal Dubh, the Black Castle, and just to the west of it is Torr Chomhairle, Council Knoll. Mention must also be made of a Stone Circle by the old path to Loch Tummel. There are four stones, on a magnificent site, and they are named na Clachan Aoraidh, the Stones of Worship.

That fairies had their home here is shown by the place-name given to the wooded knoll south-west of the Mains of Fincastle. This is still named an Sìthean, the Fairy Hill, and west of it is Edintian, which in reality is Aodann an t-Sìthein, Face of the Fairy Hill.

A belt of rock in the district is limestone, and in old days, when many people lived here, the lime was industriously burned and spread on the fields. There are limestone quarries, and a big limekiln at Tom an Rathaid. Old ruins show the extent of the former population in this district, but at the present day few people remain ; indeed one of the farmers has been forced to give up his farm, for he can get no one to help him in the work, because of the so-called remoteness of the place.

The old road from Blair Atholl to Loch Tummel passes over the hill near Fincastle, and on an evening of late September, after a day of rain, I walked along that grass-grown road to the water-shed, where I looked down on to Blair Atholl and the glen of the Garry.

The air was clear after rain, and a pink glow shone upon Ben Vrackie and Beinn a' Ghló. Away to the west rose Schiehallion, a cloud fired by the setting sun resting on its picturesque summit. Schiehallion is in Gaelic Sìdh Chailleann, the Fairy Hill of the

Caledonians (Caledonii),[1] and, from whatever quarter it may be viewed, it is one of the most picturesque mountains of the Scottish Highlands.

Below Fincastle flows the Tummel. At the Falls of Tummel a great basket was formerly fixed in position to catch salmon as they endeavoured to leap the falls and fell back towards the pool. The basket has long been removed, but the practice of taking salmon in this manner was at one time widespread on Highland rivers with falls : on the Shin, for example, a great number of salmon were taken in this way each season.

[1] Cf. Dùn Chailleann, Dunkeld

Loch Rannoch

CHAPTER XVIII

THE COUNTRY OF RANNOCH AND ITS LEGENDS

" By Tummel and by Rannoch and Lochaber I will go."

GLEN LYON of the ancient yew tree and the valley of Rannoch
are not far from each other : they are linked by one of General
Wade's old roads which leaves Glen Lyon near the Keltney burn.
As it passes over the high country between the two straths this
road winds near the old Castle of Garth, in Gaelic Caisteal Gairt.
It was sometimes called Caisteal a' Chuilein Chursta, the Castle
of the Cursed or Excommunicated Puppy. " An Cuilean Cursta "
is said to have been the term applied to the notorious Wolf of
Badenoch — he who fired the Cathedral of Elgin and was excommunicated for so doing. His son held land in the districts
of Glen Lyon and Rannoch, and from him the Stewarts of Garth
claim descent. It was Colonel David Stewart of Garth who wrote,

in the year 1822, that classical work *Sketches of the Character, Manners and present State of the Highlanders of Scotland.*

The traveller as he crosses the watershed by Wade's road and descends to the valley of the Tummel and the lands of Rannoch realises that the valley of Rannoch is broader by far than the glen of the Lyon, and is of a quite different character. If he travels west along the Rannoch road he passes near Dùn Alasdair, the ancestral home of the Struan Robertsons. The first of the Struan family was, according to the tradition of the country, Donnchadh Reamhar, Duncan the Stout : he was an ardent supporter and follower of Robert the Bruce, and was given land in the district in the fourteenth century. It is from their ancestor that the Robertsons receive their name, Clann Donnchaidh, Children of Duncan.

At Kinloch Rannoch [1] — it is here that the road reaches Loch Rannoch — Dugald Buchanan, religious poet of the Gael, lived and laboured in the eighteenth century, and his memorial is seen in the village of Kinloch Rannoch.

One branch of the road here crosses the Tummel (where it leaves the waters of Loch Rannoch) by an old bridge, on which is the following quaint inscription :

ERECTED AT THE SOLE EXPENSE OF HIS MAJESTY
OUT OF THE ANNEXED ESTATES   1764

The feeling of admiration at King George III's generosity which the passer-by experiences is abruptly qualified on reading the second line, and he feels that things could have been put just a little less bluntly !

It was on a grey misty morning of late September that I visited Rannoch. A thin cap of mist clothed the summit of Schiehallion and as the mist rose and fell it showed at times a faint golden gleam as the sun lit up the fringes of the cloud. It was 1938, a time of the most tense international crisis, and the air

[1] The name Kinloch Rannoch is strangely applied to this village. The prefix Kinloch, which is found in many Highland names, means " Head of the Loch," yet Kinloch Rannoch is at the foot of the loch of that name.

was heavy with forebodings, which called to mind the early days of the first Great War. That day the *Queen Elizabeth* was to be launched, and in Rannoch, far from the sea, the thoughts of men for a brief space turned to the launch of that great ship (which they could follow on their wireless sets), but the shadow of war, apparently approaching inexorably, fell upon even that memorable event. A police car was distributing gas masks : the constables talked quietly one to another as though they could scarcely credit this menace of imminent war. Yet as I crossed the River Tummel, travelled along the road that leads by the south bank of Loch Rannoch, and entered the celebrated Black Wood of Rannoch, I forgot for a time the evil days through which Europe was passing in the strength and beauty of the old pines which form the Black Wood.[1] One of the pines at the edge of the loch had been sawn off near the base, and out of curiosity I counted the rings of that great tree. Each ring of a tree denotes one year of its growth and this tree showed by its rings that it had lived 214 years.

There is a sense of security in the Black Wood. These great trees, centuries old, seem to tell of wisdom and peace. The wood is a relic of the old Caledonian Forest, and none of the trees have been planted by human hands. Some of them were well-grown when the Fiery Cross was sent round the district in 1745 and the men of the country rose to support Prince Charles Edward in his great adventure. In these natural-grown pine forests the trees do not grow so densely as to destroy the lesser vegetation, and the heather, this day of late September, was purple beneath the old pines. A wandering tramp, having made a careful and (as he hoped) furtive inspection of my two companions and me, now picked a sprig of heather and, appearing in our full view, offered it ingratiatingly for sale. The little comedy was well played, with the assurance which a tramp in the course of a hard life necessarily acquires.

---

[1] As I revise this chapter (1942) many of the finest trees have been felled in the Black Wood.

After a time the road leaves the Black Wood and retreats a little from the edge of the loch. Between the loch and the road is the small burial-ground of St. Michael's and, at the west side of its entrance, a large stone may be seen. This is Clach nan Ceann, the Stone of the Heads, and Alexander Cameron in his valuable book, *A Highland Parish*, thus tells the tragic story of the stone :

A Duncan woman of great beauty was wooed by a Cameron of Camghouran and a MacIntosh of Moy. Cameron, the successful suitor, took her to his home in Camghouran. There they lived happily and had a fine family of boys. But MacIntosh did not forget his unsuccessful suit, and an accident which occurred at Perth re-kindled his wrath against Cameron. One Saint Muchael's Day, while attending a market at Perth, MacIntosh went into a shop and bargained for a bunch of arrows. He did not take the arrows with him, but said that he would call for them before returning home. Cameron was at the same market, and went into the same shop in quest of arrows. The bunch bought by MacIntosh was the finest in the shop, and when Cameron saw them he wanted to buy them. He was told that they had already been bought by MacIntosh, but in the end he overcame the shopkeeper's scruples and prevailed on him to hand over the arrows. When MacIntosh returned and learned that Cameron had carried off his arrows his slumbering resentment against Cameron was roused to fever-heat. In characteristic fashion he swore, kissed his dirk, and vowed that he would have his revenge. He gathered his men who were at the market and made straight for Camghouran. On arrival there he told Cameron's wife that she would have to leave her husband and go with him, but she refused. " If you don't," said MacIntosh, " I will brain every one of your sons." " And if you dared," she replied, " I should not shed a tear." (For she believed all the while that he would not dare.)

But the infuriated MacIntosh took the boys one by one and dashed their heads against a large stone till the mother broke down and begged him to desist. According to some accounts he had already killed three, according to others, six boys. He consented to spare the other boy or boys on condition that the mother would go with him. But ere he could carry her away Cameron arrived, and a fight between MacIntoshes and Camerons ensued. In the end every MacIntosh was slain save one, who escaped by swimming across the loch : when he reached the opposite shore he was cut down by a MacGregor.

The stone against which the boys' heads were dashed can be seen to this day on the left side of the entrance to the graveyard.

The road continues west up the south side of Loch Rannoch to a small post-office (the postmistress was " listening in " to the launch of the *Queen Elizabeth* when I called there), then crosses the river to meet the road on the north side of the valley. Here the traveller looks west and sees the high tops of the Blackmount Forest and of Glen Coe, and if he should continue his journey westward for a few miles he reaches the railway station of Rannoch, on the West Highland Railway from Glasgow to Fort William and Mallaig.

The north side of Loch Rannoch is known to the old Gaelic-speaking people of the district as An Slios Mìn, the Smooth Slope, and was formerly Menzies country. Near Dunan, one of the shooting lodges of the district, is a small burn known as Caochan na Fala, the Streamlet of Blood. In the fifteenth century a travelling merchant, a Stewart from Appin, was robbed and murdered here by a tribe known as Clann Iain Bhuidhe, Children of Yellow John. The Stewarts came in force from Appin to avenge his death, and with the help of a party of Mac-Gregors utterly routed Clann Iain Bhuidhe.

North of Slios Mìn is Loch Ericht, a long loch, some sixteen miles in length. It was said in olden times that the early parish of Feadaill which traditionally disappeared during a great earthquake was deeply submerged in Loch Rannoch, and that all its inhabitants perished. It used to be said that on a very clear, calm day the steeple of the church could be seen (as one passed near it in a boat) rising from the depths of the loch.

I have mentioned that the family of Menzies held much land in the Rannoch and Glen Lyon districts. Menzies of Culdares of the '45 (he was usually known as Old Culdares) was at heart a Jacobite. He perhaps felt himself too old to take an active part in the campaign, but to show his sympathy with the cause he sent his best horse as a present to Prince Charles Edward. His personal servant, John MacNaughton, took this handsome gift to the Prince and later served under him. He was taken prisoner and was brought to Carlisle, where an offer was made to spare his life if he should tell the name of him who had gifted the horse. He stoutly refused. Again, during the last few minutes of his life, the offer was renewed and was again scornfully rejected, and that modest hero, John MacNaughton, cheerfully went to his death.

At the mouth of Loch Rannoch Robert the Bruce, according to the tradition of the country, defeated the MacDougalls, who at the time held great power in that district. The battle is commemorated in the place-name Dalchosnie, the Winning Field.

There is a curious tradition concerning a stone in a field east of Dalchosnie. The name of the stone is A' Chlach Sgoilte, the Split Stone, and the boulder is said to have split from top to bottom on that cold April day when the Jacobite cause was lost on the Moor of Culloden. In a house near the stone a Stewart woman, whose husband was " out " with the Prince, was living. She exclaimed when the stone split — " The cause of the Prince is lost, and I myself am a widow."

Loch Laggan

CHAPTER XIX

THE COUNTRY OF LOCH LAGGAN AND LOCH ERICHT

LOCH LAGGAN lies in the high country, between Badenoch and Brae Lochaber, and the road from Newtonmore in Badenoch to Fort William skirts the loch. There are two islands on Loch Laggan and both of them have associations with the ancient kings of Scotland — or rather it ought perhaps to be said that there *were* two islands. One of the great water-power schemes in the Highlands has considerably raised the level of Loch Laggan so that its isles are now hidden, yet there are times, in dry weather, when the loch sinks lower than ever it was before. On the island marked on the map as Eilean an Rìgh, the King's Isle, King Fergus is said to have had his hunting lodge. King Fergus and four other early kings are said to be buried in what is now the garden at Ardverikie. The other island is Eilean nan Con, the Island of the Hounds, where the dogs were kept.

A few years ago, when the loch had been drained to a very low level, the remains of an ancient canoe were found embedded in the mud of its shore. Near the east end of Loch Laggan are the ruins of an old church, named St. Kenneth's Chapel, which gives the parish of Laggan its name. The Gaelic word *lagan* is a hollow, and it is said that the *lagan* where St. Cainnech or Kenneth lived was near this ruined church. The church is said to have been built by Ailean nan Creach, of the family of Lochiel, and was one of seven churches he was ordered to erect to expiate his misdeeds. Cainnech was the friend and helper of Columba, and died about the year 600. The Life of the saint records that he dwelt in a desert place at the foot of a certain mountain in Britain, and that the sun did not shine on this place because of a hill that rose in its track.

On the north side of Loch Laggan the road winds through birch-clad country : on the opposite shore of the loch is Ard-verikie, where silver fir, spruce and pine grow in dense forest to the water's edge. These trees rise to the foot-hills of Ben Alder : here the wild cat and the golden eagle have their home and conditions have changed little (except that the wolf has gone) since the days when the kings of Scotland hunted here.

Beneath Ben Alder, to the south of it, lies Loch Ericht, a long, narrow loch. To see Loch Ericht from Dalwhinnie in early summer with the snowy corries at its head gleaming in the sun's strong rays, and the loch a deep blue beneath a clear serene sky, is to realise that in beauty it ranks high among Highland lochs. In Gaelic, according to Professor Watson, the loch is named Loch Eireachd, Loch of Assemblies or Loch of Meetings — a place of rendezvous. Cf. " 'San Eireachd Molaim Thu " (" I shall praise Thee in the congregation "), Psalm xxii, 22.

Ben Alder, in Gaelic Beinn Allair, rises steeply from Loch Ericht to a height of just short of 3,800 feet above sea level. The name Allair or Alder refers to a stream on the hill, which flows down the south face. Blaeu in the seventeenth century calls the hill " Bin Aildir ". The derivation of the Alder Burn, according

M

to Professor Watson, is from the old Gaelic *alldhobhar*, rock water, from *all*, a steep or precipitous rock, and *dobhar*, water. The Alder Burn flows in great cataracts to Loch Ericht, 1,600 feet below the hill-top. Its course is near a rude shelter marked, on the Ordnance Survey, as Prince Charles's Cave. " Cave " is a misleading word for this rough shelter formed by great boulders leaning one against the other. This may be the site of Cluny's Cage, where Cluny MacPherson sheltered after the '45. The " cage " is known to have been on a south spur of Ben Alder, in a thicket of holly. Professor Walter Blaikie in his *Itinerary of Prince Charles Edward Stuart* mentions that :

All traces of the shanty (an artificial structure of two storeys) have naturally disappeared, but the site of the cave fulfils the necessary conditions, excepting that of the thicket of holly ; yet, as trees have disappeared from many parts of the Highlands, the holly may have died out here.

An old MS. believed to have been written ten years after the Prince's visit to the Cage tells that :

About five miles to the south westward of his (Cluny's) chateau commenc'd his forrest of Ben Alder, plentifully stock'd with dear, red hares, moor foul, and other game of all kinds, beside which it affords fine pasture for his numerous flocks and heards. There also he keeps a harras of some hundred mares, all of which after the fatal day of Culloden became the prey of his enemies. . . . It was in this forrest where the Prince found Cluny with Locheill in his wounds and other friends in his care. He was afraid that his constitution might not suit with lying on the ground or in caves, so was solicitous to contrive for him a more comfortable habitation upon the south front of one of these mountains, overlooking a beautiful lake of 12 miles long. He observed a thicket of hollywood ; he went, viewed, and found it fit for his purpose ; he caused immediately wave the thicket round with boughs, made a first and second floor in it, and covered it with moss to defend the rain. The upper room served for salle a manger and bed-chamber, while the lower served for a cave to contain liquors and other necessaries. At the back part was a proper hearth for cook and baiker and the face of the mountain had so much the colour and resemblance of smoke, no person cou'd ever discover that there was either fire or habitation in the place. Round this lodge were placed their sentinels at proper stations, some nearer and some at greater distances, who dayly brought them notice of what happened in the country and even in the enemie's camps, bringing them likewise the necessary provisions, while a neighbouring fountain supplied the society with the rural refreshment of pure rock water.

For six days (September 6 to 12) the Prince remained in this shelter, then, since he had news brought him that a French vessel had arrived at Loch nan Uamh on the western seaboard, he immediately made his way towards the west.

In the *Lyon in Mourning* (vol. iii, pp. 41 *et seq.*) an account is given of the Prince's life during his stay in the Cage :

His Royal Highness then removed to a very romantic comical habitation made out for him by Cluny, called the *Cage*. It was really a curiosity, and can scarcely be described to perfection. 'Twas situate in the face of a very rough high rockie mountain called Letternilichk, which is still part of Benalder, full of great stones and crevices and some scattered wood interspersed. The habitation called the Cage in the face of that mountain was within a small thick bush of wood. There were first some rows of trees laid down in order to level a floor for the habitation, and as the place was steep this rais'd the lower side to equall height with the other ; and these trees, in the way of jests or planks, were entirely well levelled with earth and gravel. There were betwixt the trees, growing naturally on their own roots, some stakes fixed in the earth, which with the trees were interwoven with ropes made of heath and birch twigs all to the top of the Cage, it being of a round, or rather oval shape, and the whole thatched and covered over with foge. This whole fabrick hung as it were by a large tree, which reclined from the one end all along the roof to the other, and which gave it the name of the Cage ; and by chance there happen'd to be two stones at a small distance from the other in the side next the precipice resembling the pillars of a bosom chimney, and here was the fire placed. The smock had its vent out there, all along a very stonny plat of the rock, which and the smock were all together so much of a colour that any one could make no difference in the clearest day, the smock and stones by and through which it pass'd being of such true and real resemblance. The Cage was no larger than to contain six or seven persons, four of which number were frequently employed in playing at cards, one idle looking on, one becking, and another firing bread and cooking.

Here His Royal Highness remained till he was acquainted that the shipping for receiving and transporting him to France was arrived. In the meantime of his Royal Highness's having his quarters in the Cage, he sent Cluny and Doctor Cameron on some private affair to Locharchaick a part of Lochiel's country, who in their way, before they left Badenoch, in a very dark night, had the good luck to meet with John M'Pherson, alias M'Coilvain, he having been sent by Cameron of Cluns to find out Cluny, that if it was possible he might fall on some way to get his Royal Highness acquainted of the arrival of the ships. And this chance meeting was certainly a very good providence, since if it had happen'd otherwise the Prince would not have known of the Shippings' arrival till the return from Locharchaick, which delay, as the arrival was sometime before, might have proved of very bad consequence. But it pleased God to dispose better for his Royal Highness, who seemed to be still the Almighty's particular care. For tho' the night was the very darkest, as is before observed, the express met the other gentlemen in the teeth, and was known by 'em, whereupon, having got his news, and knowing him to be trustee and might be believed, Cluny immediately provided a trustee guide, one Alexander M'Pherson, son to Benjemin M'Pherson in Gallovie, who brought the express directly to the Cage, where they arrived about one in the morning the thirteenth of September, on which minute his Royal Highness began his journey for the shipping, and against daylight arrived at his old quarters in Uiskchilra.

Hills of Laggan

As, one day of early summer, I looked down from the summit plateau of Ben Alder upon those great stones which, according to tradition, mark the site of the Cage, it was possible to visualise the life of the Prince during his hiding here. I thought that the waters of Ben Alder must have sparkled then as they did on the day when I was on the hill, and that the ancestors of the deer which I saw, and of the croaking ptarmigan, must have been seen, and perhaps been shot, by the Prince and Cluny. To the few remaining people of the old generation this is still spoken of as Cluny's Country, but in that country are now new men, and new ways, for few of the chiefs who rose with the Prince in 1745 recovered the possessions which they forfeited after the failure of that rising.

I thought that, since the view from the Cage was obstructed

by the hillside to the north, Cluny's men must have kept watch, night and day, not from the Cage itself, but from the top of Ben Alder. In those days men did not carry stalking telescopes, but trusted in the unaided keenness of their sight ; yet nothing could have escaped their eyes as they watched from the stony plateau of the great hill. A short distance from the hill-top are still to be seen the ruins of three rude shielings. Can they have been built during the time of the Prince's concealment on the hill two hundred years ago ? Surely they cannot be the ruins of summer shielings, which would have never been built at so great an elevation. In those days men were less interested in hill views than now. Did the sentinels observe the twin spires of Cruachan Beann rise faint in blue haze beyond the hills of the Blackmount Forest where Buachaille Eite, the Herdsman of Etive, towered from the unseen waters of its sea loch ? Did they see with un-conscious pleasure beyond the snow-scarred slopes of Ben Nevis the steep Ardgour Hills rise to the heavens ? Was their imagina-tion kindled when the mist and haze lifted and the sunset flushed three far-distant peaks on the north-west horizon — the Cuillin Hills of the Isle of Skye ?

On the June day when I was on Ben Alder the plateau was green with young hill grass and yellow with marsh-marigolds in damp places where the clear new-born waters of many a hill stream sparkled in the sun. As I was " spying " Ben Nevis through my glass a golden eagle crossed the field of the telescope. The bird was perhaps four miles distant from me. Higher and higher the eagle climbed, then slanting into the rays of the sun, soared high above the waters of Loch Ossian, which shone like burnished gold far beneath me. In clear light were the sharp-pointed Sisters of Kintail, but away to the south-west a thunder-cloud was gathering behind Ben Dòrain, and above Schiehallion's cone white shafts of hail were descending earthward. East, the Cairngorm Hills rose in haze, newly coated (no rare thing on that high hill range) with the snow of a June storm.

Ben Alder summit may be said to be almost a tableland, and

on this very lonely plateau a lochan lies — Lochan a' Gharbh Choire, the Tarn of the Rough Corrie (the corrie lies beneath the loch). This lochan must dispute with Lochan Buidhe on Ben MacDhui the right of being called the highest lochan in the Highlands. They are both over 3,700 feet above the sea, and both in Alpine country. On the June day when I saw this lochan of Ben Alder a great snow-field of the past winter still lay on its western shore and a glistening white wall rose sheer from the depths of the crystal-clear waters, ruffled by the hill wind and sparkling in the sun. Autumn frost must come early here and for more than half the year that lochan must be hidden deep beneath ice and snow. But no eye sees the plateau during winter storms, save perhaps that of a wandering eagle, or a fox, or a snow bunting — for even the hardy clan of the ptarmigan have then gone to their winter quarters in the shelter of the snow-filled corries.

In the corrie beneath this mountain lochan is a larger loch, of singular beauty. Its name is Loch a' Bhealaich Bheithe, the Loch of the Birch Pass. Though it lies nearly 1,000 feet beneath Lochan a' Gharbh Choire, it is nevertheless high above the sea — almost 2,400 feet. From the shore of this loch — the home of many trout — I looked back that evening upon the dark corries and rock walls of Ben Alder, where much snow is always present in June, and where it may indeed remain throughout the year.

As I walked beside the lonely, silent shore of that hill loch a sandpiper fluttered from her nest, placed in a little clump of sphagnum moss from which water was oozing. Yet, so beautifully fashioned was that small nest, the four speckled eggs rested upon a perfectly dry bed. Rosettes of cushion pink blossomed beside the nest and hill violets held their pale blooms toward the sun, now low in the north-west.

Even in fine summer weather the country of Ben Alder is a lonely one. In mid-winter, when hill, glen and corrie are deep beneath the snow, and when the wind catches up clouds of this dry powdery snow and whirls it far over the land, how stern a scene is this ! And yet, even during the heaviest snowfall or the most intense frost, the waters of Loch Ericht remain unfrozen. Whether it be owing to the depth of the loch, or to the springs which have their birth here, or to the action of the winds which in winter continually agitate the loch's surface, it is a strange fact that none has ever seen the waters of this hill loch in the cold Central Highlands imprisoned by the frost that almost always reigns here during the period known to the Gael as the Dead Months

CHAPTER XX

EAST of Fort William, on the long ascent from Loch Linnhe to Loch Laggan in Badenoch, is the Highland district known as Brae Lochaber, a land of hills and glens and old legends. The Macintoshs and the MacDonells [1] of Keppoch long disputed for its possession and the Grants of Strathspey raided it : through the hills to the south it lay at no great distance from the hostile Campbells.

Famous men have come out of Brae Lochaber, and the memory of one of its most renowned sons — Iain Lom, the immortal bard — still lives in the district, although his time was almost three hundred years ago. Iain Lom was great-grandson of Iain Aluinn (Handsome John), chief of Keppoch. It is believed that he was educated in Spain for the priesthood, but because of some youthful misdeed was sent home. Iain Lom was the intimate friend of the Great Montrose, and was present at the battle of Inverlochy, when Montrose and his Highland force gained a brilliant victory over the Campbells. He celebrated this victory in what some consider to be his greatest poem, " Lathà Inbhir Lòchaidh " (" The Day of Inverlochy ").

Iain Lom was made Poet Laureate by Charles II, died full of years and was buried in Cill Choireil in Brae Lochaber.

The ruins of the house where Iain Lom lived are still to be seen, although there are few people in the district who can now

---

[1] MacDonell is a variation in the spelling of MacDonald and should be correctly pronounced with stress on the " *Don* " and not, as it frequently is, on the " *ell* ".

point them out. They stand — if such a word can be applied to the few stones that remain — a short distance north of the main road from Fort William to Newtonmore and Kingussie near the " march " between Lochaber and Badenoch, and overlook the great reservoir that has been made recently here. The well which provided the house with water is on the opposite side of the road, where a burn of considerable size enters the reservoir.

After the Keppoch murders Iain Lom was driven from house and home by the murderers. He made a poem on this, in which he says that he " is being banished from Clachaig, with no ground nor place to live in — and it is not that the rent is beyond my power ".

Much of the home country of Iain Lom is now flooded by the artificial heightening of the level of Loch Laggan, and the district is now almost uninhabited. Quietness broods over the secluded burial-ground of Cill Choireil, where lie the mortal remains of Iain Lom and other illustrious sons of Brae Lochaber. Beside the burial-ground stands the small chapel, which has been restored. The bell of the chapel is musical : the rafters of the roof are sweet-scented pine, and indeed the whole chapel is pervaded with this pine scent, which, unlike incense, retains its strength. About fifty years ago a stone was erected to the memory of Iain Lom and stands beside the chapel, but it is said by the old people of the district that the stone was placed in error where it now stands, and that the grave of Iain Lom is actually some way higher up the burial-ground — which is on a slope. It is said that the stone is erected actually on the grave of another Lochaber bard, Domhnall mac Fhionnlaigh nan Dàn, Donald MacFinlay of the Poems. This bard is said to have been of great strength, and to have carried his own grave-stone down from the hill on his back before his death ! According to one account, his father was standard-bearer to Mac 'Ic Iain, the son of MacDonald of Glencoe.

Cill Choireil is above the road, from which it is hidden by trees, and, curiously enough, it is not marked on the ordinary half-inch map of the district. It is believed to be one of seven churches built by an early chief of Clan Cameron named Ailean nan Creach in expiation for his misdeeds (*vide* Chapter XIX). Another of his churches was Cill Choinnich at the east end of Loch Laggan. In that churchyard is an interesting old gravestone to the memory of " Donald MacPherson ", with a galley under sail incised upon it. Because of the churches which Ailean nan Creach built in various districts, he was sometimes (perhaps with slight irony) called Ailean nan Eaglais, Allan of the Churches.

There is a curious story told of the burial-ground at Cill Choireil. It seems that at first only those of the Catholic faith were buried here, and there was a great outcry among the spirits of the departed when the first Protestant burial took place. At that time there was a small township at Achluachrach near the burial-ground, and the people who lived here were unable to sleep at night because of the clamour which was heard over the churchyard from midnight until cock-crow. The spirits of the Catholics, it seems, hotly (if this term may be applied to a ghost) resented the presence of a Protestant, and indeed this resentment often ended in blows among themselves. At length the people of the township could stand this state of affairs no longer. They sent for the priest and begged him to exorcise the spirits. At that time there was a lochan beyond the churchyard, and the priest filled one of his shoes with water at the tarn, and carried it, in his shoe, up the brae. He blessed the water and sprinkled it over the graves, but especially over the grave of the Protestant. When he returned to his servant, whom he had forbidden to accompany him, he was silent as to what he had seen or heard, and could never afterwards be induced to talk of his experiences, except to say " Poor man, but they were troubling him ". On the night following the priest's visit to the burial-ground there was silence, and the people of the township slept undisturbed, nor did the spirits again quarrel amongst themselves, nor disturb their brother of the Protestant faith.

In the days when the western clans made forays to the east,

to raid the cattle of the fertile lands of Moray, and also of Strath-spey and Upper Deeside, the MacDonells of Keppoch and the Grants of Strathspey formed, unknown to one another, a plan to raid each other's cattle. The MacDonells had proceeded some little way towards Spey when they received word that the Grants were " lifting " their own cattle in their rear. They hurriedly returned, came upon the raiders without warning and killed them almost to a man. The survivors, a small band of three or four weary and dispirited men, struggled south along the shore of Loch Tréig, and at Loch Ossian came upon another party of MacDonells. To them the Grants, apparently ignorant of the identity of those with whom they conversed, told the story of their defeat. When they had ended the MacDonells, saying to them " A pity you should not join your friends ", put them there and then to the sword, so that not one of the cattle-lifting band returned to Strathspey.

This event presumably happened before the battle of Mulroy, fought in 1688 on a small height above Roy Bridge, between the Macintoshs and the MacDonells of Keppoch. This is said by some to have been the last of the inter-clan fights in the High-lands. The story of the battle of Mulroy is somewhat as follows : Macintosh,[1] chief of Clan Chattan, and MacDonell of Keppoch had long been at variance, and Macintosh, with the assistance of a party of Government troops, marched west to Brae Lochaber, with the intention of driving the MacDonells from the district. In this attempt he was almost successful : the day seemed lost for the MacDonells when a herdsman — a gigantic fellow with long red hair — who had been told to watch the cattle in the neighbourhood of the field of battle, seeing that things were going badly for his clansmen, rushed furiously into the fight and, swinging a gigantic club, mowed a path through his enemies. When they saw his magnificent valour the MacDonells, weary and dispirited, gained fresh heart and laid about them so success-

---

[1] I have kept to the spelling " Macintosh " throughout, as being the form of spelling nearest the Gaelic.

fully with their claymores that the Macintoshs fled from the field, leaving their chief a prisoner. Their standard-bearer is said to have leaped, carrying the standard, across the River Roy at a spot where the most courageous of his enemies did not dare attempt to follow.

The old house of Keppoch has disappeared, but the garden, which Iain Lom in his poem on the Keppoch murders refers to as the "garden of pears", remains. The garden of Keppoch was renowned, and one of the seven wonders of Scotland (my authority for this is Professor W. J. Watson) was " a' chraobh a tha fàs an garradh na Ceapaich ", the tree that grows in the garden of Keppoch.

A more modern house, built about the year 1780, stands near the old garden, but it is vacant and derelict. Around this house grow fine trees, leafless and sombre on the winter morning when I visited the place. To the south rose Aonach Mór and Ben Nevis, closely shrouded in a mist that neither rose nor fell, but hung motionless in the damp air. Had Iain Lom seen the house and the garden, his heart would have been sad, for he would have realised that the glory of the MacDonells had departed ; but he would have been cheered had he crossed the Spean to Achnacarry, for he would have found there the old allies of his clan, the Camerons of Lochiel, still in possession of their lands. Lochiel would have doubtless put a warm welcome before him, and his heart would have lifted as he heard a *fàilte* played on the *piob mhór* by one who is as skilled in the playing of the old classical pipe music as were the pipers of the time of Iain Lom.

A reminder of these old times may still be seen at Spean Bridge. It is a dirk in the possession of Miss MacKenzie, Inverour, and was used by her great-great-grandfather at the battle of Prestonpans in the time of Prince Charles Edward. The owner of the dirk was Donnchadh Mór, Big Duncan, of the Camerons of Glenfintaig or Dochanassie. The Prince's army, hurrying to surprise the Hanoverian army under Sir John Cope at daybreak, in leaping the last ditch which separated them from the enemy, lost touch with one another in the half light. It is said that Lochiel, wishing to get the men into order before attacking, called out " Halt ! " Big Duncan, in his excitement, called out in reply "An Deamhan Halt — the Devil a Halt, but let us get at the enemy ! " The attack was immediately pressed home and was successful, else the consequences for Big Duncan in questioning the authority of his chief might have been serious.

I have said that there are many old legends in this hill country. Here is one of them :

At the foot of Aonach Beag (its sharp summit whitened with the first snows of winter when I visited the place) is the remote farm-house of Lianachan. Near the house are the ruins of an older dwelling beside Allt an Lòin, the Burn of the Marsh : behind these ruins is a small green mound. There is a ford beside the house, and according to the legend, a supernatural creature called a glaistig had her home here. One day a traveller on horseback arrived at the ford. The glaistig asked him if he would carry her across the stream and the traveller agreed to take her over but, his suspicions aroused, made her sit in front of him on his horse ; he also bound her " with the holy girdle of Saint Fillan " in order that she might put no spell upon him. When they had crossed the ford the horseman set her down, still bound, upon the ground, and when she asked that she might be liberated he said that she must first consent to build him a house. This she agreed to do. She called, and at her call innumerable fairy workers appeared, and so hard did the fairy host labour that the house was completed before the first pale glow of dawn shone in the eastern sky. The glaistig all the time had encouraged the small workers, giving them careful and practical hints on the laying of the stones.

When the house was finished Kennedy (for this was the traveller's name) lit the first fire on the hearth, although the glaistig, who apparently had been made to stay out in the cold, begged him to allow her to do this. When he refused her request she thrust a long skinny hand through the window, saying that at least she hoped that he would shake her hand and allow her to congratulate him on his fine new house. But Kennedy knew that a glaistig was a dangerous being, and had no intention to allow her to grasp his hand. He therefore heated a plough coulter in the fire until it was red-hot and thrust the coulter into her hand. Since she could not see into the room the glaistig was unaware of the deception, and grasped the plough coulter tightly. There was a fearful shriek, a smell of burnt flesh, and the glaistig fled to the grassy knoll and from it uttered a malison upon Kennedy and all his descendants : " Grow as the rush ; wither as the bracken," shrieked she, " and may the greyness of age fall early on your children." She then vanished from his sight in a green flame.

It may be interesting to give in full the curse of the Lianachan glaistig upon Kennedy :

> Leum i air cloich ghlais
> Na Foich, a thoirt binn air ;
> Thug i mollachd an t-sluaigh air,
> Is mollachd nan uamhlach
> Is ma chreidear na chuarlas
> Gun d' fhuair i a h-impidh,
> " Fàs mar an luachair,
> Crìonadh mar raithnich
> Liathadh nur leanbain
> Caochladh 'n ur treun neart,
> Cha ghuidhe mi gun mhac 'n ur n-aite ".

The Gaelic spelling of this old curse has been given me by Professor Watson, who has also been kind enough to supply the English translation, as follows :

> She leaped on the grey stone
> Of Foich, giving doom on him.
> She invoked the curse of the Fairy Host on him,
> And the curse of the Monsters,
> And if what has been heard is believed
> She obtained her petition —
> " May ye grow like the rushes,
> May ye wither like the bracken,
> May ye grow grey while yet children,
> May ye die in your full strength,
> I will not pray that ye be without a son in your place ".

This curse, it is said, is still seen in the Kennedys of Lochaber, who become grey before their time and are not a long-lived race.

From Lianachan, over Tom na Teine, the Knoll of Fire, to the High Bridge across the River Spean is no great distance. The old Gaelic name for this bridge is An Drochaid Bhàn, the White Bridge, and it is said to have been built by General Wade. The swift Spean here flows through a narrow gorge where aspens, birches and alders grow, and the High Bridge at the narrowest part of the gorge spans the torrent. This bridge, strong and enduring as it appears to be, has failed to withstand the onset of the years, and one of the arches has given way and been carried away by the river. But the High Bridge still presents an imposing appearance, and a touch of the picturesque is given by the larches, which have grown from seed (perhaps blown on the wind) and which flourish with their roots clinging to the old moss-grown stones.

On the west side of the bridge is an old house that was the inn or stage-house behind which Keppoch's men hid before what was the first real engagement of the '45 (the first blood was actually spilled earlier in the same day, on the opposite shore of Loch Lochy from Kilfinnan, when three Government troopers were killed). There is an interesting account of what is called the Rout of the High Bridge in the Memoirs of John Murray of Broughton :

He (Murray) then observed several persons "running towards the river of Lochy, and throwing away their plaids as they run, which he att last came to understand from one he mett by the road was owing to an alarum being given that some of the people who belonged to Cappoch had attacked two companys of Gn. Sinclair's Regiment upon their march from Fort Augustus to Fort William. These two companies had been quartered att Perth, and were ordered by Gn. Cope to reinforce the garrison at Fort William, but Cappoch . . . sent Mr. M'Donald of Tirrendrish, a near relation of his own, with eleven men and a Piper to a little Inn at Highbridge to waite their comming till he should gett some of his Clan together. Mr. M'Donald, to make the best of a small number of men, had placed them behind the Inn to wait for the approach of the enemy, and as soon as they appeared upon the opposite bank above the Bridge he ordered his Piper to play, and rushed out from behind the house with a loud huzza. By this sudden and unexpected attack ye troops were struck with such an unaccountable panick as with one consent to run of without so much as taking time to observe the number or quality of the enemy. They continued to retreat or more properly to run, for about five or six miles."

The troops finally surrendered to Keppoch, who had come up with more men. In that engagement the enemy lost three or four men killed and a dozen wounded ; there was no loss among the Highlanders.

At the time of this engagement the High Bridge must have been almost new and an object of great admiration. Now there are few persons who know even where the bridge stands, and I saw no mark of recent footsteps on the old road, grass-grown but firm, along which a frightened band of men hurried westwards that summer day of 1745. On the late autumn afternoon when I stood beside the bridge Ben Nevis rose snow-covered to the blue sky. The rough moorland grasses were orange and gold, but in sheltered hollows the fern was still green.

Glen Roy, a few miles east of the High Bridge, is a glen of great charm, and retains much of its early simplicity, for its road is no thoroughfare, but ends at a shooting lodge near its head. Where the road ends an old right-of-way crosses the watershed eastwards, passes Loch Spey, the source of the River Spey, and then continues east to join General Wade's road over the Pass of Corrieyaireag.

I will here describe a crossing of the watershed by this right-of-way from the Badenoch country in the east on a grey October day. After a night of rain my friend and I set our faces to the west and passed the old barracks which still stand at Garvamore and the lonely stalker's house at Meall Garbh Ath. Our destination, Roy Bridge, was twenty miles distant, and to reach it we had to cross the head-waters of the Spey and traverse a country all of which is lonely and almost desolate.

It is strange that the sister rivers, Spey and Dee, should have their sources in country so different. The Dee, from its cradle on the summit plateau of Braeriach, falls in a white flood nearly 2,000 feet to the depths of Làirig Ghrù. The Spey rises beside

Loch Spey, which is a placid loch, without distinction, no more than 1,400 feet above the level of the sea : yet throughout its lower reaches the Spey is swifter by far than the Dee, rising at 4,000 feet.

All around, as we traversed the bank of Loch Spey and then stood beside the infant river which trickles into it, red deer were watching us. There were stately stags and mild-eyed hinds, and the roaring of the stags was the only sound to be heard. Far up on the heights small drifts of recent snow showed white against a sombre background. Uisge nam Fichead, the Water of the Twenty (Tributaries), foamed white through the high corries, but that impetuous stream was hurrying not to the valley of the Spey but to Glen Roy and the western ocean.

It was cheering, after walking for miles along the almost flat country where the Spey has its source, to find, as we descended to Glen Roy, grander and more beautiful scenery. The lower reaches of Glen Roy we knew, but the head of the glen was un-known to us, and it was therefore pleasant, when we had begun to feel weary as the result of heavy going through the soft, peaty ground at the head of Spey, to find ourselves entering a district of greater attraction.

The first house we reached was a shepherd's dwelling, now uninhabited. It stood beside a tributary of the Roy, and this tributary, peat-stained and foaming, was a formidable barrier until, a few hundred yards up the stream, we found a footbridge spanning the burn above a deep pool.

Soon we saw ahead of us the shooting lodge at Turret Bridge, and here, at a friendly stalker's house, we found the road. We were now following the track of Montrose on his famous forced march before the battle of Inverlochy. Montrose, it will be remembered, crossed the hills from Fort Augustus in the dead of winter and, descending unheralded to Lochaber, routed the Government troops of the garrison of Inverlochy. At the stalker's cottage at Turret Bridge we saw a tame stag standing on a knoll beside the path, and a beautiful young collie at the doorstep ;

N

here we were given a most kindly welcome by the stalker and his wife, whom we met as strangers and left as friends. As we rose from their fireside rain was filling the sky to the south and was descending in Glen Roy, where the renowned Parallel Roads of Glen Roy led away across the hill face into the distance like roads made by human hands.

Colonel Stewart in his *Sketches*, written in the year 1822, has some interesting things to say of the Parallel Roads of Glen Roy, for he wrote when the old traditions of the glen were still alive. Let me quote what he says on the subject :

Since strangers and men of science have traversed these long-deserted regions, an irreconcileable feud of opinions has arisen between the Geologists and the Highlanders, regarding an uncommon conformation in Glenroy, a glen in Lochaber, remarkable for the height and perpendicularity of its sides, particularly of one of them. On the north side, at a considerable elevation above the stream, which flows along the bottom of the glen, there is a flat, or terrace, about seventy feet broad, having the appearance of a road formed on the side of the mountain, and running along, on a perfect level, to the extremity of the glen. Five hundred feet above this, there is another of these terraces, and still higher a third, all parallel, and of similar form. IN ENGLISH THEY ARE NOW CALLED PARALLEL ROADS : THE INHABITANTS KNOW THEM BY THE NAME OF THE KING'S HUNTING ROADS.

Geologists say that the glen was once full of water, up to the level of the highest parallel, which must have been formed by the action of the waters of this lake on the side of the hill. By some violence, however, an opening was made in the lower end of the glen, which confined the water, in consequence of which it immediately fell as low as the second parallel, and formed it in the same manner as the first. Another opening of the same kind brought down the surface of the water to the third parallel, when, at length, that which confined the water giving way entirely, it subsided to the bottom of the glen, where it now runs, in a rapid stream, without obstruction.

To this opinion the Highlanders object, that it is not probable that water, after the first declension, would remain so perfectly stationary as to form a second parallel of the same breadth and formation as the first, or that the second declension would be so regular in time, and the water so equal in its action, as to form a third terrace of form and breadth perfectly similar to the two others ; that the glen is too narrow to allow the waves to act with sufficient force to form these broad levels ; that, in the centre of the glen, which is narrow, the levels are the broadest and most perfect, whereas, on the upper end, which opens to a wide extent, allowing a large space for the wind to act with a superior force, the levels are contracted and less perfect ; that on one side of the glen these terraces are broad, and of perfectly regular formation, while, on the other they are narrow, and not so well formed; and that, unless the wind blew always from the same quarter, waves would not roll with more force to one side of a piece of water than to another. In Glenspean, which is in the immediate neighbourhood, and in which similar appearances present themselves, the hills recede from each other, leaving a wide expanse, on the sides of which, if the hollow had been filled with water, the waves would have acted with considerable force, and yet these roads, or terraces, are by no means so well formed, continuous, and distinct, as in Glenroy. The Highlanders also urge the impossibility of water having ever been confined in Glenspean, without an improbable convulsion of nature, the lower end being of great width, and open to the ocean. After stating these reasons, they triumphantly conclude by a query, Why other glens 'and straths in the Highlands do not exhibit natural appearances similar to those in the vicinity of the ancient residence of their kings.[1] Their own account, which they believe as they do their creed, is, that these roads were made for hunting of the kings when at Inverlochay; that they were palisadoed on each side; and, that the game was driven through, affording the Royal Hunters time to destroy numbers before they could get to the end. As a confirmation of this account they quote the names of the circumjacent places, which all bear an analogy to these huntings.

To these opinions, so opposite and difficult to reconcile, it is probable that each party will adhere.

I have quoted Stewart's interesting old account in full, because it seems to me that the Highlanders and the geologists may both have been correct in their contentions. May it not be that the Parallel Roads were indeed made by the action of water, yet may it not be equally true that the kings of Scotland from their castle at Inverlochy did indeed use the "roads" in the hunting of game?

Sir Archibald Geikie in his *Scenery of Scotland* brings his expert knowledge to bear on the subject of the Roads. He believes that they mark successive levels of a great loch which almost filled Glen Roy. At that time a vast glacier in Glen Tréig stretched right across Glen Spean and mounted its north bank, and the valley of the Caledonian Canal was filled to the brim with ice which choked the mouth of Glen Roy and the mouth of Glen Spean. A great lake must at that time have filled Glen Roy and the neighbouring glens, and at the time the uppermost "beach" or parallel road was formed (1,155 feet above the sea) the overflow from the loch in Glen Roy emptied itself not into

[1] This would seem to refer to the Castle of Inverlochy, where the ancient Scottish kings lived.—AUTHOR.

the Atlantic as at the present day, but eastwards from the head of Glen Roy into the Spey. When the Glen Tréig glacier, and with it the glacier lake, shrank, the middle " beach " (1,077 feet above the sea) was formed. The overflow now no longer flowed east to Strathspey, but through the head of Glen Glaster, through Loch Laggan, into the Spey. The Glen Tréig glacier continued to melt, and at last receded from Glen Spean. The level of the lake was again reduced, and the lowest of the Parallel Roads was formed. The level of the Glen Roy lake was now reduced to 862 feet above sea level, and it now joined Loch Laggan, forming a long, winding loch, with its outflow through what is now the head of Glen Spean, into Strathspey. The great glacier further shrank, the drainage of Glen Roy, Glen Spean and their lesser glens was no longer held back, and at last the great lake of Glen Roy disappeared, " a phantom lake which came into being with the growth of the glaciers, and vanished as these melted away ".

It is likely that Montrose and his men, weary as they must have been after their long expedition through the hills, made use of the Parallel Roads on their march down Glen Roy. There is a tradition that as they passed they saw red flames curling from the thatched houses of the township of Bohuntine which had been fired that day by a party of Campbells on the Government side, and that on seeing these flames they forgot their weariness in their fury and hurried forward to the attack at Inverlochy with black vengeance in their hearts.

A desperate character once lived near the head of Glen Roy. His name was Iain Odhar, in English Dun-coloured John, and he did not scruple to kill any man who might enter his territory. At last Iain Odhar lay on his death-bed, and a neighbour called to see whether he could do anything for the poor man. As he leaned sympathetically over the bed, the dying man grasped his *sgian dubh* and attempted to kill his neighbour. Shocked at this behaviour, the neighbour asked him what had made him attempt his life. His reply, uttered in a hoarse whisper, was, " The river has slain twenty ; I have killed only nineteen."

There is an old belief that certain Highland rivers claim a life at certain times, and the dying man had perhaps this tradition in his mind when he spoke.

The River Roy has seen strange sights, and surely one of the most grim was of Iain Lom, the bard, hurrying to Glengarry, his chief, with the seven heads of the Keppoch murderers "slung by the ears to a withy". The heir of Keppoch and his brother, on their return from abroad, where they had received their education, were massacred by their cousins. Iain Lom appealed to Glengarry for armed help to avenge the murder, but Glengarry could not see his way to give the assistance sought. Iain Lom then addressed himself to Sir Alexander MacDonald of Sleat, who was more sympathetic, or perhaps bolder, than Glengarry and commissioned another bard, Archibald MacDonald of North Uist, a poet better known by his Gaelic name An Ciaran Mabach, to take a company of chosen men to Brae Lochaber, there to place themselves at the disposal of Iain Lom. The murderers of Keppoch and his brother, after a brave resistance, were seized and beheaded, and Iain Lom in triumph carried their heads to Glengarry. On the way, the heads were washed in a well beside Loch Oich (on the main road from Fort William to Inverness) and to this day the well is known as Tobar nan Ceann, Well of the Heads.

About half-way down the romantic and very beautiful Glen Roy the traveller as he descends the valley from the east sees, at the left-hand side of the road near a sharp bend (and there are many in the glen), a stone which at first glance might be a milestone. But if he looks more closely he will see, incised with rare skill on the stone, a chalice, and a wafer of bread on which are the letters I H S. This stone commemorates an event which took place about the year 1770. At that time a *bòcan* or spectre of ill-repute haunted the burn which crosses the road about five hundred yards up the glen from the stone. So malevolent was the sprite (he had, it is said, murdered more than one person) that the people of the glen hesitated to cross the burn after dark.

It was therefore without surprise that Aonghus Mór (Big Angus), the strong man of the district, on passing that way one night heard from out the gloom a sepulchral voice call out, " Aonghus Mór shall not pass." But a more friendly voice answered the first, and said, " Aonghus Mór SHALL pass." Thrice came the words " Aonghus Mór shall not pass," and thrice, in answer to them, came the words " Aonghus Mór SHALL pass." Big Angus took courage. He shouted boldly, " Three for me, and three against me, and I for myself, and I SHALL pass." He did indeed cross the burn unharmed, but the people of the glen, when they heard his experience, decided that the time had come when they must ask the priest to help them rid the place of the hobgoblin. The priest went to the haunted burn, offered up Mass on a stone in the bed of the stream where the voices had been heard, and exorcised the *bòcan*.

All in the glen knew the site of the sacred stone on which Mass had been offered up, and whenever they passed that way looked on it with veneration. For a century it lay undisturbed, then, about seventy years ago, when the road was being widened by men who did not know the history of the stone, it was removed from its bed in the burn and was broken in two, in order to be placed in a strengthening wall for the widened road. A young man named MacPherson, a native of Glen Roy, who was studying for the priesthood, on hearing what had happened, rescued one of the halves of the stone and carried it a little farther down the road, where he set it up as a memorial and chiselled out the graceful chalice which may be seen to this day.

At Briagach, half-way up Glen Roy, it is said King James V spent a night when hunting. For blankets he had goats' skins, and was looked after so well that he exempted from rent all the goats in Scotland.

It was in earlier times than these that the Maid of Keppoch was taken by the fairies in Glen Roy. She was an Irish girl, little more than a child, and had become the wife of MacDonell of Keppoch. But the wedding rejoicings were scarcely over when the bride, wandering into the oak woods which still clothe the lower slopes of Glen Roy, disappeared mysteriously. It was believed that, like the Rev. Robert Kirk (whom I have mentioned in Chapter IV), she had been spirited away by the fairies. If indeed she was abducted by the Little People they held her closely, for from that day to this no trace has been found of the fair Maid of Keppoch.

The October clouds rose slowly from Aonach Mór, revealing traces of an early snowfall fringing the corries. Flurries of leaves, golden and delicate, were being shaken by a fitful wind from the trees. Blue smoke rose from the old township of Bohuntine, the birth-place of more than one distinguished Highlander. A pair of ravens flew overhead and grey crows cried harshly as they may perhaps have welcomed Montrose when he hurried down to Inverlochy to avenge those burning roofs which he had seen in lonely Bohuntine of Glen Roy.

Badenoch, near the Corrieyaireag Pass

CHAPTER XXI

CORRIEYAIREAG : A HIGHLAND PASS

NEAR the headwaters of the Spey a road, made by General Wade and now long disused, leads through the heart of the hills from Badenoch to Fort Augustus on Loch Ness. This old road, skilfully constructed, crosses the Pass of Corrieyaireag 2,500 feet above sea level, a wild and lonely country, far beyond the sight of any house. The place-name Corrieyaireag has puzzled Celtic scholars. The late Alexander MacBain, in his *Place-Names of the Highlands and Islands of Scotland*, suggests that the second part (yaireag) of the name may be a corruption of Gearrag, the Short One, here applied to a stream. Mr. J. M. Mathieson, an authority on Gaelic place-names, who made the last survey of St. Kilda and was familiar with the whole of the Highlands, was inclined to think that the word Gearrag might be applied to the corrie itself, and not to the stream flowing from it, and suggested that the original place-name was Coire Earrag (Coire Gearrag), the Short Corrie. In support of his suggestion he mentioned (a thing which

I also noticed) that the climber crossing the pass from the south seems to enter the corrie very quickly and, as it were, strike right up against it. One of the earliest spellings of the name is Cori Gherrag. This occurs in a MS. account of the parish of Boleskine and appears to have been written around 1720.[1]

The road across the Pass of Corrieyaireag seems to have been completed in the summer of the year 1731, for a gentleman of the name of MacLeod — perhaps MacLeod of Dunvegan, or a near kinsman of that chief — who crossed the pass in the autumn of 1731, saw six great fires, at which six oxen were being roasted whole as a treat for the five hundred soldiers who had that summer completed " the great road for Wheel-carriages between Fort Augustus and Ruthven, it being October 30, His Majesty's Birthday ".

The Hon. Mrs. Murray, who has left a record of her travelling in the Scottish Highlands in the year 1798, crossed Corrieyaireag by coach in the late summer of that season. Before she began her journey she met, at breakfast with the Governor of Fort Augustus, an Oxonian who had crossed the pass on horseback the previous day. He gave her a depressing account of Corrie-yaireag, a pass

of wild desolation beyond anything he could describe ; and the whole of the road rough, dangerous and dreadful, even for a horse. The steep and black mountains, and the roaring torrents rendered every step his horse took, frightful ; and when he attained the summit of the zigzag up Corrie-yaireag he thought the horse himself, man and all, would be carried away, he knew not whither ; so strong was the blast, so hard the rain, and so very thick the mist. And as for cold, it stupified him.

Mrs. Murray tells of a woman with an infant at the breast who succumbed when endeavouring to cross the pass ; the infant, being covered with snow, was still alive when found, and the governor's lady at Fort Augustus restored it to health. The same chronicler mentions that soldiers often perished on the pass, partly because " they over-refreshed themselves with whisky before the climb ".

[1] MacFarlane's *Geographical Collections*, vol. i, p. 220.

Prince Charles Edward crossed Corrieyaireag at the end of August 1745, at the beginning of his campaign. He had heard that Cope was encamped at Garvamore, on the Badenoch side of the pass, and was anxious to engage him as soon as possible. That morning, as he pulled on a new pair of brogues, he said happily, " Before I throw these off, I shall meet with Mr. Cope." The Prince sent ahead two of his officers to see whether they could get into contact with Cope's force, but when they reached the watershed "not a creature was to be seen", although a little later in the day forty deserters from General Cope's force were viewed ascending the zigzags on the Badenoch side of the pass : these deserters at once took up service with the Prince. Cope, thinking discretion the better part of valour, had turned aside near Dalchully at a place still known as " Cope's Turn", and was now making towards Ruthven Barracks. Lochgarry, one of the Prince's officers, remained for three days in ambush near the summit of Corrieyaireag, and had with him a party of Glengarry men. Lochgarry in his *Narrative* writes :

While I lay in ambush on Corierick there passed one Capt. Switnam, who commanded the barracks at Ruthven in Badenoch, and was going to Fort Wm. as he was recon'd a very good ingineer. I detached four of the Glengarry Kennedies to apprehend him, which they did effectively, horses, baggage and servant.

At Corrieyaireag the Prince was joined by "Ardshiel (commanding the Stewarts of Appin), Glengarry and Glenco ".

A hundred years before the stirring events of the '45, Montrose, in his historic march over the hills to Inverlochy, set foot on Corrieyaireag, but did not actually cross the pass (although some accounts of his campaign state that he did so), for his route to Glen Roy, which he traversed, is believed to have been southwest over the hill, starting from a point near Newton in the Great Glen, between Loch Oich and Fort Augustus.

It is a century and more since the road across Corrieyaireag carried the last of its wheeled traffic, but it is not so long since sheep and cattle were driven over it to the markets of the south.

Mrs. Grant of Laggan, in her *Letters from the Mountains*, writes
in 1781 from Fort Augustus :

> This district is divided from ours (Laggan in Badenoch) by an immense
> mountain called Corryarrick. That barrier is impassable in the depth of
> winter, as the top of it is above the region of clouds, and the sudden
> descent on the other (Spey) side particularly dangerous not only from
> deep snows concealing the unbeaten track of the road, but from whirlwinds
> and eddies that drive the snow into heaps ; besides an evil spirit which
> the country people devoutly believe to have dwelt there time out of mind.

Garva Bridge, between Laggan and Fort Augustus

I was twice on Corrieyaireag in 1938. In the spring of that
year I climbed to the summit of the pass on a cold April morning,
when I met beside the Spey a party of motor-cyclists who (unknown to me at the time) had that day made history by crossing
the pass from Fort Augustus : the wheel-tracks of their machines
remained for many a day to tell of their exploit.

That morning I approached Corrieyaireag from the east.
General Wade's road is still in use in the Spey valley, for about
ten miles from its junction with the main Fort William–New-

tonmore road to the stalker's house at Meall Garbh Ath, the Hill
of the Rough Ford.   The old road leaves the main Newtonmore–
Fort William road rather more than a mile west of Laggan Bridge,
passes near Dalchully, one of the hiding-places of Cluny Mac-
Pherson of the '45, then follows the Spey past Glen Shirra and
Loch Crunachan and crosses the river (here is a particularly fine
Wade's bridge) beside the old barracks at Garvamore.   At the
present day the road is rough, and there are a number of gates
to open and close again, as far as Meall Garbh Ath or, as it is now
written, Meall Garbha ; beyond that house the track is not in
use ; it is grass- and heather-grown, and usually very wet.

The scene ahead of me was wild and lonely as I set out into the
heart of the hills.   Even the glen of the Spey was bare and wintry,
although here I had seen golden plover and heard the trilling of
curlews.   From now onward to the summit of Corrieyaireag I
saw no bird, save a skylark which flew ahead of me low above the
track, but when I had almost reached the summit of the pass I
saw and watched a pair of ptarmigan dozing on a warm, grassy
bank.

At a time when, in certain parts of the Highlands and Islands,
the Ministry of Transport were narrowing the existing roads as
they reconstructed them, to a width of 10 feet, it was interesting to
discover that General Wade made this road over the hills a width
of 14 and in some places 15 feet.   Here and there a cloud-burst
had carried down earth and stones on to the track : perhaps the
same flood washed away the first stone bridge after the stalker's
house is passed, and did its best to sweep away the second.
When I had rounded a bend in the old road I saw ahead of me
the corrie which gives the pass its name.   Icicles hung from the
rocks of the corrie, and a cold northerly wind was bringing into
the corrie the smoke of a distant heather fire, which burned
far out of my sight somewhere beyond the watershed in the
neighbourhood of Loch Ness.

Scars heal slowly in hill country, and I saw gravel-pits, and
banks and passing places, and even old metal broken to repair

the track. At one place a very old grass-coated cairn lay half in ruins beside the road : it was, perhaps, the memorial of one who had met his death here. The road is well engineered, and there are few steep gradients, except at the zigzags where, as I have mentioned earlier in this chapter, Prince Charlie's men from the summit saw Cope's deserters making their way toward them.

When I reached the summit, 2,500 feet above sea level, the wind was so cold that I could not long remain to admire the view. To the north-west I could see Loch Garry, and the high hills beyond the loch, half hidden by snow showers, while south-west Aonach Mór and Ben Nevis raised their snow-filled corries to the passing clouds. Through a gap south of these two great hills a high top of the Blackmount Forest, perhaps Clachlet or Buachaille Eite, showed darkly.

I returned to Meall Garbha with the wind at my back, and was overtaken by more than one snow shower which for a time whitened the hill slopes.

Very different were the conditions on the October day when a friend and I crossed the pass from Fort Augustus to Glen Truim in Badenoch. That autumn was continuously wet and stormy ; our walk was through rain and mist, and the most pleasant memory of the day was the hot bath provided, along with a dram of *uisge beatha*, by our Highland host. It was already noon when we stood in the small room in Fort Augustus Abbey where Lord Lovat of the '45 was for some days a prisoner, and saw the old tree outside the abbey planted by Government officers to com- memorate Cumberland's victory. A late start on a long walk is rarely justified, and throughout that day we were hurrying to reach Badenoch before the darkness of a moonless night closed in on us. It is not at all an easy matter to locate the track after leaving Fort Augustus. The old right-of-way has in places been absorbed in private property and the newer path in these places is winding, difficult to find, and even when found difficult to follow until the original track is again reached. The way is first along Glen Tarff, and in the mist and gloom which held the pass ahead of us it was impossible to tell, so devious was the track, through which upland glen we were ultimately to climb in order to cross the watershed to the Spey beyond. Following weeks of rain, the track was sodden and the hills ran water. The most pleasant part of the climb was at Lagan a' Bhainne, Dell of the Milk (called by the Government troops Snugborough). Here weeping birches were scattering golden leaves on the autumn wind and into the peat-stained stream, and a golden eagle, rising from near the ruins of old houses, flew close past us down the glen, showing clearly (it was a young bird of the year) the white marking on wings and tail.

General Wade's bridge spanning the stream at Lagan a' Bhainne has fallen away at the centre, and a foot-bridge has recently been erected here by the Scottish Rights of Way Society. We now climbed more steeply, and before we entered the mist saw the last tree, a rowan, flame dull red below us. Through dense mist we plodded, wind and rain driving in our faces, and as we traversed this country of gloom heard invisible stags roaring about us. Our view was restricted to a few yards, but the old road was a sure guide, and at length we found ourselves descending into Badenoch. As we reached the fringe of the cloud we felt a sudden strengthening of the light : again the cloud enveloped us, but as we descended the steep zigzags, now running water, we finally passed out of the fog and saw ahead of us a sombre country which lay dark and dreary in the dusk of a day of rain. In the half light a peregrine falcon rose from a knoll where she had perhaps decided to spend the night : she flew backwards and forwards low above the moor, then swung high into the air and was lost to view in the deepening dusk.

Making the best speed possible, we reached the stalker's house and were glad to see the lights of the car which our kind host and hostess of Glen Truim had sent to meet us at Meall Garbha.

Ahead of us, scarce discernible in the gloom, was Garvamore

(Garbh Ath Mór, the Big Rough Ford), and Wade's old bridge. It is said that when a death was to occur in the family of MacPherson of Garva, Tom Mór, a hill in this neighbourhood, would be seen lighted up.

John MacDonald of Garva Mór was a noted strong man. Dr. Longmuir in his *Speyside* (published in 1860) gives an interesting anecdote relating to John MacDonald. The account is as follows:

A Mr. Lumsden of Aberdeenshire laid a bet with Glengarry that there was not a Highlander on Glengarry's estate who could jump, put the stone, or throw the hammer with him. The challenge was accepted, and the contest was to take place on Corryarrick. Glengarry attended at the time with a numerous retinue of his tenantry; but Lumsden sent a message that he would not come to such a place unless his life was insured for £3,000. The Marquess of Huntly bantered him that he was afraid of losing his bet, and told him that his life was as safe in Badenoch as at home. Lumsden then challenged anyone on the Marquess's estate — the parties being restricted to seven throws of the hammer. The Marquess wrote to John MacDonald of Garvamore to come and enter the lists with Lumsden. MacDonald requested Captain MacDonald to take care of his wife and children, as he declared that he would never return to Badenoch were he unsuccessful! He then proceeded to Huntly (in Aberdeenshire) and arrived there three days before the competition. On that day Lumsden, for the first three throws, took the lead; but MacDonald was ahead of his antagonist for the next three, and beat him by twenty inches. The Marquess rewarded him with a jug of considerable value, and sent him home happy in having worthily maintained the honour of the district.

Were it possible to recall the past, there would surely be stirring sights to see on Corrieyaireag — the Prince's army streaming, to the loud strains of the great Highland pipe, eastward into Badenoch, travellers on horseback breasting those same slopes, and now and again a stately, horse-drawn vehicle belonging to some dignitary slowly making its way up the steep zigzags, or perhaps some lonely soldier, during a wild winter crossing, toiling onward until slowly overwhelmed by the choking drift and lying down to sleep the sleep that knows no earthly awakening. Surely this hill pass keeps many secrets in its bosom, but now its busy life has gone, and it sees only the red deer and the hardy ptarmigan, and perhaps a wild cat stalking a red grouse. A strange visitor of late did indeed for a time make its home in the neighbourhood of Meall Garbha. This white-plumaged bird, large and unusual in appearance, preyed on the partridges which live beside the Spey here. It was unfortunately shot, and was found to be a Greenland falcon, a wanderer from that distant snowy land which gave it birth.

Insh on the Spey

CHAPTER XXII

THE COUNTRY OF BADENOCH

BADENOCH is the heart of the Central Highlands. Its western border is the historic Druim Alban; the Monadh Liath hills guard it on the north and the high Cairngorms and their western spurs rise to the south. Through Badenoch flows the River Spey, a river which, says Timothy Pont, is

accounted the longest river in Scotland: in its cours it is swyft above them all, running throw hills and cuming from hie countrey, it is most myld and calme in the courss as it runneth through Badenoch, afterward lower down, a great deal more furious.

Another old description of the Spey, believed to date from about 1630, in describing the " Speay " mentions that

Oftymes this river in tyme of speat or stormie weather will be alse bigg as if it were a Logh, and also als broad and overflowes all the low corne lands of the Countrey next to itself.

O

Badenoch is well wooded and the old tradition which accounts for the escape of its woodlands from fire in early days is as follows: The King of Lochlann, being envious of the fine forests of the Highlands, sent across the sea from Norway a witch who, beginning her murrain in the north, miraculously rained down fire on the great forests of Sutherland. Like the Luftwaffe, she was skilled in concealing herself in the clouds, and as she moved slowly south, setting fire to all the woods, she remained always invisible. Her devastating fires had reached the edge of the country of Badenoch when a man of the district hit upon a plan for making the witch reveal herself. He gathered an immense number of cattle, sheep and horses, then separated the cows from their calves, the sheep from their lambs, the foals from the mares. The result of this subterfuge produced an outcry so tremendous that the witch in alarm and astonishment thrust her head through the cloud of her making, and the wise man of Badenoch, who of course had taken the precaution of having his gun loaded with a silver sixpence, made no mistake in his aim and brought her down to earth.

In the thirteenth century the Cummings or Comyns, a proud Norman family who came over with William the Conqueror, were Lords of Badenoch. The early fourteenth century saw the fall and forfeiture of the Comyns, and in the year 1371 Alexander Stewart, Robert the Second's son, was made Lord of Badenoch. He was known as Alasdair Mór Mac an Rìgh, Big Alexander the King's Son, and from the ferocity of his character was named the Wolf of Badenoch. It was in the time of the Wolf that the battle of Invernahaven between the MacPhersons and the Camerons was fought in the year 1388 at the confluence of the Spey and the Truim. The Wolf of Badenoch had one of his seats in the castle of Ruthven, and from there, in 1390, he set out on an expedition eastwards against his enemy the Bishop of Moray and burnt Elgin Cathedral — a crime for which he was forced to do penance in the Blackfriars Church in Perth. In the year 1394 he died, and his tomb in Dunkeld Cathedral can be seen at the

present day.[1] The Wolf of Badenoch's eldest son became Earl
of Mar.

In 1451 the Lordship of Badenoch was granted to Alexander,
Earl of Huntly, by James II. The Earl of Huntly was ancestor
of the last Duke of Gordon, who died in 1836, and at that time
the family still held great possessions in Badenoch. It is therefore noteworthy that from a very early period the Clan Chattan
in Badenoch — the Macintoshs and the MacPhersons — were
under the superiority first of the Comyns, then of the Gordons —

Roy Castle, Inverness-shire

both Norman nobles and considered foreigners in race and blood
by these Celtic inhabitants of Badenoch.

The main road from Inverness to Perth strikes through the
heart of Badenoch. Beyond Aviemore it passes near, but out of
sight of, Kinrara, an attractive house and property which until
recently belonged to the Duke of Richmond and Gordon. On the
hill of Tor Alvie, near Kinrara, may be seen the memorial erected
to the last Duke of Gordon.

Kinrara was the favourite residence of that celebrated beauty,
Jane, Duchess of Gordon, who, it will be remembered, assisted in
raising the 92nd or Gordon Highlanders. "The Duchess", says
one account, "is said to have had a wager with the Prince Regent
as to which of them would first raise a battalion, and the fair lady
reserved to herself the power of offering a reward even more

[1] *Vide* p. 123.

attractive than the king's shilling. The Duchess and Lord
Huntly started off on their errand, and between them soon raised
the required number of men. The mother and son frequented
every fair on the countryside, begging the fine young Highlanders
to come forward in support of king and country, and to enlist in
her regiment ; and when all other arguments had failed, rumour

Spey, near Lynwilg

stated that a kiss from the beautiful Duchess won the doubtful
recruit."

Mrs. Grant of Laggan, in one of her " Letters ", writes that

> The Duchess of Gordon is a very busy farmeress at Kinrara, her beauti-
> ful retreat on the Spey. She rises at five in the morning, bustles incessantly,
> employs from twenty to thirty workmen every day, and entertains noble
> travellers from England in a house very little better than our own.

As a girl the Duchess, it is said, was deeply in love with a
young officer, who went abroad on active service and was later
reported as killed. Lady Jane Maxwell, as she then was, was
overwhelmed with grief, but her beauty was such that she was

admired by all, and when the Duke of Gordon proposed to her she accepted him, partly, it is said, from family pressure. On their honeymoon, at Ayton House, the Duchess received a letter addressed to her, by her maiden name, from her lover, the officer. In it he said that he was hastening home to marry her. The unfortunate bride was half crazed by this terrible news, and when she had at last recovered from the shock hid her sorrow in gaiety and excitement, although an abiding grief was always deep in her heart.

At Lynwilg the road skirts the shore of Loch Alvie, a quiet loch with birch-clad banks. The church of Alvie is believed to go back to a very remote period. Towards the close of the nineteenth century, when the building was renewed, during the excavations no fewer than one hundred and fifty skeletons were found beneath the floor of the church " lying head to head ". It is believed that they were the remains of Highlanders killed in some unrecorded battle. The skeletons were re-interred in the burial-ground surrounding the church, and a granite stone, with the following inscription upon it, was placed over them :

BURIED HERE
ARE
REMAINS OF 150 HUMAN BODIES
FOUND, OCTOBER 1880,
BENEATH THE FLOOR OF THIS CHURCH.
WHO THEY WERE,
WHEN THEY LIVED
HOW THEY DIED,
TRADITION NOTES NOT

" Their bones are dust, their good swords rust,
Their souls are with the saints, we trust."

There are some curious old church records of Alvie. Here are two :

September 20, 1729. Delated this day Ann Down and Kate Fraser, in Kannachil, for prophanation of the Lords Day in going to the wood for pulling nuts.

September 7th, 1730. Delated John Meldrum and Alexander M'Intyre, in Dalnavert, for prophaning the Lord's Day by fishing upon the watter of Feshie.

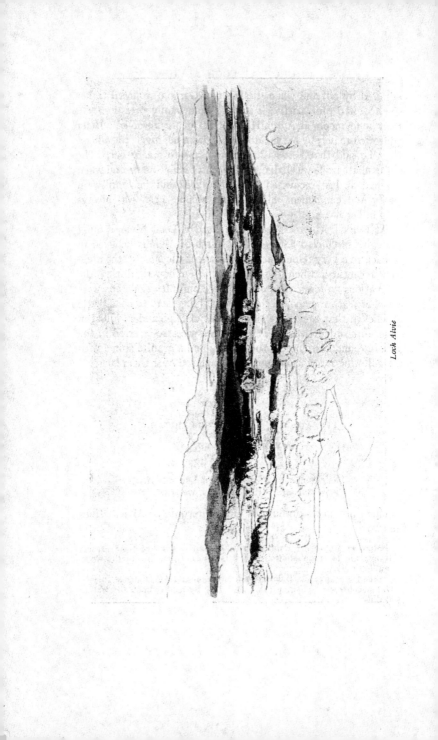

Loch Alvie

From the high ground north of the loch a graceful burn, Allt na Crìche, the March or Boundary Burn, falls into the loch. This stream an old account of the sixteenth or seventeenth century speaks of as "Alt Chriachie or the Marching Burn".

Some three miles south-west of Loch Alvie the main road

St. Adamnan's Bell, Church of Insh

reaches Loch Insh, through which the River Spey flows. Loch Insh is the Loch of the Island, and receives its name from a mound on the south-east side of the loch. This is a peninsula (an island only in times of high floods), and its old name is Tom Innis. The same old account from which I have quoted (Mac-Farlane's *Geographical Collections*, vol. ii, p. 577) mentions that "upon a half Yland in Loch Inche is Tome Inche, a seat and kirk ".

There is a very old bronze bell in this church, believed to be St. Adamnan's bell. The mound on which the church stands is Tom Eunan or Eónain, and Eónan, as I have elsewhere noted,

is the name by which Adamnan is usually known in the Highlands. Adamnan was biographer of St. Columba and ninth
abbot of Hy (Iona), and dedications to Columba and Adamnan
are usually found near one another — the old church of St.
Columba at Kingussie is not far from Loch Insh. There is a
legend that the bell, being on one occasion stolen and taken across
the hills to the south, refused to keep silence until it was returned
to its rightful place, and as it crossed the Pass of Drumochter
it rang out indignantly its name, "Tom Eónan! Tom Eónan!"

The old legends are fast disappearing in Badenoch, but surely
the spirit of the past is seen again in the skeins of whooper swans,
white and graceful, which each year fly south-east from Iceland
to winter upon the waters of Loch Insh : surely their cries have
affinity with the music of Adamnan's bell which, like the saintly
bell upon Eilean Fhìonnain on Loch Shiel, was held to have
magical properties.

The place-names around Loch Insh recall the early days of
Christianity in the Highlands. Dunachton is Dùn Neachdain, the
Dùn of Nechtan, an early saint, or it may be an early Pictish
king. Below Dunachton House (*vide* MacBain's *Place-Names of
the Highlands and Islands*) is St. Drostan's chapel, the "capella
de Nachtan" of 1380. It is believed that the Drostan commemorated was a Pictish saint before the time of Columba.

The chapel of St. Drostan probably stood within the walled
burial-ground of ancient date. There is an ivy-clad erection in
this old cemetery : on it are two inscriptions, one on each side
of the doorway. The inscription on the right-hand side commemorates Captain George Macintosh of the 60th Regiment,
who died in 1780 in his sixty-sixth year. On the other side of the
doorway is a record showing that "this Tomb was erected at
the wish and at the expense of Captain George Macintosh of the
Sixtieth Regiment". This George Macintosh may have been
an unmarried brother of William of Balnespick who was tacks-
man of Dunachton at that time. The old burial-ground is situated in the Chapel-park, below the ruined castle and present

shooting lodge of Dunachton, and the tomb is itself in the form of a chapel, with a large window in the east gable.

The barony of Dunachton was formerly held by the MacNivens, and the last of this family were two heiresses, one of whom, Isobel, married William Macintosh, cousin of the chief and himself in after years chief of Clan Chattan.

Above the road, between Loch Insh and Kingussie, is the house of Belleville or Balavil, celebrated as the home of "Ossian" MacPherson — he who according to his own account gave to the world the ancient songs of Ossian. Whether the "Ossian" of James MacPherson is a forgery from an historical point of view, or an original literary work showing great talent, its publication brought Celtic literature prominently before the world, and caused the value to be realised of old Gaelic MSS. which ignorance was allowing to disappear.

Balavil or Belleville House (according to the old *Statistical Account*) stands on the site of Raits Castle, but there is some doubt about this, for Shaw, a reliable chronicler, writes of the "Castle of Rait in the parish of Nairn". The name is plural to denote that three Raits existed — Easter, Middle and Wester. In the year 1603 the form of the name is Reatt, and Blaeu in his atlas spells it Rait.

When the Comyns and the Macintoshs were at variance the Comyns, pretending to wish to restore better relations between the two clans, invited the Macintoshs to a great feast in the castle of Rait. Fortunately for the men of Clan Chattan, a Comyn, who was friendly with a Macintosh, took him to Clach an t-Sandis, Stone of the Whisper, near the church of Croy, and addressing the stone in the hearing of his friend, revealed the plot.[1] The Macintoshs, thus forewarned — " repaired to the castle at the appointed hour, and before the Comyns could give the signal for attack each Macintosh plunged a dagger into the bosom of a Comyn, and only saved the life of the man who communicated

[1] It may be remembered that a similar procedure was adopted to warn the MacDonalds of Glencoe of their approaching massacre.

the treachery to the Stone ". In another account of the legend the signal of the massacre of the Macintoshs by the Comyns was to be the appearance at the feast of a boar's head, and in yet another, or perhaps the same, legend the disclosure is made by the daughter of the chief Comyn to her lover, one of the Macintoshs. The castle of Rait, to which the legend refers, is not, be it noted, in Badenoch, but in the neighbourhood of Nairn.

About two miles east of Kingussie and north of the high road is the historical cave known as An Uaimh Mhór, the Great Cave. Sir David Brewster, son-in-law of the translator of Ossian's poems, thus described the cave in a communication to the Society of Antiquaries in 1863 :

> The cave is situated on the brow of a rising ground in the village of Raitts on the estate of Belleville. It is about two miles from Kingussie, and about half a mile to the north of the great road from Perth to Inverness. In 1835, when it was first pointed out to me, it was filled with stones and rubbish taken from the neighbouring grounds. Upon removing the rubbish I was surprised to find a long subterraneous building, with its sides faced with stones, and roofed in by gradually contracting the side walls and joining them with very large flattish stones. The form of the cave was that of a horse-shoe. Its convex side was turned to the south, and the entrance to it was at the middle of this side by means of two stone steps, and a passage of some length. The part of the cave to the left hand was a separate appartment with a door. A lock of an unusual form, almost destroyed by rust, was found among the rubbish.

The cave is sometimes called the MacNivens' Cave, the tradition being that the MacNivens who owned that district anciently were at variance with the Clan Chattan. They treated Cluny MacPherson's daughter on one occasion in a shameful manner, and in revenge the MacPhersons by night murdered all the MacNivens with the exception of eighteen men, who secretly constructed the Great Cave under the floor of their subterranean dwelling-house.

In what seems to be an earlier tradition the cave is said to have been fashioned in the course of a single night by men of gigantic stature from overseas, who in their attempt to conquer Scotland were defeated and almost annihilated. The survivors for some time eluded capture in this cave.

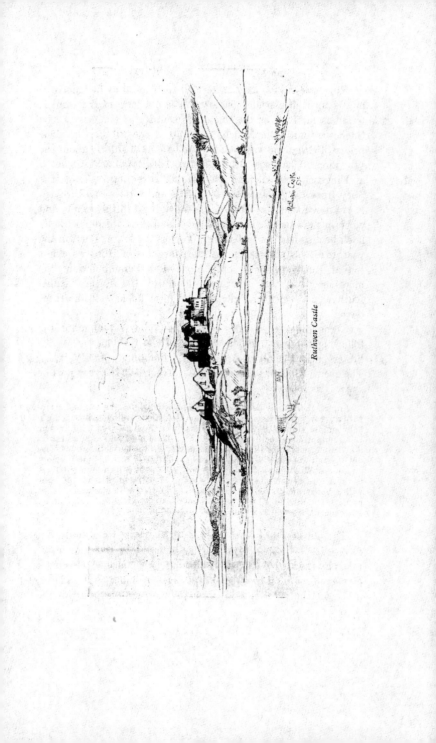

Ruthven Castle

Kingussie, which may be termed the capital of Badenoch, is now a town of considerable size. The old form of the word is found as far back as the thirteenth century as Kingussy. The Gaelic is Cinn Ghiubhsaich, the End of the Fir Forest. The priory of Kingussie was founded by the Earl of Huntly about the year 1490. There was an ancient chapel dedicated to St. Columba at Kingussie, but all that remains now is the font. Across the Spey from Kingussie is the old castle and fortress of Ruthven. It is known that the Wolf of Badenoch lived in this castle, and when in 1451 the Earl of Huntly received the Lordship of Badenoch he also had his seat there. Taylor, the Water Poet, in the year 1618 was entertained by the Marquess of Huntly's eldest son at Ruthven, for in his " Moneylesse Perambulation " he mentions that " in a strong house of the Earle's, called Ruthven in Bagenoch ", he had a " most noble welcome three days ".

Skene in his *Highlanders of Scotland* (vol. i, p. 228) quotes the following from an old MS. history of the Gordons by W. R., preserved in the Advocates' Library, Edinburgh (Jac. V, 7, ii). The event, which is believed to have occurred in the year 1591 or 1592, is as follows :

Angus, the son of Lauchlan Mackintosh, chiefe of the Clan Chattan, with a great party, attempts to surprise the castle of Ruthven in Badenoch, belonging to Huntly, in which there was but a small garrison ; but finding this attempt could neither by force nor Fraude have successe, he retires a little to consult how to compass his intent. In the meanetime one creeps out under the shelter of some old ruins, and levels with his piece at one of the clan Chattan cloathed in a yellow warr coat (which amongst them is the badge of the chieftanes or heads of clans), and piercing his body with a bullet, strikes him to the ground, and retires with gladness into the castle. The man killed was Angus himself, whom his people carry away, and conceills his death for many yeirs, pretending he was gone beyond seas.

The old castle of Ruthven has seen stirring times and grim days. It was, as a royal castle, besieged in the year 1451, taken by the Earl of Ross and immediately demolished (Gregory's *History of the Western Highlands*, p. 43). A hundred years later, in 1546, Huntly, it is said, through the instrumentality of the

Captain of Clan Chattan, imprisoned Lochiel and Keppoch in Ruthven Castle, before they were convicted of high treason at Elgin and beheaded (Gregory, p. 179).

In 1594 Argyll laid siege to Ruthven Castle — held for Huntly on this occasion by the MacPhersons — but the defence was so valiant that the young Earl of Argyll was forced to desist in his investment of the fortress, and passed eastward, to the battle of Glen Livet, at which he was defeated.

About fifteen years before that event King James of Scotland, when hunting in Atholl, was decoyed to the castle of Ruthven by a group of Protestant nobles, headed by the Earls of Mar and Gowrie, and made a prisoner there.

Although Ruthven Barracks were not built on the site of the old castle until 1718, troops were quartered in the castle itself at an earlier date. In the year 1689 General MacKay of Scourie, who commanded the Government forces in Scotland, placed a garrison in the castle under John Forbes, brother of Forbes of Culloden. But they had not been installed long when the castle was besieged by a part of Dundee's forces, and its garrison surrendered, on condition that the men should be allowed to return to their homes on parole. The castle seems to have been set alight by the besieging force, and to have remained a ruin until, thirty years later, Ruthven Barracks were built on its site, and doubtless of the same stones. In *The Chiefs of Grant* (1883, 313, 314) is a vivid account of the castle's surrender :

In the end of May or beginning of June about 60 of the Clan Grant, under their Captain, John Forbes of Culloden, marched into MacKay's camp, bringing the intelligence that the Castle of Ruthven in Badenoch, they had lately garrisoned, was now a smoking ruin. On the 29th May, Dundee had summoned the Castle to surrender ; and a few days later, after a sharp encounter, the defenders, weakened by want of provisions, and succours, yielded to Keppoch. The garrison were allowed to march out with the honours of war, but the Castle was given to the flames.

Indeed the castle of Ruthven does not seem to have been a private residence since it was captured from the Marquess of Huntly by General David Leslie in the year 1647. In the year 1650 " thirty men of the Marquis of Argyll's Regiment were appointed to be left in the Ruthven of Badenoch ". After the battle of Worcester Ruthven Castle was garrisoned by the English. In July 1654 Monk addressed a despatch to Cromwell from Ruthven Castle. In his despatch Monk craves that

care may be taken that the Irish forces that are att Loughaber may continue there, for a yeare. . . . Truly the place is of that Consequence for the keeping of a garrison there for the destroying of the stubbornest enemy wee have in the Hills, that of the Clan Cameron's and Glengaries, and the Earle of Seafort's people.

In the Jacobite rising of 1745 Lochgarry, Dr. Cameron and O'Sullivan of the Prince's army were sent to take the barracks. Neither side had cannon, and the Highland party endeavoured to set fire to the door, but the soldiers, firing through holes in the door, killed one man and mortally wounded two others. The Highland party then retired (*The Lyon in Mourning*, vol. i, p. 249). The garrison of Ruthven Castle consisted at that time of twelve men, under Serjeant Molloy. The little garrison defended the castle for three days in February 1746 and obtained an honourable capitulation, the serjeant being promoted to lieutenant (Shaw's *History of Moray*). The Prince's attacking force is said to have numbered upwards of three hundred men, led by Gordon of Glenbucket. Prince Charles Edward himself apparently stayed the best part of a week in the barracks in the early part of 1746. Two days after Culloden the Prince's forces assembled at Ruthven, ready and eager to take the field once more. This meeting of Prince Charlie's followers at Ruthven after Culloden is the last historical incident connected with Ruthven Castle. Here assembled Lord George Murray and other chiefs and their followers — a force in all of between 2,000 and 3,000 men. The Chevalier Johnston writes of this event in his *Memoirs* :

I arrived on the 18th (of April) at Ruthven, which happened, by chance, to become the rallying point of our army, without having been previously fixed on. There I found the Duke of Atholl, Lord George Murray, the Duke of Perth, Lord John Drummond, Lord Ogilvie, and many other chiefs of clans, with about four or five thousand Highlanders, all in the best possible disposition for renewing hostilities, and for taking their revenge. The little town of Ruthven is about eight leagues from Inverness, by a road through the mountains, very narrow, full of tremendously high precipices, where there are several passes which a hundred men could defend against ten thousand, by merely rolling down rocks from the summit of the mountains. Lord George Murray immediately despatched people to guard the passes, and at the same time sent off an aid-de-camp to inform the Prince that a great part of his army was assembled at Ruthven ; that the Highlanders were full of animation and ardour, and eager to be led against the enemy, that the Grants and other Highland clans, who had until then remained neutral, were disposed to declare themselves in his favour, seeing the inevitable destruction of their country from the proximity of the victorious army of the Duke of Cumberland ; that all the clans who had received leave of absence would assemble there in a few days ; and that instead of five or six thousand men, the whole of the number present at the battle of Culloden — from the absence of those who had returned to their homes, and of those who had left the army on reaching Culloden on the morning of the 16th, to go to sleep — he might now count upon eight or nine thousand men at least, a greater number than he had at any time in his army. Everyone earnestly entreated the Prince to come immediately, and put himself at the head of this force. We passed the night 19th at Ruthven without any answer to our message, and in the interim all the Highlanders were cheerful and full of spirits, to a degree perhaps never before witnessed in an army so recently beaten, expecting, with impatience, every moment the arrival of the Prince ; but on the 20th Mr. M'Leod, Lord George's aid-de-camp, who had been sent to him returned with the laconic message, " Let everyone seek his own safety in the best way he can ". This answer, under existing circumstances, was as inconsiderate in Charles as it was heart-breaking to the brave men, who had sacrificed themselves to his cause.

Chevalier de Johnstone's account continues :

Our separation at Ruthven was truly affecting. We bade one another an eternal adieu. No one could tell whether the scaffold would not be his fate. The Highlanders gave vent to their grief in wild howlings and lamentations ; the tears flowed down their cheeks when they thought that their country was now at the discretion of the Duke of Cumberland, and on the point of being plundered, whilst they and their children would be reduced to slavery and plunged without resource in a state of remedyless distress.

Near Ruthven the River Tromie enters the Spey. Glen Tromie in summer is a delightful glen, but has been described by a Gaelic bard familiar with it also in winter as " Gleann Tromaidh nan Siantan, Glen Tromie of the Stormy Blasts ". Birches and alders clothe the sides of the glen, and through it flows the Tromie, in times of rain a raging torrent.

At a narrow, rocky gorge, Leum na Féinne, the Fingalians'
Leap, was enacted a tragedy of long ago — an event that
until recent years was still spoken of by the people of the district.
The tradition is somewhat as follows : Lord Walter Comyn, one
of the Comyns of Ruthven, a profligate young fellow, decided,
for his sensual amusement, to force the women of Badenoch to
work naked in the harvest fields. He went through the hill
country to Atholl, and the day of his return was fixed for this
infamous exhibition. But Comyn never did return, although his
mare arrived, terrified and foaming at the mouth, at Ruthven
Castle with no rider on her back, but dragging one of his legs
hanging from the stirrup. Search was made, and the body was
found at Leum na Féinne, with a couple of eagles preying upon it.
Comyn's end was attributed to witchcraft, and the two eagles
were believed to be the mothers of two of the girls who were to
be forced to go naked to the harvest. Even to this day the
retribution which overtook the criminal is recalled by the Gaelic
curse in Badenoch, " Dìol Bhaltair an Gàig ort ! " (" Walter's
fate in Gaick on you ! ").

A different account of what would seem to be the same
event is given in MacFarlane's *Geographical Collections* (vol. ii,
p. 598) :

> There is a way from the yate of Blair in Athoil to Ruffen in Badenoch
> maid be David Cuming Earle of Athoill for carts to pass with wyne, and
> the way is called Rad na pheny or way of wane wheills. It is laid with
> calsay in sundrie parts. Whair this Cuming built a castell, his wyf built
> a kirk ; he ended miserablie being torne in pieces with a hors in Badenoch,
> whair falling from his horse, his fute stak in the stirrup and ane of his
> thighs stiking in the styrrop wes brocht to Blair be the said hors. Whilk
> Blair he built and the castell of Mowlin.

Glen Tromie leads up to Gaick, one of the highest lodges in
Scotland. Of Gaick I have happy memories and of expeditions
to its high tops in the time of Robert Hargreaves, one of the
finest sportsmen in Scotland, a man who acted as his own stalker
and knew the corries of his forest better than any living man.
We used to see the peregrine fly from her eyrie on Loch an Dùin,

and the golden eagle sail high above Loch Vrodin, the home of many trout.

There is an attractive legend on the naming of this loch: it is to be found in MacBain's *Place-Names*, pp. 246 and 247. A hunter in some way became the owner of a litter of fairy pups, but before they grew up a fairy or demon took from him all except one. The hunter was left with a single jet-black *cuilean* which the demon for some reason first handicapped by breaking its leg. The name of the pup was Brodan. At this time a white fairy deer lived on Ben Alder, and, with his black, supernatural hound Brodan, the hunter determined to hunt it. Together they went to Ben Alder and found the deer above Loch Ericht. A long and stern chase began, and when they reached Loch Vrodin of Gaick the dog was close to the fairy deer. Almost together the two plunged into the loch, and half-way across Brodan overtook the elfin deer and seized it in his strong jaws. On the instant deer and dog disappeared for ever, and the loch is named Loch a' Bhrodain (the genitive of Brodan, and anglicised into Vrodin) after the hound.

In my chapter on the western Cairngorms I have mentioned the derivation of Beinn Bhrodain, and since loch and hill are within an easy day's journey for one of the strong hunters of olden times it seems likely that both are named after the same hound.

Gaick through the ages was ever supposed to be the haunt of the occult and the supernatural. Of the appearance of the Witch of Badenoch to a hunter in Gaick Forest, and of her fate thereafter, a vivid account is given in Stewart's *Lectures on the Mountains*, 2nd series (1860). An interesting feature of this account is that the witch describes herself as responsible also for the drowning of Iain Garbh MacLeod of Raasay, in a great tempest which she conjured up over the Minch. Here is the story of the witch's doings in Gaick:

A hunter in the forest had taken refuge from the fury of the storm in a lonely bothy. As he and his two hounds listened to the roar of the tempest without, a faint scratching was heard on the door and when this was opened a bedraggled cat entered the bothy. The hounds were about to rush in upon the cat when she spoke in human language, telling the hunter that she was indeed a witch, but one which repented of her misdeeds and, being treated with the utmost harshness by her sisters in witchcraft, had fled to the hunter for protection. The hunter thereupon invited her to the fire, but she said that she feared to approach unless he should tie his hounds with a hair which she would give him. He pretended to agree, but merely tied the hair to the beam which supported the roof of the bothy. The cat then came to the fire, and as she sat there she increased in size until she was as large as a hound. Then, in an instant, she assumed the form of a woman, and the hunter to his dismay saw that this was one who was believed to be an upright woman, a neighbour of his, known as the Good Wife of Laggan. "Hunter of the hills," exclaimed she, "your hour is come. Long have you been the enemy of my sisterhood. Our chief enemy is no more: this morning I saw him overwhelmed by the waves[1]—and now, hunter, it is your turn." So saying, she sprang with fury upon him, and the hunter's hounds, which she supposed to be bound with her hair, flew at her breast and throat. The dogs clung to her, and one of them tore off the greater part of one of her breasts. The combat was waged with the utmost ferocity, and at length, uttering blood-curdling shrieks, the witch assumed the form of a raven, and flew off towards her home in the valley of the Spey. The two hounds, lying on the floor, were able to lick the hands of the hunter before expiring of their terrible wounds. The hunter, himself uninjured, returned to his home beside the Spey, exceedingly sorrowful at the loss of his hounds, his mind full of his strange experience. His house was empty when he reached it, but a little later his wife arrived, and told him that she had come from the bedside of the good wife of Laggan, who had been suddenly taken ill that day and was now at death's door. The

[1] This refers to the drowning by witchcraft of MacLeod of Raasay.

hunter at once hurried to the good wife's house, and to the astonishment of those who stood around her, mourning her plight, he tore off the bed-clothes and showed to those assembled the wounds upon her person. The " good wife " then sadly confessed that she had conjured up the storm which had drowned Iain Garbh MacLeod of Raasay, and had attempted to kill the hunter also ; having finished her confession she expired.

A spirit that was said to have her home in the hills of Gaick was known as the Leannan Sìth, or Fairy Sweetheart, who came to hunters in the forest, and it was believed that the earthly wife of the hunter who fell in love with the Leannan Sìth was in great danger of being hurt by her supernatural rival.

In more recent times Gaick was unenviably renowned because of an event which is known by the Gaelic-speaking natives of Badenoch as Call Ghàig, the Loss of Gaick. The story is a strange one. It is given in Scrope's *Days of Deer Stalking* (p. 119) and in other Highland records.

Captain John MacPherson of Ballachroan, with four attendants and several strong deer-hounds, at Christmas-tide of the year 1799 went up to a bothy in Gaick on a deer-hunting expedition. The day after the party had gone, a fearful storm of wind and snow broke over the hills, and when the hunters did not return a search party set out up the glen. Through gigantic snow-wreaths they fought their way, but when at last they reached the site of the bothy — somewhere below Loch an t-Seilich, beneath a steep slope, now partly covered with birch — they saw no sign of it. After a careful search they found that the bothy was

not merely blown down, but quite torn to pieces : large stones, which had formed part of the walls, were found at the distance of one or two hundred yards from the site of the building ; and the wooden uprights appeared to have been rent asunder by a force that had twisted them off, as in breaking a tough stick. From the circumstances in which the bodies were found, it appeared that the men were retiring to rest at the time the calamity came upon them. One of the bodies, indeed, was found at a distance of many yards from the bothy ; another of the men was found upon the place where the bothy had stood, with one stocking off, as if he had been undressing.

Captain Macpherson was lying without his clothes upon the wretched bed which the bothy had afforded, his face to the ground and his knees drawn up. To all appearance the destruction had been quite sudden ; yet the situation of the building was such as promised security against the utmost violence of the wind : it stood in a narrow recess, at the foot of a mountain, whose precipitous and lofty declivities sheltered it on every side excepting the front, and here, too, a hill rose before it, though with a more gradual slope.

The annihilation of the party, so sudden and complete, was ascribed by many to supernatural causes. It was remembered that when Captain MacPherson had been staying in the bothy about a month before, some of the party who were outside saw a fire on the hill-top above it. So surprised were they to see a fire in that unlikely place that they climbed the hill ; but when they reached the top the mysterious fire had disappeared. Then it was remarked that the Captain, although his friends attempted to dissuade him from this mid-winter hunting expedition because of the inclemency of the weather, was singularly obstinate. " He said he MUST go, and was resolved to go." The fact that in so sheltered a spot the bothy was swept away seems to have been taken as a clear instance of the supernatural : no one apparently thought of an avalanche, and yet it seems certain than an avalanche caused the disaster. Indeed in or about the year 1922 an avalanche swept down the hillside at this same place and killed several hinds.

There is a right-of-way from Gaick through the hills to Dalna-cardoch in Atholl. This old track, through which sheep and cattle were doubtless driven to the markets of the Lowlands, skirts Loch Vrodin of the fairy hound and reaches the watershed between Badenoch and Atholl at Loch an Dùin. From this loch to the main road at Dalnacardoch the scenery is less grand than in Badenoch. The hills are more rolling, yet in the month of August, when the heather is in bloom and the scent of thousands of acres of blossom permeates the air, the contrast between the dark, wind-swept rocks of Loch an Dùin is a pleasing one.

The less adventurous traveller, who prefers to keep the main road, continues west along the Spey valley from Kingussie as far as Newtonmore, then south along birch-clad Glen Truim to more wind-swept country at Dalwhinnie, near which place Johnny Cope drew up his army in expectation of being attacked by the Prince's forces in 1745. From Dalwhinnie the road gradually ascends to the Pass of Druim-uachdar or Drumochter, the Pass of the Ridge of the Upper Ground, where the elevation is 1,500 feet above sea level, and in winter the highway is often impassable through snow. On the right-hand side of the pass, as one travels south, are the two hills known as the Boar of Badenoch [1] and the Sow of Atholl, and from Dalnaspidal at the county boundary between Inverness and Perth, Loch Garry (which must not be confused with the Loch Garry in western Inverness-shire) is seen to the west.

From Newtonmore there is a good road which connects Badenoch with Tulloch and Fort William in the west. This road passes beneath Craig Dhubh to Cluny Castle, thence to Laggan Bridge and along the shore of Loch Laggan. The route may be varied by taking the secondary road, which leaves the main Perth road about three miles south of Newtonmore, crosses the River Truim and, passing near Glen Truim house, reaches the main west road at Laggan Bridge. On this side road, between two and three miles west of Glen Truim, the Ordnance Survey placed a stone in the wall to mark the actual centre of the Highlands of Scotland — that part most distant from either the North Sea or the Atlantic.

The parish of Laggan was the home for some years of the celebrated Mrs. Grant, whose *Letters from the Mountains*, written between the years 1773 and 1806, give a clear and simple account of life in the Highlands during that period. Mrs. Grant met the famous Dr. Samuel Johnson, and in one of her letters she refers to him as " that surly sage ". Another letter, dated December 25, 1788, is headed " Ink frozen by the Fire ". The letters, which are published in three small volumes, are delicately written, and form a valuable commentary on the times in which the authoress

[1] An Torc, as this hill is known in Gaelic, was considered by the Mac-Phersons of Crubin to be their supernatural home.

lived. In the days when she had her home at Laggan as the wife of the minister of the parish, the people of that district (the custom is continued until the present day in the Isle of Lewis) went up to the high glens at the beginning of each summer, to the summer shielings. Mrs. Grant writes thus of that annual event :

One of the great concerns of life is setling the time and manner of these removals. Viewing the procession pass, is always very gratifying to my pastoral imagination. I rise early for that purpose. The people look so glad and contented for they rejoice at going up ; but, by the time the cattle have eat all the grass, and the time arrives when they dare no longer fish and shoot, they find their old home a better place, and return with nearly as much alacrity as they went.

Mrs. Grant during the latter years of her long life was in receipt of a pension granted to her by George IV, at the representations of Sir Walter Scott and other distinguished persons, who in their petition to the king declared that Mrs. Grant had

produced a strong and salutary effect upon her countrymen, who not only found recorded in her writings much of the national history and antiquities which would otherwise have been forgotten, but found them combined with the soundest and best lessons of virtue and morality.

A couple of miles west of the manse of Laggan, on a hill guarding the pass where the Fort William road leaves Wade's road through Corrieyaireag, is an old fort, Dùn Dà Làmh, the Fort of (the) Two Hands. This fort is considered by one expert on the subject to be the most perfect relic of a British stronghold of this kind in the country. It stands 600 feet above the valley, the River Spey passing on the north side, and the river Mashie on the south. Mr. MacNab, who was for many years tenant of the farm of Dalchully, found that the dimensions of the *dùn* within its surrounding wall were — length, 420 feet ; breadth at the west end, 250 feet ; at the centre, 110 feet ; and at the east end, 75 feet. The wall appears to have varied considerably in height and in thickness, and at the time when Mr. MacNab made his observations the wall was from 2 to 5 feet high and 14 feet thick. At the west side the wall was 17 feet thick, and in the north-west corner no less than 25 feet thick — the north-west being the most vulnerable part of the hill. The wall here would appear to have been at one time about 20 feet high. But on the south side of the *dùn*, where the rock is almost inaccessible, the wall, it seems, was built only where there were gaps in the rocks, and here it could nowhere have been more than 6 feet high. The wall, like all ancient walls, was built with great care and skill, apparently without lime or cement.

The *dùn* seems to have had two approaches, one on the north side, the other on the south. The approach from the north is up a straight, steep gully. Mr. MacNab noted that half-way up this gully was a large stone which seemed to have had the ground cleared away from it and to have been supported to a slight extent by small stones, so that it could have been sent crashing down the gully in the event of enemies endeavouring to make their way up it. The south approach ascended in a zigzag, partly natural. About half-way up the zigzag was a large heap of iron slag or cinder, and a large circular hole faced with stone and filled with ashes and charcoal. This, thought Mr. MacNab, had been used for smelting iron. He said that the heaps of cinder showed evidence of much greater heat than could have been produced by a smith's forge.

The tradition of the country is that the *dùn* was built and lived in by the Fingalian hunters : on page 224 I have mentioned that their hill, Tom na Féinne, stands a few miles farther down the Spey.

CHAPTER XXIII

CLUNY MACPHERSON'S COUNTRY

In the heart of Badenoch, far from the sea, the traveller from Newtonmore to Fort William, when he has journeyed perhaps a couple of miles west from Newtonmore, notices, on the right-hand side of the road, a steep hill that is birch-clad on its lower slopes but ends in a steep rock face. Craig Dhubh [1] is the name of this hill; from it the MacPhersons took their war-cry and, as they rushed into the heart of the fight, threw their challenge, " Craig Dhubh, Craig Dhubh ", across hill and glen. The wild cat, which is the crest of the clan, has her home here, and, like the wild cat, the Clan Chattan (to which the MacPhersons and Macintoshs belong) claimed to be fearless and unconquerable.

But Craig Dhubh, the Black Rock, is memorable chiefly as the hiding-place of Cluny MacPherson of the '45 — he who, after Highland hopes had been blighted on Culloden field, hid in Badenoch for nine years until, in 1755, he escaped to France and died there, a broken-hearted man, in the year 1756.

Uamh Chluanaidh, Cluny's Cave, is high up on the rocky face of Craig Dhubh. It is a small cave and is not easy to find. Woodcock flit about it : the badger has his den near it : the darkness of a winter night may be made more eerie by the shriek of unseen wild cats fighting grim and merciless battles. The pointed, death-dealing wing of the peregrine falcon sometimes throws a transient shadow on the cave's entrance, and Cluny, as he hid in the cave, must have seen the raven at the season of courtship

[1] " Creag " is the usual spelling of this word, but Sir Stewart Mac-Pherson tells me that the Badenoch spelling is " Craig ".

turn on his back and, like a skilled airman, glide upside-down for a few breathless seconds before righting himself with a movement so swift as to be barely perceptible.

It was, perhaps, while hiding in his eyrie that Cluny saw the smoke of his burning castle, fired by Government troops, rise slowly into the air, and pondered, we may doubt not, on the fate of the Green Banner, with which the fortunes of the clan are mystically united, and of the fairy pipe chanter which dropped from heaven to give immortal music to the clan in time of stress.

On the grey winter morning when I climbed to the cave the clouds drifted low above Craig Dhubh and a soft wind from the south-west stirred the leafless boughs of the birches where owls hoot at dusk. The withered bracken was dry ; the ground, newly released from the grip of the frost, was soft and crumbly ; yet in sheltered nooks the bell heather (*Erica cinerea*) was still in blossom.

My companion, the last of the house of Glen Truim, first led me up a steep slope, then diagonally across the face of the cliff, following a ledge that narrowed, broadened, then narrowed again with a drop into space beneath us. The ledge abruptly ended, and it seemed to me that we must now be precipitated over the sheer face of the cliff when my companion, who was leading, suddenly jumped down and called out that we had arrived at Cluny's Cave. Yet until I too had made that leap I could see nothing of the cave nor of its entrance, and realised that the place of concealment was indeed hidden in a remarkable manner.

In order to enter the cave it was necessary to stoop low, but, once inside, I saw that the interior was more roomy than might have been supposed. Two or three persons might find conceal-ment here, and perhaps Cluny had at least one trusty follower who shared the cave with him and stood watchful at the small opening near the roof half-way down the cave. This small " window " seems to have been made by human hands, in order, no doubt, that the watcher at it might have warning of the approach of danger. At the far end of the cave is a second narrow opening to the surface, smaller than the " window ". This is believed to have served as a chimney, and a broad ledge beside it, a little above the level of the cave's floor, is said to have been the fireplace. At the entrance to the cave a pillar-like stone is set in the ground, apparently in order to render the cave's entrance more difficult to detect. Even at the present day Cluny's Cave on Craig Dhubh is not easy to find, but tradition has it that in 1746 the face of the hill was more thickly wooded than it is now, and the cave must therefore at that time have been quite invisible from any view-point and must have afforded a safe refuge. The ledge which leads to the cave is so narrow that a determined man might have held the place against great odds, had the occasion arisen.

Though hidden from prying eyes, this cave, set high on the face of Craig Dhubh, gives a wide view. In the subdued light of a winter morning I looked away to the east and saw the snow-scarred slopes of the western Cairngorms rise to the clouded sky, and west to the lesser hills which hide the lonely acres of Ben Alder where Cluny's Cage is an abiding memorial to another of the fugitive's hiding-places. I looked down upon the Spey flowing quietly far below me, and saw the remains of the sub-terranean dwelling where, during his nine years as an outlaw, Cluny sometimes hid. His clansmen prepared this second hiding-place for their chief, working always at night to avoid suspicion. Sobieski in his *Lays of the Deer Forest* mentions that the sand and gravel excavated from this retreat under cover of darkness was invariably thrown before dawn into the River Spey, which is here sluggish and muddy and would have speedily hidden any trace of the sand thrown into it. There is a tradition in the Glen Truim family that Cluny in his underground retreat beside the river was one day surprised by the roof of his hiding-place suddenly collaps-ing as a startled man dropped in beside him. The man was a stranger, and Cluny, as he grappled with the fellow and rendered him helpless, thought at first to kill him with his dirk. These thoughts gave place to kindlier ones, and Cluny asked the stranger whether he would swear an oath never to reveal the hiding-place to any person, whether friend or foe. The man readily agreed, and was permitted to go his way; but Cluny in thinking the matter over began to mistrust that promise, and a little later left the shelter and travelled west to another secret hiding-place in the old house of Dalchully. When in hiding there he heard that not long after his departure Government troops had raided the subterranean shelter — to find that their bird had flown.

It was near Dalchully that General Cope made his camp in 1745. The place is still known as Johnny Cope's About-turn, because Cope here decided that discretion was the better part of valour and, instead of engaging the Prince's army on Corrieyaireag as had been expected, retreated toward Inverness. The camp was on a grass-covered outcrop of rock near the junction of Wade's road to Corrieyaireag and the main Newtonmore–Fort William road. The site is on the right bank of the Mashie near its confluence with the Spey, and near Dalchully house. There is a fenced enclosure on the traditional spot where Cope's tent was pitched, and in the enclosure grow birches, pines and a few unhappy larches.

Throughout the nine years Cluny was in hiding a reward of £1,000 was offered by the Government to any person who should give information as to his hiding-place. Although upwards of one hundred of his clansmen always knew where their chief was concealed, these devoted men scorned to make money at the expense of him they loved. The Government, knowing that Cluny was hidden somewhere on his own estate, had eighty soldiers permanently stationed in the district to intimidate the clansmen: these men were in addition to those who daily searched hill and glen for the wanted man.

Yet Cluny preserved his safety although he was more than once almost taken, and in the end, like Lochiel, escaped to France. Browne, in his standard work, *A History of the Highlands*, writes as follows:

Sir Hector Munro, at that time a lieutenant in the thirty-fourth regiment was entrusted with the command of a large party, and continued two whole years in Badenoch, for the purpose of discovering Cluny's retreat. The unwearied vigilance of the clan could alone have saved him from the vigilance of this party, directed as it was by an officer, equally remarkable for his zeal, and his knowledge of the country and the people. The slightest inattention, even a momentary want of caution or presence of mind on the part of the MacPhersons, would infallibly have betrayed his retreat ; yet so true were the clan, so strict in the observance of secrecy, and so dexterous in conveying to him unobserved the necessaries he required, that, although the soldiers were animated by the hope of reward, and a step of promotion was promised to the officer who should apprehend him, not a trace of him could be discovered, nor an individual found base enough to give a hint to his detriment. Many anecdotes have been related of the narrow escapes which he made in eluding the vigilance of the soldiery, especially when he ventured to spend a few hours convivially with his friends : and also of the diligence, fidelity and presence of mind displayed by the people in concealing his retreat, and baffling the activity of his pursuers, during a period of no less than nine years. At length, however, wearied out with this dreary and hopeless state of existence, and taught to despair of pardon, he escaped to France in 1755, and died there the following year.

About fifty years ago (this chapter was written at the close of 1937) Sandy MacDonald, piper of renown and devoted and trusted friend and companion of the Glen Truim family (his skill in the piping of Ceòl Mór is still recalled), was ferreting rabbits about one hundred yards from the site of that old underground hiding-place of Cluny MacPherson beside the river. In his work he moved some large stones, and found concealed below the surface of the ground six old claymores. It is believed that these claymores would have been brought into use if Cluny had been in danger of capture (there is no doubt that some of his clansmen were always near to guard that hiding-place in which the chief at the time happened to be in hiding), and that even if those wielding them had lost their lives, their sudden, desperate onslaught would have diverted the attention of the Government troops, and in the excitement Cluny would have been able to make his escape.

The first visit of Queen Victoria and the Prince Consort to the Highlands was in the late summer of the year 1847. The royal party landed from the royal yacht at Fort William, and drove to Ardverikie lodge on the south shore of Loch Laggan. Here they stayed for some time, and one day rode on ponies across to Cluny Castle, where they honoured Cluny MacPherson with a visit. There is a tradition in the country that Queen Victoria had intended to buy Cluny Castle for her Highland home. But there was so much bad weather during her visit to those parts that the project was abandoned, and a little later Balmoral, in a less humid climate, was acquired.

When at Ardverikie, Prince Albert stalked the Ben Alder corries with Catanach, the head stalker. One day stags were spied, and an argument ensued between the Prince and Catanach as to the best method of getting within shot. The argument ended by Catanach remarking heatedly, " Your Royal Highness may be king in Westminster, but I am king in Ardverikie Forest !"

The Green Banner of Clan Chattan, with its proud motto " Touch not the Cat but a Glove ", still hangs from the hall of Cluny Castle,[1] but the Black Chanter, gift of the fairies, has gone from its old place. Gone, too, are the days when Calum Pìobair, Malcolm the Piper, with proud bearing and long, flowing locks, was accustomed to tune his *pìob mhór* and of an evening, after a long day spent on the hill after grouse or deer, to play, in the warmth of the old, friendly rooms, some *pìobaireachd* composed by the great pipers of long ago. The piper has gone ; the pipe chanter has also gone : no longer does Cluny live in his castle, which was rebuilt after the passions of the '45 had cooled. Truly the glory of the house of Cluny MacPherson has gone on the hill wind.

Beneath Craig Dhubh, at the confluence of the Truim and the Spey, is the site of an old clan battle that was fought long before the day of Cluny of the '45. As I stood on a mound beside this river confluence and saw the mellow winter sunshine weave patterns on the crisp brown bracken beneath leafless birches, I heard, from one learned in the history of the country, the

[1] This chapter was written before the sale of the historic clan possessions and their re-purchase by a committee of representative clansmen in 1943.

tradition concerning that ancient fight known as the battle of Invernahaven.

It was about the year 1370 that the Clan Cameron from Lochaber, on their way east to harry Macintosh's country, found themselves opposed by the MacPhersons, Macintoshs and Davidsons. Before the fight the MacPhersons claimed their traditional right of being placed on the right wing, but were told that on this occasion the Clann 'ic Dhàidh (the Davidsons) were to have that honour. On hearing this the MacPhersons, considering themselves insulted, left the line of battle, crossed the River Spey and, on the birch-clad knoll immediately north of the confluence of the two rivers, leisurely and contemptuously ate their midday meal as (now disinterested spectators) they watched the course of the fight. They saw the day go badly with their allies. They saw MacDhàidh, the Davidson chief, and seven of his sons, fighting valiantly, slain within two hundred yards of their own house ; the Macintosh line waver and break. They heard the clash of claymore upon targe ; the whistle of arrows through the keen sunlit air of that May day. They watched the defeat become a rout — yet remained proudly, disdainfully aloof.

Late on the same day Macintosh successfully endeavoured by a subterfuge to incite the defecting MacPhersons against the victorious Camerons. He summoned his bard, and ordered him to compose a satire upon the MacPhersons, taunting them with cowardice. The satire was composed, and the bard was then instructed to go to the MacPherson chief, and to recite that satire to him, but he was enjoined to say that he who had sent him was not Macintosh, but the Cameron chief. The office of bard was an almost sacred one, and when he announced himself to the MacPherson outposts he was received with the respect befitting his high office, and was conducted to the chief of the MacPhersons, to whom he claimed his ancient privilege of delivering a message, whatever its import might be. He then recited the satire taunting MacPherson and his clan because it was not friendship which had restrained them from fighting that day, but cowardice.

When they heard this taunt, flung at them by the bard of the victors, the MacPhersons were naturally infuriated. They forgot their fancied grievance and immediately set out in pursuit of the Camerons. By this time it was night, but in May the hours of darkness are short and did not hinder their pursuit. It was believed that the Camerons were encamped at Briagach, a mile or two lower down the Spey, but when the MacPhersons reached that place before sunrise they saw that their foes were gone, and a little later had news that they were in retreat — the reason for this retreat has never become clear — toward the west. The MacPhersons, having ascertained the line of retreat, at once hurried in pursuit. Past Phoness to Dalanach they hurried, and at Dalanach overtook their enemies and attacked them. That sudden and unexpected attack was disastrous to the Lochaber men, and one of their leaders was slain in a corrie, known to this day as Coire Thearlaich (Charles's Corrie) after the officer who lost his life here. From this place a running fight was fought through the hills to Loch Patag. Near that lonely loch was fought the epic duel between two renowned bowmen, Mac Dhomhnuill Duibh, chief of the Camerons (he who would now be called Lochiel), and one of the leaders of the MacPhersons — he who was known to his clan as Mac Iain Ceann Dubh. These two renowned archers were close friends, and when this historic duel in archery began Mac Iain Ceann Dubh called out to his adversary, as he drew the bow, "Tharam—is tharad—a Thearlaich!" ("Over me — and over you — Charles!"). Lochiel (as we should now call him), seeing the arrow fall beyond him, understood the signal, and in his turn shot his arrow over his adversary's head. The arrows subsequently exchanged did no more than kill those men standing behind the archers, and when the MacPherson chief came up and saw his men lying dead behind Mac Iain, he cried out tauntingly to him, "Where is your old skill, Ceann Dubh? Surely you had a Cameron for your mother!" Stung by that taunt, Mac Iain called out loudly to his friend, "Umam — is umad — a Thearlaich!" ("For me — and for you —

Charles !"). Both then shot their arrows in grim earnest and both fell to the ground, mortally wounded. Not far from Loch Patag, at Dal an Lungairt, by Loch Ericht side, is — or was until recent years — a moss-grown cairn marking the spot where the Cameron chief fell. The cairn is called Carn Mhic Dhomhnuill Duibh.

As I looked, that winter day of sunshine, upon the level grassy land where the battle of Invernahaven was decided, I thought of the Davidsons fighting desperately within sight of their home, of which scarcely a stone now remains. I thought of the eager shouts of the victors ; the groans of the mortally wounded ; the clear waters of the river rising in silver spray as the MacPhersons, moody and defiant, splashed their way across it as the fight began. Old graves have been found on that battlefield, and MacPherson of Glen Truim, on whose land it is, showed me a flint arrow-head which he had found here. But that must be a memorial of a still earlier fight, commemorated, it may be, in the name Tom na Féinne, Hill of the Fingalians — a hill which stands west of Invernahaven's field.

The Clann Dàidh or Davidsons never recovered their losses in the fight at Invernahaven, and from that day almost disappeared from their ancestral country ; but it was not until far later that evil times came to the MacPhersons. Rabbits and sheep now close-crop the fine turf of the ancient battle-ground, and away to the east, across sun and shade on the moors, I could see the hills of Glen Feshie which lead up to the high Cairngorms. Such is the story of a fight waged six hundred years ago, when a proud family of Badenoch achieved glory followed by extinction in sight of their homes and dear ones.

Loch Ruthven, near Inverfarigaig

CHAPTER XXIV

INVERNESS

INVERNESS, commonly called the capital of the Highlands, stands on the River Ness, about five miles below Loch Ness.

It is believed that Inverness was made a royal burgh so far back as the time of David I. The privileges of the burgh were defined and confirmed by King William the Lion, who granted four charters in its favour. In the second of these charters, dated 1180, the King agreed to make a *fosse* round the town, which the burgesses were to enclose with a good paling.

Shipbuilding from very early times was an Inverness industry. In 1249 Matthew Paris, writing of the armament of a crusade, mentions and describes a great ship built at Inverness for the Earl of Saint Pol. The Saint Pols, who still survive as a respected family in France, conducted themselves with bravery and distinction at the various crusades in which they took part; their crest, a simple, unadorned cross, testifies of this.

But long before the time of William the Lion, King Brude ruled in his fortress beside Inverness. It will be remembered that this proud king was converted to Christianity by St. Columba. In the words of Adamnan, his biographer :

At another time, when the saint made his first journey to King Brude, it happened that the king, elated by the pride of royalty, acted haughtily, and would not open his gates on the first arrival of the blessed man. When the man of God observed this, he approached the folding doors with his companions, and having first formed upon them the sign of the cross of our Lord, he then knocked at and laid his hand upon the gate, which instantly flew open of its own accord, the bolts having been driven back with great force. The saint and his companions then passed through the gate thus speedily opened. And when the king learned what had occurred, he and his councillors were filled with alarm, and immediately setting out from the palace, he advanced to meet with due respect the blessed man, whom he addressed in the most conciliating and respectful language. And ever after from that day, so long as he lived, the king held this holy and reverend man in very great honour as was due.

Again we are told that Columba

in that same country took a white stone from the river, and blessed it for the working of certain cures ; and that stone, contrary to nature, floated like an apple when placed in water. This divine miracle was wrought in the presence of King Brude and his household. In the same country, also, he performed a still greater miracle, by raising to life the dead child of an humble believer, and restoring him in life and vigour to his father and mother.

The distinguished Celtic scholar Reeves believed that King Brude's fortress was the modern Craig Phadrick (where, some time ago, a massive silver chain was found), about two miles south-west of Inverness. Craig Phadrick is a natural eminence, of considerable height and well defined. On the summit, 453 feet above the sea, are the remains of a vitrified fort, and it is inspiring to think that St. Columba may well have performed miracles here in the days when the world was young and the faith of men was great. But, according to some authorities, the site of King Brude's palace was on Torvean, a small hill, or perhaps rather a very large mound, which rises directly from the main Inverness–Fort William road less than two miles west of Inverness (as you travel west from Inverness to Fort William the hill is on the left of the road, between it and the Caledonian Canal).

William MacKay (*Transactions of the Gaelic Society of Inver-*

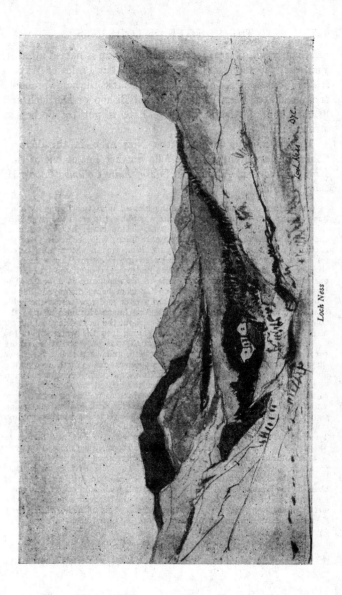

Loch Ness

ness, vol. xxvii, p. 152) records that Torvean is named after St. Baithene, the successor of St. Columba, but Professor Watson (*Celtic Place-Names of Scotland*, p. 311) thinks the name probably commemorates Beyn or Bean, styled Bishop of Mortlach and first Bishop of Aberdeen, whose date is put by Forbes at A.D. 1012.

That a monster haunted the Ness even in the days of Columba is apparent from the following account of one of that saint's miracles in Adamnan's *Life of Saint Columba* (Book II, chap. xxviii) :

> On another occasion also, when the blessed man was living for some days in the province of the Picts, he was obliged to cross the river Nesa (Ness) ; and when he reached the bank of the river, he saw some of the inhabitants burying an unfortunate man, who, according to the account of those who were burying him, was a short time before seized, as he was swimming, and bitten most severely by a monster that lived in the water ; his wretched body was, though too late, taken out with a hook, by those who came to his assistance in a boat. The blessed man, on hearing this, was so far from being dismayed that he directed one of his companions to swim over and row across the coble that was moored at the farther bank. And Lugne Mocumin hearing the command of the excellent man, obeyed without the least delay, taking off all his clothes, except his tunic, and leaping into the water. But the monster, which, so far from being satiated, was only roused for more prey, was lying at the bottom of the stream, and when it felt the water disturbed above by the man swimming, suddenly rushed out, and, giving an awful roar, darted after him, with its mouth wide open, as the man swam in the middle of the stream. Then the blessed man observing this, raised his holy hand, while all the rest, brethren as well as strangers, were stupified with terror and, invoking the name of God, formed the saving sign of the cross in the air, and commanded the ferocious monster, saying, " Thou shalt go no further, nor touch the man ; go back with all speed." Then at the voice of the saint, the monster was terrified, and fled more quickly than if it had been pulled back with ropes, though it had just got so near to Lugne, as he swam, that there was not more than the length of a spear-staff between the man and the beast. Then the brethren seeing that the monster had gone back, and that their comrade Lugne returned to them in the boat safe and sound, were struck with admiration, and gave glory to God in the blessed man. And even the barbarous heathens, who were present, were forced by the greatness of this miracle, which they themselves had seen, to magnify the God of the Christians.

On another occasion when Broichan the Druid became aware that Columba wished to sail down Loch Ness, he raised a contrary wind (Adamnan, Book II, chap. xxxv). The Druids, seeing that the weather had become dark and threatening and that the wind was very violent and contrary, exulted greatly, but Columba was unperturbed :

Our Columba, therefore, seeing that the sea was violently agitated, and that the wind was most unfavourable for his voyage, called on Christ the Lord and embarked in his small boat ; and whilst the sailors hesitated, he the more confidently ordered them to raise the sails against the wind. No sooner was this order executed, while the whole crowd was looking on, than the vessel ran against the wind with extraordinary speed. And after a short time, the wind, which had hitherto been against them, veered round to help them on their voyage, to the intense astonishment of all. And thus throughout the remainder of that day the light breeze continued most favourable, and the skiff of the blessed man was carried safely to the wished-for haven.

Inverness in those days was the capital, or at all events an important centre, of the Pictish kingdom. Columba, a Gael, was therefore a foreigner to the Picts, for, in the opinion of the leading authorities of the present day, not only St. Columba but all Scottish Gaels originally came from Ireland.

From very early times the castle at Inverness is prominent. At the close of the thirteenth century Edward I of England seized the castle, and appointed as captain Sir Reginald le Chen, who, however, was unable to hold it long against the Scots. In 1303 King Edward again travelled north with his army, and from the fortress on Lochindorb, which he had captured, marched against the castle of Inverness, which he took without difficulty. About ten years later Robert the Bruce laid siege to and captured the castle, which he was able to hold during his reign. In 1335 Edward III of England with a strong force invested the castle of Inverness, which was unable to withstand him. In the year 1451 John, Lord of the Isles, marching east, seized the fortress of Inverness, summoning the people of the surrounding district to pay their taxes to him and not to King James. For some years the Lord of the Isles held Inverness Castle, and when at last he was driven out by the King, and it was hoped that quieter times were in store, the nephew of John

of the Isles made himself master of the castle in the year 1494.
This transitory achievement was a bad thing for him, for he was
defeated and his Lordship of the Isles forfeited and annexed to
the Crown — since then it has been one of the titles of the
Prince of Wales.

James II spent a considerable time in the Highlands of Scotland, and James III in 1470 remained in the town for a month,
his visit no doubt bringing much prosperity to the district.

In 1562 Queen Mary of Scots rode on horseback from Edinburgh to Inverness. The castle at the time was held by a
representative of the Earl of Huntly, who denied the Queen
admittance. But the Clan Chattan, Monros and Frasers came
to her aid, overpowered the castle garrison, and hanged the
representative of Huntly from the battlements. Randolph thus
describes the event :

> At the Queen's arrival at Inverness, she, proposing to have lodged in
> the castle, which pertaineth to herself, and the keeping only to the Earl of
> Huntly (Lord Gordon), being sheriff by inheritance, was refused there to
> have entry, and enforced to lodge in the town. That night, the castle
> being summoned to be rendered to the queen, answer was given by those
> that kept it in Lord Gordon's behalf, that without his command it should
> not be delivered. The next day the country assembled to the assistance
> of the queen. The Gordons also made their friends come out. We looked
> every hour to see what shall become of the matter. We left nothing
> undone that was needful. And the Gordons not finding themselves so well
> served, and never amounting to above 500 men, sent word to those who
> were within, amounting to only twelve or thirteen able men, to render the
> castle ; which they did. The captain was hanged, and his head set upon
> the castle ; some others condemned to perpetual imprisonment ; and the
> rest received mercy. In all these garbulles, I assure your honour I never
> saw the queen merrier ; never dismayed ; nor never thought I that stomach
> to be in her that I find. She repented nothing, but, when the lords and
> others at Inverness came in the morning from the watche, that she was not
> a man, to know what life it was to lye all night in the fields, or to walk
> upon the causeway, with a jack and knapsack, a Glasgow buckler, and a
> broadsword.

On a Sunday morning of the month of May in the year 1649
the good people of the burgh of Inverness were perturbed by the
entry of Lord Reay and 1,500 Highlanders into the town. The
castle was speedily captured and, in the words of the minister
of Kirkhill :

They crossed the bridge of Ness on the Lord's Day in time of divine service and alarmed the people of Inverness, impeding God's worship in the town. For instead of bells to ring into service I saw and heard no other than the noise of pipes, drums, pots, pans, kettles, and spits in the streets to provide them victualls in every house. And in their quarters the rude rascality would eat no meat at their tables until the landlord laid down a shilling Scots upon each trencher, calling this argiod cagainn (chewing money), which every soldier got, so insolent were they.

Just a year later a noble prisoner was led captive through Inverness. No reader can fail to be moved by the contemporary account, by the minister of Kirkhill, of the nobility of Montrose's bearing during what for him were most tragic days :

I set down that which I myself was an eye witness of. On 7th of May at Lovat, Montrose sat upon a little shelty horse without a saddle, but a bundle of rags and straw, and pieces of ropes for stirrups ; his feet fastened under the horse's belly, and a bit halter for a bridle. He had on a dark, reddish plaid, and a cap on his head ; a muscateer on each side, and his fellow-prisoners on foot after him. Thus he was conducted through the country ; and near Inverness, on the road to Muirton, where he desired to alight and called for a draught of water, being then in the first crisis of a high fever, the crowd from the town came forth to gaze. The two ministers went thereupon to comfort him. At the end of the bridge, stepping forward, an old woman, Margaret M'George, exclaimed and brawled, saying, " Montrose, look above, see those ruinous houses of mine, which you occasioned to be burned down when you besieged Inverness " — yet he never altered his countenance, but with a majesty and state beseeming him, kept a countenance high. At the cross was a table covered, and the magistrates treated him with wine, which he would not taste till alloyed with water. The stately prisoners, his officers, stood under a fore-stair and drank heartily. I remarked Colonel Hurry, a robust, tall, stately fellow with a long cut on his cheek. All the way through the streets he (Montrose) never lowered his aspect. The provost, Duncan Forbes, taking leave of him at the town's end, said, " My lord, I am sorry for your circumstances." He replied, " I am sorry for being the object of your pity."

At the end of 1651 the forces of Cromwell occupied Inverness. They built a citadel, and a frigate capable of holding sixty men. This they dragged overland to Loch Ness and launched her there. During this great feat three cables, each of seven inches, snapped. After the craft was launched, four pieces of ordnance were set in position on board of her and she then sailed up and down Loch Ness, to act as a deterrent to the lawless Highlanders of the district and of Lochaber in the west.

On the restoration of Charles II, Cromwell's fortress in Inverness was razed to the ground and the frigate on Loch Ness was no doubt demolished.

About seventy years later General Wade, then commanding the royal forces in Scotland, placed on Loch Ness a successor to Cromwell's " frigate ". This craft carried as armament six or eight *patteroes* (J. Cameron Lees, *History of Inverness-shire*, p. 127) and

was employed to transport men, provisions, and baggage from Inverness to Fort Augustus. Cromwell's soldiers sailed a vessel on Loch Ness, but she was built at Inverness and transported overland. That of Wade was built on the banks of the lake. " When she made her first trip she was mightily adorned with colours, and fired her guns several times, which was a strange sight to the Highlanders, who had never seen the like before."

Thomas Tucker, who visited Inverness in 1655, writes thus of the town and district (Hume Brown, *Early Travellers in Scotland*, p. 174) :

The last port northerly, is Invernesse, lyeing at the head of the Firth of Murray, not farre from Loquh Nesse, where the towne is a small one, though the cheife of the whole north, and would bee yett worse, were it not for the large cittadell, built there of late yeares. This port hath for its district all the harbours and creekes of the shires of Murray, Rosse, Southerland, and Caithnes, with the Isles of Orkney ; in which, although there bee many large rivers which, riseing in the hills, runne downe into the sea, and the ocean hath indented many more creeks and inletts, with its stormy waves still beateing on the shoare, yett few of them are serviceable, and those few much too bigge for any trade that is or may be expected in these parts. For as the roughnesse of the sea and weather lye constantly on the east of them, soe on the west they have the hills for theyr portion. The inhabitants beyond Murray land (except in the Orkneys) speake generally Ober garlickh,[1] or Highlands, and the mixture of both in the towne of Invernesse is such that one halfe of the people understand not one another.

The trade of this port is onely a coast trade, there being noe more than one single merchant in all the towne, who brings home sometimes a little timber, salt, or wine. Here is a collector, a checque, and one wayter, who attends here, and lookes (as occasion serves) to Garmouth and Findorne in Murray-land, two small places, from whence some 60 lasts of salmon in a yeare are sent out, for which salt is brought in from France, and sometimes a small vessell comes in from Holland or Norway.

---

[1] Apparently Gaelic is meant.

Around the year 1735 Captain Burt, an officer of Engineers, wrote to his friend in London a number of *Letters from the North,* which gives an interesting, and it is believed faithful, description of the Highlands at that time. Burt, who, it seems, was in the service of General Wade, lived chiefly in the town of Inverness. Of this town in one of his letters he says :

Inverness is one of the Royal Boroughs of Scotland, and jointly with Nairne, Forres, and Channery, sends a Member to Parliament. The Town has a military Governor, and the Corporation a Provost and four Bailies, a kind of Magistrates little differing from our Mayors and Aldermen : besides whom, there is a Dean of Guild who presides in Matters of Trade ; and other Borough Officers, as in the rest of the corporate Towns of this Country. It is not only the Head Borough or County-Town of the Shire of Inverness, which is of large Extent, but generally esteemed to be the Capital of the Highlands : but the Natives do not call themselves High-landers, not so much on Account of their low Situation, as because they speak English. Yet although they speak English, there are scarce any who do not understand the Irish Tongue ; and it is necessary they should do so, to carry on their Dealings with the neighbouring Country People ; for within less than a Mile of the Town, there are few who speak any English at all. What I am saying must be understood only of the ordinary People, for the Gentry, for the most part, speak our Language in the remotest parts of Scotland.

The bridge (over the Ness) is about 80 yards over, and a piece of good workmanship, consisting of seven arches, built with stone, and maintained by the toll of a Bodle, or the sixth part of a penny for each foot-passenger with goods, a penny for a loaded horse, etc. . . .

From the Tolbooth or County Gaol, the greatest part of the Murderers and other notorious Villains, that have been committed since I have been here, have made their Escape ; and I think this has manifestly proceeded from the Furtherance or Connivance of the Keepers, or rather their Keepers. When this Evil has been complained of, the Excuse was, the Prison is a weak old Building, and the Town is not in Condition to keep it in Repair : but, for my own Part, I cannot help concluding, from many Circumstances, that the greatest Part of the Escapes have been the Consequence, either of Clan-Interest or Clannish Terror. As for Example, if one of the Magistrates were a Cameron (for the Purpose), the Criminal (Cameron) must not suffer, if the Clan be desirous he should be saved.

Of the churches of Inverness Burt writes :

Near the extreme Part of the Town, toward the North, there are two Churches, one for the English and the other for the Irish Tongue, both out of Repair, and much as clean as the other Churches I have seen.

One of these churches at least stands at the present day — the High Street church. In the churchyard of this church are two old tombstones of curious shape. These, according to tradition, were put to sinister use less than twenty years after Burt had written his *Letters*. It is said that after the suppression of the rising of 1745 Jacobite prisoners were forced to sit on one of these stones, and from the other, which, from its shape, acted as an excellent rest for a musket, the executioner shot down the condemned prisoners one after another. Against the wall of this church other Jacobite prisoners were shot. Captain William MacKay of Inverness (son of the author of the masterly work *Urquhart and Glen Moriston*), in giving me this information, told me also that the Jacobite prisoners of the '45 were confined in the tower of the church, which is still a prominent landmark.

In the days of Burt a number of the Highland chiefs and leading families owned town houses in Inverness, and he sarcastically writes that " the Wife of a Laird of fifteen pounds a Year is a Lady ; and treated with your Ladyship ".

In his day Macintosh had a house in Inverness — Prince Charles Edward lodged in it during his campaign — Grant of Glenmoriston owned a house on the bank of the Ness and Lord Lovat's house was just off Church Street. Glenmoriston's house is now a boarding-house, and Lovat's house is also used for a more humble purpose than formerly. There is nothing to tell you as you walk down Church Street that Lord Lovat's house is here, for it is invisible from the main street and you must enter it through a close. Here lived that celebrated character, Lord Lovat of the '45 — he who had armed clansmen always at the gate to guard him from intrusion and who, when an old and hunted man, was captured on an island of Loch Morar and a little later lost his head by the executioner's axe. His old home remains, surrounded by mean dwellings which have encroached upon it, and almost hide it from view, yet it stands aloof and silent like a proud prisoner among an idle, vulgar throng, awaiting the moment when it must be condemned.

In the days when Lord Lovat's armed Highlanders mounted

guard over his house there was great poverty in Inverness. Let us read what Burt writes (Letter IV) :

To return to Town after my Ramble : here is a melancholy appearance of Objects in the Streets ; — in One Part the poor Women, Maid-servants, and Children, in the coldest Weather, in the Dirt or in Snow, either walking or standing to talk with one another, without Stockings or Shoes. In another Place, you see a Man dragging along a half-starved Horse little bigger than an Ass, in a Cart, about the Size of a Wheel-Barrow. One Part of his Plaid is wrapt round his Body, and the Rest is thrown over his left Shoulder ; and every now and then he turns himself about, either to adjust his Mantle, when blown off by the Wind or fallen by his stooping, or to thump the poor little Horse with a great Stick. The Load in this Cart, if compact, might be carried under his Arm ; but he must not bear any Burden himself, though his Wife has, perhaps, at the same Time, a greater Load on her Loins than he has in his Cart : I say on her Loins, for the Women carry Fish, and other heavy Burdens, in the same Manner as the Scots Pedlars carry their Packs in England. . . . Here are four or five Fairs in the Year, when the High-landers bring their Commodities to Market : but, good God ! you could conceive there was such Misery in this Island.

One has under his Arm a small Roll of Linen, another a Piece of Coarse Plaiding : these are considerable Dealers. But the Merchandise of the greatest Part of them is of a most contemptible Value, such as these, viz.— two or three Cheeses, of about three or four Pounds weight a-piece ; a Kid, sold for Sixpence or Eightpence at the most; a small Quantity of Butter, in something that looks like a Bladder, and is sometimes set down upon the Dirt in the Street ; three or four Goat-skins ; a Piece of Wood for an Axle-tree to one of the little Carts, etc. With the Produce of what each of them sells, they generally buy something, viz.— a Horn, or Wooden Spoon or two, a Knife, a Wooden Platter, and such-like Necessaries for their Huts, and carry home with them little or no Money.

P.S. You may see one eating a large onion without salt or bread ; another gnawing a carrot, etc. These are rarities not to be had in their own parts of the country.[1]

But the food prices in Inverness at this time were very low :

Mutton and beef are about a Penny a Pound ; Salmon, which was at the same Price, is, by a late Regulation of the Magistrates, raised to Two-pence a Pound, which is thought by many to be an exorbitant Price. A Fowl, which they, in general, call a Hen, may be had at Market for Two-pence or Two-pence-Halfpenny, but so lean they are good for little. The little Highland Mutton, when fat, is delicious, and certainly the greatest of Luxuries.

---

[1] When Burt was driving through the Highlands he says that his carriage occasioned so great a veneration on the part of the natives that they ran from their huts to doff their bonnets to the coachman, " little regarding us that were within ".

Concerning the dress of the people, Burt writes that

The Highland Dress consists of a Bonnet made of Thrum without a Brim, a short Coat, a Waistcoat, longer by five or six Inches, short Stockings, and Brogues, or Pumps without Heels. By the way, they cut Holes in their Brogues, though new made, to let out the Water, when they have far to go and Rivers to pass : this they do to preserve their Feet from galling. Few besides Gentlemen wear the Trowze — that is, the Breeches and Stockings all of one piece, and drawn on together ; over this Habit they wear a Plaid, which is usually three Yards long and two Breadths wide, and the whole Garb is made of chequered Tartan, or Plaiding : this, with the Sword and Pistol, is called a full Dress, and, to a well-proportioned Man, with any tolerable Air, it makes an agreeable Figure.

The common Habit of the ordinary Highlanders is far from being acceptable to the Eye ; with them a small Part of the Plaid, which is not so large as the former, is set in Folds and girt round the Waist, to make of it a short Petticoat that reaches half way down the Thigh, and the rest is brought over the Shoulders, and then fastened before, below the Neck, often with a Fork, and sometimes with a Bodkin, or sharpened Piece of Stick. The Stocking rises no higher than the Thick of the Calf, and from the Middle of the thigh to the middle of the Leg is a naked space, which being exposed to all weathers, becomes tanned and freckled. This dress is called the Quelt ; and, for the most part they wear the Petticoat so very short, that in a windy day, going up a Hill, or stooping, the Indecency of it is plainly discovered.[1]

Writing of the country Gaelic-speaking people round Inverness, Burt records that they

are in Winter often confined to their Glens by swollen Rivers, Snow, or Ice : have no Diversions to amuse them, but sit brooding in the Smoke over the Fire till their Legs and Thighs are scorched to an extraordinary Degree, and many have sore Eyes, and some are quite blind. The long Continuance in the Smoke makes them almost as black as Chimney-Sweepers ; and when the Huts are not Water-tight, which is often the Case, the Rain that comes through the Roof and mixes with the Sootiness of the Inside, where all the Sticks look like Charcoal, falls in Drops like Ink. To supply the Want of Candles, when they have occasion for more Light than is given by the Fire, they provide themselves with a Quantity of Sticks of Fir.

This graphic description of an old Highland " black house " might apply to homes still in use at the present day in Skye and the Outer Hebrides, yet despite (or more correctly, I believe, because of) the peat smoke the better type of " black house " is

---

[1] Burt mentions that " the Bonnet is frequently taken off and wrung like a Dish-clout (in wet weather), and then put on again ".

more healthy than many of the modern crofters' houses of dressed stone, wood floor, two stories and slated roof.

An interesting observation of Burt in one of his letters is that it was " by Law no less than transportation to take the Salmon-Fry ".

On February 25, 1746 (according to the account in a contemporary issue of the *Scots Magazine*, Thursday, February 20), Prince Charles Edward and his Highlanders occupied the town of Inverness and its castle, Lord Loudon and his men having abandoned the town as they received news that the Prince's force was approaching. At Inverness (as I have mentioned earlier in this chapter) the Prince took up his quarters " in the house of his benefactrix, old Lady Macintosh ". Entries in the household of that time show that " 8 dozen egges cost 1/4 and 2000 oysters 10/– ".

During the Prince's stay in the Highland capital there was much gaiety. By day he hunted and in the evening graced with his presence balls and concerts. Then came the day when, to the cheers of the folk of Inverness, he marched out to Culloden, and, in a few hours, the Jacobite hopes crashed to the ground. Inverness was to know terrible days after the Highlanders' defeat at Culloden. Bradeshaw's account (*The Lyon in Mourning*, vol. i, p. 49) sheds some light on what the prisoners and wounded had to suffer :

I was put into one of the Scotch kirks together with a great number of wounded prisoners who were stript naked and then left to die of their wounds without the least assistance, and though we had a surgeon of our own, a prisoner in the same place, yet he was not permitted to dress their wounds, but his instruments were taken from him on purpose to prevent it ; and in consequence of this many expired in the utmost agonies.

Cumberland — " Butcher Cumberland " as he was commonly called — had his headquarters in Inverness at a hotel just round the corner of Church Street, beside the town hall. The hotel has long disappeared, but the ancient stone of Clachnacuddin beside it was old and venerable even in his day. This stone can be seen outside the town hall. Its correct name, according to the Celtic scholar MacBain, is Clach nan Cùdainn, Stone of the Tubs, for in the old days, when the women of Inverness had to fetch their water from the river, it was customary for them to stand their tubs on the flat surface of this stone while they rested.

General Wolfe, who was afterwards the hero of Quebec, was stationed in Inverness in 1751. He complained of the weather, the food, indeed of most things, but he writes :

> We have an assembly of female rebels every fortnight, entirely composed of MacDonalds, Frasers, and MacIntoshes. I had the honour to dance with the daughter of a chieftain who was killed at Culloden, the Laird of Kippock. They are perfectly wild as the hills that breed them, but they lay aside their principals for the sake of sound and movement. They make no converts, which I chiefly attribute to a strong dialect of the Erse that destroys the natural softness of their notes.

The celebrated traveller Pennant visited Inverness in 1769. In his *Tour in Scotland* (vol. iii, p. 177) he writes :

> Inverness is finely seated on a plain, between the Firth of Murray, and the river Ness : the first, from the narrow strait of Ardersier, instantly widens into a fine bay. . . . The town is large and well built, very prosperous, and contains about eleven thousand inhabitants. This being the last of any note in North Britain, is the winter residence of many of the neighbouring gentry : and the present emporium, as it was the ancient, of the north of Scotland. Ships of five or six hundred tons can ride at the lowest ebb within a mile of the town ; and at high tides vessels of 200 tons can come up to the quay. The present imports are chiefly groceries, haberdasheries, hard-ware, and other necessaries from London : and of late from six to eight hundred hogsheads of porter are annually brought in. The exports are chiefly salmon, those of the Ness being esteemed of more exquisite flavor than any other. Herrings, of an inferior kind, taken in the Firth from August to March. . . . The commerce of this place was at its height a century or two ago, when it engrossed the exports of corn, salmon, and herrings, and had besides a great trade in cured codfish now lost ; and in those times very large fortunes were made here.
>
> The opulence of this town has often made it the object of plunder to the Lords of the Isles ; and their dependents. It suffered in particular in 1222, from one Gillispie ; in 1429, from Alexander, Lord of the Isles ; and, even so late did the antient manners prevale, that a head of a western clan, in the latter end of the last century, threatened the place with fire and sword, if they did not pay a large contribution, and present him with a scarlet suit laced ; all which was complied with.
>
> On the North stood Oliver's fort, a pentagon, those form remains to be traced only by the ditches and banks. He formed it with stones purloined from the neighbouring religious house.
>
> On an eminence south of the town is old Fort St. George, which was

taken and blown up by the rebels in 1746. It had been the antient castle converted by General Wade into barracks. According to Boethius, Duncan was murdered here by Macbeth : but according to Fordun, near Elgin. This castle used to be the residence of the court, whenever the Scottish Princes were called to quell the insurrections of the turbulent clans. Old people still remember magnificent apartments embellished with stucco busts and paintings. The view from hence is charming of the Firth, the passage of Kessock, the river Ness, the strange-shaped hill of Tomman-heurich, and various groups of distant mountains.

At Inverness was a house of Dominicans, founded in 1233 by Alexander II : and in Dalrymple's collection there is mention of a nunnery. . . . Cross the Ness on a bridge of seven arches, above which the tide flows for about a mile. A small toll is collected here, which brings to the town about £60 a year.

In August 1773, four years after Pennant's visit, Johnson and Boswell arrived in Inverness, and on Sunday, August 29, they went to church there, but Boswell remarks that

the chapel was but a poor one. The altar was a bare fir table, with a coarse stool for kneeling on, covered with a piece of coarse sail cloth doubled by way of cushion. The lofts were at each end, and one before the pulpit. At the left hand of it, when you looked up to the loft you saw just the un-covered joists.

After church we walked down to the quay, where I met at Oliver's fort, Mr. Alves the painter, whom I had not seen since I was at Rome in 1765. We then went to Macbeth's Castle. I had a most romantic satisfaction in seeing Mr. Johnson actually in it. It answers to Shakespeare's description — " This castle hath a pleasant ", etc. ; which I repeated. When we came out of it, a raven perched on one of the chimney-tops and croaked. Then I repeated, " The raven himself is hoarse ", etc.

No history of Inverness would be complete without a short account of the construction of the Caledonian Canal — that great water-way which links the Atlantic with the North Sea. Mr. Telford, the celebrated engineer, estimated that the undertaking would cost £350,000 and would take seven years. Actually the work lasted considerably longer, and cost the huge sum of £1,300,000. Mr. Telford proposed that the canal should be large enough to admit the largest class of British and American traders (Cameron Lees, *History of the County of Inverness*, p. 253) or a 32-gun frigate, fully equipped.

The length of the Caledonian Canal is sixty miles, of which forty are the lochs of Ness, Oich and Lochy ; the summit level (at Loch Oich) is 100 feet above the sea. In the construction of the canal it was found necessary to raise the level of Loch Lochy 9 feet, and to cut a new passage for the River Lochy in the solid rock, where the famed Mucomer salmon-pool now is. The dredging of Loch Oich proved both difficult and costly, because a great number of oak trees, which during the ages had been carried down

Loch Lochy

the River Garry in times of flood, had to be removed, and some of these old trees were as much as 12 feet in diameter.

The first passage from sea to sea was when, in October 1822, a steamship reached Fort William from Inverness in thirteen hours, but although the Caledonian Canal was then opened for traffic it was by no means completed, and it was not indeed until 1843 that the work was finished.

We have thus seen how, through the centuries, Inverness has grown and changed. The latest change has been the construction of the great highway between Inverness and Fort William, called the Glen Albyn road, from which the Loch Ness monster has been often seen.

During many centuries the River Ness has flowed unchanged yet ever-changing through the town. This river, so short in its course, is nevertheless in times of flood one of the most mighty in the Highlands. Its waters never freeze, even at the margins, and on a morning of hard frost it is interesting to see the majestic Ness flowing seaward, with waters steaming like those of a hot spring in Iceland. Here in winter many water ouzels fly backwards and forwards, or sing their low song, or plunge beneath that rapid tide and search the stones of the river-bed for aquatic larvae. In December, January and February eager salmon, fat and silver-sided, from the deeps of the Atlantic enter the Ness and pass swiftly through to Loch Ness, thence to the clear foaming waters of the Garry, where they are sometimes caught with the fly on days of January so cold that the angler's line freezes to the rings of his rod. They are also taken in Loch Ness at this chilly season, but the Loch Ness salmon are believed to be a different race from those which enter the Garry.

With associations of ancient days — of the Lord of the Isles ; of Montrose, proud and noble even in defeat ; of Prince Charles Edward and the gallant men who shared his fortunes and saw their hopes crash at Culloden — Inverness may well claim to be the capital of the Scottish Highlands, and to occupy a position unique as it is illustrious.

R

Glen Doe, near Fort Augustus

CHAPTER XXV

THE COUNTRY AROUND INVERNESS

ALONG the south bank of Loch Ness there is a good road from Inverness as far as Inverfarigaig and Foyers (where the splendid Fall of Foyers supplies power for aluminium works), but at Foyers the road leaves the loch-side and climbs to Whitebridge, continuing on high ground until Fort Augustus is almost reached.

The road from Inverness first skirts the River Ness, and reaches the loch at Dores. Before Loch Ness was deepened for the passage of ships and its level considerably raised for the Caledonian Canal, the loch could be crossed at Dores at the Bona Ford. There is at Dores an old stone, Clach nam Mèirleach, Stone of the Robbers, which is now hidden by the water,[1] but in

---

[1] On a winter day in January 1941 when I passed, the loch was unusually low and the great stone was just awash.

old days it was possible to tell, by the height of the water on this stone, whether the ford was passable. The old Gaelic name for this ford is Am Bàn Ath, the White Ford, a name given to it because of its white pebbles.

The Dores–Foyers road was made by General Wade, and near Dores is the General's Well, and also the site of the grave of two Highlanders who, as they were attempting to drag themselves, badly wounded, from the field of Culloden to their homes in the west, died of their wounds and were buried here. Until recent years a stone, with the date 1745 cut on it, marked the place of their burial.

About five miles west of Dores, at Whitefield, is the site of the old house thus described by Dr. Samuel Johnson in 1773 :

Near the way, by the water side, we espied a cottage. This was the first Highland Hut that I had seen ; and as our business was with life and manners, we were willing to visit it. To enter a habitation without leave, seems to be not considered here as rudeness or intrusion. The old laws of hospitality still give this licence to a stranger.

A hut is constructed with loose stones, ranged for the most part with some tendency to circularity. It must be placed where the wind cannot act upon it with violence, because it has no cement ; and where the water will run easily away, because it has no floor but the naked ground. The wall, which is commonly about six feet high, declines from the perpendicular a little inward. Such rafters as can be procured are then raised for a roof, and covered with heath, which makes a strong and warm thatch, kept from flying off by ropes of twisted heath, of which the ends, reaching from the center of the thatch to the top of the wall, are held firm by the weight of a large stone. No light is admitted but at the entrance, and through a hole in the thatch, which gives vent to the smoke. This hole is not directly over the fire, lest the rain should extinguish it ; and the smoke therefore naturally fills the place before it escapes. Such is the general structure of the houses in which one of the nations of this opulent and powerful island has been hitherto content to live. Huts however are not more uniform than palaces ; and this which we were inspecting was very far from one of the meanest, for it was divided into several apartments ; and its inhabitants possessed such property as a pastoral poet might exalt into riches.

When we entered, we found an old woman boiling goats-flesh in a kettle. She spoke little English, but we had interpreters at hand ; and she was willing enough to display her whole system of economy. She has five children, of which none are yet gone from her. The eldest, a boy of thirteen, and her husband, who is eighty years old, were at work in the wood. Her two next sons were gone to Inverness to buy meal, by which oatmeal is always meant. Meal she considered an expensive food, and told us, that in Spring, when the goats gave milk, the children could live without

Dun Deirdre at Inverfarigaig on Loch Ness

it. She is mistress of sixty goats, and I saw many kids in an enclosure at the end of her house. She had also some poultry. By the lake we saw a potatoe-garden, and a small spot of ground on which stood four shucks, containing each twelve sheaves of barley. She had all this from the labour of her own hands, and for what is necessary to be bought, her kids and her chickens are sent to market. With true pastoral hospitality, she asked us to sit down and drink whisky. She is religious, and though the kirk is four miles off, probably eight English miles, she goes thither every Sunday. We gave her a shilling, and she begged snuff ; for snuff is the luxury of a Highland cottage.

Near Inverfarigaig rises Dùn Dearduil, an ancient *dùn* or fort that is connected with the Celtic heroine Deirdre, or Dearduil as she is sometimes called. The tale of Deirdre is known as one of the Three Sorrows of Story-telling. It describes the giving and taking of great love, and the deep sorrow that followed.

The tale has been many times told in the ancient language of the Gael. Through the centuries it has been recited at the *céilidh* or social gathering beside glowing peat fires in the Highlands and Islands of Scotland, and in Eire also. The tale describes the romantic life of Deirdre, fairest of women, and her pre-ordained meeting with Naoise of the raven-black locks, one of the sons of Uisneach, he who in manly beauty was supreme and in stature exceeded his fellow men by head and shoulders. The three sons of Uisneach are sometimes known as the Three Falcons of Sléibhe Cuillinn (or the Cuillin Hills) because they were trained under the amazon queen Aife at Dùn Scathach in Sleat of Skye, which looks across Loch Eiseord on to the dark Cuillin. Deirdre against her will had been betrothed to Conchubar, King of Eire, and Naoise, because of his loyalty to his King, was at first unwilling to fly with her. But at length she prevailed upon him to save her from an unhappy marriage, and Naoise, with his brothers Ardan and Ainnle, sailed with her to Scotland (poetically described in Deirdre's Lament as " Alba of the east "). The anger of King Conchubar was great, but he bided his time, and then sent Fergus, one of his nobles and a great friend of Naoise, to bid the fugitives return, since all had been forgiven them. Fergus, believing that his King acted in good faith, gladly took the message across the sea, yet Deirdre, with her fore-knowledge of the future, was full of foreboding and mistrust when she heard it, and endeavoured to persuade Naoise to remain in Scotland, but he laughed at her fears, and as they sailed away and saw the Highland peaks recede on the eastern horizon she composed the Lament that has come to us with undimmed beauty through the centuries.

Her premonition of disaster was fulfilled. On their return to Eire they were treacherously seized by King Conchubar, and although they escaped from prison the King caused his Druid to conjure up a magic sea in their path as they fled. As the water deepened Naoise and his brothers lifted Deirdre upon their shoulders. The enchanted sea deepened yet further, and now they were swimming over its angry, crested billows. One of Naoise's brothers became exhausted, and they bore him with them although death was laying his hand upon them all. At last Naoise and the two brothers were lifeless : the Druid now recalled his phantom sea, and Deirdre was seen lamenting, in a grassy meadow, over her beloved. A grave was dug, and in it were placed brave-hearted Naoise and chivalrous Ardan and Ainnle. Then Deirdre called to the dead to make room for her beside Naoise, and when the lifeless bodies, hearing her, did this, she sprang into the grave, laid herself beside Naoise, and died. The King, reluctant to permit her to obtain her last wish, caused her to be buried in a separate grave. Then, in the words of the teller of this old tale of sorrow :

A young pine grew from the grave of Deirdre, and a young pine grew from the grave of Naoise, and the two young pines bent towards one another, and twined together. The King commanded that the two young pines should be cut down, and this was done twice, but they grew again, and the wife whom the King married persuaded him to cease his persecution of the dead.

During their time in Scotland Deirdre and Naoise, with a retinue of " 150 men, and 150 women, and 150 hounds ", lived chiefly in Glen Etive at Dalness in the Royal Forest. Here (as I have described in *Highways and Byways in the Western Highlands*) Deirdre from her *grianan* or sunny bower was so near the river that she could catch a salmon from her window. But in some versions of the old story they lived for a time also in Dùn Dearduil, the *dùn* which stands high above the south shore of Loch Ness (a loch which is sometimes said to derive its name from Naoise) in the neighbourhood of Inverfarigaig. I know of no *dùn* in the Scottish Highlands in more inspiring surroundings than Dùn Dearduil. The hill on which it is built is cone-like and on three sides a sheer precipice. Beneath the hill flows the River Farigaig, a Highland river of swift rushes and deep, peat-stained pools, and along the river weeping birches sway graceful boughs.

I saw Dùn Dearduil on a winter's day, when the leafless birches and cold ground, iron-hard from long-continued frost where the snow had gone from it, increased the heroic character of the scene.

The ascent of Dùn Dearduil should be made from the south-east, for the ascent is comparatively easy from that quarter, and the rocky bluff on which the *dùn* is built is seen at its best. Little is now left of the actual *dùn*, but the great stones which formed its outer foundations are still in place. Because of the view alone, the ascent of the bluff will more than repay him who makes it. I know of no view which brings out so clearly the grandeur of Loch Ness, which is seen stretching away east and west into the haze of distance. Nor have I found a view which gives a greater dignity to the ruins of Castle Urquhart, although they are some miles distant and on the far side of the loch. On the winter day when I stood on Dùn Dearduil I thought that Castle Urquhart rose like some magic castle, dark and mystical, upon a promontory that from my view-point seemed very lonely, and almost surrounded, so it appeared, by dark storm eddies which moved across Loch Ness on the icy breath of the winter wind.

Rather more than a mile to the west of Inverfarigaig and Dùn Dearduil is the Fall of Foyers (now harnessed for industrial purposes) where Dr. Johnson found " all the gloom and grandeur of Siberian solitude ". He writes :

We desired our guide to show us the fall, and dismounting, clambered over very rugged crags, till I began to wish that our curiosity might have been gratified with less trouble and danger. We came at last to a place where we could overlook the river, and saw a channel torn, as it seems, through black piles of stone, by which the stream is obstructed and broken till it comes to a very deep descent, of such dreadful depth, that we were naturally inclined to turn aside our eyes.

In MacFarlane's *Geographical Collections* (vol. i, p. 219) the writer looks upon the Fall of Foyers almost with awe. Thus he describes it :

The River runs very rapid about two miles, then falls down a precipice and makes a great Linn, then it runs six miles and a half and then falls down a greater precipice and Linn and a quarter of a mile downward falls down a third precipice, the most terrible and greatest of all, and for any thing we know, in the highlands, and then with great noise and rapidity falls a quarter of a mile downward into the Lake of Ness. His Excell: G. Wade, Colonel Spotiswood and Capt. Romer hath lately the curiosity to take a view of these last two. . . . We have seen this Fechlin[1] so big and rapid that it stopped the march and stages of the King's troups and other passengers : many have perished by this water, but not within these ten years past.

Later in the same account the writer quaintly observes that there are in the parish

many other hurtfull creatures, such as eagles, ravens, of all sorts, foxes, wild cats, serpents, toads and frogs.

When I visited the Fall of Foyers it was a winter's day during a spell of very severe weather. Although Foyers itself has changed greatly during the past twenty-five years, the scene at the great fall has lost nothing of its dignity and grandeur. On this winter day the beauty of the scene was enhanced by the fairy-like wall of ice which had been built up on either side of the cascade, and the falling water, filling the deep gorge with tumult, disappeared almost at once beneath the ice which held the pool below. I was interested to see that the water lying above the ice at its edges was deeply stained with peat, and I thought this noteworthy, because there are few Highland rivers or burns

[1] This name at the present day seems to be given the river only along its upper course.

which maintain their peaty character after a prolonged spell of frost.

The mansion-house of Foyers was situated near the river, beneath the fall. The first of the Frasers of Foyers was named (*vide* p. 256) Hùisdean Frangach (French Hugh) ; the name may have been given him because, after having killed his half-brother, he fled to France, or perhaps because when in France he married a French wife, who it is said on one occasion saved his life. The race of Hùisdean Frangach for centuries lived in the house of Foyers. James Fraser of Foyers was " out " with Prince Charlie, and, like Cluny MacPherson, was in hiding in his own country for a number of years after Culloden. For most of this time he was in concealment in a cave near Foyers, on the high ground. On one occasion he narrowly escaped with his life. A woman of the district was bringing him food, and was, unknown to her, followed by one of Cumberland's soldiers. Fraser, realising that either his own life or the soldier's life would be forfeit, shot the man dead. On another occasion a local boy was carrying to the fugitive a small cask of beer. He was met by a party of redcoats, who, suspecting the lad's mission, seized him, and insisted that he should tell them his secret. The boy was at the time above the Fall of Foyers, and when he was roughly stopped the cask fell from his shoulder and rolled down the steep bank into the river. But the brave lad refused to betray Fraser of Foyers, and one of the soldiers thereupon cut off one of his hands with his sword. The place where this happened is named the Cask's Leap.

In the old burying-ground of the parish church of Boleskine are ancient tombstones. In Neil Fraser-Tytler's *Tales of Old Days* is an interesting account of one of those old stones :

Regarding as east the wall flanking the road, we have let into the south wall a tombstone to Donald Fraser of Erchit, who died in 1729. A burial was taking place near the spot shortly after Culloden. While the funeral party were at the grave, a cart with military provisions was passing to Fort Augustus. One of the mourners seized a loaf of bread from out of the cart and threw it to the dogs ; he was immediately arrested and taken to the Fort. The soldiers fired a volley indiscriminately into the funeral party. The marks of the bullets are still plain to see in the above tombstone.

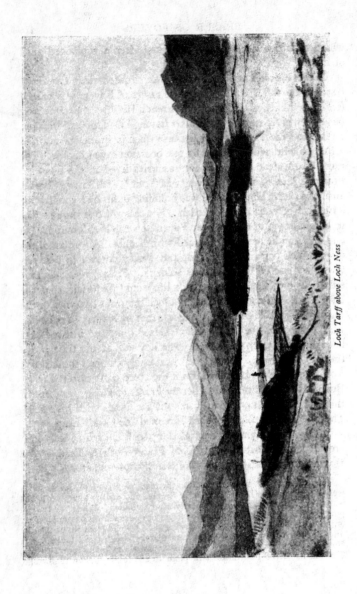

Loch Tarff above Loch Ness

Next morning the minister of Boleskine, who, like that of Dores, was an ardent supporter of the Government, appeared at the Fort an at early hour and had a long interview with the Duke of Cumberland, walking backwards and forwards on the green. Finally the minister took his leave, and was allowed to take his parishioner home along with him.

From Foyers the road rises, and crossing high ground and passing near Loch Tarff, descends again abruptly to the level of Loch Ness at Fort Augustus.

The original name of Fort Augustus was Cill Chuimein (named after Cummein, abbot of Iona). The fort was built by General Wade, and the name Augustus is traditionally said to have been given it to honour the Duke of Cumberland. In the early part of 1746 the fort was captured by the Jacobites. When Johnson and Boswell made their " tour " they stayed a night at Fort Augustus where, writes the learned doctor, " Mr. Trapaud, the governor, treated us with that courtesy which is so closely connected with the military character ". He continued :

In the morning we viewed the fort, which is much less than that of St. George. It was not long ago taken by the Highlanders. But its situation seems well chosen for pleasure, if not for strength ; it stands at the head of the lake, and, by a sloop of sixty tuns, is supplied from Inverness with great convenience.

Fort Augustus as a military station has disappeared. Where the fort stood is now a well-endowed Benedictine abbey. Lord Lovat bought from the Government the fort and the farm attached to it, and the present monastery was completed and opened in 1878. The old fortress has now become part of the abbey, and the room where Lord Lovat was confined as a prisoner can be seen. The old tree planted in memory of the battle of Culloden is still alive. The tradition that Jacobite prisoners were hanged on this tree is, I understand, incorrect ; they were shot on a piece of level ground which is now the cricket field of the abbey.

The return journey to Inverness can be made along the north side of Loch Ness, by the new high-road from Fort William to Inverness. The scenery along this road, particularly in late spring or early summer, is particularly fine. The graceful weeping birches leaf here earlier than in most parts of the Highlands, and are in all the beauty of their young foliage when the trees of Glen Moriston and Glen Urquhart are bare as at mid-winter. Broom beside this road comes into flower early. I have seen golden fields of broom here in April, although on the higher ground this plant does not flower until June. When, on damp rocks beside the Loch Ness road, broom and primroses are blossoming together, the blending of gold and yellow is most attractive.

The road passes above the grand old ruin of Urquhart Castle, a ruin now in the care of the Government department of Ancient Monuments. Little is known with certainty concerning the early history of this great castle, stately in its ruins. Pennant writes that it was " the seat of the once powerful Cummins, and was destroyed by Edward I."

In a seventeenth-century MS. (MacFarlane's *Geographical Collections*, vol. ii, p. 550) it is described as " the Castal of Urquhart very fair, sumtyms perteyning to the Lords of the Yles, and built be them as is alledged very fair in situation ".

Cameron Lees in his *County History of Inverness* mentions that Edward I of England subdued the castle of Urquhart and placed in charge of it Sir William Fitz Warrine, a knight of renown. But that knight was unable to hold the castle for long against Highland attacks, and it reverted to the Scots. In the year 1303 the English King once more appeared in the north with a great army, and again the castle of Urquhart fell to him, this time after a long siege. Some years later Robert the Bruce in person besieged Urquhart Castle and captured it, and during his reign the castle was held by him. In 1335 Edward III of England laid siege to Urquhart Castle, whose captain at that time was Sir Robert de Lauder — a brave knight who succeeded in holding the stronghold against the forces of the English King.

In 1509 King James IV gifted the Lordship of Urquhart to John Grant of Freuchie (or as it would now be called, Castle Grant), who was bound to repair or build at the Castle a tower, with an outwork or rampart of stone or lime, for protecting the lands and the people from the inroads of thieves and malefactors ; to construct within the castle a hall, chamber and kitchen, with all the requisite offices, such as a pantry, bake-house, brew-house, barn, ox-house, kiln, cot, dove-grove, and orchard.

In the revolution of 1689 the castle was held by a Whig garrison consisting of three companies of Highlanders under the command of Captain James Grant.

In February 1715 it is recorded that the " castell of Urquhart is blowen down with the last storme of wind " : it has since then remained roofless and a ruin.

During recent excavations numerous articles of interest have been found, among them mediaeval brooches and a penny of Edward I.

Before leaving the neighbourhood of Urquhart Castle it may be of interest to record that Pennant, writing of the Urquhart and Glen Moriston district, has an observant natural history note on the capercaillie.   He writes :

Above is Glen Moriston, and East of that Straith Glas, the Chisolm's country ; in both of which are forests of pines, where that rare bird the Cock of the Wood is still to be met with.   Formerly it was common throughout the Highlands, and was called Capercalze, and Auercalze ; and in the old law-books, Capercally.

Not so many years after Pennant visited the Highlands the old race of the capercaillie did indeed become extinct, and the breed which inhabits the Highland pine forests at the present day was introduced into Scotland from Sweden.

From the neighbourhood of Urquhart Castle of recent years the strange but now well-attested creature, the Loch Ness monster, has on a number of occasions been seen.   There is in my mind no doubt that such a creature — there may be more than one — does exist in Loch Ness.   Among a number of reliable witnesses who told me that they saw the monster was the late Captain Grant, of the MacBrayne paddle steamer *Pioneer*, which regularly plies on Loch Ness during the summer months.   From Captain Grant's observations — and from the observations of other reputable witnesses — it would seem that the strange creature is timid, and that the sound, or vibration, of a steamer's screw or paddles causes it to submerge while the ship is yet a considerable distance off. Mr. Goodbody of Invergarry House and his daughter watched the creature for forty minutes through a stalking-glass. The Loch Ness monster is indeed no recent " find ", although at the present day it is known to a much larger number of people than ever before. The chief reason, I believe, why many more people now see it is that the new high-road along the north shore of Loch Ness gives a much better view of the loch. But there is another reason. Before the monster became, so to speak, public property, those who saw the "unchancy" creature decided that the less said about it the better. They realised that they would be laughed at, or pitied, or would be set down as addicted to a " dram ". So long as half a century ago, to my own knowledge, children were told by their nurses that if they persisted in naughtiness the loch monster would take them. I heard of a well-known resident on Loch Ness-side who one day, after rowing down the loch in his small boat, appeared at a friend's house white and shaken, and asked for brandy. His friend for some time vainly endeavoured to ascertain the cause of his distress, to receive as answer, " It is no use my telling you, for even if I did you would not believe me." But in the end, when prevailed upon to unburden himself of his secret, he said to his friend, " As I was rowing down the loch some creature came to the surface beside me — and all I can say is that I hope I may never see the like again."

Most of the large and deep Highland lochs harbour, in the legends of the country, creatures which, as described in old books and writings, in their appearance resemble the Loch Ness monster. A peculiarity common to them all would appear to be their humps. The monster of Loch Morar, deepest loch in Scotland with a depth of 1,080 feet, and a floor no less than 1,050 below sea level, had a special name ; it was known to the Gaelic-speaking Highlanders of the district as Mhorag (pronounced Vorag), and appeared only before a death in the family of MacDonell of Morar. May it not be that in the monster of Loch Ness we have a survival of an ancient race which, living for the most part under water and being of a timid disposition, has existed in comparative obscurity during successive centuries ?

Hills rise steeply from Loch Ness throughout the length of its northern shore. Looking west up the loch from the neighbourhood of Inverness, the most prominent of these hills is graceful Mealfourvonie (2,264 feet). Geikie describes this hill as " one of the most elevated masses of Old Red Sandstone in the country ", and points out that its position shows how old the valley of the Great Glen (the country traversed by the Caledonian Canal) must be. Professor Watson gives the Gaelic name of the hill as Meall Fuarmhonaidh, Hill of Cold Moor. It doubtless received its name because of the cold, upland country which lies around it on every side, except toward Loch Ness.

Looking up Loch Ness, it can be realised how straight is the depression of the Great Glen, a depression which Geikie considered to coincide with a line of fracture of great geological antiquity, and one which has been subjected again and again to disturbance and displacement. Even at the present day, earthquake tremors are more frequent here than elsewhere in the Highlands.

Let us now return to Dores, and instead of travelling along the shore of Loch Ness, ascend the hill road to Kildrummond, then make our way east along the moor road which ends at Inverness. In the neighbourhood are the high-lying lochs, Ashie and Duntelchaig. On the moor near Loch Duntelchaig [1] are cairns which are believed to mark ancient graves of warriors. The late Neil Fraser-Tytler of Aldourie in an interesting booklet, *Tales of Old Days*, notes that on the moor east of this loch a ghostly battle has often been seen. Soon after dawn on a May morning is the most propitious time for watching that ghostly fight. In 1870–71 it was clearly seen, and the suggestion was made

[1] Gaelic Dùn t-Seilcheig, Fort of (the) Snail.

that it was a mirage of the fighting in France. But the battle has been seen since that time. " Large bodies of men in close formation and smaller bodies of cavalry facing an attacking force advancing from the east, wounded men clapping sphagnum moss to their wounds and tearing off strips from their shirts to bind it on — all this has been seen. On one occasion a man cycling to Inverness saw three horsemen on the road in front of him. He followed them for some distance and then, when rounding a sharp bend in the road, he ran into and through them. He fell off his bicycle in astonishment, and on getting up he beheld the phantom armies."

A couple of miles to the south lies Loch Ruthven. Near Loch Ruthven is Tom na Croiche, Gallows Knoll, where it is said that long ago Lord Lovat hanged those who had been convicted of wrongdoing, or had incurred his displeasure. On Leac Bhuidhe, above Loch Ruthven, Hùisdean Frangach, first of the Frasers of Foyers, in a duel mortally wounded his half-brother, John Fraser of Lovat, about 1420.

The country around Loch Ruthven is wild and attractive, and in spring and early summer the air is filled with the trilling songs of curlews. The cuckoo calls from the birches, and lapwings wheel and somersault. It is a country very different from that of Loch Ness, and in winter may be for weeks snow-bound and in the grip of frost when on the shores of Loch Ness, 800 feet below, the ground is snowless and the air comparatively mild.

The main road from Inverness to the south winds past Culcabock, then, at Inshes, quickly climbs to moorland country. At Daviot, descending slightly, the road crosses Strath Nairn and the River Nairn, then climbs again to Moy (which I have described in Chapter XXVII.). As the road winds among the old pines which grow beside Loch Moy a good view is had of the historic loch, and of Moyhall, standing beside it. From Moy the road continues south to Tomatin, near which place it crosses Strath Dearn and the River Findhorn. Still rising, the road and the railway, which here are close together, reach the watershed at bleak Slochd, 1,200 feet above sea level. I remember one spring day seeing a flight of wild swans passing north high over Slochd, and very lovely did the great birds look as they flew with strong, measured flight, their course set for Iceland, where they nest.

As the road begins to descend after Slochd an excellent view is had of the Cairngorm range of hills, from Sgòran Dubh and Braeriach in the west to Ben A'an and Beinn a' Bhùird in the east. At Carr Bridge, a renowned curling centre, the road divides, the main road continuing toward the south and a branch road, of excellent quality, turning east to Grantown-on-Spey.

Culloden

CHAPTER XXVl

THE COUNTRY AROUND INVERNESS : CULLODEN MOOR

SOUTH of Inverness, on high ground overlooking the Moray Firth, is Culloden Moor ; here, in April 1746, was fought the battle which brought irretrievable ruin to the Jacobite cause. The country has greatly changed since the time of the battle of Culloden. Woods have sprung up : a number of fields have replaced the heather : a modern road has been driven through the heart of the burial-place of the ancient dead. But the King's Stables and the Well of the Dead remain, to bring back a memory of the fight, and the memorial stones raised in memory of the clansmen that fell are seen beside the road.

For many years after the battle these graves had no stones to mark them ; they were distinguishable only by small mounds of green grass, short-cropped by rabbits and sheep. It must have been difficult, after so many years, to identify the resting-place of the various clans. On one stone are the names MacGillivray, MacLean and MacLachlan ; others record Clan Cameron, Clan Macintosh and Clan Stewart of Appin. Two graves have the inscription " Clans Mixed ". On the Great Cairn is the following inscription :

The Battle of Culloden was fought on this moor, 16th April, 1746. The graves of the gallant Highlanders who fought for Scotland and Prince Charlie are marked by the names of their clans.

Culloden, as Shaw, writing a few years after the battle, picturesquely puts it, broke " the charm of the broad sword and target, and may convince the Highlanders that, in the way of fighting now practised, their undisciplined, though brave militia, cannot stand before well-disciplined troops, conducted by a proper general ".

Culloden Moor on a spring day can be a very bleak country, for it lies high, and is full open to the north-east. On a bitter April day the Prince's army, cold, weary and hungry after an all-night march, faced a Hanoverian force twice their number — men who had eaten and slept well and were supported by strong artillery. Snow squalls were driving across the moor, and in these conditions famished and weary men lacking a night's sleep could not do justice to themselves.

An incident of ill-omen had preceded the battle. That careful historian, Browne, puts the matter as follows (Browne's *History of the Highlands*, vol. iii, p. 241) :

There had been, a day or two before, a violent contention among the chiefs about precedency of rank. The MacDonalds claimed the right as their due, in support of which claim they stated, that as a reward for the fidelity of Angus MacDonald, Lord of the Isles, in protecting Robert the Bruce for upwards of nine months, in his dominions, that prince, at the battle of Bannockburn, conferred the post of honour, the right, upon the MacDonalds — that this post had ever since been enjoyed by them, unless when yielded from courtesy upon particular occasions, as was done to the chief of the MacLeans at the battle of Harlaw. Lord George Murray, however, maintained that, under the Marquis of Montrose, the right had been assigned to the Athole men, and he insisted that that post should be now conferred upon them, in the contest with the Duke of Cumberland's army. In this unreasonable demand, Lord George is said to have been supported by Lochiel and his friends. Charles refused to decide a question with the merits of which he was imperfectly acquainted ; but, as it was necessary to adjust the difference immediately, he prevailed upon the commanders of the MacDonald regiments to waive their pretensions in the present instance. The MacDonalds in general were far from being satisfied with the complaisance of their commanders, and as they had occupied the post of honour at Gladsmuir and Falkirk, they considered their deprivation of it, on the present occasion, as ominous.

In vain the leading men of the MacDonalds — Keppoch, Lochgarry, Scothouse — had pleaded for the recognition of their traditional right. The MacDonalds were undoubtedly men with a strong grievance when they took up their position on the left of the line, but there seems to be no contemporary evidence that the clan refused to fight and, as a modern historian puts it (without evidence), " cut the heather tops with their claymores ". In the contemporary accounts of Culloden which appear in *The Lyon in Mourning* it is certainly noteworthy that not one word of blame is placed on the MacDonalds for their behaviour on the field of Culloden. Surely if that behaviour had been as selfish, proud and altogether indefensible as later historians have found it, there would be some mention of this in a contemporary account given by those who actually fought in the battle. Surely there would have been reproach against the MacDonalds in the statement of some eye-witness. Yet there is no mention even that the MacDonalds resented being placed on the left wing.

Later historians of repute have done much to vindicate the MacDonalds. Dr. Evan M. Barron, who knows more of the battle of Culloden than any living man, believes that the left wing of the Prince's army did not advance so speedily as the right because the MacDonalds were confronted by a marsh between them and Cumberland's forces. Dr. Barron indeed crossed swords with the late Mr. Lloyd George some years ago on this very matter.

In his *History of Scotland* (vol. iv) Andrew Lang also supports the MacDonalds. He writes :

The account by Yorke and Cumberland, who were on the spot, and as between Jacobite clan and clan had no prejudice, decides the question as to the conduct of the MacDonalds. They attacked at once, but, being out-flanked, and under a heavy fire of grape, they did not come to the shock. The narrative of Colonel Whitefoord (who stood alone by Cope's guns, and fired them at Prestonpans) corroborates the versions of Cumberland, Yorke, and Lord George Murray. " Their right column, and the left of our line, shocked at one corner of the park of Colwhineach. Nothing could be more desperate than their attack, or more properly received. Those in front were spitted with the bayonets ; those in flank were torn in pieces by the musketry and grape shot : their left column made several attacks on our right but as the battalions there never fired a shot, they (the Highland left) thought proper not to come too near, and in about a quarter of an hour . . . the whole first line gave way, and we followed slowly."

It is of course well known that certain of the MacDonalds behaved most valiantly on the field of Culloden : indeed the heroic conduct of Keppoch has often been described to show that he was heart-broken at receiving no support from his clansmen. So far as is known, the legend that the refusal of the Keppoch regiment to charge led Keppoch to exclaim, " Children of my heart ! Has it come to this that you will not follow me ? " appears first in Scott's *Tales of a Grandfather* in 1830. But Home in his *History of the Rebellion*, published in 1802, writes that

when the MacDonalds' regiment retreated, without having attempted to attack sword in hand, MacDonald of Keppoch advanced with his drawn sword in one hand and his pistol in the other : he had got but a little way from his regiment when he was wounded by a musket-shot, and fell.

It will be noticed that there is no mention that the MacDonalds REFUSED to attack, though this might be inferred from his state-ment.

Sir Walter Scott, adducing no real evidence, seems to be the first historian to make that serious charge against the Mac-Donalds although Home mentions that the Duke of Perth in vain implored the MacDonalds to advance: it is upon this account, which is amplified, and apparently exaggerated, by Sir Walter Scott, that we are obliged to rely.

I am inclined to think that the MacDonalds, rightly vexed and dispirited that their hereditary right had been ignored, fought with less impetuosity and *élan* than if they had been placed in their hereditary station, yet the legend that they refused to attack has no foundation. Nothing, indeed, is heard of it for more than fifty years after Culloden, and in fifty years error and exaggeration are very liable to creep into the account of any incident in a battle. It is known beyond doubt that many MacDonalds behaved most valiantly at Culloden. It is good that the bravery and devotion to duty of MacDonald (or Mac-Donell) of Keppoch has never been disputed. The chief of Keppoch, a man greatly loved by all who knew him, was the son of that chief, Coll, who defeated the Macintoshs in the last clan battle in Scotland (1689) at Maol Ruadh, and who fought also at Killiecrankie and Sheriffmuir. Keppoch, who died gallantly at Culloden, was for at least ten years a regular officer of some distinction in the service of the King of France.

But Keppoch did not fall alone at Culloden. A number of the leading clansmen of Glengarry were also killed, and that although a considerable number of the MacDonells of Glengarry were not engaged at Culloden, but were at the time on active service in the northern Highlands under Colla Bàn MacDonald or MacDonell of Barisdale, fighting the northern Whigs.

The history of the sword carried at Culloden by Keppoch is an interesting one. It was handed down from generation to generation, passed through the female line by marriage to persons of different names, including MacRaes and Chisholms, and is now in the West Highlands in the house of a Chisholm who greatly honours it. The sword is not of the ordinary basket-hilted or Highland type, but is a shortish, curved sword, with a hall-marked silver and ivory handle. The steel is of the finest quality, and the edge is still keen.

The story of the battle of Culloden has often been told, but a brief account of the fight should, perhaps, be given here. The Highlanders had a force of 5,000 men, deployed in two lines, and a thin reserve of Lord Ogilvy and his men. The first line consisted of the Atholl men on the right and next them the Camerons. Then in turn were drawn up the Appin Stewarts, John Roy Stewart, the Frasers (all of whom had not yet arrived), Mac-intoshes, Farquharsons, MacLeans, MacLeods (for not all the

MacLeods fought *against* the Prince), Chisholms, Clanranald, Keppoch, Glengarry's men and the Duke of Perth. In the second line were a few horse, Gordon of Glenbucket, a few of the French Royal Scots, Lord Lewis Gordon, French picquets and Fitz-James's few French horse. The Prince was in the centre. He had expected Cumberland to attack, for a tempest of wind and snow was blowing on the backs of his force, and in the faces of the Highland army. But, since no attack came, the Prince gave orders for the MacDonalds, who were under the command of the Duke of Perth, to begin the attack. In the words of Cumberland, " The whole (Highland) first line came down to attack at once ". The MacDonalds came down " three several times within a hundred yards of our men, firing their pistols and brandishing their swords, but the Royals and Pulteneys hardly took their firelocks from their shoulders, so that after these faint attempts they moved off ".

Whatever may be said of the conduct of the MacDonalds on the day of battle on Culloden Moor, it is universally agreed that Lochiel and his Camerons bore themselves most gallantly. It is recorded that the men under Lochiel, Lord George and MacGillivray in their onslaught " bore their opponents from their ranks, intermixing with them everywhere ". MacGillivray, mortally wounded, later dragged himself to die beside the Well of the Dead. Heavy flank fire stopped the Atholl Highlanders, while Stewarts, Camerons, MacLeans and Macintoshes " fought, without intermission, hand to hand, bayonet against broadsword ", although as they gallantly advanced they were "torn to pieces by musketry and grape ". The MacLeans were stationed near the MacDonalds. They certainly charged with great gallantry, and of their original number (200) no more than fifty survived.

The plight of the Highlanders in the front line was desperate. They were blinded by the snow which, accompanied by the smoke of battle, drove in upon them. In front and on their flank a withering fire was directed upon them, yet they broke Barrel's regiment, swept over the foremost guns in an irresistible line of tartan, and died on the bayonets of the second line of Cumberland's troops.

A celebrated engraver, Sir Robert Strange, was with the Prince at Culloden, and thus describes the fight (Dennistoun, *Memoirs of Sir Robert Strange*, vol. i, p. 62):

The right of our army, commanded by Lord George Murray, had made a furious attack, cut their way through Barrel's and Munro's regiments, and had taken possession of two pieces of cannon; but a reinforcement of Wolfe's regiment, etc. coming up from the Duke's second line, our right wing was obliged to give way, being at the same time flanked with some pieces of artillery, which did great execution. Towards the left the attack had been less vigorous than on the right, and of course had made but little impression on the Duke's army; nor was it indeed general, for the centre, which had been much galled by the enemy's artillery, almost instantly quitted the field. The scene of confusion was now great; nor can the imagination figure it. The men in general were betaking themselves precipitately to flight; nor was there any possibility of their being rallied. Horror and dismay were painted in every countenance. It now became time to provide for the Prince's safety: his person had been abundantly exposed. He was got off the field and very narrowly escaped falling in with a body of horse which, having been detached from the Duke's left, were advancing with incredible rapidity, picking up the stragglers, and, as they gave no quarter, were levelling them with the ground. The greater numbers of the army were already out of danger, the flight having been so precipitate. We got upon a rising ground, where we turned round and made a general halt. The scene was, indeed, tremendous. Never was so total a rout — a more thorough discomfiture of an army. The adjacent country was in a manner covered with its ruins. The whole was over in about twenty five minutes. The Duke's artillery kept still playing, though not a soul upon the field. His army was kept together, all but the horse. The great pursuit was upon the road towards Inverness. Of towards six thousand men, which the Prince's army at this period consisted of, about one thousand were asleep in Culloden parks, who knew nothing of the action till awaked by the noise of the cannon. These in general endeavoured to save themselves by taking the road towards Inverness; and most of them fell a sacrifice to the victors, for this road was in general strewed with dead bodies. The Prince at this moment had his cheeks bedewed with tears; what must not his feelings have suffered!

Thus, more swiftly than can be conceived, came the end to the high hopes of the Jacobite cause: thus, at a stroke, was happiness changed to mourning in many a Highland home. Thus fell upon the Highlanders and the Highlands an inconceivable calamity from which they have not to this day recovered, nor indeed will ever recover.

CHAPTER XXVII

MOY

That never the son of a chief of Moy
Might live to protect his father's age,
Or close in peace his dying eye,
Or gather his gloomy heritage.
                        (" The Curse of Moy ",
                            by Morritt of Rokeby)

SOME ten miles south of Inverness, and 900 feet above the level of the Moray Firth, is Moy Hall, ancestral seat of the Macintoshs,[1] chiefs of Clan Chattan.

The house of Moy stands near the shore of Loch Moy, and is the third house built in that district by the chiefs. Macintosh's Gaelic title is Tighearna na Moighe (Lord of Moy). This Moy must not be confused with the Moy which stands at the west end of Loch Laggan, but the two place-names are the same : they are from the Gaelic word *magh*, signifying a plain.

The earliest seat of Macintosh of Moy was a castle built upon the larger island of the loch. It was to raid this castle that Clanranald and his men once travelled all the way from Castle Tioram in Moidart, but the island castle is best remembered in local tradition because of the brave deed of a Macintosh. The powerful Comyns had long been at feud with the Macintoshs, and on this occasion were besieging their island castle. The Comyns dammed the loch in order to submerge the island and drown its occupants, but the scheme was defeated by the bravery of one of the Macintoshs who, under cover of darkness, swam ashore from the

---

[1] I have throughout kept to the older spelling of the name.

Moy

island and succeeded in demolishing the turf bank that was damming the loch. The released water, rushing out with irresist- ible force, carried the daring man to his death, but also swept away the Comyn force who were encamped on level ground below the dam.

Shaw in his *History of the Province of Moray* (vol. ii, p. 198) mentions that

in an island on the Loch of Moy the Lairds of MacIntosh had a house, as yet entire, where they resided in times of trouble. Now they have Moyhall, a good house and convenient summer-seat, at the west end of the loch. So rich is the loch of delicious red-bellied trouts, called Red-wames[1] that I have seen near 200 taken with one draught of a small net.

The lands of Moy were purchased from the Bishop of Moray: and MacIntosh took a new right from Bishop Hepburn in October, 1545.

Shaw, whose *History* is believed to have been ready for the press as early as 1760, although it was not actually published until 1776, evidently held char in greater esteem than they are held at the present time.

In the *Survey of the Province of Moray*, published in the year 1798, is the following interesting description of Moy:

The Lake of Moy is somewhat more than a mile in length, and rather less than one in breadth. It abounds in char, and a variety of other trout of various size and colour. Near its middle is an island, about two acres in extent, nearly in the shape of a violin: on its southern end are the ruins of ancient buildings, of considerable extent: the remains of a street, the whole length of the island, and the foundations of houses on each side, are readily distinguishable. In the year 1762, two ovens were discovered, each capable of baking 150 lb. avoirdupois of meal. In the year 1422 it con- tained a garrison of 400 men, and here, the chief of Mackintosh resided, except during the winter, when the country was inaccessible. The walls of a more modern building remain pretty entire: an Inscription over the gate imports, that it was built in 1655 by Lachlan, the 20th chieftain of the clan. The garden, stocked with fruit trees and bushes, is still in cultivation.

At the distance of several hundred yards, is another small island, formed by the accumulation of common rounded stone. It was the prison, when the punishment of malefactors was vested in the Chiefs. The miser- able prisoner could scarcely stand with dry feet, when the lake was at the lowest; but in the season of rain, if the surface was then no higher than

---

[1] Evidently char, for which the Gaelic name is *tarrdheargan*, literally " little belly-red ".

now, the water rose nearly to his middle ; but within the space of 24 hours he was condemned or set free.

After leaving their island home the chiefs of Clan Chattan built a house on the north-west shore of Loch Moy, and it was here that Prince Charles Edward was entertained. The bed which the Prince used is still to be seen in Moy Hall, and other priceless relics are the table at which he dined and the blue Highland bonnet which he wore — perhaps the same bonnet which he crammed on to his head over his nightcap when obliged to take flight in the middle of the night. It may be remembered that Macintosh of the '45 was, in name at all events, a supporter of the Government, but his wife, who was a Farquharson of Invercauld and at the time (although she had already been married four years) an accomplished and beautiful girl of no more than twenty, took command of the clan, and was a heroic figure at what is usually called the Rout of Moy. Lord Loudon, who was at Inverness with the Government troops, on hearing that the Prince was at Moy, at once marched there with his forces, hoping to take His Royal Highness prisoner.

MacLeod's piper, Donald Bàn MacCrimmon, was killed at the Rout of Moy. A few days before the engagement Donald Bàn was walking with other pipers in the town of Inverness, when his companions noticed that he appeared to shrink to the size of a child, and realised by this sign that the piper's end was near. It was a tragic thing that Donald Bàn should have lost his life in an engagement against a Prince to whose cause he was devoted. Indeed MacLeod had difficulty in raising his men to fight against Prince Charlie, for the Jacobite instinct was strong in Skye. It has been stated in a contemporary account (*The Lyon in Mourning*) that the MacLeod militia marched through Glen Moriston with white cockades on their bonnets, and the inference is that the clansmen were under the impression when they left Skye that they would be fighting for the Jacobite cause, for the white cockade, the white rose of Scotland, was the Jacobite emblem. Yet the sacrifice of Donald Bàn MacCrimmon's life was not in vain, if only for the lament composed on his death, which is one of the finest pieces of classical pipe music in existence.

A contemporary account of the happenings at Moy is given in *The Lyon in Mourning* (vol. ii, p. 134). Old Lady Macintosh, the mother of the chief, had her home in Inverness, and having in some way received a warning that Lord Loudon was to attempt to make the Prince prisoner,

dispatched a boy (Lachlan Macintosh) about fifteen years of age, to try if he could get past Lord Loudon's men, and to make all the haste he could to Moy to warn the Prince of what was intended against him. The boy attempted to pass by Lord Loudon and his command, but found he could not do it without running the risque of a discovery ; and therefore, as he said, he lay down at a dyke's side till all Lord Loudon's men past him, and, taking a different road, came to Moy about five o'clock in the morning. And though the morning was exceedingly cold, the boy was in a top sweat, having made very good use of his time. He said that Lord Loudon and his men (to use his own words) were within five quarters of a mile of Moy-hall. Immediately the Prince was awaked, and having but about thirty men for a guard, he marched two miles down the country by the side of a loch, till his men should conveen. There was not the least suspicion entertained of any danger, otherwise there would have been a much stronger guard about the Prince's person ; and there is no doubt to be made but that Lord Loudon had got certain information (perhaps from Grant of Dalrachny) of the small number of men who were to mount guard upon the Prince that night, which had induced him to try the experiment. Lady Macintosh (junior) was in great pain to have the Prince safe off from Moy when she heard of the alarm. The Prince returned the same night (Monday) to Moy and slept there. Mr. Gib, upon the alarm, having been sleeping in his cloaths, stept out with his pistols under his arm, and in the close he saw the Prince walking with his bonnet above his nightcap, and his shoes down in the heels ; and Lady Macintosh in her smock petticoat running through the close, speaking loudly and expressing her anxiety about the Prince's safety. Mr. Gib went along with the Prince down the side of the Loch, and left several waggons and other baggage at Moy, about which Lady Macintosh forbad Mr. Gib to be in the least anxious, for that she would do her best to take care of them. And indeed she was as good as her word ; for upon the Prince's return to Moy, Mr. Gib found all his things in great safety, the most of them having been carried off by Lady Macintosh's orders into a wood, where they would not readily have been discovered, though Lord Loudon and his men had proceeded to Moy. But they were most providentially stopt in their march, which happened thus. A black-smith and other four, with loaded muskets in their hands, were keeping watch upon a muir at some distance from Moy towards Inverness. As they were walking up and down, they happened to spy a body of men marching towards them, upon which the blacksmith fired his piece, and the other four followed his example. The Laird of MacLeod's piper (reputed the best of his business in all Scotland) was shot dead on the spot. Then the blacksmith (Fraser) and his trusty companions raised a cry (calling some particular regiments by their names) to the Prince's army to advance, as if they had been at hand, which so far imposed upon Lord Loudon and his command (a pretty considerable one), and struck them with such a panick, that instantly they beat a retreat, and made their way back to Inverness in great disorder, imagining the Prince's whole army to be at their heels. This gallant and resolute behaviour of the five, which speaks an uncommon presence of mind, happened much about the same time when the boy (Lauchlan Macintosh) arrived at Moy to give the alarm.

Another account (*ibid.* p. 269) mentions that the Prince, by rising hastily and going outside with light clothing, contracted

such a cold as stuck to him very long, and I may ev'n say endanger'd his life, which was one great reason of his staying so much at Inverness afterwards, to the great detriment of his affairs in other places.

In yet another account (*The Lyon in Mourning*, vol. ii, p. 246) it is mentioned that

Norman M'Leod (the Laird) who was upon the advance guard with about 70 men with him lying in a hollow not knowing what to doe by reason of the flashes of lightning from the heavens, that was confounding all their desines : for which a blacksmith, one of the five men that my Lady M'Intosh sent out as spies, fired upon them and killed M'Leods pyper hard by his side and wounded another of them, and then they all tooke the flight and returned to Inverness, halling the pyper after them till they got a horse and cart to cairrie him of.

The " pyper " was the celebrated Donald Bàn MacCrimmon, and I have somewhere read that a stone was raised to his memory near where he died, but if that is indeed so, Macintosh of Macintosh, who kindly made enquiries for me on the subject about the year 1930, found that his oldest tenants had no knowledge of any memorial.

The Rout of Moy took place on the night of Sunday, February 16, 1746, and Donald Fraser, the smith of Moy, was the hero of that fight. The night was a wild one, and on the westerly gale hurried dark thunder clouds. Loudon's advance guard, under MacLeod of MacLeod, lying in a hollow near Moy, found themselves unable to proceed farther without discovery, by reason of the flashes of lightning. The storm passed, and MacLeod's men moved forward. Donald Fraser had with him four men, and as the MacLeod militia approached them Donald and his companions fired their pieces, and ordered, at the tops of their voices, imaginary MacDonalds and Camerons to advance on the right and on the left, and to give no quarter. This subterfuge of the smith of Moy was aided by the presence of a number of peat-stacks standing on the ground, which were no doubt mistaken for men by the attacking force. Because of his gallant behaviour on that February night Donald Fraser was afterwards known locally as Captain nan Cóig, Captain of the Five, because with his little army of four men he had routed a large force.

A few hours before that strange fight the Prince had dined at Moy, his meal being " exceedingly genteel and plentiful ". A few days later he established his headquarters at Inverness, where he was entertained from the end of February until the middle of April by the dowager Lady Macintosh in her house in Church Street.

The anvil of Donald Fraser, the strong smith of Moy, is still to be seen outside Moy Hall. There is also preserved at Moy Hall a large family bible, with the date 1703, which has a romantic history. Together with family deeds and other valuables the bible was placed in troublous times in an iron chest which was sunk deep in the waters of Loch Moy. There it rested for many years, but the chest was so skilfully and strongly made that no water found its way into the bible, which was in Moy Hall, and in a perfect state of preservation when I was there in the summer of 1939. Among other valuable relics at Moy Hall are a set of dominoes used by the Duke of Cumberland, and two miniatures of Prince Charles Edward.

The legend of the Curse of Moy has been variously told, but although there are several versions of the events which led up to the curse, the curse itself is clear. It is that the lands of Moy and the chiefship of Clan Chattan shall never pass directly from father to son. It is indeed remarkable that only on very rare occasions since the uttering of that curse has Moy descended from father to son, and now Macintosh and his lady are no more, nor has their only son lived to succeed his father as chief. Gone are the days when the piper played of a morning and again at night, and when kings and queens were entertained here. It was at the time said that, with the passing of the last chief, a great Highlander and a great Highland gentleman, Moy lost its soul. Thus, within a few years, the Macintoshs and the Mac-Phersons have lost the head of their clan, and more than that, for neither Cluny nor Macintosh left an heir. One thinks of these lines from the past :

> Macintosh of Macintosh,
> The Laird of Moy Hall,
> He never had a baby
> And never never shall

Loch Pityoulish, near Aviemore

CHAPTER XXVIII

THE COUNTRY OF GRANTOWN-ON-SPEY

IF you cross the watershed at Slochd beyond Moy, you arrive at
Aviemore, from which Grantown-on-Spey is distant down the
Spey valley some twenty miles.

East of Aviemore is a broad, heathery country, comparatively
level. Here and there are small woods of Scots pine, or graceful
weeping birches, but the country is chiefly heather and very dry,
so that the railway, which passes through it, often sets wide
areas ablaze. In spring and early summer it is a pleasant
place, for many birds have their nesting haunts here. Curlews
sail overhead, uttering their trilling love-song, or (when their
young are hatched) shrieking raucous defiance at the human
intruder ; golden plovers pipe mournfully and oyster-catchers
utter their high-pitched whistling cries. There is one heathery

knoll in that country where is held each day the "lek" or fighting display of the blackcock of the district. From a hide my wife and I have watched the birds fly in at earliest dawn, and display until sunrise. When seen at close quarters (sometimes they have

Spey at Broomhill

displayed actually on the roof of our hiding tent) the blackcock is a handsome, even noble bird. The wings with deep blue glossy sheen are held slightly open and drooping, and the white inner coverts are spread fan-wise as the birds "spar" in couples or run lightly over the short heather in crouching attitudes, the while uttering a succession of low bubbling notes, very fast and eager. Even at mid-winter, when this moorland country is austere and snow-clad, the blackcock still hold their dawn tourneys, for they are strong, virile birds, impervious to cold.

Black-headed gulls have their colonies on reed-grown tarns on these moors; they arrive in March and nest in late April and May. They are handsome and apparently innocent birds, yet are

Upper Spey Valley

not above sucking one another's eggs, and I suspect the eggs of the red grouse also.

Near Kinveachy, where the birches are of singular beauty, the road divides as you travel down the Spey. One branch continues to Inverness by way of Carr Bridge (it passes Moy before reaching Inverness); the other winds down the Spey valley and approaches closely the village of Boat of Garten on its way.

Various place-names beginning with the word " Boat " are characteristic of the Spey valley. These places commemorate the sites of ferries which plied on the river in the days before there were bridges. To this day the place-names Boat of Garten, Blacksboat, Boat of Cromdale, Boat of Insh, and perhaps others, remain, but the majority of these names are found only in old records. Colonel Grant Smith, who was for many years Commissioner on the Seafield estates, informed me that the ferry-boat at Boat of Garten continued to ply until the present bridge was built in 1899, and that the Boat of Insh was abolished when the bridge was erected here in 1879. In his letter he mentioned that Boat of Cromdale was superseded by a suspension foot-bridge in 1881. This bridge was swept away in January 1920, when the present iron bridge, for foot and vehicle traffic, was made. Few of the Gaelic names of these " Boats " survive, but Boat of Garten in Gaelic is Coit Ghartain, and Boat of Insh is Coit Innse. Professor Watson, who sends me this information, writes that *coit* is Gaelic for a small boat, and is often used to designate a ferry-boat.

In a description of the district written in the year 1723 (Mac-Farlane's *Geographical Collections*, vol. i, p. 230), the names of some of the old Boats are given, in the free spelling of the period :

> Three myles above the boat of Spey at Fochabirs is another passage called boat of Budge, thence 3 myles furder up is another passage boat called boat of Fiddigh wher goes in the water of Fiddich into Spey running from S. to north : then 2 miles furder up, ther is the passage boat called boat of Skirdustan or Aberlour : thence 3 myles furder up, there is another passage called boat of Delnapot, below which enters in the water of Awin to Spey and runs from S. to North and has a ferry boat also. The next passage boat is called Cromwell six miles furder up within a myle of Castle Grant to the North.

Shaw (*History of Moray*, vol. i, p. 252) names the " passage boat of Gartenmore ". He tells us that here stood the house of Cumming of Glenchernich " as yet called Bigla's house, because Bigla, heiress of Glenchernich, married to the Laird of Grant, was the last of the Cummines that enjoyed that land ". Shaw continues :

> A current tradition beareth that at night a salmon net was cast out into the pool below the wall of the house, and a small rope, tied to the net and brought in at the window, had a bell hung at it, which rung when a salmon came into and shook the net.

The tradition of Bigla's House and its salmon-pool no longer survives in the district.

Bigla is also mentioned in an old MS. in the MacFarlane

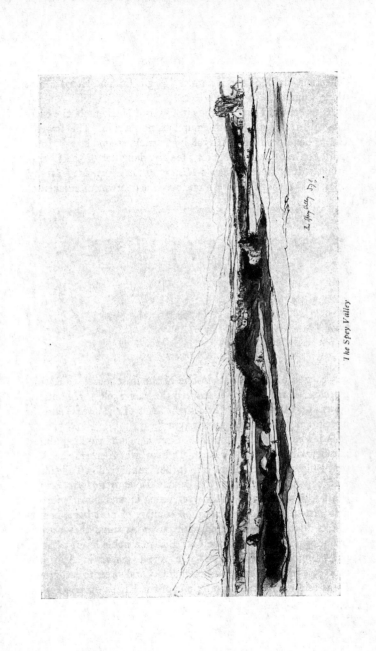

The Spey Valley

Collection, in which she is named " Beglit Cumine Heir to Lord Alexr. Cumin ".

Near Boat of Garten is the old tower of Muckerach, the early home of the Grants of Rothiemurchus, now a ruin. This tower is said to have been built in 1598 by Patrick, second son of John, Laird of Grant, and Margaret Stewart, daughter of the Earl of Athole. It is stated (Shaw's *History of the Province of Moray*, vol. i, p. 253) that the lintel stone over the doorway of Muckerach

The Dulnan

was carried off, and exists in one of the farmhouses at Rothie-murchus. On the stone is marked the year 1598, three antique crowns and three wolves' heads (the arms of the owner) and the inscription " IN GOD IS AL MY TREST ".

A few miles to the west of the Spey here, and running almost parallel with it, is the Water of Dulnan, which enters the Spey near Dulnan Bridge. Shaw calls it the " rapid rivulet Tuilenan ". At Sluggan, two miles up the Dulnan River from Carr Bridge, is a fine Wade bridge. This river, rising in, and flowing for the first part of its course through, a country of peat bogs, has its waters almost always tinted with peat : at times they are the colour of port wine. Above Carr Bridge a noble forest of Scots pine approaches the river. On forest tracks in April the chocolate-brown Morell mushroom, tasty and sweet to eat, grows. I was told many years ago by one of the King's deerstalkers at

Balmoral that this mushroom was a great favourite with the old Duke of Edinburgh.

Salmon are late in entering the Dulnan in any numbers, but from olden times the river has been celebrated for its autumn salmon. In an old description of the district (quoted in Mac-Farlane's *Geographical Collection*, vol. iii, p. 241) we have an interesting sidelight on the illegal fishing for salmon at their spawning season in the Dulnan centuries ago. The account is as follows :

There comes no salmon in this Water (in this account called the Water of Dullan), but extraordinary much Kipper, that is salmon in the forbidden time which are in such abundance, that a gentleman thinks nothing to kill 160 in a night. They used to feast the Sheriff, and so escape the fine, but the Commonalty pay some little thing.

The old name of the valley of the Dulnan is Gleann Cheathair-nich, Valley of the Hero or Freebooter.

Not far from the estuary of the Dulnan the river Nethy enters the Spey, on its opposite bank. The Nethy, which has its source high in the Cairngorms, is a swift stream, subject to violent spates. It derives its name from the ancient Celtic word *necht* which, according to Cormac, means pure or clean. Like other Highland streams, the Nethy was believed to be haunted by water spirits. There used to be a saying in the district when the Nethy began to rise rapidly, " Tha na Neithichean a' tighinn " (" The Nethy sprites are coming ") — vide *Celtic Place-Names of Scotland*, p. 210.

Near the Nethy is the old gallows tree at Lynstock. On this tree criminals were hung, and beneath it are said to be the marks of old graves. This tree is sometimes called the Tree of the Brothers, a name given it because, according to tradition, two brothers were hanged on it, and their graves, side by side, are, or were, to be seen beneath it.

The forest of Abernethy is a part of the old Caledonian Forest. Here the old Scots pines seed themselves so freely that beneath the trees are seen innumerable seedlings, fresh and strong, growing fast in their parents' shade.

In Abernethy forest are to be seen a few excellent specimens of the rare weeping variety of the Scots pine. Here the caper

Spey at Cromdale

caillie displays at dawn, and greyhens nest on the forest outskirts: here crossbills flit in small parties from tree to tree, tearing the pine cones to pieces with their strong, crossed bills and extracting the seeds.

On the Spey, perhaps eight miles below Nethy Bridge, is
Cromdale. The battle of Cromdale, which is commemorated by
the song " The Bonny Haughs o' Cromdale ", was fought in 1690,
the year after Claverhouse was slain at the battle of Killiecrankie.
At Cromdale Colonel Sir Thomas Livingstone, King William's
general, defeated what was left of Claverhouse's army commanded
by General Buchan. Buchan's force consisted mainly of Highlanders — MacLeans, MacDonalds, Camerons, MacPhersons and
Grants of Glenmoriston.

Livingstone and his troops came from Inverness, the Highlanders from the south-east. The Highland force had camped
the previous night at the farm of Lethendry, at the foot of the
Hill of Cromdale, and near the old kirk of Cromdale. Very early
on the morning of May 1, 1690, their outposts saw Livingstone's
troops fording the Spey at the ford below Dellachaple, but the
dragoons were upon them before the majority of those in camp
had time to put on their clothes. They retired to the Hill of
Cromdale where they fought valiantly, but were at length broken
and utterly defeated, leaving on the field 400 slain and prisoners.

The road from Grantown which leads south-east through the
hills to Strathdon and Balmoral passes less than three miles from
the site of the battle of Cromdale. This road, winding across the
high moor, passes through some very fine scenery. Descending
a steep hill at Bridge of Brown, its winding course then ascends
to Tomintoul, which shares with Braemar the dignity of being
the highest village in the Highlands. From Tomintoul the road
still climbs, by way of the Conglass Water, to the Lecht, which
it crosses at a height of 2,048 feet above the sea. On the descent
to the inn at Cockbridge (1,322 feet above the sea) a grand view is
had of the eastern Cairngorms, and on a July day of great heat I
have seen from here the extensive snowfield in the north-east
corrie of Ben MacDhui gleaming in the sunlit air. A short
distance below Cockbridge the road again climbs across the hills
to the Gairn, and thence over further high ground to join the
main Deeside road just above Balmoral.

From Nethy Bridge to Grantown-on-Spey is a distance of five miles. Grantown is on the north bank of the Spey, and on the

Castle Grant

rising ground above the town stands Castle Grant, the ancestral home of the chiefs of Grant.

Castle Grant, or Freuchie as it was called of old, is one of the most historic castles in the Highlands. As far back as the fourteenth century the family of Sir John Grant are denominated "of

Freuchy ", for it appears that about this time Sir John received as a gift from the King of Scotland a part of the Strathspey lands of the Cummings. A century later another Sir John Grant was Sheriff Principal at Inverness, and his musket is preserved among the arms which find a resting-place in Castle Grant. On the barrel of the musket is the Latin inscription "Dominus Johannes Grant, Miles, Vicecomes de Inverness, anno 1434 ".

In the year 1694 Ludovick Grant, 8th Earl of Freuchie, received a charter from William and Mary, ordaining that the castle of Freuchie be called the castle of Grant.

I like Shaw's description of Castle Grant, written only a few years after the rising of 1745, " The house is a grand building, environed with gardens, inclosures, and much planting ". Indeed the strongest impression I received as I climbed, one morning of early June, toward the old grey-harled castle was the beauty of its trees, and their grateful shelter. Although the day was young the sun was shining with intense power and heat, and a magnificent avenue of old limes afforded pleasant shade.

The house of Freuchie or house of Grant, now known always as Castle Grant, is an austere, four-storied building. The towers, of which there were four originally, are the oldest part ; they date from around the year 1200. One of the towers is named Lady Barbie's Tower, and there is a tradition that it is haunted by the ghost of one of the family, Lady Barbie or Barbara, who for some misdeed was walled-in alive here. In the eighteenth century, in the time of Adams, the castle was added to, and the front is now the back. The simple austerity of the building is heightened from the fact that there is no garden beneath the castle, and if you look out from it you see only grass fields and stately trees — very green and pleasant on the June day when I visited the place.

The hall of Castle Grant is full of weapons, belonging mainly to the Grant Fencibles, who were disbanded in the year 1756. An enormous musket is known as " Lady Anne Grant's Pocket Pistol ". In the hall is hung a portrait of a fine wild type of

Highlander, dark-featured and eager. This portrait is named "Alasdair Grant Mór 1714". There is also a striking portrait, by Watt, of the family piper, also dated 1714. There is a tradition that this piper walked, piping all the way, from Inverness to Castle Grant, a distance of more than thirty miles, perhaps for a wager. He was approaching Castle Grant and was doubtless being acclaimed by his supporters, when he dropped dead. The bag of his pipes was found to be full of blood. It is said that a cross marks, or marked, the spot where he fell. When I heard this tale, I was reminded of the story of the great MacArthur piper who marched (with other competitors) up the steep slopes of Arthur's Seat, Edinburgh, piping all the way. The piper who first reached the hill-top was to receive as a prize a hatful of gold which had been placed there. MacArthur arrived first. To show his contempt for the gold he kicked the hat down the hill. But he received a permanent injury in accomplishing his feat, and was not the same man again.

I thought that, if there was any truth in these two traditions of famous pipers, the skill of those who piped in olden times must have been little appreciated by their patrons, if they permitted the highland pipe to be lowered to an instrument of mere feats of endurance.

As one enters through the door of Castle Grant one steps at once into a world of the past. The fine organ in the castle was given by Queen Anne to one of her ladies-in-waiting on her marriage to the chief of Grant. Here one is surrounded by old portraits, by old furniture. Great beams of pine, erected centuries ago, remain in their full strength: there is to be seen the Lochindorb Beam, from which prisoners were hanged for sheep-stealing. In some of the upper rooms the old wooden floors are nailed down with pegs of wood, and on the floor boards are marks showing that they were cut with an adze, for the surface is still uneven.

Many of the pictures in Castle Grant are of great value. One which, though not among the most precious, is nevertheless of

unusual interest, bears the title " Portrait of Hen Wife 1706 ".
This shows a shrewd and determined old woman, one who held
an office that was of considerable importance in the families of
Highland chiefs. The tenants in those days paid a part of their
rent in hens. When the hens were brought to the castle the Hen
Wife carefully examined them, and if they were below the
required standard made the tenant bring more hens. The

Lochindorb

receipts for the hens are still kept in Castle Grant ; they show
that the tenants paid twenty hens at intervals of six months.

Although it is some little distance away from the country of
Grantown-on-Spey, a few words should perhaps be written on
the historic castle on Lochindorb. This loch lies about midway
between the rivers Findhorn and Spey, and the castle stands on
a small island in the loch. For centuries the castle has been a
ruin, yet its strong walls remain. Shaw mentions that in the year
1335, when the Earl of March defeated and killed David de
Strathbogie, Earl of Athole, at Kilblain, and raised the siege of
Kildrummy Castle, the Earl of Athole's lady fled to the castle of
Lochindorb. Sir Alexander Gordon laid siege to it, but next
year King Edward (Edward the Third) of England obliged him
to desist. In the year 1606 the Earl of Moray, Superior of the
district, disponed to Sir John Campbell of Calder certain lands,

" together with the Loch of Lochindorb, with the houses in it, and the neighbouring Shielings ".

At the time of Edward I, the castle of Lochindorb was a strong fortress in the possession of the Comyns. King Edward (grandfather of Edward III who later besieged it) captured the castle, and occupied it for some time. He did not indeed take the castle without a hard struggle, but his investing force time and again hurled their engines of war at the massive building on its small island, and at last breached its walls. The site on the south-east bank of the loch where the besiegers encamped is still known.

In Shaw (vol. i, p. 235) it is mentioned that within the walls of the castle are the vestiges of houses and those of a church. In the same volume and page is an interesting account of a plant, known locally as Lochindorb kail, which grows on the castle island. This is said to be a mixture of red cabbage and common turnip, sowed by the last possessor of the place. These plants were used as greens at the tables of the country people, and were transplanted into their gardens : young cattle were also ferried to the island in order to feed upon them. Some of the turnip-shaped roots of the plants were, it is said, almost one pound in weight in favoured situations.

Loch Morlich

CHAPTER XXIX

THE APPROACHES TO THE CAIRNGORMS

THE Cairngorm hills rise from a vigorous remnant of the ancient Caledonian Forest, and among the old pines weeping birches show a more tender shade of green of a summer's day. The old forest north of the Cairngorms holds varied and beautiful lochs. Loch Morlich and Loch Eanaich are described in Chapter XXX. Loch an Eilein, Loch of the Island, which some people consider to be the most beautiful loch in Scotland, is accessible even to the aged and infirm, for a road leads up to it through Rothiemurchus forest from Aviemore — from which centre it can be reached in half an hour.

Loch an Eilein lies in the depths of the forest and is not seen the road, or indeed from any part of the low country, until its wooded shore is actually reached. Behind the loch rise the wooded foothills of the Cairngorms, and some of the high summits are also seen. On the island from which Loch an Eilein takes its name is an ancient ruin. Timothy Pont (of whom James Gordon, Parson of Rothiemay, warning his readers, writes that " in Mr.

287

Timothies Papers thur manie things false ") speaks of Loch an Eilein as " Rothumurcus loch a myl long ". He also mentions that on it " is a tour in ane Inche " but does not describe the "tour", of which the ruins still remain. This old tower, on which was one of the last nesting-places of the osprey in the Scottish Highlands, is believed to date back to the days of Robert the Bruce and to have been built by the Red Comyn. The Shaws, said to be descended from the Thane of Fife, subsequently owned the lands of Rothiemurchus, but Allan Shaw, the last of the Shaws of Rothiemurchus, was outlawed for the murder of his stepfather, Sir John Dallas. This happened in the sixteenth century, and between 1570 and 1580 the chief of Grant purchased the estate, or rather the right to hold it if he could, and bestowed it on his second son, Patrick, the direct ancestor of the present Grants of Rothiemurchus. Macintosh, as Shaw's chief, considered that the defaulter's property should have fallen to him, and Patrick's possession was by no means an easy one. But he and his descendants have retained these lands ever since, without the loss of a single acre. The Shaws of Rothiemurchus claim descent from Shaw, the leader of Clan Chattan at the battle of the North Inch of Perth in 1396. The original grave-stone of this leader, sometimes called Shaw Mór, with the five small stones upon it, can be seen in Rothiemurchus burial-ground. There are markings on the stone, now much weathered. Mr. MacKenzie Shaw, a descendant of Shaw Mór, tells me that the old stone, which had been moved, has now on his advice been restored to its original resting-place.

Even as far back as the sixteenth century the castle on Loch an Eilein was a ruin, but the first of the Grants of Rothiemurchus restored it lest the Shaws should not submit to his ownership of their ancient lands ; he also destroyed an old fort of the Shaws on the Doune hill. In 1690 Grizzel Mhór, wife of James Grant of Rothiemurchus, successfully defended the castle of Loch an Eilein when it was attacked by General Buchan after the battle of Cromdale.

More than a century before, in or about the year 1524, the strong tower on Loch an Eilein was the scene of a grim revenge. Lauchlan Macintosh of "Dunnachton," chief of his clan, a "verrie honist and wyse gentleman", had been murdered by a near kinsman. The clan Macintosh, enraged at this murder, pursued the murderer and his followers to the castle on Loch an Eilein, and put them to the sword to a man. Another account says that

Loch an Eilein

the three chief murderers were kept in chains in the fortress on Loch an Eilein until 1531, when they were tried by the Earl of Moray and found guilty. The chief murderer (Malcolmson) was beheaded and quartered : the two Davidsons were first tortured, then hanged and their heads fixed on poles at the scene of the crime.

In MacFarlane's *Geographical Collections* (vol. iii, p. 240) is an interesting account of Loch an Eilein, apparently written in the late sixteenth century :

Rothemurcus belongs to Patrick Grant, a Cadet of Grant's family; but formerly it belonged to the Schaws, who yet possess the Parish, Alexander Schaw of Dell being Head of the Tribe. The Schaws are able fighting

U

men, and acknowledge Mackintosh to be their Chieftain, and go under his Banner. The Schaws killed the Cumins that dwelt here, who built a Castle in the middest of a great Loch called Loch Iland (Loch an Eilein). This Castle is usefull to the Countrey in time of troubles or wars : for the people put in their goods and children here, and it is easily defended, being environed with steep Hills, and Craigs on each side, except towards the East.

After the battle of Cromdale on May 1, 1690, Colonel Mac-Donald or MacDonell of Keppoch and his men " attempted to reduce the Castle of Lochinelen in Rothiemurchus, and were by that laird and his tenants beat off with loss " (Shaw's *History of the Province of Moray*, vol. iii, p. 130).

Loch an Eilein in more recent times was celebrated because of its ospreys, and as the osprey became rare great efforts were made by collectors to steal the eggs, one hardy man swimming out in the cold of an April night and bringing back the eggs in his cap — the only article of clothing he wore ! Now, alas, the osprey has gone from the Scottish Highlands as a nesting bird, although stragglers on migration to and from Scandinavia are still at times seen on Strathspey sometimes in April and May.

Near Loch an Eilein is Loch Gamhna, and between the two Rathad nam Mèirleach, the Caterans' Road, wanders through the forest. This old Thieves' Road begins in Lochaber in the west, winds through Rothiemurchus, then along the south side of Loch Morlich toward the east through the pass of Lochan Uaine, the Green Loch. There is, I imagine, no man living at the present day who can follow that old track throughout its course, which must be close on a hundred miles. But along the shore of Loch Gamhna, thence to the south shore of Loch an Eilein, it is still easy to trace. Between Loch an Eilein and Loch Morlich many tracks lead through the forest and tend to obliterate Rathad nam Mèirleach, but along the south shore of Loch Morlich it is not difficult to find. The Thieves' Road was used by the Camerons and Macintoshs from Lochaber, the MacPhersons from Cluny, and other Highlanders in Badenoch and the upper parts of Strathspey when they made forays to the east, to raid the lands of the fertile Laich of Moray of their cattle, which they considered

to be their lawful booty. This is well shown in a letter from
" Allan Camerone of Lochyll " written in 1645 to the Laird of
Grant. In this letter Lochiel, in apologising for injuries and

Loch Morlich

indignities inflicted on one of the chief of Grant's men, mentions
that the raiders did not know that the man " was ane Graunt,
but thocht that he was ane Morrayman ", and elsewhere in the
letter records that the raid was intended to be " to Morrayland,
quhair all men taks their prey ".

The Rev. W. Forsyth, D.D., in his book *In the Shadow of*

Cairngorm, mentions that on one occasion the Camerons from Lochaber made a raid on the lands of the men of Tulloch, who had gone to Forres for a millstone. When the worthies of Tulloch returned with their millstone — which they had rolled all the way from Forres by means of a pin thrust through the hole in the stone's centre — they found their cattle gone. The day was Sunday, and the men of Rothiemurchus were in church when their kinsmen from Tulloch, or a messenger from them, burst into the church with the news of the raid. It was known that the thieves were likely to return with their booty over high and unfrequented ground, and they were found near the head of Glen Eanaich, where, after a sharp encounter, they were driven off and the stolen cattle recovered. The only man who fell in that fight was Fear nan Casan Caol, the Man with the Thin Legs, and he is commemorated in a small loch below Loch Eanaich named Lochan mhic a' Ghille Chaoil. Another version of this raid and its abrupt termination tells of the naming of Lochan mhic a' Ghille Chaoil. This version makes the raid directed on the cattle of Glen Eanaich. The day being Sunday, the Rothiemurchus men had journeyed from their shielings in Glen Eanaich down to Rothiemurchus to attend the kirk, the men wearing the kilt, blue jackets and blue bonnets, the women in homespun gowns, each man and woman wearing the plaid. When word was brought to the church of the raid a swift-footed youth named Mac a' Ghille Chaoil, the son of the Thin Lad, was the first to reach the raiders and engaged them single-handed beside the lochan until his friends arrived. He was killed, and a rusted dirk found near the loch may confirm the tradition. It is said that Mac a' Ghille Chaoil buried treasure in Rothiemurchus, where it remains hid to this day. But it is averred that if a white snake should be seen to enter a hole, there will be found the treasure of Mac a' Ghille Chaoil.

Across the Spey from Rothiemurchus rises, from terraces of weeping birches, the bold rock of Craigellachie. The ancient war-cry of the Clan Grant was " Seas buan, Creag Eileachaidh "

("Stand Fast, Craigellachie"). Ruskin in his *Two Paths* gives a delicate pen-picture of this rock and its associations :

> In one of the loneliest districts of Scotland, where the peat cottages are darkest, just at the western foot of that great mass of the Grampians which encircles the sources of the Spey and the Dee, the main road which traverses the chain winds round the foot of a broken rock called the Crag, or Craig Ellachie. There is nothing remarkable in either its height or form ; it is darkened with a few scattered pines, and touched along its summit with a flush of heather ; but it constitutes a kind of headland, or leading promontory, in the group of hills to which it belongs — a sort of initial letter of the mountains ; and thus stands in the mind of the inhabitants of the district, the Clan Grant, for a type of their country, and of the influence of that country upon themselves. Their sense of this is beautifully indicated in the war-cry of the clan — "Stand fast, Craig Ellachie". You may think long over those few words without exhausting the deep wells of feeling and thought contained in them — the love of the native land, and the assurance of their faithfulness to it. . . . You could not but have felt, had you passed beneath it at the time when so many of England's dearest children were being defended by the strength of heart of men born at its foot, how often among the delicate Indian palaces, whose marble was pallid with horror, and whose vermillion was darkened with blood, the remembrance of its rough grey rocks and purple heaths must have risen before the sight of the Highland soldier ; how often the hailing of the shot and the shriek of battle would pass away from his hearing, and leave only the whisper of the old pine branches — "Stand fast, Craig Ellachie".

In the old *Description of Strathspey* (from which I quoted the interesting account of the castle on Loch an Eilein) mention is made of Craigellachie :

> The River Spey taketh its beginning at a great Craig called Craig I'lachie, which divideth this Countrey from Badenoch. This word Craig Ilachie is the Laird of Grant's Slugan. When ever the word is cryed through this Countrey, all the Inhabitants are obliged under a great Fine or Mulct, to Rise in Arms and repair themselves to a meeting place in the middest of the Countrey lying on the Rivers side called Bellentone and there to receive the Lairds Commands.

The derivation of the place-name Craigellachie has provided material for discussion among Celtic scholars, but Professor Watson has shown (*Celtic Place-Names of Scotland*, p. 478) that the original name is Craigeileachaidh, Rock of the Rocky Place.

The place-name Aviemore (Craigellachie rises close to the

village of Aviemore) has been shown by the same authority to be in its original form Agaidh Mhór, Great Gap or Cleft.[1] " A little knowledge is a dangerous thing ", and when the average Gaelic-speaking man, unfamiliar with the district, is asked the meaning of the name he usually answers, " Oh, yes. It is Amhuinn (Avon) Mór, the Great River." That this plausible derivation is incorrect is shown by the early form of the name, Agaidh Mhór.

Some seven miles down the Spey, on the north bank of the river, is Tullochgorm, a name familiar to pipers and dancers because of the famous Highland dance air or strathspey called after the place. In an old MS. account of the district mention is made of Tullochgorm :

> The Chief family here is that of the Clanphadrike,[2] Tullachcorume being the Head of that Tribe of the name of Grant. In old times there frequented this Family a Spirit called Meg Mulloch.[3] It appeared like a little Boy, and in dark nights would hold a candle before the Goodman and show him the way home, and if the Goodwife would not come to bed, it would cast her in beyond him and if she refused to bring what he desired, it would cast it before him.

In another account Meg or Mag Mulloch was said to have had " the left hand all over hairy ".

The Shaws of Rothiemurchus at their ancestral house, The Doune, sheltered a being of this kind. This sprite was known as Bodach an Dùin, and it is said that when the Grants of Rothie-murchus displaced the Shaws, the Bodach, chanting a Gaelic rhyme, left his old home and afterwards guarded the tomb of the Shaws in Rothiemurchus churchyard. Tutelary fairies were at times in the form of a *glaistig* — a thin grey little woman, dressed in green, with long yellow hair which reached to the ground : they sometimes took the form of a *gruagach*. Milk was each night poured into a hollow stone known as Clach na Gruagaich, and the *gruagach* drank the milk during the hours of darkness. Unless this was done, no milk was to be had at the next milking.

---

[1] Cf. Gealagaidh (Gallovie) where the burn comes down foaming white.
[2] Clann Phadraig.   [3] Properly *molach*, hairy.

A couple of miles east of Coylum Bridge is Loch Pityoulish, which has associations with the past. At the east end of the loch is a hollow known as Lag nan Cuimeanach, the Hollow of the Cummings, where it is said Shaw of Rothiemurchus waylaid and slew a party of the hated clan who had ruled the district before the Shaws.

The water horse lived in this loch, and enticed children to their doom.

Near here, and almost opposite Kinchurdy, the church of Kincardine stands above the south bank of the Spey. The walls of this church are very old, and when, in 1897, the building was restored, these walls had stood unchanged since the fatal day in the fifteenth century when the Grants took summary vengeance upon the Cummings here. The tradition of that grim revenge is in danger of being lost in the mists of antiquity : there are features in the tale which recall the burning of the church at Trumpan in MacLeod's country of Skye, by the men of Clanranald.

Chapman, in his *MS. History of the Grants* (quoted by Forsyth in his book *In the Shadow of Cairngorm*), describes that old tragedy enacted in the church of Kincardine. When on a visit to Stewart of Kincardine (the first Stewart, a son of the Wolf of Badenoch, received a charter of the lands of Kincardine from Robert the Third of Scotland in the year 1400), the Laird of Grant was murdered by his hereditary enemies the Cummings. After the crime the Stewarts and the followers of the murdered chief pursued the Cummings furiously, and were fast overtaking them when the fugitives, believing that there they would find sanctuary, took refuge in the church. The Grants and the Stewarts held a consultation as to what should be done. They were reluctant to desecrate the holy place, yet they were resolved that the murderers should not escape. Most of the churches in the Highlands at that time had thatched roofs, and it was resolved to fire the building by shooting a burning arrow into the thatch. That arrow had scarce found its mark when a dense cloud of smoke, quickly followed by red flames, rose into the clear air of Strathspey. The Cummings were trapped beyond all hope of escape, yet one of their number, a man of gigantic stature, forced his way out and, mad with rage and half blinded with smoke, defended himself manfully. But he was slain by a mighty blow from a two-handed sword, " which sword ", writes Chapman, " to this day lies in the representative of Clan Cheran's

Leper's Window, Kincardine Church

house ". It seems that this house must have been named Dellachaple, for Shaw in his *History of Moray* records that " in Cromdale is Dellachaple, the seat of the head of the Clan Chiaran ".

It was thus that the church of Kincardine became a ruin : its building goes back to very ancient times. The legend is that the Laird of Kincardine and the Laird of Tulloch contended for the honour of having a church on their lands. The Laird of Tulloch gained his point, but the stones which were taken to Tulloch for the building of the church were miraculously moved over to

Kincardine during the hours of darkness. At last the Laird of Tulloch, recognising that it were better for him to bow to the will of Heaven, agreed that the church should be built where it now stands. According to the tradition of the country, the church is dedicated to a Celtic saint named Tomhaldaidh, of whom there seems to be no record elsewhere in the Highlands.

In the south wall of the church of Kincardine is a small opening. This is known as the Leper's Window, and through it those whose infirmities did not permit them to enter the church were able to watch the celebration of the Mass.

The country in which the church of Kincardine stands has changed little since the days when the old church with its heather-thatched roof was a harmonious part of that earlier world. It was on an evening of early summer that I visited the place. The Spey, shrunken by the drought, flowed leisurely between its high banks, the haunt of many sandmartins. In the air was the scent of birches — that most delightful of all Highland scents — and in a field of young oats a green plover could be seen brooding her eggs. Through the warm, perfumed air came the husky call of an invisible cuckoo. I entered the small burial-ground and saw a gnarled laburnum tree, centuries old, which may have been there on the day the church was fired. That ancient tree was a glory of golden blossom which drooped in clusters from the main stem, which had withstood the snow, the frost, and the gales of many, many winters.

Near the Leper's Window lay the old font, a symbol of an earlier but no less sincere form of worship.

I looked south, and through the haze of evening saw, beyond the wooded slopes of the Slugan, white snow-fields lit by the sinking sun on the high Cairngorms. That weathered font, that Leper's Window, and most of all that venerable laburnum tree with its pendulous, fragile flower clusters, spoke of a past from which we have much to learn ; when the restless speed of the present mechanical age was undreamed of, and simple things gave pleasure. At ten o'clock the sun dipped behind the

Monadh Liath to the north-west, yet sandpipers continued to fly above Spey, and oyster-catchers piped shrilly near the river, where curlews drifted on wings quickly and delicately driven.

In the forest which clothes the foothills and the approaches to the Cairngorms are many walks — many byways where the walker without interfering with sport may wander for hours with never a sight of a house or human being. His companions are the capercaillie which flies rocket-like through the trees, and the small crested titmice which flit like tiny elves among the upper branches of the pines. The hot summer sun draws a perfume from the old trees, and as the traveller sits on some sun-warmed bank in a little clearing in the forest he sometimes sees, on an early summer day of cloudless sky and brilliant sun, strange waves of mist drift past him on the breeze. The ground is dry and sun-baked and for a minute he is perhaps puzzled — then investigation shows him that this is no vapour but rather clouds of pollen dust which wandering airs have shaken from the pines. Beneath these pines he may find, if fortune favours him, that rare and lowly plant *Linnaea borealis* — a plant which the great naturalist Linnaeus named after himself, for in lowliness and self-effacement he found himself in affinity with it. The blossoms of this eagerly-sought plant are very delicate, of a pale-pink colour and sweet-scented. More common, and more robust, are the pink or white china-like blooms of the bearberry and the cowberry which grow in, and on the outskirts of, the old forest. The true cranberry — with which bearberry and cowberry are often confused — is rare, and the flowers, smaller and more delicate, are found in boggy ground ; they do not grow on the sun-dried knolls loved by the cowberry and trailing bearberry.

" The old order giveth place to new ", and even the character of the old pine forest is changing. Large areas of late years have been replanted by the Forest Commission. Douglas firs and spruces in places grow evenly and closely, and the distinctive character of the old open forest has been lost. During the war of 1914–18 Canadian foresters felled great areas of old pines in

Glen More. Many of these trees were never taken away, and at the close of that war lay with bleaching stems where they had been cut down in their venerable age yet in the vigour of their growth.[1] The planting of young trees has been a bad thing for the stock of native blackcock. These hardy birds are justly accused of doing damage to the leading shoots and their numbers have been greatly reduced by shooting : their decrease must be regretted by all nature lovers. Beside the forest lochs the melancholy whistle of the greenshank is heard in spring, and the liquid notes of courting curlews fall pleasantly on the ear. Sometimes the red flash of a greater spotted woodpecker is seen as the bird flies through the trees. Sandpipers court over the forest streams, and the goosander, in handsome black-and-white plumage, fishes in the tree-girt lochs of a summer evening. High over the scene the lordly golden eagle sails, and red deer when autumn comes make harsh music in the corries. Winter approaches. At first she lays her cold fingers on the hill-tops, whitening them with snow and binding the springs with frost. Gradually she draws near the forest, and one morning, when the laggard sun peeps behind the ridge of Cairngorm, the trees rise no longer dark but clad in a delicate dress of white. Each bough glistens as the sun shines on the ice crystals of this virgin snow, and the old trees stir gently in their winter sleep, then, shaking themselves free of the snow, hold up their resinous needles to the grateful warmth of the low winter sun.

[1] Again during the war of 1939–45 great inroads were made on the old trees, so that some of the glens are entirely altered.

Strathavon, near Tomintoul

CHAPTER XXX

A PASS OF THE EASTERN CAIRNGORMS

LÀIRIG LAOIGH is in English Calf's Pass and has apparently received its name because, in the days when drove roads crossed the Cairngorms, calves were driven through it on their way to the south markets. The pass is an easier one than Làirig Ghrù and thus would naturally have been chosen by drovers who had young beasts to drive.

At the present day Làirig Laoigh is often crossed by hikers, who undertake the walk for the fine air and the healthy exercise, but in olden times the pass was used by good walkers of Upper Strathspey for a more practical reason — because it was the shortest way back to their homes from the south. Tragedies sometimes occurred on this hill track in winter. One of these disasters is chronicled at the beginning of January in the year 1805. It appears that late the previous December a party of seven soldiers, natives of upper Strathspey, set out from their quarters in Edinburgh to walk home on leave. They rested a night at Braemar, and as the morning on which they left that township was threatening they were warned of the danger of attempting to cross Làirig Laoigh that day. Deep snow covered the hills, but the men, anxious to return to their families, could not be dissuaded from setting out. They toiled up Glen Derry, but before they had reached the head of the glen snow began to fall. They crossed the River A'an, invisible beneath the snow, below Loch A'an. They reached the small loch, Lochan a' Bhainne, and here, at fault in the choking drift, they followed the Glas Allt instead of breasting the gradual slope of Làirig Laoigh. Gradually their strength left them : one by one they sank down and died in the snow, and of the seven who set out through the hills, only two survived that terrible walk. The two men who came safely through the ordeal were Donald Elder and Alexander Forsyth. At the height of the blizzard the travellers became separated, but the two brothers Forsyth kept together, and when the younger grew faint and lay down in exhaustion his brother lifted him on to his shoulder, toiling grimly with his heavy burden against the fury of the storm. The rest revived the younger man, and he reached his destination, but his brother, exhausted by his gallant action, failed to reach safety.

It must be nearly a century since Làirig Laoigh was used as a drove road, yet the track is still distinct, and it is interesting to see that on a dry and gently-sloping face it divides into many branches, showing that here the beasts spread out and perhaps fed a little. When boggy ground is approached the tracks again converge, for the cattle evidently walked here in single file.

Làirig Laoigh can be reached from Nethy Bridge, by Forest Lodge and Rynettin, or from Aviemore, by Coylum Bridge and Glen More. From Nethy Bridge the road winds through the beautiful pine forest of Abernethy, then out on to the open moor at Rynettin and across a country of moor and loch until the old shieling of Revoan [1] is reached. Làirig Laoigh leaves the road about half a mile beyond Revoan.

[1] Gaelic Ruighe a' Bhothain, Ridge of the Hut.

If the Làirig be approached from Aviemore, the main road along the south bank of the Spey is left at Coylum Bridge and a rough forest road is followed through the old pine trees to Loch Morlich, a beautiful loch of considerable size which lies beneath Cairngorm. The derivation of the place-name Morlich has proved a hard nut for Gaelic scholars, but Professor Watson tells me that the name is Loch Mórthulaich, Loch of the Big 'Tulach', or ridgy hill.

On the shore of Loch Morlich a formidable spectre had his haunt. In MacFarlane's *Geographical Collections* (vol. iii, p. 242) is the following account (apparently written in 1670) of this spectre :

Above this Parish (Kincardine) lyeth the Glen-More, where is a great Firr Wood with much Birch. Here is a great Loch, out of which runneth a Water, which runneth through Rothiemurcus, called Druie & runneth into the Spey. They use to bring down their timber on this Water. Here is the famous Hill called Kairne Gorum, which is four miles high. Here, it is said, there are Minerals : for Gold hath been found here. This Hill aboundeth with excellent Crystall. Much Deer and Roe here. The people of this Parish much neglect labouring, being addicted to the Wood, which leaves them poor. There is much talking of a Spirit called Ly-Erg (Làmh-dhearg) that frequents the Glen-More. He appears with a red hand in the habit of a Souldier and challenges men to fight with him, as lately in '69 he fought with three Brothers one after another, who immediately dyed thereafter.

A knoll near the west shore of Loch Morlich was the home of Domhnall Mór Bad an t-Sìthein, Big Donald of the Clump of Trees of the Fairy Knoll. Donald was reputed to be the King of the Fairies, yet was a harmless sprite without the sinister record of Bodach Làmh-dhearg, the Spectre of the Red Hand. But Red Hand appears in a more kindly light in the following story :

The wraith was said by tradition to be connected with the family of Stewart of Kincardine. One of that family when hunting in Glen More killed a hind. He was about to *grallach* the animal when he found that his *sgian dubh* or hunting knife which he had laid on the ground beside him had disappeared. Wondering at this, he took the knife from his dirk, but scarcely had he laid it on the ground when it too vanished. He was mystified, and perhaps suspected the Red-handed Spectre, but it was not until some time later that he met the ghost. He was on the shore of Loch Morlich when he observed an old man wrapped in a grey plaid and with one of his hands red and blood-stained. The spectre returned the two knives to the hunter, but upbraided him for killing the hinds of Glen More.

Of the Red-handed Spectre Scott (*Marmion*, canto iv, 22) writes as follows :

> Marvell'd Sir David of the Mount ;
> Then, learn'd in story, 'gan recount
>   Such chance had happ'd of old,
> When once, near Norham, there did fight,
> A spectre fell of fiendish might,
> In likeness of a Scottish knight,
>   With Brain Bulmer bold,
> And train'd him nigh to disallow
> The aid of his baptismal vow.
> ' And such a phantom, too, 'tis said,
> With Highland broadsword, targe, and plaid,
>   And fingers, red with gore,
> Is seen in Rothiemurcus glade,
> Or where the sable pine-trees shade
> Dark Tomantoul, and Auchnaslaid,
>   Dromouchty, or Glenmore.
> And yet, whate'er such legends say,
> Of warlike demon, ghost, or fay,
>   On mountain, moor, or plain,
> Spotless in faith, in bosom bold,
> True son of chivalry should hold,
>   These midnight terrors vain ;
> For seldom have such spirits power
> To harm, save in the evil hour,
> When guilt we meditate within,
> Or harbour unrepented sin.'

Sir Walter gives the following note :

The forest of Glenmore, in the North Highlands, is believed to be haunted by a spirit called Lham-dearg, in the array of an ancient warrior, having a bloody hand, from which he takes his name. He insists upon those with whom he meets doing battle with him ; and the clergyman, who makes up an account of the district, extant in the MacFarlane MS in the Advocates' Library, gravely assures us, that, in his time, Lham-dearg fought with three brothers whom he met in his walk, none of whom long survived the ghostly conflict.

The east shore of Loch Morlich is of golden sand, hot to the naked feet when the strong summer sun shines down upon it and causes the wavelets of the loch to sparkle. At such a time it is pleasant to rest beside the loch, for the air is sweetly perfumed with birch and fir, and the birds of the loch — sandpiper and oyster-catcher, curlew and ringed plover — make music. There are good trout in Loch Morlich, and the osprey, which formerly nested on an old pine beside that loch as well as on the castle of Loch an Eilein, must in its day have captured many of them.

The juniper, which in most Highland districts grows in the form of a bush, is, I think, found at its greatest height around Loch Morlich. There is one juniper on the south side of the loch which stood no less than 24 feet high when I measured it in or about the year 1927.

Half an hour's walk east of Loch Morlich is Lochan Uaine, the Green Loch. It lies, sheltered by old pines, in a wooded defile between Meall a' Bhuachaille, the Herdsman's Hill, to the north and Craig nan Gall to the south, and is one of the most beautiful of the lesser lochs of the Cairngorms.

At the head of the pass beyond the loch, near the deserted shieling of Revoan, the track across Làirig Laoigh leaves the old road from Loch Morlich to Abernethy and leads east into the hills, passing above Loch a' Gharbh Choire with its wooded islands and its black-headed gull colony. To the west rise abruptly the rocky slopes of Mam Suim. The upper reaches of the Nethy are crossed by a good footbridge, and after the Nethy is left behind the track travels south-east, at a height of 2,600 feet above sea level. Below the shoulder of Bynack Mór (3,574 feet) Làirig Laoigh crosses exposed moorland, then traverses a green, moist corrie where cloudberries grow thickly. In the corrie is Fuaran nan Granntach, the Grants' Well, named because a party of the Grants rested here on an expedition to Deeside.

Almost as soon as it leaves this corrie (Coire Odhar) the Làirig enters the county of Banff and continues in that county until, at the head of Glen Derry, it reaches the shire of Aberdeen. Beneath Bynack Mór the track passes below remarkable out-crops of rocks which are named the Barns of Bynack, perhaps because of their fancied resemblance to giant barns. A mile beyond the Barns is a small loch, Lochan a' Bhainne, the Tarn of the Milk. The Làirig then descends to the A'an and crosses that river rather less than a mile below Loch A'an, at Ath nam Fiann, the Ford of the Fianna, or Fingalians.

The view from Làirig Laoigh is less grand than from the sister pass Làirig Ghrù, but where it crosses the watershed between the Nethy and the A'an a good view is had of Beinn a' Bhùird and Ben A'an, and of Culardoch (2,953 feet) rising beyond them.

After the Làirig has crossed the A'an it rises gradually to the watershed between Strath A'an and Deeside, reaching this water-shed at the head of Glen Derry. Here the pass becomes narrower. West is the high rock-covered hill Beinn Mheadhon and east is Beinn a' Chaorainn, the Hill of the Rowan. Near the county march a large boulder rests near the track ; here one looks down into Glen Derry and across to the hills which rise to the south of that glen.

In Glen Derry can still be seen the remains of the old dam constructed for floating timber from that high glen to the Dee. The dam was made by Alexander Davidson, a noted character and strong man of Upper Deeside. It is recorded of Sandy, as he was affectionately called, that on one occasion (the only one, I believe) when he was lost on the hills during a heavy snowstorm he found a small burn and resolved to follow its course, knowing that in time it would lead him to the low ground and safety. He was very tired and, try as he might, he could not tell which way the stream was flowing. He threw small snowballs into the stream and to his astonishment they apparently floated *up*hill ! Fortun-ately he realised that his weariness had brought on hallucinations, and as he felt sure that the burn was right and he was wrong he

x

followed the snowballs on their strange uphill course and at last reached safety.

Làirig Laoigh at Derry Lodge joins Làirig Ghrù and, as I have elsewhere recorded, traverses Gleann Laoigh (Glen Lui) and reaches the Deeside road at the Linn of Dee, about five miles west of Braemar.

Lairig Ghru

CHAPTER XXXI

THE CAIRNGORM AREA : LÀIRIG GHRÙ

IN the previous chapter I have mentioned that there are two
passes through the Cairngorm hills — Làirig Laoigh, Calf's Pass,
and Làirig Ghrù. In its grandeur and in the beauty of its scenery
Làirig Ghrù is perhaps unequalled in all Scotland. It is a right-
of-way, centuries old, and through it in former days cattle were
driven from Strathspey to a market that was held each year at
Braemar, and also no doubt to the great Falkirk tryst. In those
days the people of Rothiemurchus — this district is immediately
north of Làirig Ghrù — often crossed to Braemar, and the late
Colonel Charles Grant of the Rothiemurchus family told me that
the young women of Rothiemurchus used to cross in threes and
fours to the Braemar district. Each woman on these occasions
would carry on her head a basket of fresh eggs to sell to the

housewives of Mar, who, we may infer, were less successful with their poultry than the people of Rothiemurchus. In those days Làirig Ghrù was kept in good repair, especially at the watershed, where the ground is now so rough and boulder-strewn that no girls with baskets of eggs on their heads, nor even the most sure-footed cattle, could cross it. Bob MacBain from Achnahatnich in Rothiemurchus told me that as a boy he had seen the last flock of sheep driven through Làirig Ghrù. Old John Stewart from Tulloch had driven the sheep and MacBain had accompanied him " so far ".

As a place-name Làirig Ghrù remains an enigma. Làirig means a hill pass, and the map-makers of the nineteenth century solved the problem to their own satisfaction by substituting for Ghrù the word Ghruamach, for which they had apparently not the slightest authority. Ghruamach means forbidding or surly, and forbidding the Làirig often is in wild weather. Other fanciful suggestions are Làirig Cruidh, the Cattle Pass, and Làirig Ruadh, the Red Pass, because of the deep sandstone screes at the watershed. But the authorities on place-names reject these suggestions, and are obliged to leave the name Ghrù a mystery, although it seems to contain the same root as the Allt Dhrù burn which drains it to the north. MacBain, a distinguished philologist, writes that the name is " probably the Pass of Druie river, from root *dru*, flow, as in Gaulish Druentia ".

Làirig Ghrù may be said to begin at Coylum [1] Bridge in Rothiemurchus about two miles from Aviemore. At Coylum Bridge, which spans the hill torrent, is, or was, the home of the spectre known as Bodach Cleòcain Deirg, the Carlin of the Little Red Cloak. This, it seems, was a different spectre from Bodach Làmh-dhearg, the Red-handed Carlin, who haunted the shore of Loch Morlich a few miles away and suddenly appeared from the gloom of the old pines to challenge the traveller to fight.

---

[1] The word Coylum, says Professor W. J. Watson, is a corruption of *cuingleum*, " defile-leap ", a compound of *cong*, a narrow gut in a river or between rocks in the sea, and *leum*, a leap.

The old right-of-way to Braemar crosses the stream known as Allt na Beinne Móire at an iron footbridge (from which salmon may often be seen swimming in the clear water of the hill stream), then continues toward the south, through the old forest of firs. Here is the haunt of black-game and capercaillie. A few birches grow among the pines, and in autumn the orange and russet tints of these drooping birches are the more lovely because of the background of dark firs.

Làirig Ghrù winds near a conical hill, Carn Eileirg or Elrick. Professor Watson tells me that the hill derives its name from the old Gaelic word *eileirg*, meaning a V-shaped defile, natural or artificially made, that was used as a deer trap. The deer were rounded up by Highlanders from near and far, and as they rushed terrified through the *eileirg* they were shot at with bows and arrows, or guns, at close range. There is a deep defile, through which the stream known as the Beanaidh flows, at the foot of Carn Elrick, and the hill perhaps takes its name from this defile.

At each season of the year Làirig Ghrù has its own charm — in winter when the drifting snow eddies, white and mysterious, about it ; in the brilliant, cold sunshine of spring, when the snow at its crest is yet unmelted ; in summer, when the scent of hill plants perfumes the quiet, fresh air ; in autumn, when the high surrounding hills are dark with hurrying storm wrack.

Many times, and in almost every month of the year, I have made the journey through Làirig Ghrù, and recall a recent October crossing with a friend who was familiar with western passes, but not with those of the Cairngorms. A night of rain had cleared as we reached Rothiemurchus from the west. As we began our walk the wind suddenly veered from south to west, a light mist strangely formed and drifted over the moor, and when this unexpected low cloud, with its attendant drops of rain, had vanished, the sun shone out and sparkled on the rain-drenched heather, still bearing the dried and withered flowers of its summer glory. Below the pines the cowberry (*Vaccinium Vitis Idaea*) was in its second bloom, white flowers and red fruits

showing side by side. In the forest the air was still, but as
we reached the higher ground and left the last of the trees
behind us the wind freshened and backed toward the south, and
ahead of us the watershed of Làirig Ghrù was in gloom. Mist
raced across the rocks of Craig an Leth-choin, the Rock of the
Half-dog, or Lurcher. The name of this hill commemorates a
great deer hunt (according to another version of the story a great
fox hunt) on the Cairngorms. The hunt began at Revoan, east
of Loch Morlich, and ended on Craig an Leth-choin, where a
lurcher in the eagerness of pursuit fell to its death over these high
rocks and gave the hill its name.

Craig an Leth-choin, where a herd of wild goats had their
home in the early years of the present century (I have not seen
them of late), rises above Làirig Ghrù to the east of the pass : on
its west side are the great slopes of Braeriach. Beyond, and
south of, Craig an Leth-choin is Ben MacDhui, where a climber
standing on the summit cairn is just 4,300 feet above sea level.

After leaving the road at Coylum Bridge the walker passes (so
long as he continues in Inverness-shire) in sight of no inhabited
house, but he perhaps notices, in a little clearing in the forest, a
ruin which has an interesting history.

For generations the MacGregors and the Grants of Rothie-
murchus were close friends. In his classic book *In the Shadow of
Cairngorm* Forsyth mentions that Rob Roy used to visit Grant
of Rothiemurchus at his house The Doune, and that his friend
Rothiemurchus, perhaps because of his friendliness with Rob
Roy, perhaps as a mark of distinction given him by that re-
nowned Highlander, was always known as MacAlpine (the
MacGregors are sometimes known as Clan Alpine).

In her *Memoirs of a Highland Lady ; the Autobiography of
Elizabeth Grant of Rothiemurchus*, the author describes how the
Macintoshs set up a mill just beyond the Rothiemurchus west
march, and threatened to divert the water from the Rothiemurchus lands. MacAlpine, who had received a promise of support from Rob Roy, sent a haughty letter to Macintosh, who

determined to raid Rothiemurchus in revenge and to set fire to
The Doune. MacAlpine each day expected to have some message
of encouragement from Rob Roy but no messenger came, and at
length the laird of Rothiemurchus received word that Macintosh
and his men would carry out their threatened raid on the following day. In numbers the Macintoshs were greatly superior to the
Grants of Rothiemurchus, and the laird, anxious at the prospect
of the coming fight, was seated in his room in great perplexity
when he felt a hand on his shoulder and, looking up, saw the
sturdy figure of Rob Roy MacGregor standing over him. Rob
Roy was alone, and when the laird of Rothiemurchus asked him
where his men were his answer was to call for a piper and tell him
to play the " MacGregors' Gathering ". As the piper played,
the lands of Kinrara, on the opposite side of the Spey, were
deserted no longer.

Two MacGregors, and then three MacGregors, and then two MacGregors
appeared, till at last a hundred and fifty of the prettiest men in Rob Roy's
band were standing there, fully armed. The piper had orders not to stop
playing till all were out, and it nearly burst him. And as the MacGregors
came out by twos and threes the Macintoshs on the opposite side stole off
by fours and fives until, as the last MacGregor took his place, the last
Macintosh disappeared.

Rob Roy, before he left the district, told the laird of Rothiemurchus that he was not to hesitate to call on him when he
should again feel the need of a strong friend, and he said that he
would leave in Rothiemurchus two of his men who were very
fleet of foot — " for," said he, " it is a far cry to Balquhidder, and
no one here knows the way." Two young men accordingly remained : to one of them the laird of Rothiemurchus gave the
farm of Allt Dhrù and he and his descendants lived there for
many years. The last of the race, Hamish MacGregor, died in
1890, and now the old house is a ruin.

The highest ground of Làirig Ghrù, at the watershed between
Spey and Dee and at the march between the great deer forests of
Rothiemurchus and Mar, is 2,800 feet above sea level, yet even at
this height the walker is in a deep defile, and sees on either side

of him hills that rise almost sheer to the clouds. On the October day when we crossed it a strong, cold wind from the south was sweeping through the Làirig and the clouds swiftly rose and fell on Craig an Leth-choin and Ben MacDhui. The clouds drove through the dark rock gullies of Craig an Leth-choin at the speed of an express train, giving the illusion that vast volumes of smoke were rising from some invisible fire ; yet the mist at times evaporated with astonishing speed, and during these short clear intervals the hill stood out dark against a gloomy sky. At the crest of Làirig Ghrù the storm spirits held high revelry. Across the uneven ground, strewn thickly with granite boulders, the wind, cold and damp, raced toward the north. I have almost always seen ptarmigan when crossing Làirig Ghrù, and on this autumn day a flock of twenty or thirty of these mountain dwellers were on the hillside about a hundred yards above the path. Strong, sturdy birds, the rough wind inconvenienced them not at all. Over the uneven ground they ran, feeding with quick pecks at the young shoots of the blaeberry plants, which in Làirig Ghrù are their favourite food. Their wings were white and their breasts were also snowy white, but the backs and shoulder feathers of the birds were a delicate shade of grey, a colour which closely harmonised with the lichens on the stones. One cock ptarmigan, more advanced in his moult than the rest of the flock, had already assumed the winter dress of white, and this made him very conspicuous against the dark hillside. On a rock beside the track a dead ptarmigan was lying. The bird was fresh, and it may have been killed that day — struck down by the eagle which often pursues ptarmigan above the Làirig. The white wings, now that the spirit had left them, waved rather pathetically in the breeze.

I remember being in the Làirig with the Prince of Wales (as he then was) in the autumn of, I think, 1922. The Prince, wearing Highland dress with a kilt of MacDonald of the Isles tartan, had left Dunrobin Castle early in the morning, and at Rothiemurchus was escorted by Colonel Grant of Rothiemurchus, who

walked part of the way over to Luibeg Cottage in Mar with him.
I recall that a ptarmigan with a broken wing was killed on that
occasion by Rothiemurchus with his stick near the watershed of
the Làirig, and that the Prince took the ptarmigan home with
him to Balmoral. His father, King George V, afterwards told me
at the Braemar Gathering that year that he ate the bird, but
found it very tough ! I remember that day on Làirig Ghrù well ;
partly because of the Prince's kindly thought for the Rothiemurchus gamekeeper, George Duncan, in insisting that he should
share his lunch with him, partly because of the old Dunrobin
whisky which we drank with the ice-cold water at the source of
Allt Dhrù. As we sat near the crest of the pass the Prince
remarked that no scenery in the Sutherland country could
compare with Làirig Ghrù in grandeur.

The Pools of Dee lie in the Làirig rather more than 100 yards
south of the watershed. There are, under normal conditions,
four pools — two of them small, two larger. So clear is the water
that the pools appear less deep than they in reality are, and in
the two larger tarns are many small trout, which rise to an
artificial fly without suspicion. It is said that the Pools of Dee
have never been frozen over, even during the most intense and
prolonged hill frost : certainly I have never seen them frozen.
One April day, when the ground at the Pools of Dee was covered
with several feet of hard-pressed snow, and even the boulders
were hidden beneath this snowy covering, I noticed a small dark
object lying on the snowy surface. Curious to see what it might
be, I walked across to it, and to my astonishment found a dead
robin. The bird had presumably been caught in a snow blizzard
as it was on migration across the Cairngorms ; it had lost its way,
and had been suffocated by the drift — and now it lay in death
in ptarmigan country, far from the usual homely haunts of Robin
Redbreast.

From the watershed of Làirig Ghrù, beside the Pools of Dee,
the view on a clear day extends far to the north. Morven, a hill
of Caithness, easily recognised by its delicate, sharp-cut summit,

is seen, and early one very clear September morning I saw, at a considerable distance beyond Morven, a cloud which I believe was mist lying above the Pentland Firth.

From Ben MacDhui a burn falls steeply to the Làirig. Until late in summer a snow bridge usually spans this, the March burn, in Gaelic Allt na Crìche. Shortly before it reaches the floor of the Làirig the burn disappears underground, and it has never, I believe, been proved whether it flows underground to the Spey side of the watershed, or whether it appears once more on the surface as the Pools of Dee. I myself believe that it feeds the Dee, and that it shows itself at the Pools before disappearing underground once more until, some little distance below and to the south of the Pools, the young Dee begins to flow southward through the Làirig. On a day of storm this country 'twixt Spey and the upper reaches of the Dee can be grand and even awe-inspiring. In the dim light the red granite screes are the colour of blood : green grasses and yellow mosses contrast strongly with these deep-red areas, and the darker screes beside the Pools of Dee assume the colour of a ripe grape. No more fitting country for eagle and ptarmigan can be imagined.

As the walker begins to descend into Glen Dee he sees ahead of him the noble summit of Cairntoul (powdered that autumn day with the first snows of what deer-stalkers call the "back-end"), and behind it the lower but equally prominent peak Bod an Diabhail, politely translated as the Devil's Point. To the east of the Làirig are the pleasing ridge and summit of Carn a' Mhaim.

At a distance of perhaps a mile south of the Pools of Dee the traveller sees a great corrie of sublime grandeur gradually appear to the west. This is An Garbh Choire, the Rough Corrie, and there is no corrie in all Scotland that is more beautiful or more utterly lonely. An Garbh Choire is mentioned in one of the songs of the Cairngorm poet William Smith, whose *duan* on Allt an Lochain Uaine, the Burn of the Green Tarn, holds an assured place in Gaelic verse. At the head of An Garbh Choire, and visible from the track through Làirig Ghrù, is a great snow-bed which I have never known entirely to disappear, although (as I shall narrate in another chapter) in the early days of October 1938 the fragments of the drift had become very small.

As the walker through the Làirig looks into the Garbh Choire he sees, rising from the north side of the corrie, a great, flat-topped hill. This is Braeriach, in Gaelic Am Bràigh Riabhach, the Brindled Hill, second highest of the Cairngorms, rising to an altitude of 4,248 feet above sea level. Immediately beneath, and to the south of, the hill-top is a vast corrie where boulder is piled upon boulder in sublime confusion. The name of the corrie is Coire Bhrochain, the Corrie of Gruel,[1] and upwards of forty years ago Donald Fraser of the Derry, a Mar stalker who had much ancient lore, told me the history of this place-name. According to him, the naming of the corrie came about in this way. Long ago, cattle from the shielings were accustomed in summer to pasture right up to the summits of the Cairngorms. One day, when the mist was very close, certain cattle lost their way and fell to their death over the 1,000-feet precipice into Coire Bhrochain, where, after their fall, they were reduced to the consistency of *brochan* or gruel. This derivation of the name of the corrie for a long time seemed to me to be rather fanciful, but about the year 1927, when a companion and I were in the corrie very early one summer's morning, after a night spent on the hills, we saw along the rocks what seemed to be the ancient skeleton remains of two deer. My companion sent one of the jaw-bones to Edinburgh to be identified and it was pronounced to be the jaw-bone of an ox. The bones were lying on ground so rough that no cattle could have *walked* to the spot where they were found, and our discovery corroborated in a remarkable manner the tradition concerning the naming of the corrie. Grigor Grant, the deer-stalker, also had heard of this tradition. He told me he thought the cattle had come from Glen Eanaich. He said that in those days cattle were pastured in Glen A'an and in Glen Eanaich and

---

[1] *Brochan* (of which the genitive is *bhrochain*) is usually gruel, but in some districts is porridge.

that, during a great snow-storm one June, a number of them went over the rocks at Faindouran in Strath A'an.

The play of the clouds on Braeriach on a day of south wind is inspiring. Mist holds all the upper slopes of the hill until, without warning, the cloud rises. The black gullies smoke for a moment, then are clear, and, in less time than it takes to describe in print, the summit of the hill is free of cloud. Five minutes later the traveller perhaps looks again at Braeriach. Surely a magician's wand has been waved here, for the top is clear no longer and mist has descended even more closely about the upper slopes than before.

Not far from the bothy at the foot of the Devil's Point a large rock is to be seen beside Làirig Ghrù. The rock is Clach nan Tàillear, the Tailors' Stone, named after certain tailors who for a wager attempted to dance, during the hours of a winter day, at the " three Dells " — the Dell of Abernethy, the Dell of Rothiemurchus and Dalmore in Mar. They danced at Abernethy and at Rothiemurchus and had crossed the most exposed miles of the Làirig when a blizzard overtook them in Glen Dee, and they succumbed as they vainly sought shelter behind the stone that is their memorial.

The bothy on the opposite side of the Dee to the Tailors' Stone is known as the Corrour Bothy, receiving its name from the corrie behind it.[1] In the lifetime of the late Duke of Fife, a deer-stalker or deer-watcher lived in the bothy from July to October. When first I knew the Cairngorms an old watcher named Charles Robertson, a great character, inhabited the bothy, and was succeeded by John Macintosh, known as the Piper. He was a fine figure of a man, and was pipe-major of the Duff Highlanders, succeeding the famous piper Colin Cameron. Many a night John and I piped in the Corrour bothy, by the glow of the friendly fire of peat and bog fir ; and it was good, of a dark evening when still some distance from the bothy, to hear his pipes echo through the lonely glen. I remember that one summer

[1] Coire Odhar, Dun-coloured Corrie.

evening a herd of stags came down from the slopes of Cairntoul
and began to jump and dance on their hind legs near the piper —
whether they had an ear for music or were merely excited by the
strange sound I know not, but the effect was so remarkable that
I have never forgotten it.

In the summer of 1893 a cloudburst which struck the Devil's
Point almost overwhelmed the Corrour bothy, and Charles
Robertson, who then lived in it, told me that he thought his last
hour had come.

That old shieling at the foot of the Devil's Point has many
pleasant memories for me.   There were summer evenings,
calm and serene, when the air was drenched with the honey scent
of the heather, and early summer mornings when the sky was
blue and the red deer grazing on the green dew-drenched grass
showed a warm red-brown in their new coats.   There were moon-
light nights in winter when the moon in a frosty sky climbed
slowly in cold beauty above the ridge of Carn a' Mhaim.   I retain
a vivid memory of a mid-winter storm at the bothy, when water
in a basin froze in the small room, although the fire was piled
high with peat and bog fir, and when drifting snow swept past
the bothy in a dense, suffocating cloud that would have brought
speedy death to the man or beast who faced it.

Above the bothy the golden eagle often soars, and one summer
day, when a breeze from the north was drifting through Làirig
Ghrù, I watched an eagle rise higher and higher on the air currents
until even that great bird was invisible to the unaided eye.   With
the aid of a stalking telescope the eagle was picked up again, and
was closely watched as it continued to mount, with no perceptible
movement of its broad wings, until even in the field of the
telescope, which gave a magnification of × 26, the eagle became
no larger than a speck of dust and finally disappeared entirely
from view.   The bird must then have been at least 10,000 feet
above the ground, and 12,000 feet above the sea, and from that
great height (for the day was fine) the whole of the Scottish
Highlands, and even the Isle of Skye and the Outer Hebrides,

must have been visible. From the door of the Corrour bothy there is a fine view across the young Dee with its clear water to Coire nan Tàillear, the Tailors' Corrie (named after the Tailors' Stone) on Ben MacDhui. During winter and early spring, storms from the north-east drift the snow across Ben MacDhui plateau into this corrie, where it may lie to a depth of 50 feet and more. The slope where the snow lies is steep and leans to the south, and in July an avalanche usually falls from this snow-bed. I was once crossing the Làirig when the avalanche took place, and saw great blocks of frozen snow leap with the rumble of thunder down the steep stony slope.

By the time he has reached the shieling at Corrour the traveller has walked upwards of twelve miles from the pines of Rothie-murchus, but Làirig Ghrù still shows him new and unexpected views of beauty and grandeur. A short distance south of the bothy the track leaves the glen of the Dee and winds toward the east round the shoulder of Carn a' Mhaim. As he looks back from this hill shoulder the traveller sees a broad and deep glen lead-ing away westward — Glen Giùsachan, the Glen of the Pine Wood. This glen, the deer sanctuary of the Forest of Mar, is now treeless, but the roots and stumps of the great fir trees that formerly grew here can still be seen in the glen up to, and rather above, the 2,000-foot level. At the head of Glen Giùsachan is a large flat-topped hill named Monadh Mór, and the east slope of this hill sometimes holds snow throughout the summer (*vide* Chapter XXXIII).

Where the track rounds the shoulder of Carn a' Mhaim the view, for the first time during the crossing of the Làirig, opens toward the east, and on the horizon are seen the peaks of Loch-nagar on the Balmoral forest and, still farther east, the sym-metrical summit of Mount Keen. The path soon descends, and crosses, by a wooden bridge, the strong hill stream, Allt Gleann Laoigh Beag, anglicised to Luibeg burn. This stream has its source in a loch high up on Ben MacDhui, and during the melting of the snows in early summer is a milk-white torrent. It is beside the Luibeg burn that the outposts of the Mar Scots firs are reached. They are strong and stately trees, and must be of a great age ; they have indeed scarcely altered since the day, now over forty years ago, when first I saw them. It is regrettable that these fine trees should have left no descendants behind them : red deer are so numerous in Mar forest that each fir seedling is devoured as soon as it is visible. If small areas were fenced in, here and there, the young trees would be quick to grow and establish themselves.

On the south side of Luibeg burn, not far from the footbridge, is a cluster of pines known to the old Gaelic-speaking people of Mar as Preas nam Mèirleach, the Robbers' Thicket. It is said that cattle raiders from Lochaber once hid here. Opposite this thicket and farther down the glen, a solitary and very old pine may be seen on the slopes of Carn Crom. This pine has a Gaelic name, Craobh an Oir, the Tree of the Gold, or Treasure. MacKenzie of Dalmore in Mar had been west to the Lochaber country on a raid, and had " lifted " considerable treasure. This gold he first buried in the wilds of Garbh Choire Dhé of Brae-riach, but later on, as he thought that the gold was too far away from him in that lonely corrie, he dug it up and re-buried it below the Tree of Gold. According to the version told me by John Macintosh the piper (and he had a considerable store of old lore), even then MacKenzie of Dalmore was not easy about his treasure : perhaps he thought that some of the drovers crossing Làirig Ghrù might discover it. At all events he dug up the gold, and this time finally buried it near the summit of Carn Geldie, a hill about four miles to the south, where it remains to this day. It is said that the site where the treasure was buried was visible from Dalmore house. The tradition is that a great stone, on which MacKenzie of Dalmore had incised a horse-shoe, was placed above the treasure, and if any wanderer on Carn Geldie, above the Chest of Dee, is fortunate enough to discover this stone his fame and fortune are assured.

From the footbridge across the Luibeg burn there is a fine

view up Glen Luibeg to Ben MacDhui and Derry Cairngorm to the right of it : nearer at hand is the striking summit of Carn a' Mhaim.

The track now passes eastward beneath splendid old Scots pines with red gnarled bark and graceful boughs which have withstood many a storm. On the heathery banks and clearings between the old trees cock grouse sun themselves of an autumn morning and antlered stags graze at sunrise. In the clear pools of the hill stream the rings of rising trout may be seen of a calm summer's evening, and a pastoral touch is given to the lonely scene by the cattle slowly returning from the hill grazing to their milking at the deer-stalker's cottage that stands amid shelter-ing trees, with a small garden where scented roses climb to the windows, and where Sandy MacDonald, most kindly of men, was accustomed to give a warm welcome to the weary traveller.

A few hundred yards west of the stalker's house a large stone lies on the grass beside the burn, and near the track. The stone is said by old people of Mar to commemorate an historic occasion. The men of Rothiemurchus — whether the Grants, or the Shaws who held Rothiemurchus before them, is not recorded — had crossed to Deeside to assist the Earl of Mar on some warlike expedition and were now returning home through Làirig Ghrù. The Earl of Mar, and some of his vassals, were as a mark of friend-ship accompanying them during the first part of their journey through the Làirig. One of the men from Rothiemurchus was of remarkable strength, and the laird, in order to impress the Earl, called upon this man to lift a great stone that lay near the track. Without difficulty the Rothiemurchus clansman threw the stone from him, and when the Earl, accepting the implied challenge, called upon Fionnlagh Mór, Great Finlay, his own champion in feats of strength, the atmosphere became tense and the men of both parties waited eagerly to see whether he also would be able to lift the stone which was beyond the strength of an ordinary man to raise. Fionnlagh Mór stooped down and with no effort, and with an affected carelessness, he lifted the stone and, holding it in his hands as an ordinary mortal might have held a stone of lesser size, asked his master what his wishes were regarding it. " Throw it," was the reply, " across the neck of the pony that stands yonder." This Big Finlay did, to the astonishment of the men from Rothiemurchus, and from that day to this the stone has lain where he threw it.

Zeppelins are not associated with hill passes of the Cairngorms, but on May 2, 1916, Zeppelin L.20 left Germany under the command of Captain-Lieutenant Stabert on a raiding voyage to the British Isles. The great craft reached the Scottish coast at Lunan Bay, turned inland past Montrose, then set a course which brought her over the Forest of Mar. Travelling in the darkness of night over Ben MacDhui, the Zeppelin then sailed across Strathspey and over the Monadh Liath hills and the Caledonian Canal. She was perhaps searching for the fleet at Invergordon but did not apparently locate them, and now endeavoured to return to her German base. But a storm arose and, driven out of her course, she collided with high ground on the Norwegian coast and sank in the deep water of a fjord.

The sequel to the Zeppelin's visit to Mar is interesting and has not perhaps been put in print before. In the summer of 1921 Sandy MacDonald, stalker at Luibeg and a man beloved by all who knew him, found on the hill above his house what he thought was a bomb dropped by the Zeppelin (which had been heard but not seen in the darkness as the great airship passed over Mar). In the autumn of 1921 the Prince of Wales was out stalking with Sandy, who showed him the supposed bomb. The Prince took it back with him to Balmoral, and sent it to the Air Ministry for identification. There it was recognised as a " flare " of calcium carbide used by an airship to ascertain whether she was over the land or the sea (if dropped on land the carbide would remain unlighted, but if dropped in water it would flare up). For the month of May the night must have been a very dark one for the Cairngorms to have been invisible to the wandering Zeppelin, and that " flare " dropped on the Forest of Mar was perhaps the last trace of her that is known.

At Derry lodge, Làirig Ghrù may be said to end, for the track here broadens to a motor road to Braemar, ten miles farther on. The road from Derry lodge to the Linn of Dee (as I have mentioned in another chapter) is a private one, but the motorist can use it by paying a small toll.[1] This system of toll is an excellent one, and might with advantage be followed in other places, for the money received goes to the upkeep of the road, and motorists are not prohibited from enjoying the beauties of a Highland glen.

At Derry lodge the two streams, Derry and Luibeg, join and as one river flow down Glen Lui, through which the road is made. There are now no people living in Glen Lui, but many small ruins in the glen tell of the time when it must have been a comparatively populous district. In the *Records of Invercauld* an interesting letter is published, written in the year 1726 by Lord Grange to James Farquharson of Balmoral. The rising of 1715 had ended disastrously for the Highlands. The Earl of Mar's estates had been forfeited and his honours and superiorities had been taken from him. Mar forest was now in the possession of Lord Grange, who decided with ruthless determination to clear Glen Lui of its inhabitants. The letter written by Lord Grange is as follows :

ALLOA, 15 *Septer.* 1726

SIR,— . . . As to Glenluy, Ld. Dun and I find your letter of the 26th of August at this place when we came to it last week. The directions formerly given as to the ejection are so particular that we need only refer to them, and we desire you to act according to them, and to eject those people after their harvest is over . . . and the more you have along with you there will be the less opposition, these people perceiving it will be vain for them to resist.

The evictions were the more reprehensible and inexcusable, for Lord Grange was the Earl of Mar's brother, and eleven years earlier these same people, ordered to be driven from their

[1] This refers to the period up to 1939 ; since the end of the war the gate has remained locked during the summer and early autumn months.

ancestral homes, had risked their lives in the service of the Earl of Mar at the Jacobite rising in 1715.

The day of the evictions must have been a sad one for Glen Lui, the old people mourning and lamenting as they were herded like cattle from the glen which was associated with all the joys and all the sorrows of their simple lives. In Arrowsmith's map (1807) four houses are marked in Glen Lui. On the west side of the water of Lui are " Knockinted " and " Dalgwnich ", and on the east are " Alt Vattigally " and " Achavadie ".[1]

The old people of Mar are passing from the mortal scene. Donald Fraser of the Derry, Charles Robertson who tamed the mice in Corrour bothy, John Macintosh the piper and Sandy MacDonald of Luibeg — these men no longer climb to the high tops nor tell of the romance of ancient times. Most of their successors in the forest have little or no Gaelic, nor have they the same interest in old lore as the older generation. The wireless is taking the place of the *céilidh* in the glens. Yet the high Cairngorms remain unchanged, and almost as unchanging as the hills is the storm-scarred Tree of Gold which saw MacKenzie of Dalmore bury his treasure and the Lochaber raiders hide from the men of Mar in Preas nam Mèirleach.

[1] Alt Vattigally is for Allt a' Mhadaidh Allaidh, Burn of the Wild Dog (Wolf). Achavadie is Ach' a' Mhaidaidh, Field of the Dog.

Cairngorms, from Strathspey
Làirig Ghrù with Ben MacDhui (left) and Braeriach (right)

CHAPTER XXXII

THE HIGH TOPS OF THE CAIRNGORMS : I. THE CENTRAL AND EASTERN CAIRNGORMS

In Scotland there are six mountains which reach a height of 4,000 feet or more, and of the six, four are Cairngorm summits.

The Cairngorms do not give the impression of great height when they are seen from their approaches — from Aviemore in Upper Strathspey, or from Braemar on Upper Deeside. This is partly because their summits are rounded and not sharp-pointed like many hills on the western seaboard, and partly because the glens of the Cairngorms are themselves over 1,000 feet above sea level and in some instances approach the 2,000-feet contour.

The 4,000-feet summits of the Cairngorms are — Ben MacDhui (4,296 feet, and second only to Ben Nevis in height), Braeriach (4,248 feet), Cairntoul (4,241 feet) and Cairngorm (4,084 feet). Beinn a' Bhùird and Ben A'an almost reach the 4,000-feet level, and several other of the summits (Beinn Bhrodain and Monadh Mór, Sgoran Dubh and Derry Cairngorm) exceed the 3,500-feet level.

It is difficult to say which is the finest summit of the Cairngorms. Each has its own distinctive charm. For sheer savage wildness I should say that the north-east slopes of Ben MacDhui are supreme. The great corrie rising from the head of Loch A'an, immediately below Ben MacDhui, is also as fine as anything to be seen in the Cairngorms. For symmetry of outline Cairntoul is distinctive among Cairngorm summits, and in the charm of its plateau, where alpine flowers and bright green grass grow beside the low banks of the infant Dee, Braeriach perhaps excels its fellows.

Cairngorm, from which the range takes its name, is the easiest hill of 4,000 feet to ascend in this country. One of the charms of the high Cairngorms is the long distance it is possible to walk at a great height above the sea. The distance from the summit of Cairngorm to the summit of Ben MacDhui is, as the walker walks (as the eagle flies it is shorter), a matter of between four and five miles, yet the traveller is always at a height of over 3,000 feet, and sometimes of 4,000 feet, above the sea.

If the Cuillin of Skye be *par excellence* the climber's hills, the Cairngorms are no less certainly the walker's hills, for all the summits can be gained with little exertion. The Cairngorms rise near the centre of the Scottish Highlands, and in fine weather the view from the summits extends from Bennachie on the eastern Aberdeenshire coast (I have never actually seen the North Sea from Ben MacDhui, but in exceptionally clear weather it may be visible) to the Kintail hills on the Atlantic seaboard.

The high tops of the Cairngorms form the boundary between several Highland counties. Braeriach is the dividing line between Inverness-shire to the west and north and Aberdeenshire to the south and east. The summit of Ben MacDhui is the county march between Aberdeen and Banff.

Besides forming county boundaries, these high hills are the
" marches " between different deer forests. On Cairntoul is the
march between the two great deer forests of Mar and Glen Feshie.
Braeriach forms the march between the forests of Mar and
Rothiemurchus, and on the summit of Ben MacDhui the forests
of Mar and Inchrory meet.

Deer are very rarely shot on the high tops or plateaus of the
Cairngorms, but since the owner or tenant of a deer forest rightly
expects that the stags should not be disturbed during the stalking
season, I have always suggested in my writings that climbers
should as far as possible avoid the hills during the six weeks of
that season, which begins on or about September 1. But
there are certain rights-of-way, and a climber can ascend Ben
MacDhui and Cairngorm at any season of the year. I was told
an amusing story of the tenant of the Forest of Glen More a
number of years ago. The right-of-way to the summit of Cairngorm runs through his forest, and one day, late in the morning,
after many people had climbed the hill, the first (and only)
climber that day to ask permission called at the lodge and said
that he hoped he would not disturb the deer if he climbed
Cairngorm. The stalking tenant replied, " I greatly appreciate
your courtesy in consulting me on the matter, but I have been
' spying ' the hill to-day through my stalking-glass, and as I
have already counted 143 persons either on, or approaching the
top, and as my stalking is entirely spoiled for the day, I am sure
that one more climber will make no difference. At the same
time I cannot complain, for there is an undoubted right-of-way
to the top, and anyone who wishes to climb the hill is at perfect
liberty to do so."

The Cairngorms are far from the sea, and snow usually lies
unbroken on their summits until late in May. But the winter of
1937–8 and the spring of 1938 were unusually mild, and on Good
Friday of 1938, when a friend and I climbed Cairngorm, crossed
the high ground from that hill to Ben MacDhui and then returned
to Loch Morlich, from which we had begun the climb, the hills

were almost free of snow. Indeed not in the memory of old people of the district had so little snow been seen on the Cairngorms in April, when the high plateaus and corries are usually more deeply covered than at any time during the winter months — for the snowy covering increases gradually from November until April.[1] On Good Friday 1938, there was indeed considerably less snow on the high tops than is seen in June — or even in July, in an average season. The Red-handed Spectre did not bar the way beside the golden sands of Loch Morlich as we crossed the stream and entered the old pine forest — where the Forest Commissioners were planting large areas with spruce and fir — which clothes the foot of Cairngorm. The grey clouds of early morning had partially dispersed, and here and there the sun shone on hill, glen and corrie, and on the low country of Aviemore away to the north. It was a remarkable tribute to the mildness of the season that even in this glen beneath Cairngorm some of the old birches, growing more than 1,000 feet above sea level, were already clothing themselves with delicate green. The burn from Coire Cas and Coire an Lochain of Cairngorm, instead of thundering bank-high through the glen, as is usual in early spring when the snows begin to melt, was at summer level. I looked up at the great snow-drift, known to the old people of Strathspey as Cuithe Crom, Bent or Crooked Wreath, which seems to hang (so steep is the ground on which it rests) in a graceful bend at the top of the high corrie immediately west of, and a little below the summit of Cairngorm, and saw that it was already shrunken and broken at the middle, and no larger than it might be expected to appear in late July.

The north wind, blowing behind us, was fresh and eager as we climbed the slopes of Cairngorm and, without once walking on snow, reached the summit cairn which stands 4,084 feet above the level of the sea. The only Arctic reminder during the long walk

[1] That year Sgùrr nan Gillean in Skye was entirely snow-free by the beginning of April: in 1942 snow lay in its north corrie till the last days of June.

across the high Cairngorms was this cairn. The north wind, damp and mist-laden, of the two previous days had given birth to feathery fog crystals of remarkable delicacy, grace and beauty. The crystals extended horizontally into space from the windward side of the cairn ; one which I measured was over two feet in length. Yet a few yards south of the hill-top the air was comparatively warm and the sun shone upon a flock of snow-buntings which rose on white wings from the stony ground and, flying low over the hill face, gave the illusion of a sudden snow flurry. These small, white-winged birds were very lovely ; they were natives of the high north — of Greenland perhaps or of Iceland — and on the Cairngorms were awaiting the day when they would set out overseas to their distant nesting country. These snow-bunting flocks on the high Cairngorms are restless and timid in spring, and are sometimes seen as late as May. The local snow-buntings — and they are very rare — are tamer and when disturbed do not usually fly far.

We lunched behind a rock, high above Loch A'an, where the wind gently played on clear, dark waters. From the loch the River A'an (at one time known as An Uisge Geal, the White Water) flowed toward the east. The great hills in that direction — Ben A'an and Beinn a' Bhùird — had scarcely a snow-drift upon their western slopes, which alone were visible to us. Beinn Mheadhon was without snow and Loch Éiteachan high on Ben MacDhui was unfrozen — a rare sight in April and even during the first fortnight of May.

The white, fleecy clouds were now dissolving in the rays of the strong noonday sun and revealing the sky, hazy and of a delicate blue, beyond them. Round us ptarmigan were croaking, the male birds, with tails spread fan-wide, sometimes driving off rivals from their " territories ".

We crossed the high country which joins Cairngorm and Ben MacDhui. This is a truly Arctic tableland and in April is usually so deeply snow-covered that the walker cannot traverse it without the protection of snow-glasses, unless he is prepared to

risk snow-blindness. But, this memorable April of 1938, instead
of deep snow there was crisp, sun-warmed grass pleasant to walk
upon. Even Lochan Buidhe, a small loch 3,800 feet above the
sea and the highest tarn in Scotland, was ice-free, although it is
usually buried so deeply beneath ice and snow until late May as
to be invisible.

From Lochan Buidhe to the summit of Ben MacDhui the rise
is gradual, but the ground is covered with stones and boulders of
granite which make walking irksome. On this ground Cairngorm
crystals have been found, and a " character " of former years,
Cailleach nan Clach, the Old Woman of the Stones, spent much
of her time searching for these crystals. She discovered some of
great size and considerable value, and one of the largest I saw
some years ago in the house of Invercauld. The old woman was
once asked whether she were not afraid to be on the high Cairngorms day after day, and sometimes night after night, with no
companion near her, and whether she did not fear that she might
see one of the spectres which were reputed to haunt that lonely
country. She replied that so far she had seen nothing worse than
her own reflection in the clear pools over which she had stooped
to quench her thirst, and since God was as near her there as elsewhere, her mind was easy. Another searcher after Cairngorms
was James Grant, who lived at Revoan. He found, beside the
Fèith Bhuidhe, a huge Cairngorm crystal, upward of 50 lb. in
weight, for which Queen Victoria paid the sum of £50. Cailleach
nan Clach doubtless passed many a night in the dark recess below
the Shelter Stone, and perhaps watched the moon sparkle on the
great Cairngorm crystal which has from time to time been seen
high up on the precipice on the north side of Loch A'an, but has
never been reached.

As we approached the summit of Ben MacDhui we were surprised to see a gathering of people on the hill-top — children and
their elders, and even dogs moving about the cairn. Here was
the parish minister of Crathie, living up to the standard of the old
days when the minister of a Highland parish walked farther than

any of his parishioners, and with him were His Majesty's Commissioner at Balmoral and his good lady.

Leaving a friendly gathering on this, the second highest hill in Scotland, we walked to the edge of the Ben MacDhui plateau, and looked south into Glen Dee, more than 2,000 feet below, and west into Garbh Choire Mór and its snows, vast even in that snowless season. Here the steep, stern slopes, facing mainly east, had been screened from the warm influence of the mild south-westerly gales of early spring, and snow still lay here in great fields. Shafts of sun, piercing the clouds, played upon this grand and very lonely corrie.

We were standing at a height of over 4,000 feet, yet even at this great altitude the rosettes of the cushion pink were already tinged with green.

Evening was approaching as we turned toward the Spey. In the keen air was the scent of distant heather fires. We passed Allt na Crìche, the March Burn, and looked down on to the Pools of Dee in Làirig Ghrù where men, no larger than ants, were traversing the Làirig. The Pools of Dee were shrunken : of the four, two were dry or almost so, and the third, where many small trout have their home, was less than half full. The March burn was a mere trickle of water, and the young Dee was also very low.

Crossing the west slope of Carn Lochan (the north spur of Ben MacDhui), we rested awhile toward sunset on the *miadan* or meadow of Craig an Leth-choin and watched the sun's light, soft and rosy, on the west slopes of Cairngorm, above which a golden eagle sailed slowly, quartering the ridge. The breeze had gone to rest as we looked into Coire an Lochain, and as we descended towards Loch Morlich we saw red flower-buds already showing on *Azalea procumbens* and delicate green leaves on the cloudberry. We reached the low country at dusk, to find the evening air fragrant with the scent of young birch leaves.

I do not think that an early spring in the Highlands is often followed by a fine summer ; certainly the summer that succeeded the exceptional spring of 1938 was boisterous and without

warmth, save for a hot spell in August. June on the high Cairngorms is, at its best, a month of light, fragrant airs and long
sunny hours, and when, as in this June of 1938, snow on more
than one occasion whitened the Cairngorm plateaus and the wind
blew with the cold strength of autumn, the finest season of the
year is lost. We were anxious to see the effect of an early spring
followed by a cold summer on the hills, and on a mid-June
morning, when the sun was high in the heavens and the red ants
of Rothiemurchus forest were full of activity beneath the old
pines, my wife and I crossed Allt na Beinne Móire, the Stream
of the Great Hill, above Coylum and entered the lower reaches of
Làirig Ghrù. Here weeping birches grew among the pines, and
were renewing their youth with young, scented leaves.

We climbed to Craig an Leth-choin where the ground was
carpeted with the crimson buds and rose-coloured flowers of
Azalea procumbens, a charming plant that is faithful to the high
ridges of a hill, and is happy only on granite formation. The
strong sun was drawing from the leaves and flowers of this lowly,
creeping plant a fragrant characteristic scent, honey-sweet.

Although the sun was warm, the north wind was cool as we
crossed Miadan Craig an Leth-choin, the Meadow of the Rock of
the Lurcher : on this level, grassy land we realised that the
season, despite its early promise, was now unusually late at high
altitudes. The hill grass was dry and brown as in March : a
match could have kindled a fire with ease here. We crossed the
shoulder of Carn Lochan to the highest tarn of the Cairngorms —
Lochan Buidhe — and saw that the alpine willow had scarcely
begun to unroll its green leaves and that no flower-buds (let alone
flowers) appeared on the rosettes of the cushion pink which in
April had shown such early growth — yet in a favourable season
the cushion pink may be in flower by the first week in June. The
air was clear, as is usual with north wind. Lochnagar, the Buck
o' the Cabrach, and Bennachie to the east, and Ben Nevis far to
the west, were distinct. Above the abyss of Làirig Ghrù, Cairntoul and the Devil's Point rose : the great rocks on Beinn

Mheadhon were so plain that they seemed but a stone's-throw distant. Clear and ice-cold was the small stream which flowed from Lochan Buidhe. Across the high, exposed slopes swept the rugged north wind, and the ptarmigan, sheltering from it behind stones and boulders, were reluctant to move. A golden plover on taking wing was the plaything of the breeze : creamy clouds were hurrying south across the blue zenith.

Ahead of us, beyond many acres of granite screes, rose the rounded summit of Ben MacDhui, perhaps 500 feet higher than where we sheltered on a sun-warmed slope from the wind. Beside a small stream issuing from a clear spring we made our evening meal of tea and eggs, our tablecloth the young plants of *Gnaphalium supinum*, growing closely together.

There was little inducement to remain on the high tops this June evening. The north wind sought us out wherever we sheltered, and in the cold evening light the great snow-beds still remaining in the Garbh Choire of Braeriach were austere. We turned our faces to the north, and when we had crossed the rounded top of Carn Lochan and come in sight of Loch Morlich could see at a great distance the reflection of its encircling pines in waters that were turquoise in the evening light. A bank of cloud, black as night, was forming over the high summits behind us. Coire an Lochain was in deep shade, and its snow-fields served only to accentuate its gloom. In gulleys above those snow-beds was the only verdure we had seen during all our long walk over high ground that day. It was nine o'clock when we reached Làirig Ghrù, and in the north-west sky the evening sun still shone, lighting up the green heather slopes above the Làirig, and shining radiant almost to the cloud that was already resting lightly on the summit of Braeriach. The cloud increased, and a few minutes later when we looked back we saw that all the hills were in shade except where, in a small pool of primrose light, the sun burned high on the slope of Craig an Leth-choin. In the invigorating air of evening was the scent of heather, blaeberry and crowberry. There was peace at the heart of nature that night. From the glen beneath us a cuckoo called, and a wood-cock flitted gnome-like above a forest clearing, uttering his evening cry. From the hill stream a mallard rose and as, at eleven o'clock, we approached a forest lochan a lapwing wheeled overhead, young rabbits ran before us, and trout were rising to the midges that made their unwelcome presence felt in the windless hollows below the firs that swayed gently in the breeze of a June night.

I have mentioned that Loch A'an lies immediately beneath Cairngorm. The loch is not quite so near Ben MacDhui, but the north-east slopes of that hill slope gradually away to a great corrie that lies at the head of Loch A'an. By following the stream marked on the Ordnance map as Garbh Uisge, the Rough Water, which rises immediately north-east of Ben MacDhui summit, it is not difficult to descend to Loch A'an : the descent through the corrie is steep, but is mostly over grassy ground, and a foothold is never wanting. At Loch A'an the grand and the beautiful join hands. There is no more splendid loch in all Scotland. To each man his own tastes. Myself, I believe that I would rank Loch A'an, Loch Coruisk and Loch Sloy as the three finest lochs in the Scottish Highlands and (perhaps this is partly because of its remoteness) I would place Loch A'an first.

Although Loch A'an lies at a greater distance from the nearest road or track than any other large Scottish loch it is well known to those who explore the Cairngorms on foot ; of these hill-lovers there are few who have not seen (even if they have not passed the night beneath) Clach Dhìon, the Shelter Stone. This huge boulder stands near the loch at its upper end. From a precipice south of the loch great rocks in a past age have been hurled and now lie in sublime confusion beneath the parent cliff. One enormous boulder rests upon several others, in such a manner that a recess or hollow capable of sheltering or concealing a number of persons has been formed. This is Clach Dhìon (now usually known by its anglicised name, Shelter Stone) which for centuries served as a sleeping-place for hunters of the red deer, and which is now made use of as a shelter by lovers of the high and solitary country of the Cairngorms, where is to be found the most exhilarating air in all Scotland.

On the occasion when my wife and I remained for a night beneath the Shelter Stone we found that a " Visitors' Book " had been for some time here. In this book, placed inside a tin, were many signatures, but I do not remember that the signature of Ramsay MacDonald was among them, although the Prime Minister of that time knew the Cairngorms well, and on one occasion when I lunched with him at 10 Downing Street gave me an interesting account of his experiences on the hill.

A recent tragedy is linked with the Shelter Stone. At New Year 1933, two inexperienced climbers rashly passed a winter night below the Stone. We shall never hear of their discomforts during that night of snow and intense frost, for the following day, as they were crossing Cairngorm on their return to Strathspey, they were caught in a blizzard and died of exposure, exhaustion and suffocation in the snow beside the burn of Coire Cas, when the worst part of that long journey lay behind them, and when they were comparatively near the shelter of the pine trees of Glen More.

A similar tragedy, from a similar cause, took place on Braeriach a few years previously. Here again the climbers had reached comparative shelter when, exhausted by their ordeal, they lay down in the snow, to fall quickly into the sleep of death.

The Shelter Stone stands 2,500 feet above the level of the distant sea, and the alpine vegetation which surrounds it is unusually luxuriant. It is interesting to find that the plants of the blaeberry or bilberry here are taller than in the low country of the Forest of Rothiemurchus. The great bilberry (distinguished by its glaucous leaves and wooded stems) also grows here and the neighbourhood of Clach Dhìon is almost the only place on the Cairngorms where I have seen it produce flowers and fruit, although in Iceland it flowers (and presumable fruits) freely.

Around the Shelter Stone in late July is to be seen a carpet of cloudberry plants with many fruits, already large and red, upon them. It is a peculiarity of the cloudberry that its fruits are red while yet unripe, but when fully ripened are yellow. Excellent jam can be made from them.

I have only once spent the night beneath the Shelter Stone, but that night, and the two days which preceded and followed it, are still clear in my memory. My wife and I began our climb from Aviemore when a heat-wave lay over the valley of the Spey. That July morning when we left Aviemore the thermometer in the shade registered 82 degrees Fahrenheit. We climbed first by Làirig Ghrù then over Craig an Leth-choin to Lochan Buidhe, the Yellow Tarn, on the great tableland which extends from Ben MacDhui to Cairngorm. Before we had reached this plateau clouds had hidden the sun, and a warm southerly wind was bringing refreshing rain to the high hills. Beside Lochan Buidhe a herd of perhaps one hundred and fifty hinds were feeding. Many of the hinds had their calves with them, and the high-pitched bleating of the fawns mingled with the deeper cries of the mothers as they answered their children. We walked east over a green carpet of Arctic willow, and as we reached the edge of the tableland looked down into dark Loch A'an, almost encircled by black cliffs. We stood at the head of the corrie down which the Garbh Uisge [1] thunders in white spray to the loch, but before we could enter the corrie it was necessary for us to cross a great snow-field which, despite the heat, was as hard as ice. At the edge of the snow the grass was brown, but a few yards away, where it had been released for perhaps a week from its snowy covering, it was already green and in vigorous growth. How strange for plant life must have been this abrupt transition from mid-winter to mid-summer ! Beside the snow a wheatear stood, and a pair of meadow-pipits were flying near. Below us a heavy thunder-shower formed and as it grew it drew a veil across Loch

---

[1] I have heard it said that old people named this stream Geur Uisge, Sharp Water.

A'an, but with the passing of that shower the sky was blue and the evening sun shone golden upon great thunder-clouds.

Below us Garbh Uisge Beag mingled its waters with those of a sister stream — Garbh Uisge Mór, which rises below one of the largest summer snow-fields on the Cairngorms, a short distance north-east of the summit of Ben MacDhui. This snow-field was melting so rapidly that Garbh Uisge Mór was a torrent of foaming waters. We followed this clear torrent to the cliff edge, where it fell to Loch A'an. The drop to Loch A'an looked formidable, but by beginning the descent a short distance to the north of the waterfalls we were able to walk down to Loch A'an and reach the Shelter Stone without difficulty, passing through the great corrie (which, curiously enough, is without a name on any map) that is perhaps the most magnificent in the Cairngorms and, under certain conditions, is without an equal in all Scotland. In this unnamed corrie three streams of considerable size meet. They are Garbh Uisge Mór, Fèith Bhuidhe and the white foaming burn which drains Coire Domhainn, the Deep Corrie, of Cairngorm. Near where these streams enter Loch A'an is marked on the large-scale Ordnance Survey map Meur na Banaraiche, the Dairymaid's Finger. The word Meur (here, again, I am indebted to Professor Watson) is often applied to a branch of a stream : the dairy shieling may have been at the foot of this stream. In the corrie we saw many alpine plants. Here were July violets which mingled their blossoms of intense blue with the flowers of the butterwort. Washed by the spray of the falls, the starry saxifrage held its pale petals to the evening air, and in places we saw *Arabis petraea*, harebells and globe flowers. At a height of 2,700 feet above sea level I passed a raspberry bush.

We reached the foot of the corrie and looked back upon a scene of sublime grandeur. At the head of the corrie the stream of the Fèith Bhuidhe flowed invisible below a great snow-field. Its waters emerged from an arch of snow, then hurried in a foaming tumult to where Loch A'an with serenity awaited their coming and calmed their youthful impetuosity. Close to the

Shelter Stone lay Loch A'an, opal-tinted in the soft evening light. Many small trout were rising on its waters, disturbed by no wandering air : the rings of these rising trout crossed and re-crossed one another, so that many tiny wavelets roamed over the loch's surface. At ten o'clock that night we sat beside a sandy bay where the hill torrent entered the loch, and saw many trout cruising in the clear water, and often rising to the surface to suck down some fly or midge. One dark-coloured trout in its wanderings evidently entered the " territory " of his neighbour, for that neighbour (a light-coloured trout) drove him away with vigour. At 10.30,[1] as the twilight was deepening, a goos-ander duck flew up noiselessly and with a splash alighted on the darkening water of the sandy bay. In the half light she did not observe us and after she had preened her feathers, began to fish. Beside the Shelter Stone was the " earth " of a fox, apparently unoccupied, and a cock grouse, rising from the dew-drenched heather, broke the evening silence with his cheery " becking ".

The recess — it appeared almost a cave in the subdued light — beneath the Shelter Stone on so fine a night was gloomy and depressing. We therefore chose for our couch a heather-grown shelf out in the open, but protected from dew and rain by an overhanging corner of the great stone. During the short hours between sunset and sunrise we lay on this shelf, with the noise of falling waters in our ears and the peace and silence of the hills to soothe us.

At the midnight hour the sky was clear and a star burned in the depths of Loch A'an. An hour after midnight thin mists began to form on the slopes of Beinn Mheadhon. These mists of dawn grew stealthily until, at sunrise, Loch A'an was hemmed in by a billowy cloud. An hour later this cloud reached us, and we were caught in the embrace of grey, clammy vapour which was without apparent movement : through it the murmur of the

---

[1] This would be 11.30 P.M. by Single Summer Time and 12.30 A.M. by Double Summer Time.

waterfalls above us now came more faintly. The air all that night had been extraordinarily warm, and even the mist brought with it no chill ; we therefore remained lying, but not sleeping, on our hard but dry couch, hoping that the mist would lift before midday. We were not disappointed.

Shortly after eleven o'clock the sharp summit of the great cliff known as the Sticil, which rises almost sheer from the Shelter Stone, loomed grandly through the cloud and gradually the whole precipice, dark and grim even on this summer morning, was revealed. A narrow gully in the cliff was still filled with snow, and high up on the precipice we saw a curious circular hollow which recalled to mind Ossian's Cave above Glencoe. We received the impression that a stream sometimes issued from this cavern — perhaps in early summer, when the snows were melting fast. On all sides of us the air was clearing. In soft, woolly walls the clouds hung close to the sides of the great snowy corrie of the Garbh Uisge, but gradually these clouds lessened in size and then dissolved.

We left the Shelter Stone shortly before noon. The sun could now be seen faintly above the upper clouds and a pair of meadow-pipits were carrying on a belated courtship. The burn flowing from the high corrie had ebbed, for even on the warmest night the snow melts more slowly than during the day. The previous evening we had been obliged to look carefully for a crossing place ; now we crossed without difficulty. The air was sultry but sunless as we climbed the corrie and reached the snow near its head. Although the season was mid-July the blaeberry plants near the snow were not yet in flower, and the alpine ferns were only now beginning to unroll their fronds. Violets were in blossom, or only in bud, and here and there a cushion of *Arabis* or rock-cress grew on the damp rocks.

As we climbed the corrie a fresh army of mists had formed above Loch A'an, and now they rose to the corrie and pressed in upon us so that we were again imprisoned in fog. We followed the course of Garbh Uisge Beag until my pocket aneroid showed that we had reached a height of 3,500 feet above sea level, then turned north toward where we knew the Fèith Bhuidhe flowed unseen. Soon a wall of snow rose ahead of us. Almost vertical, this great snow wall towered above us, its summit invisible in clouds. We groped our way along the foot of this snow wall, hearing, as we walked, the cries of many hinds and their calves, so loud that the animals, although hidden from us by the mist, must have been near. By compass and by aneroid we steered for Carn Lochan, and just as we were reaching that rounded top, almost 4,000 feet above the sea, we emerged above the mist. We now looked across a sea of cloud to where the rocks on the summit of Ben A'an rose above the mist and, beyond them, the dark cone of Lochnagar. West, the waves of the mist ocean flowed in upon Braeriach.

We looked over the precipice of Carn Lochan. In clear weather we should have seen from here the houses in Strathspey and, beyond the Spey valley, the Monadh Liath range of hills, but we looked instead upon a great sea of cloud, gently stirring in places.

We crossed Craig an Leth-choin, and as we gazed into the mist-filled depths of Làirig Ghrù a mutter of thunder came from a black cloud high above us to the east. It was indeed strange to walk across this lonely country with black thunder-clouds high in the heavens above us and dun-coloured clouds in the valleys and glens far below us. Above the mist-sea a swift was hawking insects, and although rain was now falling the quiet air remained unusually warm.

Reluctantly we descended into the mist, and when we reached Làirig Ghrù found there twilight gloom and a temperature at least ten degrees lower than we had experienced on the high tops. The mist was so low that even the pine trees of Rothiemurchus were hidden in it, and that evening, as we shivered over a fire in the Spey valley, we pictured the hinds and their calves grazing in summer warmth above the clouds on that lonely plateau of Ben MacDhui, 4,000 feet above the sea.

Ben MacDhui is perhaps climbed more often from Braemar on Deeside than from Strathspey. It is rather nearer Deeside, and there is a right-of-way from Derry Lodge in Mar forest up to the hill-top. Derry Lodge is ten miles from Braemar. For the first six miles the road is a public one, then a private motor road (although a right-of-way foot track) continues up Glen Lui.

In my chapter on Làirig Ghrù I have described Glen Lui. On a fine day, at any season of the year, the view as one drives or walks up the glen is grand and beautiful. Rising ahead are the high Cairngorms. Ben MacDhui is clear, with Derry Cairngorm beside it, and the summit ridge of Cairntoul is also visible, although Carn a' Mhaim hides Braeriach.

At Derry lodge the road ends, and here two very old rights-of-way lead into the heart of the hills. One becomes Làirig Ghrù, the other curves to the right and winds north, through Glen Derry. Some distance up Glen Derry this track in its turn divides, one branch continuing as Làirig Laoigh, the Calf's Pass, across to Strathspey, the other branching to the west, into Coire Éiteachan, and continuing, by way of Loch Éiteachan, to the summit of Ben MacDhui.

Glen Derry is a wide glen. It is the anglicised form of Gleann Doire, the Glen of the Grove of Trees. There are interesting old Gaelic place-names in the glen, many of them now forgotten. The old stalkers had a name for each knoll, stream and hollow, but the younger generation do not know these names. On the slope above Glen Derry, not far from the lodge, small rocks may be seen on the ridge of Carn Crom. The name of the most prominent of these rocks is Craig Bad an t-Seabhaig, the Rock of the Clump of Trees of the Hawk. I think it probable that in earlier times the goshawk nested in the old pines beneath the rock and gave it its name. The goshawk has been for many years extinct as a nesting species in Britain, but the pine woods below the Cairngorms were among its last nesting haunts.

As the walker traverses Glen Derry he may see, among the pines, a large heathery mound. This is An Toman Dearg, the

Little Red Hill ; it appears to be a moraine left by the glacier which in a past age flowed imperceptibly through Glen Derry from the Cairngorm ice plateau. On the west side of Glen Derry are three corries, their names now almost forgotten. They are Coire na Cloiche, the Corrie of the Stone, Coire na Saobhaidhe, the Corrie of the Fox's Den, Coire Easgann Fhraoich, the Corrie of the Eel of the Heather,[1] and, rising from the east side of the glen, Coire an Fhir Bhogha, the Bowman's or Archer's Corrie.

Scots pines grow almost to the head of Glen Derry, where some storm-harried veterans are found on rough stony ground just short of 2,000 feet above sea level.

High up on the west side of the glen, and invisible from the path, is Lochan Uaine, the Green Tarn. There are several lochans of this name on the Cairngorms. Pure water, where deep, has a green tinge and all these lochs are green-tinted. Besides Lochan Uaine of Glen Derry there is a Lochan Uaine on Ben MacDhui, a Lochan Uaine on Cairntoul, and a Lochan Uaine (now usually named in maps by its English translation, Green Loch) not far from Loch Morlich, beneath Cairngorm. Lochan Uaine of Glen Derry, as I have mentioned in a previous chapter, is immortalised in the Gaelic poem " Allt an Lochain Uaine ", by William Smith, bard and hunter, he who is sometimes known as the Poet of the Cairngorms.

A hundred years ago there was a great dam in Glen Derry. This dam regulated the artificial floods on which the pine timber of the glen was floated down the stream to the Dee, and down the Dee to the seaport of Aberdeen. The memorable flood of 1829 demolished the dam, and it was never repaired ; its former boundaries can be seen only with difficulty at the present day. I have mentioned that Lochan Uaine is invisible from the path up Glen Derry, but the hill burn which flows from the loch is conspicuous after rain as it foams in a milky torrent down the steep hill face. Until late summer it is spanned by a snow bridge near its source.

[1] " Eel of the Heather " is the lizard.

After it branches westward from Glen Derry the track to Ben MacDhui traverses Coire Éiteachan, where flocks of ptarmigan are almost always to be seen, then skirts Loch Éiteachan. The climb up Coire Éiteachan is steep, and as one emerges at the head of the corrie it is unexpected to find a loch lying on what is really a small plateau 3,100 feet above sea level. I believe that Loch Éiteachan is the highest British loch in which trout are found. I remember, in the years before the first Great War, an ancient boat lying near the shore of the loch. I have seen only one man fish Loch Éiteachan. That was on a day of early July, so cold that showers of wet snow drifted from Ben MacDhui across the loch. Yet despite the strangeness of that midsummer weather, which might have been a product of Greenland or Spitsbergen, the angler succeeded in landing more than one large trout, thin and lanky as the result of the spartan diet on which it was compelled to exist, for flies here must be a luxury, and so rare that it can be hardly worth while keeping a watch for them. When the wind blows strongly, the waters of Loch Éiteachan are often lifted in spindrift : as furious gusts strike the loch, the waters on the western shore are seen to flow and ebb again a full inch. On the east shore of Loch Éiteachan, between it and the small tarn known as Loch Éiteachan Beag, sea thrift grows abundantly. Some botanists of distinction are doubtful whether this thrift of the high hills is *Armeria maritima*, and suggest that it is a form of *Armeria alpina*, the thrift which grows on the western Alps at a height of 7,000 to 9,000 feet above the sea. The poetical Gaelic name for the sea thrift is Cluasag Mhuire, the Virgin Mary's Pillow.

One of the east shoulders of Ben MacDhui rises abruptly from the west shore of Loch Éiteachan. This spur is known as Sròn an Daimh, the Nose of the Hart, and perhaps takes its name from some celebrated stag which had his home or was shot here. The Gaelic word *damh* (of which the genitive is *daimh*) is correctly applied to an ox, but the older generation of Mar stalkers used the word when speaking of a stag.

The right-of-way up Ben MacDhui skirts Sròn an Daimh, and passes a small ruined bothy where sappers who surveyed the Cairngorms in the middle of the nineteenth century for a time lived. Their visit to Mar forest is even now spoken of, for they handsomely paid the crofters of the township of Inverey for the use of their ponies. The ponies carried coal and provisions up to that small dwelling on the roof of Scotland 4,000 feet above the sea — almost as high as the old observatory on Ben Nevis.

It is interesting to look across to Ben Nevis on a clear day from Ben MacDhui : I have seen from Ben MacDhui, through a stalking telescope, the cloud shadows racing across the snow-beds of Ben Nevis more than fifty miles distant. On very clear days two slender cone-like hills may be noticed to rise on the far western horizon. If the reader of this chapter wishes to see these distant hills from the cairn of Ben MacDhui, he must look across the birth-place of the Dee on the Braeriach plateau. One of these remote cone-like hills I believe to be Sgùrr Ouran, a high hill above Kintail. The other may be Ben Attow (Beinn Fhada, the Long Hill), one of the Sisters of Kintail, but I incline rather to the belief that it is Ben Sgriol, a high, sharp-pointed hill which rises from Loch Hourn. These are the two peaks which in Rothiemurchus tradition are named the Cuillin hills of the Isle of Skye, but, as I have mentioned on page 357, experts of the Ordnance Survey consider that intervening hills make it impossible to see the Cuillin from the Cairngorms.

Weather conditions change quickly on the high Cairngorms. One summer day when I reached the cairn on the summit of Ben MacDhui the sky everywhere was almost cloudless, but a little later a long line of white, billowy clouds crept inland from the south-east. The clouds touched, then flowed over, hills so far apart as Beinn a' Ghló in Atholl forest, Lochnagar, highest hill of the Balmoral forest, and Mount Keen, on the borders of Aberdeenshire and Angus. Soon black clouds gathered above Ben MacDhui itself, and as they hid the sun the air grew cold and damp. Across the bleak tableland a freshening south wind blew: each moment the clouds grew and became more ominous. The great snow-field east of the cairn no longer gleamed dazzlingly white, for the clear air had suddenly become dark and hazy, although to the north the slopes of Cairngorm were still in bright sunshine. More quickly than it can be told, that fair view of many hills and glens was blotted out and Ben MacDhui was held in the cold embrace of grey, ghostly mists. At the coming of the mists the spectre reputed to haunt the summit of Ben MacDhui might have been expected to appear. This phantom is Fear Liath Mór, the Big Grey Man. The late Professor J. N. Collie, F.R.S., a former president of the Alpine Club, asserted that he encountered this spectre and heard the crunching of giant feet which followed him with dreadful persistency across the plateau ; the late Marquess of Ailsa told me he used to hear of that spectre when he stayed at Castle Grant at the close of the nineteenth century.

We can scarcely bid farewell to Ben MacDhui without discussing the meaning of its name, which is sometimes spelled Ben Muich Dhui and sometimes Ben MacDhui. Ben Muich Dhui is in English Hill of the Black Pig, but the spelling which finds favour with Celtic scholars at the present time is Ben MacDhui (more correctly Beinn Mac Duibh) ; in English, MacDuff's Hill. I understand that in an old map " Macduff Cairn " is marked near Ben MacDhui. In the old *Statistical Account* of Scotland (vol. xii, p. 426) it is recorded that MacDuff, Thane of Fife, in the thirteenth century made a gift of the parish of Inveraven (the head springs of the Avon or A'an are on Ben MacDhui) in a charter. It is therefore probable that a part at all events of the hill was on his land, and it may well be that the mountain is named after him, or after one of his family. On the other hand, the spelling — Binn-na-Muick-Duidh — in the same *Account* is an argument in favour of " the Hill of the Black Pig " derivation. In modern Gaelic the name would be spelled Beinn na Muice Duibhe.

I have so far described what may be termed the central massif of the Cairngorms. The two most prominent of the eastern Cairngorms are Beinn a' Bhùird and Ben A'an. Beinn a' Bhùird is, in English, the Hill of the Board or Table, and Table Mountain it was well named, for the hill-top and its surrounding plateau appear flat as a table when viewed from the west — it is note-worthy that both Cairntoul and Beinn a' Bhùird should appar-ently have been named by people who knew them from the *west*. So level is the Beinn a' Bhùird plateau that with little difficulty it could be made an ideal landing-place for aircraft : the North Top is fully two miles distant from the South Top, yet the altitude of the two summits is almost the same. The North Top is 3,924 feet above the sea, and the South Top is 3,860 feet high. Beinn a' Bhùird is partly in the county of Aberdeen and partly in the shire of Banff — the county march crosses the North Top. Three great deer forests, Mar, Invercauld and Inchrory, also march on this hill, and as no right-of-way leads to the summits, the climber should avoid Beinn a' Bhùird during the deer-stalking season. The hill can be climbed from the Slugan or from Glen Quoich on Deeside, or from Faindouran on the river A'an. A third way of ascent is from Glen Lui, by way of Clais Fhearnaig, the Alder Furrow. A couple of miles up Glen Lui a track leads northward to Glen Quoich (in Gaelic Gleann Cuach, the Glen of the *Cuach* or Small Wooden Cup). In Clais Fhearnaig are a succession of small rush-grown pools. They are the home of trout, and a heron haunts them, fishing patiently. On the rocks above this pass are to be seen three interesting trees growing together — a spruce, a larch and a rowan or mountain ash. The rowan one would expect to find here, but how came the spruce and the larch to this remote place ? Neither tree is a native of Scotland, although both grow in plantations on upper Deeside. The seeds may have been carried to the rock by a bird, or may have been whirled there by some snow blizzard.

Clais Fhearnaig leads into Glen Quoich, one of the most pleasant glens of the Cairngorm country. The splendid old pines that grow here extend as high as 1,800 feet above the level of the sea, and the outposts of the forest almost reach the 2,000-feet contour line. On the hills of the western seaboard no well-grown tree would be found at anything like this height, but Glen Quoich, being in the central Highlands and in the heart of the hills, is comparatively sheltered from storms. Fierce gales do at times strike the glen, and hundreds of old pines in Glen Quoich were uprooted by a great storm from the north-west which swept the glen in December 1893. Although these old trees crashed fifty years ago, they lie at the present day with no signs of rot showing in their strong timber. They all lie towards the south, their branches and stems bleached almost white by the action of rain and sun. On that day, long ago, when they fell, the sight must have been an awe-inspiring one, and the crash of the trees and the rush of the gale must have produced a symphony of terrible grandeur. It would be interesting to know the age of the oldest pines in Glen Quoich : most of them are, I believe, well over a hundred years old, and some of them must have seen more than two centuries pass, for in these old natural forests growth is slow and each year adds imperceptibly to height and girth. Some of the old pines of Glen Quoich show clearly the phenomenon of spiral growth. The wood of the main stem has grown spirally like a corkscrew and this gives the tree increased strength to withstand storms.

In Glen Quoich on fine summer days the strong sun draws the aromatic scent from the plants of crowberry and blaeberry that grow in clearings among the old pines, and the redstart sings his song and flirts his red tail on the whitened branches of overthrown trees.

At the foot of Beinn a' Bhùird Glen Quoich divides. The greater of its two branches curves away toward the east and the lesser continues toward the north and becomes An Dubh Ghleann, the Black Glen. This leads up to Mòine Bhealaidh, the Moss of Broom, a summer home of many deer. It is possible that this place-name was given the moss because of the bright yellow colour, almost as yellow as the flower of broom, which is seen on this high-lying ground in autumn : the Mar stalkers refer to it always as the Yellow Moss. Near a watcher's bothy in the Black Glen the track to Beinn a' Bhùird crosses a shoulder known as An Diollaid, the Saddle, and keeps above, and parallel to, Alltan na Beinne, the Streamlet of the Hill, to the high ground. A tributary of this streamlet drains a steep, grassy corrie, Coire Gorm. The Gaelic word *gorm* usually means blue (cf. Cairngorm, the Blue Hill) but when applied to grass has the meaning green : in this instance Coire Gorm, the Green Corrie, is a fitting name, for on a summer day the grass here is as green as a lawn.

There is usually a snow-field until late in the summer beside the course of Alltan na Beinne, and I have seen an ice-wall here 8 feet high at the end of July.

Beinn a' Bhùird being one of the eastern Cairngorms, the view from its top is extensive to the east rather than to the west. The hills of middle and lower Deeside are distinct — Morven, Mount Keen and the hill of Craigendinny near Aboyne, and, farther east, the flat-topped Hill o' Fare near Banchory and Cairn-mon-earn on the high ground of Durris. On a clear day I have seen the North Sea, east of Aberdeen, showing as a long misty line.

Although flat-topped, Beinn a' Bhùird holds several fine corries to the east of the summit. Deep in Coire an Dubh Lochain lies An Dubh Lochan, the Black Loch, on which ice is sometimes seen at midsummer. Near the North Top is Coire nan Clach, the Corrie of Stones, wild and gloomy, with a projecting rock wall that almost divides the corrie into two. South of Coire an Dubh Lochain is Coire na Cìche, the Corrie of the Pap ; it takes its name from a great rock known as A' Chìoch, the Pap. Just south of Coire na Cìche is Coire Buidhe, the Yellow Corrie. South-west of the Yellow Corrie are the two Snowy Corries. In Gaelic they are named An Ear Choire Sneachda, the East Snowy Corrie, and An Iar Choire Sneachda, the West Snowy Corrie. In the Snowy Corries of Beinn a' Bhùird a great snow-wreath, plainly visible from the main Deeside road as one approaches Braemar from the east, frequently remains unmelted all through the summer and autumn. On very hot summer days red deer love to lie on this snow-field.

There are two corries on Beinn a' Bhùird bearing the name Coire Ruaraidh, Roderick's Corrie. It is possible that the Roderick whom the name commemorates was a noted hunter of deer, but so far as I have been able to discover, no record of this man remains in the country of Beinn a' Bhùird. Between the North Top and the eastern spur (known as Cnap a' Chléirich, the Clergyman's Knoll) Allt Dearg, the Red Burn, rises. This may be held to be the true source of the Water of Quoich, which joins the Dee a short distance above Braemar.

At the head of the glen, 2,500 feet above sea level, a great boulder lies at the end of a stalking path ; it is named Clach a' Chléirich, the Clergyman's Stone, and no doubt commemorates the same cleric as the spur.

From Clach a' Chléirich, Beinn a' Bhùird is seen as a hill of grandeur and character, very different from the unimposing flat top viewed from the west. In Coire an Dubh Lochain are two tarns bearing the name Dubh Lochan (Black Tarn), the lower lochan some 300 feet beneath the upper sheet of water. Above them, on the summit ridge, stands A' Chìoch, the giant Breast, dark and grim in summer but in winter covered with a coat of snow, so that it shines white and spotless in the sun.

Ben A'an, usually, though less correctly, spelled on modern maps as Ben Avon, is the most easterly of the Cairngorms : the source of the Don, a lowland stream during most of its course, is only two miles north-east of this great massif, which has a number of tops.

Ben A'an is no doubt named after the River A'an, which it is suggested derives its name from Fionn or Fingal and is Ath-Fhinn, Fingal's Ford. Fionn was chief of the warrior band known as the Féinne or Fingalians. When Fionn and his wife were out hunting one day and attempted to cross the river, Fionn crossed safely but his wife, slipping on the stones of the ford,[1] was carried away and drowned. Fionn thereupon named the river Ath-Fhinn, the Ford of Fionn or Fingal, to commemorate the event. Another version of the old tale is that Fionn's wife was named Ath-fhinn, the Very Fair One, and that when she lost her life in the torrent Fionn named the river Ath-fhinn after her. Those who may like to read of this strange tradition should consult vol. xii, p. 415 of the old *Statistical Account of Scotland*, published in 1794. There are no grounds, writes Professor Watson, for believing that the place-name is from Abhuinn (Avon) meaning a river, which might superficially appear to be the derivation. It is interesting that the ford at which Làirig Laoigh crosses the A'an rather less than a mile below Loch A'an is still known as Ath nam Fiann, the Ford of the Fingalians, which seems to confirm the tradition that the district has associations with the band of half-mythical heroes of whom Fionn or Fingal was the chief.

The River A'an is renowned for its clearness, and I myself have noted when crossing the ford that this clearness makes the depth of the water deceptive : even in flood the water remains unstained by peat or mud, and a drowning accident might easily occur here. In one of Timothy Pont's papers, written before the year 1600, it is mentioned that the A'an is clearer than any of the tributaries of Spey, " yea more clear and pure than anie river in Scotland whatsoever ".

Ben A'an, as I have said, is a large hill, or rather a number of summits linked by a central plateau extending from north-east to south-west and more than four miles in length. The long backbone of Ben A'an is the gathering-ground of many burns which have their sources here. To the north these streams feed the River A'an ; to the south they flow to the Gairn and thence to the Dee. Ben A'an is remarkable for its outcrops of granite. They rise here and there from the smooth face of the hill. One

---

[1] The ford where she slipped and was submerged is the Linn of A'an near Inchrory ; her grave is supposed to be two miles below that place, at Bogluachrach.

Lochnagar

of these great rocks is named Clach Bhàn, and two rough seats have been chiselled out of it. There is an old tradition that women from great distances came to sit on these rough stone seats in order that the pains of child-birth might be lessened.

One summer day the air was so clear on the Ben A'an plateau that I was able to see the smoke of a steamer on the North Sea, over fifty miles distant.

The actual summit of Ben A'an is marked by a great rock, a full 30 feet high. Beneath this rock was Leabaidh an Daimh Bhuidhe, the Bed of the Yellow Stag. Long ago must have been the day of that Yellow Stag, which may have been remarkable for his colour, as also, perhaps, for his size. From his couch, which he no doubt used only in fine summer weather, he must have looked across the Highlands of Scotland from Lochnagar and Mount Keen in Angus to the Lomonds and the Ochil Hills of Fife. To the west he may have noticed the neighbouring Cairngorms, never entirely without snow even at midsummer, and he may perhaps have looked down upon the heather-thatched houses of Ceann Drochaide, as the township of Braemar was named in his day. But there is none now living who can tell of the doings of the Yellow Stag ; even his name and the name of his couch are rarely spoken of, for Gaelic has almost died in the country of Braemar and Strath A'an.

CHAPTER XXXIII

THE HIGH TOPS OF THE CAIRNGORMS : II. THE WESTERN CAIRNGORMS

> Land of the Mountain and the Flood,
> Where the pine of the Forest for ages hath stood,
> Where the eagle comes forth on the wings of the storm
> And her young ones are rocked on the high Cairngorm.

THE Western Cairngorms may be described as the hills of the Cairngorm massif which rise to the west of Làirig Ghrù. Of these western hills the two highest are Braeriach (4,248 feet) and Cairntoul (4,241 feet), but Sgoran Dubh, Monadh Mór and Beinn Bhrodain are all between 3,500 and 3,900 feet high.

Of all the high Cairngorms Cairntoul, in Gaelic Carn an t-Sabhail, Barn Hill, is, to my way of thinking, the most alpine in appearance. It rises steeply from Làirig Ghrù in a splendid cone — and yet, like Beinn a' Bhùird, it has an entirely different appearance when seen from the west, from which view-point its summit is shaped like a great barn. It is evident, therefore, that Cairntoul, like Beinn a' Bhùird, was named by people who looked upon it from the west. There are two fine corries on the east face of Cairntoul. One is Coire an t-Saighdeir, the Soldier's Corrie ; the other, immediately below the summit, is Coire an t-Sabhail. North-west of the hill-top is Coire an Lochain Uaine, the Corrie of the Green Tarn, and deep in its recess is a small loch, its waters over 3,000 feet above sea level.

Near Coire an Lochain Uaine is the spur known usually as Sgor an Lochain Uaine, and sometimes as the Angel's Peak. I used to be told in Mar forest that the name Angel's Peak was a comparatively recent one — that it was given the peak by Mr. Copeland, a well-known climber, in order, so old Donald Fraser of the Derry told me, " to keep the Devil's Point in its place ". The old name for the hill, I always understood, was Sgor an Lochain Uaine, the Peak of the Green Tarn (Lochan Uaine lies immediately beneath it). But more recently, when I discussed the matter with the late George MacPherson Grant of the Ballindalloch family, who own Glen Feshie deer forest and the west slope of the hill, he told me that as a young man (this would be about the year 1890), when he used to stalk in Glen Feshie forest, the stalkers even at that time used always to refer to the hill as Sgor an Aingeil, the Angel's Peak, and not as Sgor an Lochain Uaine. It is of course quite possible that so distinctive and unusual a name as the Angel's Peak at once "caught on" in the district, and was translated into their own language by the Gaelic-speaking stalkers.

There are many fine walks among the western Cairngorms. Their highest peaks can be climbed with no great difficulty in a summer's day, either from Mar on Deeside or Rothiemurchus on Speyside. From Mar perhaps the best route is by the Làirig Ghrù as far as the small Corrour bothy beside the Dee, then up the slope between the Devil's Point and Cairntoul, where the ridge is reached at about 3,000 feet above sea level. Thence the " going " to the top of Cairntoul is easy. The walk may then be continued round the head of the Garbh Choire (Garrachory), crossing the summit of the Angel's Peak and reaching the Braeriach plateau near the Wells of Dee. From the Wells, the summit of Braeriach is distant perhaps a mile and a half, and a climb of no more than 250 feet. The descent may be made to Làirig Ghrù at the watershed of the pass, near the Pools of Dee, and the walk continued through the Làirig to Aviemore.

The Braeriach plateau is the nearest thing to true Arctic country that we have in the British Isles. Here, at heights from 4,000 to 4,250 feet, the plant life and character of the land resemble Iceland or Spitsbergen. Even in July I have known snow

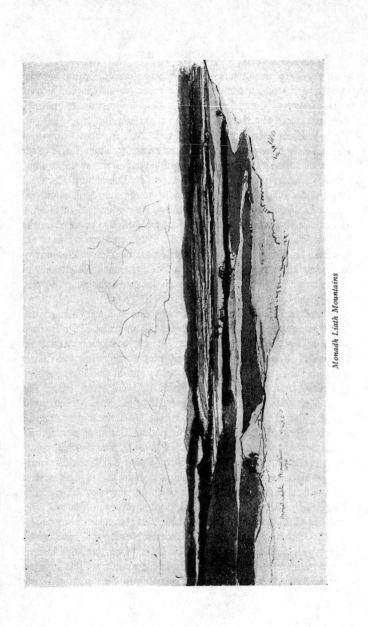

Monadh Liath Mountains

swirl before the north wind over this mountain plateau, piling up wreaths in the sheltered hollows, but in fine weather, at the season of midsummer, the green of the grass, the red of the gravel and the pink rosettes of the cushion pink are a delightful background to the cornice of gleaming snow which fringes the Garrachory until July or even later. The golden eagle, herding in play a flock of ptarmigan over the Garrachory, or a whistling golden plover speeding overhead, or perhaps a hunting party of black-headed gulls drifting on white, pointed wings high in the clear sky, are sights in keeping with the stern character and beauty of this plateau of the great hills, to which the red deer climb only during the finest weather.

Across the plateau flows the River Dee, a small stream of cold, pure water which at first moves slowly and rather aimlessly as if unwilling to leave its home on the roof of Scotland. Thus it arrives at the edge of the Garrachory, when (except for a short space in late summer when the snow has melted) it dives beneath the snow cornice which fringes the plateau and reappears at the beginning of a series of high cascades which fall in white tumult to the depths of the Garrachory. At first sight it would appear impossible for the human wanderer to descend over this seemingly sheer precipice to the Garrachory, yet there is a way of descent, not too difficult if care is exercised, to the corrie, if the climber keeps near the east bank of the river.

The Garbh Choire, or Garrachory, is without doubt one of the most splendid corries in all Scotland. The late John Mathieson, Librarian of the Royal Scottish Geographical Society, kindly sent me an interesting and very old reference to this corrie. It appears in *Collections for a History of the Shires of Aberdeen and Banff* published by the Spalding Club. On page 78 there is a footnote as follows :

The river Dee springes out of Corredee, on the confynes Badenocht at a place caled by the barbarous inhabitants, Pittindawin and Bodindeweill (that is the deivell's . . .) so speakes these wylde scurrilous people, amongst wych ther is bot small feare and knowledge of God.—*Sir James Balfour's Collections MS.*

I have sometimes seen the water-ouzel beside the River Dee on the Braeriach plateau at a height of 3,900 feet : the bird must come here in search of water larvae, for there are no small trout, or their ova, which might attract it. Fishermen often accuse the water-ouzel of devouring the ova of fish when they see it haunting the gravelly bed of a stream, but the fact that it makes the long flight to the Dee at its source, where there are no trout, is a mark in its favour.

There is usually no season of spring on the Braeriach plateau, but a sudden transition from winter to summer. This transition takes place about May 20. Up to that time the plateau has been deep in unbroken snow, and to visit this upland country at the middle of May is to have a very good idea of what the Arctic regions are like at that season. When the sun rides high in the heavens the glare from the great expanse of white is dazzling. A companion and I were on one occasion on the Braeriach plateau in late May. There had been a heavy fall of fresh snow, but the day was fine and clear. When we reached the plateau the sun was shining with power, and the newly fallen snow was so dazzling that we began to suffer from snow-blindness. We soon realised that it would be impossible for us to reach the top of Braeriach, and, sitting down on a small area of snow-free ground, we awaited a short period of cloud to permit us to return to lower levels. It is a symptom of the approach of snow-blindness that the snow in the vision of the affected person gradually loses its whiteness, and becomes pink, or violet in colour. The snowy plateau apparently changed colour as we looked on it, and our eyes soon became painful. As we returned across that plateau I walked with eyes closed and one hand pressed over them in order to protect them further from the glare, yet I felt at once, to my discomfort, the increase in the power of the light when the sun appeared from behind a cloud. It might have been thought that with the double shade of the closed eyelids and the thickness of the human hand held over the eyes no light could have reached me, let alone light so strong as to cause discomfort.

It is difficult to estimate the depth of snow which covers this plateau in spring. The cairn which marks the summit of Braeriach is on exposed ground, where much of the snow which falls must be blown away. Yet on April 3, 1925, when I crossed Braeriach, I could find no trace of the summit cairn, although I stood on the snow above the place where it was buried. I estimated that an average depth of 7 to 8 feet of snow covered the hill-top at that time.

From this plateau, 4,000 feet above sea level, the view across Scotland is wide. On page 343 I have recorded the tradition in Rothiemurchus that the Cuillin hills in distant Skye are visible from Braeriach. The cone-like hills which are held to be the Cuillin I have described in the preceding chapter; they are definitely not peaks of the Cuillin range, for I was at pains to travel from Braeriach to a view-point nearer the Cuillin and in the same line, and a careful scrutiny of the Cuillin from that view-point showed me that no summit had the same shape as the distant hills seen from Braeriach. Since local opinion in Rothiemurchus still held that the tradition of the district was justified, I resolved to ask the Ordnance Survey and put the matter beyond doubt. The Ordnance Survey were good enough to take an interest in the matter and worked out the problem carefully. Their answer was that the actual distance between Braeriach and the Cuillin (a matter of ninety-five miles) was not too great for the Skye hills to be seen, but that a hill between sixty and seventy miles distant from Braeriach rose right in the track of the Cuillin, and hid this range from Braeriach. Thus the matter at issue was put beyond doubt.

Although the Cuillin are invisible from Braeriach, there are few hills in the Highlands of Scotland which cannot be seen from its high plateau. On the south-west horizon in fine weather Ben Lawers rises, blue and clear: to the right of that hill, and at an even greater distance, are the twin tops of Stob Inneoin and Ben More above Crianlarich. West are the Blackmount tops, and Ben Nevis with the long snow-splashed ridge of Aonach Mór beside it.

In very clear weather the hills rising from Loch Linnhe, and the two sharp tops of Cruachan above Loch Etive are seen. North-west are the long range of hills which rise from the country of Glen Moriston, Glen Affric [1] and Glen Cannich. North is the great mass of Ben Wyvis, a lump of a hill, and north-east, across the blue waters of the Moray Firth, is the cone of Morven in Caithness.

The near view, too, is grand. Across the gloomy Garrachory Cairntoul rises nobly, and to the east are two other hill giants, Ben MacDhui and Cairngorm.

One of the finest walks through the Cairngorms is from Mar, by way of the Làirig Ghrù to the Garrachory, thence to the Braeriach plateau and on to Aviemore by way of Loch Eanaich. It was late October when last I did that walk. The morning mist was lifting and the sun, red and hazy, was rising above the eastern horizon as my friend and I set out from Luibeg in Mar forest. Before sunrise stags had been roaring near us : they were now grazing quietly on level ground beside the clear waters of the river. On heathery knolls cock grouse sun-bathed. By nine o'clock Glen Luibeg was warm and smiling, and away to the west the clouds were slowly rising from the corries of Beinn Bhrodain like steam from a vast cauldron. Where the Làirig Ghrù path crosses the Luibeg burn we came in sight of Ben MacDhui, the snow powdering its summit now faintly tinged with yellow in the light of the soft autumn sun. The date was October 23 of the year 1937 and this was the first autumn coating of snow on the high Cairngorms.

As we crossed the stream a pair of golden eagles sailed higher and higher above the heathery slopes of Carn Crom. The sun shone on their golden heads and on the strong primary feathers of their wings as the great birds rose without effort above the hill-top. Below the eagles a herd of stags climbed to the ridge

[1] MacBain in his *Place-Names* says that this glen takes its name from the river which has the old female personal name Afric or Oirig (Euphemia) and which was perhaps the name of the water-nymph that haunted the stream.

and appeared, one after another, on the skyline as they passed beyond our view to the high pastures. We followed the path round the base of Carn a' Mhaim : as we came in sight of Glen Dee the mist was flowing white into the Soldier's Corrie of Cairntoul and above the corrie the snow-powdered summit rose in radiance to the blue of the sky. The beauty of Glen Dee was memorable this late October morning. The great hills of the glen — the Devil's Point, Cairntoul, Ben MacDhui, Braeriach — all were in warm sunlight. We passed Clach nan Tàillear, the Tailors' Stone, where certain tailors (as I have recorded in Chapter XXXI) perished in snow in their attempt to dance — for a wager — on the same day at "the three Dells", the Dell of Abernethy, the Dell of Rothiemurchus and Dalmore in Mar, close to where Mar lodge now stands. Across the River Dee stood the Corrour bothy. Here John Macintosh, deer-stalker, piper and strong hillman, was accustomed of an evening to tune his pipes in the glow of the fire of bog-fir and peat. Now "the Piper", as he was always known in Mar, has gone to his rest and the bothy is deserted. My thoughts went back to a still earlier deer-watcher who in summer and autumn lived in the bothy — old Charles Robertson, a kindly man, and one with a quaint humour. Often he searched the hills for Cairngorm stones, and had once (*vide* Chapter XXXI), the awe-inspiring experience of seeing a cloudburst strike the rocks of Carn a' Mhaim opposite the bothy and roar down the hill in torrents so furious that now, forty years later, the scars they made are still evident. Charles Robertson tamed the mice in the bothy, and one of these mice used to come out of its hole of an evening and sit on the old man's boot, to beg for pieces of cheese.

The morning wore on, and now we had reached and entered the wild, grand Garbh Choire, or Garrachory. Above the corrie the deep-blue sky was cloudless, and the air so warm that it was hard to realise that October was nearing its close. In places the milkwort still showed blue flowers among the heather and the lousewort held its red blossoms to the sky. Across the mouth of

Coire Bhrochain of Braeriach we toiled over granite screes, and remembered the old Mar tradition of the naming of this corrie. The story I have put on record in Chapter XXXI.

Sunset came to us for a time at high noon when we passed into the great shadow cast across the Garrachory by the peak of Sgor an Lochain Uaine, and here a ptarmigan which rose ahead of us in that shadow became of a sudden luminous as its white wings bore it from shade to sunlight. On the ground were ancient bleached stems and roots of great juniper bushes, the wood aromatic and incense-scented when kindled. As we crossed the young Dee below its fall over the Braeriach precipice many ptarmigan rose from the screes, and with white wings gleaming in the sun sped across the wild country that is their home. A young golden eagle alighted not far from us and then, rising again, showed the white on the tail which is the distinguishing feature of the young golden eagle during its first year.[1] In sunshine we came in sight of the snow-beds which remain unmelted from one year's end to another in a sunless recess beneath the cliff at the extreme west end of the Garrachory. In late summer the great snow-field which is formed here each winter breaks up into three smaller beds ; on this October day the three snow-fields which lingered here were ice-hard and, so steep was the slope on which they rested, it was not easy to keep one's footing on them. My friend picked up a piece of ice and threw it idly among the rocks — and almost at his feet a mountain hare darted from its shelter. An interesting sequel to this was that, when I visited the snow-beds in October of the following year, the same hare (at least I presume it was the same animal) ran out from beneath the same rock ! During the intervening twelve months it is probable that it had seen no human being, for the west of the Garrachory is perhaps the least frequented country of the Cairngorms.

[1] The white on the tail persists until the Golden Eagle is more than three years old, for the species does not reach maturity until four years after fledging.

Near the snow-beds the hill slope was covered with a carpet of plants of *Gnaphalium supinum*, and the parsley fern grew here and there in crevices among the boulders. The droppings of a deer and the feathers of a ptarmigan lay beside a little-used deer track.

A sudden change of weather overtook us here. To the south the sky remained a deep, glorious blue, yet, on a cold north wind which had risen, mist began to spill in over the Braeriach precipices and flow like a river down the slopes of the corrie where we sat. Time after time the sun fought with and dispelled that cold cloud, but the vanguard of the mist was succeeded by an irresistible army of an ever-increasing size. We could see that another cloud was pressing in upon the snowy summit of Ben MacDhui — and then, as we climbed the steep slopes of the corrie and reached the plateau of Braeriach, we passed, in a few brief moments, from summer to winter. On the plateau the ground was lightly covered with snow and twilight succeeded the sunlight — the twilight of a dense forest after the clear air of the open country beyond it.

We walked along the edge of the precipice until we had reached the infant Dee, then crossed the plateau westward in thick mist, keeping close to the low river banks which reminded me that day of a desolate Arctic tundra rather than of a hill plateau 4,000 feet above the sea. Our hair and clothes became coated with ice crystals ; there was little wind and the mist ever grew more dense. We reached the Wells of Dee, and as we steered west (magnetic) by compass after leaving the Wells we might have been explorers in an unknown and uncharted land, for we had to rely on the accuracy of our compass course to take us down to Loch Eanaich and Speyside. I had not done the walk for a dozen years and more, and although I believed that my course was an accurate one it was with relief that, after a time, I saw through a rift which appeared in the mist the dark waters of Loch Eanaich 2,000 feet below. Professor W. J. Watson has thrown much-needed light on the derivation of this place-name. He writes to me that the loch derives its name from the old (and obsolete) Gaelic word *eanach* (of which the genitive is *eanaich*), meaning a marsh or bog. The name is therefore incorrectly spelled Einnich or Eunaich in the maps. The place-name is appropriate, for an extensive area of boggy land is found below the loch. There are many small trout, and char, in Loch Eanaich, but Sandy Mac-Kenzie, at one time head stalker in Rothiemurchus forest, told me that he had taken on a line set in Loch Eanaich a trout which, had it been in condition, would have weighed 5 lb.

The mist closed in upon us again, then finally drifted clear as we continued the descent. When we had last seen the upper sky in Glen Dee it had been cloudless : now we found ourselves beneath a canopy of dark cloud. A sombre country lay beneath us, except at Slochd, between Strathspey and Inverness, where the evening sun burned dull red, as though a heather fire had been kindled here. It was strange to have left the clear air and blue sky which had been our companions before we had entered the mist-cap on Braeriach ; we had passed not only from one county to another but from one climate to another — even the air we breathed seemed different. We descended the steep slope into Coire Dhondail [1] and looked across the corrie at the great rocks of Sgoran Dubh, dark with the shades of approaching night. Beside the small bothy (haunted, so it is said, by the spectre of a black dog) which then stood at the end of the stalking road to Loch Eanaich many red deer were grazing, and here red grouse replaced the ptarmigan of the high grounds. We had still a nine-mile walk before us down Glen Eanaich before reaching Rothiemurchus and Aviemore. Low and clear flowed the Beanaidh : a herd of stags forded the river ahead of us, and threw a shower of white spray into the dusk. Twilight had deepened as we passed the sturdy aged pine known to the old people of Rothiemurchus as Craobh Phillidh, the Tree of the Returning, and as we saw its thick canopy against the night sky

[1] Professor Watson is of the opinion that this word may have been originally Gamhandail ; in English, Stirk-dale.

above the hillside behind it we remembered the old associations with this tree. Long ago, when the people of Rothiemurchus each summer went up to the hill shielings at the head of Loch Eanaich, this tree was a landmark to them. It is said that they drove the young cattle up to the shieling country before they themselves went there, and that it was necessary to accompany the stirks only as far as this tree, for, once there, they would continue of themselves to the shieling grazings. Since the herdsman left the cattle at this tree and returned to Rothiemurchus it was known as the Tree of the Returning.

It was dark as we entered the forest, but the aurora brightened the northern sky, and when the moon rose it shone upon a country of falling leaves, for a rising north wind was shaking the birches and bringing flurries of drifting snow to the lonely country of the high Cairngorms.

Sgoran Dubh (3,658 feet) is the most westerly of the Cairngorm range. From the west it is not imposing, but from Glen Eanaich it forms a noble background to pine, river and heather. It can be climbed either from Glen Eanaich to the east or from Glen Feshie to the west. The climb from Glen Feshie is more gradual, and when the hill-top is reached there is a truly magnificent view over the east-facing precipice into Loch Eanaich, which lies, blue and smiling or inky-black according to the mood of the weather, 2,000 feet beneath. The unexpectedness of this grand scene adds to its impressiveness, for there is nothing, during the ascent of the western slopes, to give the climber any inkling of what he will see on the hill-top.

The well-known sportsman, Colonel T. Thornton, who climbed Sgoran Dubh, apparently from the west, in 1804 gives an interesting account of his day. He writes:

At 12 o'clock we got to the first snow before we were near the mouth of Glen Ennoch, and then depositing our champaign, lime, shrub, porter, etc. in one of the large snow drifts, beneath an arch, from which ran a charming spring, we agreed to dine there. In my way up I had killed an old moorcock and a ptarmigant, which I ordered to be well picked and prepared for dinner. . . . It is impossible to describe the astonishment of the whole party, when they perceived themselves on the brink of that frightful precipice, which separated them from the lake below. They remained motionless for a considerable time equally struck with admiration and horror, the mountain above them to the right chequered with drifts of snow and differing but little from it in colour, the immense rocks to the left, separated by large fissures, the safe abode of eagles, and even the precipices around, appeared to them truly majestic. Let the reader figure to himself a mountain AT LEAST EIGHTEEN THOUSAND FEET ABOVE HIM AND A STEEP PRECIPICE OF THIRTEEN THOUSAND FEET BELOW, encompassed with conical and angular rocks. Then let him imagine men and horses scrambling over huge masses of stones which though of immense size are frequently loose, and at every step seem as if the next would carry them off into the air beyond its edges, and the very idea would be enough to make him shudder. Yet the eye, having dwelt awhile on these frightful naked piles, is soon relieved, and feels an agreeable composure from the scene beneath, where the lake like a sheet of glass reflects on its extensive bosom all the objects around. This lake, bordered by soft sandy banks whose fine but partial verdure scattered over with small herds of cattle, grazing and bleating, and a single bothee, the temporary residence of a lonely herdsman, softens in some measure the unpleasant idea of danger which is apt to arise, while the solemn silence interrupted only by the hoarse notes of the ptarmigants, increasing at the approach of strangers, or by the dashing of the never-ceasing cascades soothes the mind with the most agreeable emotion. Our dinner, which was soon dressed proved an excellent one, the chief dish consisted of two brace and a half of ptarmigants, and a moorcock, a quarter of a pound of butter, some slices of Yorks ham and reindeer's tongue with some sweet herbs prepared by the housekeeper at Raits. These with a due proportion of water made each of us a plate of very strong soup which was relished with a keenness of appetite that none but those that have been at Glen Ennoch can experience. We now drank in a bumper of champaign, gentlemen and servants faring alike, success to the sports of the field, and, with the addition of a tumbler of sherbet and a cordial, were enabled to pack up our apparatus and proceed.

There is a spring on Sgoran Dubh, rather to the south of the hill-top, and near the sudden descent into Loch Eanaich, that is known as Fuaran Diota, the Dinner Spring, and I have sometimes wondered whether this is where Thornton ate his " ptarmigants " and drank his champagne and sherbet over 140 years ago. The same writer mentions that he observed many skeletons of horses beside Loch Eanaich and tells of a belief that in the glen there is " a pernicious quality of grass which poisons horses ". The grass was apparently con-taminated by " an animal, similar to a large mouse, which

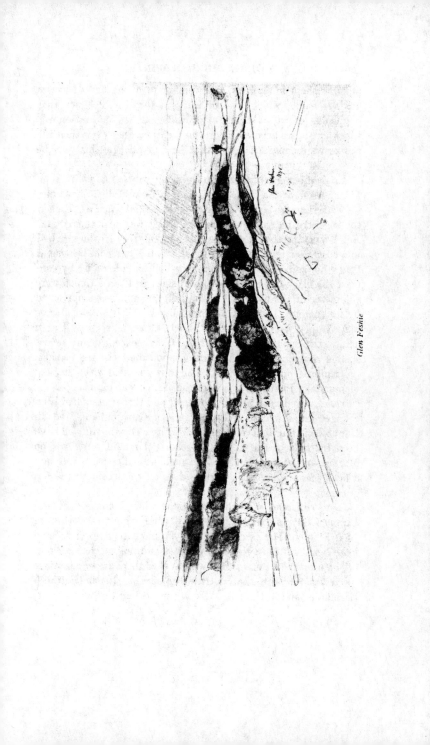

Glen Feshie

inhabits these mountains, and coming over the bent, leaves a noxious slime, which, except early in the day, has not that pernicious effect, it being afterwards exhaled by the sun ". Elsewhere in his account Thornton mentions that even then the people were emigrating, and that he remarked on this to "the laird of Rothiemurcos ".

I remember climbing Sgoran Dubh one winter's day with John MacPherson, at that time deerstalker in Glen Feshie. For miles we walked across a snow-covered expanse, and when we reached the ice-encrusted cairn of Sgoran Dubh it was near sunset, and Ben Wyvis and the hills to the north and north-west were bathed in a rosy glow that changed to violet as the sun sank beneath a frosty horizon. Snow lay deep upon hill and glen, and by contrast the black cliffs which dropped sheer to Loch Eanaich were the more formidable. The loch itself had not been imprisoned by ice (perhaps because it is in a funnel, and is almost always played upon by the hill winds, Loch Eanaich is rarely frozen across, but one day in late March, after an exceptionally severe spell, I saw many ice-flows drifting upon the loch) and lay in a profound sleep, dark and still. The snow sparkled with a myriad diamonds of frost : everywhere the silence was intense, for the cascades were imprisoned by the frost and their waters had been changed into immense icicles. Braeriach, Cairntoul and Monadh Mór rose in an unrelieved mantle of white ; they might well have been the hills of the ice-cap of some Polar land. We saw no ptarmigan that day, but a golden eagle passed over the hill, and a flock of snow-buntings were feeding on the ice-encrusted hill grasses.

Very different were the conditions when I climbed Sgoran Dubh on a day of late May, by way of the Foxhunters' Path from Glen Feshie. The birches of Glen Feshie surely never seemed more beautiful than they did on that morning of clear air and bright sunshine. Botanists now hold that there are two distinct species of birch in the Scottish Highlands. In the northern Highlands, and in the Isle of Skye, this tree is sturdy and erect, delightful because of its fragrance and its green leaves rather than its form. But in the central Highlands the birch is weeping, and here, and more particularly in the Spey valley and its tributaries, it reaches its highest perfection of beauty. To see the birches of Aviemore and Glen Feshie in their young foliage sway in the breeze of an early summer morning is to receive one of the most delightful gifts of the Highland glens.

The public road up the east bank of the Feshie leaves the main

Glen Feshie

road along the south side of the Spey valley at Feshie Bridge, close to a fine old bridge over the Feshie river : below this bridge is a very deep pool where many salmon lie in summer. The ascent of Sgoran Dubh can be made by way of the Foxhunters' Path. A celebrated family of fox-hunters named Clark lived at Achlean in Glen Feshie, and the path, I believe, received its name from them.

It is, as I have said, one of the charms of the Cairngorms that the transition from winter to summer is often swift. In the year which I describe (1939) fresh snow in mid-May had whitened the high tops of the Cairngorms, but on May 28, when I climbed

Sgoran Dubh from Glen Feshie, summer had come to hill and glen. The sky was cloudless and of a deep, glorious blue and the air almost unbelievably clear. Oyster-catchers called beside the Feshie, where the glen was melodious with songs of curlews. On heathery knolls cock grouse perched, guarding their mates which, invisible in deep heather, brooded their eggs not far away. Near the path a meadow pipit slipped furtively off her nest and fluttered low over the ground with hesitant flight. As I neared the great snow-field, gleaming in the sun, which each year lies in Ciste Mhairearad until late summer, I saw a cock ptarmigan sunning himself beside a boulder; when he flew away across the corrie his white wings moved quickly and his grunting or croaking alarm cry conveyed the knowledge of danger to his mate sitting quietly on her eggs on a sun-warmed carpet of dry moss and blaeberry plants. Crossing and recrossing the snow-field were the tracks of deer that had visited the snow to find relief from the heat.

Out on the high plateau which extends from Carn Bàn Mór to Sgoran Dubh the hill vegetation had scarcely awakened from its winter sleep. The grass was brown and dry and as yet showed no young growth; it would have burnt fiercely, and was as lifeless as the grass of the glens in February. It was curious to walk over a land reminiscent of winter on a day of midsummer warmth and brilliance.

From Carn Bàn Mór, where the Foxhunters' Path emerges on the plateau, the top of Sgoran Dubh is rather less than two miles to the north: it is a pleasing, cone-like summit rising from wide, billowy slopes. From the hill-top the ground here falls almost sheer to Loch Eanaich. There are two rock pillars facing one another on opposite sides of the corrie in which Loch Eanaich lies. One of them is named A' Chailleach, the Old Woman, the other (on the east side of the corrie) Am Bodach, the Old Man. It is said that the two figures are in the habit of conversing with each other in tremendous voices across the glen, filling with consternation the human beings who hear them, but the wild notes of a ring ouzel, invisible far down the precipice, are more frequently heard than those supernatural voices.

The summer shielings of Rothiemurchus were in the green corrie at the head of Loch Eanaich. This is a corrie of singular charm, where a few birch trees and rowans grow beside the burn that hurries down the rocky face at the head of the corrie. It was in a summer shieling here that one of the Grants of Rothiemurchus was born, and was known, because of the corrie of his birth, as Corrour Grant.

In that interesting book *Memoirs of a Highland Lady*, by Elizabeth Grant of Rothiemurchus, we are told a little of Corrour Grant :

He died a distinguished officer, though he began life by fighting a running duel, that is, challenging two or three in succession, rather than acknowledge his ignorance. He had brought with him to the south, where he joined his regiment, a horse accoutred ; the horse died, and John Corrour went looking about for another to fit the saddle, which he insisted was the correct method of proceeding, and anyone who questioned this had to measure swords with him. He had never seen asparagus ; some being offered to him he began to eat it at the white end, which provoking a laugh at the mess table, he laid his hand on that terrible sword, and declared his undoubted right to eat what best pleased him. It is said that to his dying day he always put aside the tender green points of this vegetable.

Where the stream leaves Loch Eanaich on its journey down Glen Eanaich it is possible, from the top of Sgoran Dubh, to see the remains of a sluice that was used in the days of timber floating. The pine timber felled in Rothiemurchus was dragged by ponies to the banks of the stream, and by opening the sluice at the loch and raising an artificial flood the timber was then floated down to the Spey and thence to the distant sea at the Moray Firth. It was the duty of one man to go up the glen to Loch Eanaich by night (the floating usually took place in winter) and before daybreak open the sluice so that the flood-water might reach the timber logs in time for the meeting of the woodmen in the morning. The logs were thrown into the flood and were subsequently guided down the stream by long, thin poles, each pole having a sharp hook at the thin, flexible end. This work was done by the Rothiemurchus men : once the logs had reached the Spey they were taken charge of by the Spey floaters, a race of men who had followed that calling for generations and who bound the logs into rafts and floated them down the river. These hardy men lived during the floating season in a large bothy at the mouth of the Druie river, on the opposite shore of the Spey from where Aviemore station now stands. The bothy was built specially for their use. The fire was on a stone hearth in the middle of the floor ; there was no window, but a hole in the centre of the roof allowed the smoke to escape. The floaters, after a hard day's work, lay down on beds of heather in their wet clothes — for they had been perhaps hours in the river — " each man's feet to the fire, each man's plaid round his chest, a circle of wearied bodies half stupified by whisky, enveloped in a cloud of steam and smoke, and sleeping soundly till the morning ".

It was sometimes no easy task to walk up to the head of Glen Eanaich on a winter night. The glen lies high and there is no human dwelling here. On one occasion the young man in charge of the sluice-gates left his home in Rothiemurchus on a wild night of hail, wind and snow. The stream came down in spate in the morning, so that it was known that the lad had reached and opened the sluice gates ; when he failed to return, a search-party set out to look for him and found him lifeless beside the sluice, where he had apparently sat down to rest after opening the flood-gates.

The work of floating timber is graphically told :

The logs that went straight to Spey were seized on by the Ballindalloch men, bored at each end by an auger, two deep holes made into which iron plugs were hammered, the plugs having eyes through which well-twisted wattles were passed, thus binding any given number together. When a raft of proper size was thus formed it lay by the bank of the river awaiting its covering ; this was produced from the logs left at the saw-mills, generally in the water in a pool formed to hold them. As they were required by the workmen, they were brought close by means of the clip, and then by the help of levers rolled up an inclined plane and on to the platform under the saw ; two hooks attached to cables kept the log in its place, the sluice was then opened, down poured the water, the great wheel turned, the platform moved slowly on with the log, the saw-frame worked up and down, every cut slicing the log deeper till the whole length fell off. The four outsides were cut off first ; they were called " backs ", and very few of them went down to Garmouth ; they were mostly used at home for country purposes, such as fencing, out-offices, roofing, or firing ; out-houses even were made of them. The squared logs were then cut up regularly into deals and carted off to the rafts, where they were laid as a sort of flooring. Two rude gears for the oars completed the appointments of a Spey float. The men had a wet berth of it, the water shipping in, or more properly over, at every lurch ; yet they liked the life, and it paid them well. Then they had idle times a great part of the year, could live at home and till their little crofts in their own lazy way, the rent being made up by the floating.

Near Arndilly (Arndilly is in lower Strathspey, near Rothes) there was a sunken rock difficult sometimes to pass ; this furnished a means of livelihood to several families living on the spot. It was their privilege to provide ropes, and arms to pull the ropes, and so to help the floats through a rapid current running at high floods between this sunken rock and the shore. The dole they got was small, yet there was hardly more outcry raised in Sutherland when the Duke wanted his starving cottars to leave their turf huts on the moors and live in comfortable stone houses by the sea, than my father met when some years later he got leave to remove this obstacle by blasting.

A section of a magnificent pine floated down to Garmouth from the Forest of Glen More (a few miles east of Glen Eanaich) I used to admire at Gordon Castle. It is now at the Department of Forestry, Aberdeen University. There was an inscription on the Scots pine plank as follows :

In the year 1783 William Osbourne, Esqur. Merchant of Hull, purchased of the Duke of Gordon the Forest of Glenmore, the whole of which he cut down in the space of 22 years, and built during that time at the mouth of the River Spey, where never vessel was built before, 47 Sail of Ships of upwards of 19,000 tons burthen. The largest of them 1050 tons and three others but little inferior in size, are now in the Service of His Majesty and the Honble. East India Company.

This Undertaking was compleated at the Expence (for Labour only) of about 70,000£.

To His Grace the Duke of Gordon

This Plank is offered as a Specimen of the Growth of one of the trees in the above Forest by His Grace's

Most Obedient Servant

W. Osbourne

Hull, Septr. 26th
1806.

The plank was unfortunately not cut through the centre of the tree, hence its age cannot be determined by a ring count, but

Professor H. M. Steven, of the Department of Forestry, Aberdeen University, estimates the age of the tree at about three hundred years.

As the mountaineer stands at the summit of Sgor Ghaoith, the Windy Peak (as the summit of Sgoran Dubh is sometimes called), he may reflect on the old days, when the young cattle and horses roamed the corries and men in Glen Eanaich shouted and laughed as they guided the logs Speywards in the flood of clear, ice-cold water foaming from the loch ; but the old times are gone and Glen Eanaich and its corries are now deserted except for the red deer, the eagle and the fox. The eagle scarcely holds his own, but the fox during the war years following 1939 greatly increased.

On that day of early summer in the year 1939 the view was clearer than I had ever before known. From Morven and the Scarabens in Caithness, Ben Clibreck and Ben Armine in Suther-land and the heights of Kintail, to Ben Lawers, Ben Vorlich above Loch Earn, and the hills of the Blackmount Forest — all was clear beneath a deep-blue, almost cloudless sky. The last of the morning's mists were rising from snow-capped Ben Nevis, and the snow-fields on the great hills which stand at the head of Glen Moriston, Glen Affric and Glen Cannich gleamed in the strong sun. The ground was crisp and dry : from each melting snow-field swift streams of clear water flowed, the sun glinting and sparkling on their small waves. Summer had come swiftly and the high hills rejoiced at her coming and forgot the long-sustained winter storms that had vexed them.

In very lonely country, at the head of Glen Giùsachan and at the " march " between the great deer forests of Mar and Glen Feshie, stands Am Monadh Mór, in English the Great Hill, which is the south-westerly outpost of the Cairngorm range. Monadh Mór, for the Cairngorms, is not a high hill, and since it lies off the track of those who climb the highest peaks of the range it is rarely visited. A fox-hunter out of Glen Feshie may perhaps spend a summer night's lonely vigil at some fox's den hidden deep in its granite screes, or a deer-stalker in September, when fine weather keeps the stags on the high ground, may find himself late in the day on its slopes, but even in summer there must be weeks, even months, when no human wanderer disturbs the ptarmigan in its corries or crosses its stony summit.

The morning mists were rising ahead of us as my companion and I climbed out of Glen Feshie and passed the snow-field which lies at the head of Coire Fhearnagan. Here is the hollow known as Ciste Mhearad or Mhairearad, in English Margaret's Coffin or Chest, and the legend of the Curse of Moy seems to be associated with this hollow, as also with the Ciste Mhearad which is a short distance from the summit of Cairngorm. One version of the Curse of Moy is that the chief of Clan Chattan condemned a young man to death for sheep-stealing. His sweetheart (in another version his mother) begged that mercy should be shown to the lad, but since her entreaties were unavailing she then cursed Macintosh and his successors to the chiefship with a curse that has taken effect in successive generations. That curse was that never more should the chiefship of Clan Chattan descend from father to son ; and the most recent evidence of the curse was when Angus Macintosh, only son of the chief, died in early manhood in 1918.

The following version of the curse was given me by Alice Claire MacDonell of Keppoch, great-great-granddaughter of Alexander, sixteenth chief of Keppoch, who was killed at Culloden. She writes :

Ronald Mór, VII of Keppoch about the years 1513 to 1547 was married to a sister of William Macintosh of Macintosh. In aiding his kinsman John Moidertach, chosen chief of Clan Ranald against the claims of Ronald Galda the rival claimant to the chiefship of Clan Ranald the latter was aided by William Macintosh and the government troops.

Macintosh afterwards invited Ronald Mór on a friendly visit to Moy Hall and betrayed him to the government. He was executed at Elgin. He (Macintosh) also invited his own sister and her eldest son, the sister (the wife of Ronald Mór) being ignorant of her husband's fate. Macintosh took the boy in a boat to an island in Loch Moy, submerged in time of flood and held the mother's hands whilst she witnessed the drowning of her son.

Afterwards the mother knelt down on the strand, cursing Macintosh and predicting that no son of the chief should succeed his father for 300 years at least.

According to one version of the legend, she who uttered the curse lost her reason, wandered over the Cairngorms, and is commemorated in the two hollows, Ciste Mhearad, which bear her name, Margaret. In the vicinity of Ciste Mhearad of the western Cairngorms that gem of the high ridges, *Azalea procumbens*, was opening its small red buds, and marsh-marigolds were covering the course of a small stream with gold.

We crossed a wide expanse of hill country, passing lonely Lochan nan Cnapan, the Tarn of the Humps, on which tiny wavelets twinkled as they caught the rays of the sun, now riding high in the heavens. The country around Lochan nan Cnapan is broken and full of hummocks, which have given the lochan its name : the Arctic character of the scene was emphasised by the glistening snow-wreath which lay on the west shore of the loch.

Ahead of us rose Am Monadh Ruadh (as the main Cairngorm range was formerly called by Gaelic-speaking natives of Strathspey). Braeriach with red-tinted slopes and corries stood in bright sunlight ; next to it were Sgor an Lochain Uaine, and the stony slopes of Cairntoul. In the distance Lochnagar, clear and radiantly blue, was seen in the Dee valley through a gap in the nearer hills at the head of Glen Giùsachan.

Half an hour's walk beyond Lochan nan Cnapan two pairs of nesting lapwings were passed. I do not remember having observed these birds before on the Cairngorms at a height of 2,800 feet above sea level, nesting in ptarmigan country, and their dashing flight when seen with snow-fields as a background seemed indeed strange.

Fed by melting snow, the burn which drains Horseman's Corrie of Braeriach flowed broad and clear : above this sparkling water flew a golden plover, its narrow, clear-cut wings driving it swiftly forward. Horseman's Corrie is perhaps unique among

Cairngorm corries in having an English name. The corrie is named after a Mr. Horseman who many years ago was tenant of Glen Feshie forest, and was apparently fond of stalking in this high and remote corrie. There must have been an older Gaelic name for the corrie, but I have never heard of it, for the people who knew it are all gone.

The western base of Monadh Mór is almost 3,000 feet above sea level, and the climb from the west is therefore easy, but on this early summer day the sun beat down on the hill with intense power, and there was no water anywhere near the summit except that oozing from a small snow-field, discoloured by peat dust blown on to it by winter gales. We reached the cairn that marks the summit and were refreshed by a cool breeze which drifted gently up to us from the great snow-field in Coire Creagach, the Rocky Corrie, which lies just below the hill-top and to the east of it. This snow-field is a prominent landmark from Mar, and there are years when it remains unmelted throughout the summer. On this June day it was still so deep that it curled over, at its deepest part, like a wave about to break. The scene recalled an Icelandic landscape — here were the same clear air and brilliant light, the same springs (though scarcely so strong) of ice-cold water welling from the ground of a country of virgin snows, and Arctic plants and flowers responding gladly to the magic touch of the strong sun.

The amount of snow still covering large areas of Monadh Mór showed that winter had not long left this upland district, and it was easy to visualise those winter days and nights when clouds of choking drift had been whirled mile after mile on the west wind across the great plateau which lies between Glen Feshie and Mar, and had come at last to rest in sheltered Coire Creagach, where the snow at the end of winter in some years must be 50 or even 100 feet deep.

Almost immediately beneath us lay Glen Giùsachan, a deep and lonely glen where there are old pine stumps — showing the appropriateness of the place-name — in the peat at a height of

2,300 feet above sea level.[1] There are at the present day no pines in the forest above the 2,000-feet level, but one would expect to find their traces high in Glen Giùsachan because of its sheltered character. A tradition of the country is that many of the glens, now treeless, were burned to drive out the wolves, which were not uncommon in the Highlands in bygone centuries.

In Glen Giùsachan a cloudburst had swept thousands of tons of gravel from the heights of Beinn Bhrodain to the Giùsachan river which flows through the glen : the river in one place was dammed up by this debris and a waterfall formed where none had previously existed.[2] At the foot of Glen Giùsachan we could see Glen Dee and the track of Làirig Ghrù, where it leaves Glen Dee and winds east beneath Carn a' Mhaim. The old pines of Glen Derry were distinct : beyond them the churches and houses of Braemar might have belonged to some village of the Alps. Mount Keen, Mount Battock and many lesser hills of lower Deeside rose faint in the heat haze. We turned about and, facing west, looked across to Schiehallion, Ben Lawers and the distant Blackmount hills, and also to a far-distant peak which, I think, was Ben Lui. The great snow-fields of Aonach Mór and Ben Nevis gleamed beneath the unclouded sky of the horizon.

A cloud drifted idly in the heavens above us and, as it grew, cast a shadow upon the summit of Monadh Mór and over the deep corrie between that hill and Beinn Bhrodain. This corrie is romantically named ; it is Coire Cath nam Fiann and perhaps commemorates some ancient fight waged by Fingal and his warriors. It may be remembered that Loch A'an in the eastern Cairngorms also holds Fingalian associations. Even at the present day the battle atmosphere is sensed in Coire Cath nam Fiann,[3] and on this brilliant summer day the corrie remained unsmiling.

[1] Glen Giùsachan is in English Pine-forest Glen. No fir grows there now, but three weather-beaten birches flame golden in autumn.

[2] This happened in September 1937, but the scars were still conspicuous when last I passed that way, in October 1946.

[3] Corrie of the Battle of the Fingalians.

From Monadh Mór the summit of Beinn Bhrodain is no great distance. The name of this hill has puzzled many Gaelic-speakers, but Professor W. J. Watson, our leading Celtic scholar, tells me in a letter, that *brodan* is the reduced form of *brodchú* (earlier form *brotchú*), meaning a fierce hound or mastiff. In place-names, the Professor writes, the second part of a compound word is not infrequently dropped, and in its stead the form *-an* or *-ag* is added to the first part.

In Chapter XXII I have mentioned Loch Bhrodain in the Forest of Gaick and suggested that the loch and the hill may both commemorate the same hound.

Between Monadh Mór and Beinn Bhrodain there is a descent of some 500 feet and, at 3,200 feet above sea level, a narrow pass. Two streams have their head-springs here — the burn known as Allt Dhé Móire, flowing, at first, south-west, and the streamlet Allt Cath nam Fiann, which flows into the corrie of the same name.

From the pass to the top of Bein Bhrodain the climb is stony, and when the cairn is reached it is found to be unusual, for it has a well-built wall encircling it : it may have been used as an observation post when the sappers of the Ordnance Survey were at work surveying the Cairngorms in the nineteenth century.

But on this occasion time did not permit of us climbing Beinn Bhrodain. We retraced our steps, walking north along the edge of Coire Creagach, where we soon came in sight of Loch an Stuir-teag far below us and watched a sandpiper, at this great height no larger than a midge, fly on hovering wings backwards and forwards across that small hill loch. The name Loch an Stuirteag means, as it stands, the Loch of the Black-headed Gull, but this does not seem to have been the loch's earlier name. The late George MacPherson Grant of the Ballindalloch family, in a letter to me, mentioned that when first he began to climb, in 1887, with his father and other old friends, the loch was called Lochan Suarach, the Insignificant Loch, but his brother, disliking the name Suarach, " finally fixed that it ought to be Stuirteag, and

got the Ordnance Survey people to alter it ". I mention this
instance to show how difficult it is to determine the original forms
of many of the place-names in the Highlands.

A small herd of hinds, and with them a last year's calf, were
feeding in the evening sunshine on the slopes of Loch an Stuirteag, and a party of black-headed gulls (as though to vindicate
the place-name) could be seen feeding above the loch on the
gentle slopes of Braeriach. Very graceful and beautiful did these
small, narrow-winged seagulls look as they alighted on the grass,
fed eagerly for perhaps a minute, then flew in a flock a little way
forward, in a mist of white wings, to search fresh parts of the
slopes. The gulls had been attracted to the Cairngorms by the
crane-flies or daddy-long-legs which the hot sun had brought out
in great numbers. Later in the evening we saw these black-
headed gulls rise from their feeding, circle in the sun until they
had gained a considerable height, then make off toward their
nesting haunts in the Spey valley.

As we watched the foaming burn flow through Clais an t-Sabhail of Cairntoul and looked upon the white snows cradled high in
Coire nan Tàillear, the Tailors' Corrie of Ben MacDhui beyond
Làirig Ghrù, the breeze of a sudden died away, and at once we
were surrounded by midges, which crawled over our arms and
faces, yet made no attempt to bite. I have more than once
noticed that in early summer when midges first appear they
abstain from attacks on their human victim. Is this because the
insect is a little uncertain of itself when first it takes the air, or
is it because the males of the species appear first and, like the
mosquito, leave to the females the satisfaction of sucking human
blood ?

With ptarmigan croaking ahead of us we crossed the plateau
westward, and as we approached Lochan nan Cnapan and the
rocky spur above it, known as Cnapan Alasdair Mhóir (this
commemorates the grandfather of Finlay Macintosh, head stalker
at Ardverikie), we saw Am Bodach, dark in the evening sun,
keeping his lonely vigil over Loch Eanaich. We wandered through

a maze of knolls, where lochans lay in deep hollows, and saw a great patch of *Azalea procumbens*, measuring four yards by four, in full flower. As we passed high above Loch Eanaich we felt the north-east wind blow fresh and cool from the deep hollow of the loch, already in shadow. We crossed the snow-bed which still covered the bed of Allt Sgàirnich near its source on Carn Bàn Mór, and as we reached the watershed above Glen Feshie saw the Spey beyond Loch Insh flow as a line of burnished silver in the track of the setting sun. Before we entered Coire Fhearnagan we looked north and saw a mantle of white mist creep in over the land from the Moray Firth and flow around Ben Wyvis, which rose dark as though from an aerial sea. Crowberry and heather scented the air ; a golden plover rose from her nest containing four beautifully marked eggs and fluttered low over the ground, as though she were wounded. We reached the lower ground and saw petty whin and bird's-foot trefoil golden beside the path, and butterwort and milkwort intensify in the depth of their blue flowers the serene, unclouded sky.

CHAPTER XXXIV

THE COUNTRY OF MAR

FOR some of us the history of Braemar begins in the time of Taylor the Water Poet, for it is he who first brings that hill country clearly before the mind's eye.[1] The Water Poet (he was a water-man on the Thames), for a wager set out on foot from London to travel to Edinburgh, thence through the Scottish Highlands, carrying no money on his person, and relying on the hospitality of those he met. Such was his joviality, wit and good comradeship that he made friends wherever he went, and successfully completed his journey. Of his sojourn in Mar he has a good deal to say — partly, perhaps, because here he first entered the Highlands and found himself in a country, and amid customs, which must have been very strange to him. His description of a great hunt in Mar is worth quoting in full. After describing his miseries in crossing Mount Keen (which he calls Skeene) in thick mist from Angus " so that my teeth beganne to dance in my head with cold, like virginal's jacks ", his account goes on :

Thus with extreme travell, ascending and descending, mounting and alighting[2] I came at night to the place where I would be, in the Brea of Marr, which is a large country, all composed of such mountaines, that Shooter's Hill, Gad's hill, Highgate hill, Hampsted hill, Birdlip hill, or Malvernes hill, are but mole-hills in comparison, or like a liver, or a gizard

---

[1] *The Pennyless Pilgrimage, or The Moneylesse Perambulation of John Taylor, Alias, The King's Majestie's Water-Poet : How he Travailed in Foot from London to Edenborough in Scotland, not Carrying any Money to or fro, neither Begging, Borrowing, or asking Meate, Drinke, or Lodging.*

[2] It will be noticed that at this stage of his journey the Water Poet was no longer on foot.

under a capon's wing, in respect of the altitude of their tops, of perpendicu-laritie of their bottomes. There I saw mount Benawne, with a furr'd mist upon his snowie head instead of a nightcap : for you must understand that the oldest man alive never saw but the snow was on the top of divers of those hills, both in summer, as well as in winter. There did I finde the truely noble and right honourable Lords John Erskin Earle of Marr, James Stuart Earle of Murray, George Gordon Earl of Engye, sonne and heire to the Marquesse of Huntly, James Erskin Earle of Bughan and John Lord Erskin, sonne and heire to the Earle of Marr, and their Countesses, with my much honoured, and my best assured and approved friend, Sir William Murray knight, of Abercarny, and hundreds of others knights, esquires, and their followers ; all and every man in generall in one habit, as if Licurgus had beene there, and made lawes of equality. For once in the yeere, which is the whole moneth of August, and sometimes part of Sept-ember, many of the nobility and gentry of the kingdome (for their pleasure) doe come into these highland countries to hunt, where they doe conforme themselves to the habite of the High-land-men, who for the most part, speake nothing but Irish ; and in former time were those people which were called the Red-shankes. Their habite is shooes with but one sole apiece ; stockings (which they call short hose) made of a warm stuffe of divers colours, which they call Tartane : as for breeches, many of them, nor their forefathers, never wore any, but a jerkin of the same stuffe that their hose is of, their garters being bands or wreathes of hay or straw, with a plead about their shoulders, which is a mantle of divers colours, much finer and lighter stuffe than their hose, with blue flat caps on their heads, a handker-chiefe knit with two knots about their necke ; and thus are they attyred. Now their weapons are long bowes and forked arrowes, swords and targets, harquebusses, muskets, durks, and Loquhabor-axes. With these armes I found many of them armed for the hunting. As for their attire, any man of what degree soever that comes amongst them, must not disdaine to weare it : for if they doe, then they will disdaine to hunt, or willingly to bring in their dogges : but if men be kind unto them, and be in their habit ; then are they conquered with kindnesse, and the sport will be plentifull. This was the reason that I found so many noblemen and gentlemen in those shapes. But to proceed to the hunting.

My good Lord of Marr having put me into that shape, I rode with him from his house, where I saw the ruines of an old castle, called the Castle of Kindroghit. It was built by King Malcolm Canmore (for a hunting house) who raigned in Scotland when Edward the Confessor, Harold, and Norman William raigned in England : I speake of it, because it was the last house that I saw in those parts ; for I was the space of twelve days after, before I saw either house, corne-field, or habitation for any creature, but deere, wilde horses, wolves, and such like creatures which made mee doubt that I should never have seen a house againe.

Thus the first day wee traveled eight miles, where there were small cottages, built on purpose to lodge in, which they call Lonquhards.[1] I thanke my good Lord Erskin, he commanded that I should alwayes bee lodged in his lodging, the kitchin being alwayes on the side of a banke,

---

[1] *Longphort* is a Gaelic term denoting a hunting booth or shieling.

many kettles and pots boyling, and many spits turning and winding, with great variety of cheere ; as venison bak't, sodden, rost, and steu'de, beefe, mutton, goates, kid, hares, fresh salmon, pidgeons, hens, capons, chickens, partridge, moorcoots, heathcocks, caperkellies and termigants ; good ale, sacke, white, and claret, tent, or allegant, with most potent Aquavitae.

All these, and more than these wee had continually in superfluous aboundance, caught by faulconers, fowlers, fishers, and brought by my Lord's tenants and purveyors to victuall our campe, which consisteth of foureteen or fifteene hundred men and horses ; the manner of the hunting is this : Five or sixe hundred men doe rise early in the morning, and they doe disperse themselves divers wayes, and seven, eight, or tenne miles compasse, they doe bring or chase in the deere in many heards (two, three, of foure hundred in a heard) to such or such a place, as the nobleman shall appoint them ; then when day is come, the Lords and gentlemen of their companies, doe ride or goe to the said places, sometimes wading up to the middles through bournes and rivers : and then they being come to the place, doe lye downe on the ground, till those foresaid scouts which are called the Tinckhell, doe bring downe the deere : but as the proverbe sayes of a bad cooke, so these tinckhell men doe lick their owne fingers ; for besides their bowes and arrowes which they carry with them, wee can heare now and then a harquebusse of a musket goe off, which they doe seldome discharge in vaine : Then after we had stayed there three hourse or there-abouts, we might perceive the deere appeare on the hills round about us (their heads making a shew like a wood) which being followed close by the tinckhell, are chased down into the valley where we lay ; then all the valley on each side being way-laid with a hundred couple of strong Irish grey-hounds, they are let loose as occasion serves upon the heard of deere that with dogges, gunnes, arrowes, durkes, and daggers, in the space of two houres, fourescore fat deere were slain, which after are disposed of some one way and some another, twenty and thirty miles, and more than enough left for us to make merry withall at our rendezvous.

Being come to our lodgings, there was such baking, boyling, roasting, and stewing, as if Cooke Ruffian had been there to have scalded the Devil in his feathers : and after supper, a fire of firre-wood as high as an indifferent may-pole : for I assure you, that the Earle of Marr will give any man that is his friend, for thankes, as many firre trees (that are as good as any shippes masts in England) as are worth (if they were in any place neere the Thames, or any other portable river) the best Earledome in England or Scotland either : For I dare affirme, hee hath as many growing there, as would serve for masts (from this time to the end of the worlde) for all the shippes, carackes, hoyes, galleys, boates, drumlers, barkes, and water-crafts, that are now, or can be in the worlde these fourty yeeres.

This sounds like a lye to an unbeleever ; but I and many thousands doe knowe that I speake within the compasse of truth ; for indeed (the more is the pity) they doe grow so farre from any passage of water, and withall in such rockie mountaines, that no way to convey them is possible to be passable, either with boate, horse, or cart.

But the first, and greatest hero of Mar lived six centuries before the Water Poet's day. This was Malcolm III of Scotland, called Ceann Mór, Big Head — he who was killed at the siege of Alnwick Castle in 1093. Malcolm built the castle of Kindrochit (in Gaelic, Ceann Drochaid or Bridge-head) and bestowed the Earldom of Mar on him who until then had been Captain of that district. Thus the Earldom of Mar goes back into the mists of a thousand years. It is stated that, like the Black Castle of Moulin, Kindrochit Castle at Braemar was destroyed by artillery fire because those within it were stricken with plague — the Galar Mór, or Great Plague, as it was called. It is traditionally said that a company of artillery came over from Blair Castle to batter it down, and that the cuttings made for the passage of the artillery over the Cairnwell hill were until comparatively recent years pointed out. In the old *Statistical Account* it is mentioned :

There is, upon the estate of Castletown of Braemar, the ruins of an ancient castle, built, as tradition reports, by King Malcolm Kenmore for a hunting seat. By the vestiges which still remain, it is obvious that there was a very considerable building. The house stood on the top of a rock on the E. side of the water of Cluanaidh ; and the King having thrown a drawbridge across the river, to the rock on the opposite side, the parish of Braemar derived its original name of Ceann-an-drochart from that circumstance.

Kindrochit Castle must not be confused with Braemar Castle, originally built by John, Earl of Mar in 1483. On this castle, too, the old *Statistical Account* has some interesting notes :

King William after the Revolution took possession of it for a garrison, and put some troops into it to keep the country in awe ; but this had not the desired effect, for the country being of opposite sentiments at the time, besieged the garrison, and obliged the troops to retire, under silence of night, in order to save their lives : and to save themselves from such troublesome neighbours for the future, they burnt the castle.

In this state it continued till the year 1715, when the whole Marr estates were forfeited. About the year 1720, Lords Dun and Grange purchased from government all the lands belonging to the Erskine family ; and about 1730, John Farquhar, son of Invercauld, bought the lands of Castletown from Lords Dun and Grange. About 1748, Mr. Farquharson gave a lease to government of the castle, and an enclosure of 14 acres of ground, for the space of 99 years, at 14£ Sterling of yearly rent ; upon which the house was repaired (the walls being then sufficient) and a rampart built round it, and it has, since that period [1] been occupied by a party of soldiers.

---

[1] The old *Statistical Account* was written in 1794.

In more recent years Braemar Castle has been a private residence. For a number of years prior to the first Great War in 1914 it was leased by Princess Alexis Dolgorouki, a Scottish lady who had married a Russian prince, and whose name was a byword for kindness and generosity in the Braemar district.

Although Malcolm Ceann Mór who built the castle of Kindrochit

Braemar Castle

is a legendary figure of distant days, he is modern in comparison with Martach, a Captain of Fergus I in the year 300. King Fergus is said to have bestowed the district of Mar on Martach because of his valour and devotion, and, ever since, his country has been known as Mar. The Earldom of Mar, which followed the Captaincy, is still in existence, but the family have now no active associations with the district, although the Honourable Ruaraidh Erskine, brother of the late Earl, is keenly interested in the Highlands and their people.

In modern times the two great families of the Braemar district have been the Farquharsons and the MacDuffs (who succeeded the MacKenzies of Dalmore). The Farquharsons for at least four centuries have been renowned in the district. It is said that they were descended from Farquhar, son of John Shaw of Rothiemurchus, who lived about 1370. A celebrated ancestor of the Farquharsons was Fionnlagh (Finla) Mór, or Big Finlay, a man of great stature and strength — he who was killed by a cannonball from one of the enemy's ships at the battle of Pinkie in 1547 when carrying the Royal Standard of Scotland. Of Big Finlay many stories are told in Mar — how on one occasion unawares he entertained the King, and how, single-handed, he disarmed and took prisoners five armed men from the south whom he found wandering on the Bealachbuidhe or Ballochbuie Pass. After Finla Mór's time the Farquharsons, who had until then been the Clann Fhearchair, were known as the Clann Fhionnlaigh.

The Invercauld Farquharsons (Michie's *Deeside Tales*, p. 341) were descended from Robert, second son of Finla Mór. It was in the house of Invercauld that the Jacobite lords and chiefs, with the Earl of Mar as their leader, gathered before the rising of 1715.

The last of the Farquharsons of Invercauld (writes Michie) in the direct male line died in 1805. The titular chiefship of the clan then passed to the Farquharsons of Whitehouse, where indeed it had long lain as far as right of primogeniture was concerned ; and on the death of Andrew Farquharson of Whitehouse in 1896, the Family of Finzean became the representatives of the eldest male line of Donald of Castletown, eldest of the Deeside sons of Finlay Mor.

The house of Invercauld (to give it its old name) is a large and imposing building standing on the north bank of the Dee two miles east of Braemar. There is reason to believe that there was a stronghold here before written records existed. In the *Records of Invercauld*, p. 74, I find the following :

What form the mansion presented when it first became a residential place of consequence, it would be impossible now to conjecture, but judging from the character of the masonry of the oldest portion now extant, the walls of which are from 5 ft. to 7 ft. in thickness, and comparing them with

2 C

The old Bridge of Dee at Braemar, Lochnagar rising beyond it

those of the basement walls of Braemar Castle, there are good grounds for
holding that both belong to the same period, and probably the two struc-
tures were originally of the same style of architecture and very different in
each case from what they are now. The most probable era to assign to both
is the reign of James IV (1488–1513) or perhaps somewhat earlier. . . .
There is no record of any change on, or addition to, the House of Invercauld
till the estate was several years in the peaceful and prosperous possession of
Alexander Farquharson. In 1679 measures were taken for what would
appear to have been large additions to the mansion.

A legendary hero on Upper Deeside was the Black Colonel —
John Farquharson of Inverey — he who is traditionally said to
have been in the habit of summoning his servant by firing his
pistol at a shield which hung on the wall and, when hit by a
bullet, gave out a bell-like tone.

The Farquharsons of Inverey, sometimes called the Clann
Mhic Sheumais, after Seumas, their founder, are descended from
one of the seven sons of Fionnlagh Mór, and an early head of the
Inverey branch — Uilleam Maol, William the Bald — was out
with Montrose in his campaign of 1645.[1]

A remarkable feat of the Black Colonel of Inverey, the grandson of the founder of the family, was to ride his black mare —
when seemingly powerless to escape two companies of dragoons
converging on him through the pass — up the steep, rocky hill
which rises from the north side of the Pass of Ballater. To anyone seeing the huge boulders on that hillside, and its steepness,
the feat must appear incredible, yet there is little doubt that it
was actually performed.

The Black Colonel had many narrow escapes from his enemies
the Government troops. On one occasion they burnt his castle
and he escaped, *in puris naturalibus*, not a moment too soon.
With a mighty leap he cleared the Ey, then in full flood, and the
hump-backed bridge which takes the old road across the Ey near
where he jumped is known as Drochaid an Leum, the Bridge of
the Leap. The bridge is about a mile above where the road
crosses the Ey at the present day. Farther up the river Ey is the

---

[1] It is said that, before the time of the Farquharsons, Inverey was in
possession of the Lamonts, an old family who had come from Argyll.

Colonel's Bed — a ledge in a chasm of the river where he is believed to have remained for a time in hiding after the burning of his house. A grand man must have been the Black Colonel ! He lives in history and tradition : yet even his language, the language of the Gael, has almost gone from the Braes of Mar.

Like other families of the Highlands, the Inverey Farquharsons chose the profession of arms, and when the clans rose in 1715 and the standard was raised in Mar, Peter Farquharson of Inverey was colonel of the Braemar Highlanders. In the *Records of Invercauld* interesting and valuable information is given (p. 295 *et seq.*) of the part John Farquharson of Invercauld played in the rising of 1715. The editor of the *Family Papers* points out that the power of a feudal lord over his vassal was still supreme at that time. Invercauld, as Mar's vassal, was bound to give military service, with all his tenants capable of bearing arms, when called upon by his Lord Superior, under pain of the forfeiture of his estates. The Earl of Mar at that time had no residence in Braemar, and so when he decided to come to the district to meet the clans and raise his banner he took up residence at Invercauld, " the mansion of the Laird, his vassal ". Burton in his account of the early proceedings at Mar writes as follows :

> In the course of his journey northwards he (Mar) issued instructions to the chiefs on whom he could rely, to join him in a great hunting party in his forest of Mar, and had personal interviews with those whose estates lay near his route. . . . He probably reached Invercauld's mansion on the 21st or 22nd of August.

Regarding the meeting of the chiefs with Mar at Invercauld's house the *Records of Invercauld* state that the following were present : the Marquis of Tullibardine, the Marquis of Huntly ; the Earl of Breadalbane ; the Lords Southesk, Stormont, Drummond and Ogilvie ; Lord Seaforth, and the Chief of Glengarry ; Lords Nithdale and Traquhair ; the Earls Marischal, Errol, Carnwath and Linlithgow ; the Viscounts Kilsyth, Kenmure and Kingston ; and the Lords Rollo, Duffus, Strathallan and Nairn ; with the Lairds of Auchterhouse and Auldbar. " There were also in attendance twenty-six Highland chiefs and chieftains of clans, but Invercauld was not amongst them ; he had either not been invited, or had absented himself because he disapproved of the purpose in view."

Amongst those present was the famous Rob Roy.

At length (continues the account) it was resolved to raise the banner of insurrection. The ceremony took place at Braemar on the 6th September 1715 and was solemnized by prayer and other religious exercises, though not unattended by an incident — the fall of the gilded ball at the top of the flag-staff — that more than neutralised in the Celtic mind, the influence of these propitiatory solemnities.

John Farquharson of Invercauld, having unwillingly joined a cause in which he had no heart, believing it to be doomed to failure, now conducted himself with skill and gallantry, and fought with special distinction at the battle of Preston. When the rising of 1745 took place Invercauld was an old man of seventy-two and took no part in it. There is a tradition that before the rising of 1715, and perhaps also in 1745, Invercauld had his charter chest removed to an almost inaccessible cleft in the rock on the face of Craig Cluny — afterwards named from this circumstance Invercauld's Charter Chest.

The last of the Farquharsons of Invercauld in the male line was James, who died in 1805 aged eighty-three. James and his wife (who was a daughter of Lord George Murray and was much beloved by the people of Braemar) had eleven children, but all died with the exception of the youngest daughter, Catherine, from whom the present Farquharsons of Invercauld are descended in the female line. The tragedy of that large and united family is thus told in the *Records of Invercauld* (p. 380) :

At length a gloom overcast the once happy household at Invercauld. First a little baby died, and, soon after her, another and so on, one by one as they grew up, they passed away, struck down by the fell hand of consumption, till the saddest affliction of all came ; the mother, worn out with watching, anxiety and sorrow, followed her children (1779), leaving only, of all their eleven offspring, the youngest, a little girl five years of age, to be the care and comfort of the bereaved father for the rest of his life. . . . James Farquharson survived until the summer of 1805. He had held the estates for the lengthened period of 55 years. His father before him had held them for 56 ; thus father and son in succession had continued in possession of these estates for no less a space of time than 111 years.

The celebrated traveller Pennant and, at a later date, George Gordon, Lord Byron, stayed at Invercauld. Of his visit Pennant writes graphically (Pennant's *Tour in Scotland*, vol. i, p. 127):

Pass the Castle of Braemar, a square tower the seat of the antient Earls of Mar : in later times a garrison to curb the discontented chieftains ; but at present unnecessarily occupied by a company of foot, being rented by the Government from Mr. Farquharson of Invercauld, whose house I reach in less than half an hour.

Invercauld is seated in the centre of the Grampian hills, in a fertile vale, washed by the Dee, a large and rapid river : nothing can be more beautiful than the different views from the several parts of it. On the Northern entrance, immense ragged and broken crags bound one side of the prospect ; over whose grey sides and summits is scattered the melancholy green of the picturesque pine, which grows out of the naked rock, where one would think nature would have denied vegetation.

A little lower down is the castle above-mentioned ; formerly a necessary curb on the little kings of the country ; but at present serves scarce any purpose, but to adorn the landscape. The views from the skirts of the plain near Invercauld are very great ; the hills that immediately bound it are cloathed with trees ; particularly with birch, whose long and pendant boughs, waving a vast height above the head, surpass the beauties of the weeping willow.

The southern extremity is pre-eminently magnificent ; the mountains form there a vast theatre, the bosom of which is covered with extensive forests of pines : above, the trees grow scarcer and scarcer, and then seem only to sprinkle the surface ; after which vegetation ceases, and naked summits of a surprising height succeed, many of them topped with perpetual snow. The highest is called Ben y bourd, under which is a small loch, which I was told had ice the latter end of July. As a fine contrast to the scene, the great cataract of Garval-bourn, which seems at a distance to divide the whole, foams amidst the dark forest, rushing from rock to rock to a vast distance.

Some of these hills are supposed to be the highest part of Great Britain : their height has not yet been taken, but the conjecture is made from the descent of the Dee, which runs from Braemar, the most distant from the sea of any place in North Britain, to the sea, above seventy miles, with a most rapid course.

In this vale the Earl of Mar first set up the Pretender's standard on the 6th of September 1715 ; and in consequence drew to destruction his own, and several of the most noble families of North Britain.

Rode to take a nearer view of the environs ; crossed the Dee on a good stone-bridge, built by the Government, and entered on excellent roads into a magnificent forest of pines of many miles extent. Some of the trees are of vast size ; I measured several that were ten, eleven, and even twelve feet in circumference, and near sixty feet high, forming a most beautiful column, with a fine verdant capital. These trees are of a great age, having, as is supposed, seen two centuries. Their value is considerable ; Mr. Far-quharson informed me, that by sawing and retailing them, he has got for eight hundred trees five-and-twenty shillings each : they are sawed in an adjacent saw-mill, into plank ten feet long, eleven inches broad, and three thick, and sold for two shillings apiece.

Near this antient forest is another, consisting of smaller trees, almost as high, but very slender ; one grows in a singular manner out of the top of a great stone, and notwithstanding it seems to have no other nourishment than what it gets from the dews, is above thirty feet high.

The prospect above these forests is very extraordinary, a distant view of hills over a surface of verdant pyramids of pines.

I must not omit, that there are in the moors of these parts, what I may call subterraneous forests, of the same species of trees, overthrown by the rage of tempests, and covered with vegetable mould. These are dug up, and used for several mechanical purposes. The finer and more resinous parts are split into slender pieces, and serve the purposes of torches. Ceres made use of no other in her search after her lost daughter.

> Illa duabus
> Flammifera PINUS manibus succendit ab Aetna.
> OVID, *Met.* lib. v. 7.

> At Aetna's flaming mouth two pitchy pines
> To light her in her search at length she tines.

This whole tract abounds with game : the Stags at this time were ranging in the mountains ; but the little Roe-bucks were perpetually bounding before us ; and the black game often sprung under our feet. The tops of the hills swarmed with Grous and Ptarmigans. Green plovers, Whimbrels, and Snow-flecks, breed here ; the last assemble in great flocks during winter, and collect so closely in their eddying flight, as to give the sportsman opportunity of killing numbers at a shot. Eagles — the Ring-tail Eagle, called here the Black Eagle — Peregrine Falcons, and Goshawks breed here : the Falcons in rocks, the Goshawks in trees : the last pursues its prey on end, and dashes through every thing in pursuit ; but if it misses its quarry, desists from following it after two or three hundred yards flight. These birds are proscribed ; half a crown is given for an eagle, a shilling for a hawk, or hooded crow.

I suspect, from the description, that the Dotrel breeds here. I heard also of a bird, called here Snatach na cuirn, but could not procure it.

Foxes are in these parts very ravenous, feeding on roes, sheep, and even goats.

Rooks visit these vales in autumn, to feed on the different sort of berries ; but neither winter nor breed here.

I saw flying in the forests, the greater Bulfinch of Mr. Edwards, tab. 123, 124 the Loxia enucleator of Linnaeus, whose food is the seed of pine cones ; a bird common to the north of Europe and America.

On our return passed under some high cliffs ; with large woods of birch intermixed. This tree is used for all sorts of implements of husbandry, roofing of small houses, wheels, fuel ; the Highlanders also tan their own leather with the bark ; and a great deal of excellent wine is extracted from the live tree. Observed among these rocks a sort of projecting shelf on which had been a hut, accessible only by the help of some thongs, fastened by some very expert climbers, to which the family got, in times of danger, in former days, with their most valuable moveables.

The houses of the common people in these parts are shocking to humanity, formed with loose stones, and covered with clods, which they call devots, or with heath, broom, or branches of fir : they look, at a distance, like so many black mole-hills. The inhabitants live very poorly, on oatmeal, barley, cakes and potatoes ; they drink whisky, sweetened with honey. The men are thin, but strong ; idle and lazy, except employed in the chace, or any thing that looks like amusement ; are content with their hard fare, and will not exert themselves farther than to get what they deem necessaries. The women are more industrious, spin their own husbands' cloaths, and get money by knitting stockings, the great trade of the country. The common women are in general most remarkably plain, and soon acquire an old look, and by being much exposed to the weather without hats such a grin, and contraction of the muscles, as heightens greatly their natural hardness of features.

Tenants pay their rent generally in this country in money, except what they pay in poultry, which is done to promote the breed, as the gentry are so remote from any market. Those that rent a mill pay a hog or two ; an animal so detested by the Highlanders, that very few can be prevailed on to taste it, in any shape.

Another celebrated visitor to Invercauld was the poet Lord Byron. It was in 1803 that Byron visited this district of Upper Deeside, and in the *Records of Invercauld* (p. 389) the gillie who accompanied him on his ascent of Lochnagar is quoted as saying :

We set out from Invercauld early in the forenoon, crossed the Dee by the old bridge and then up the glen of the Garawalt. His Lordship rested often and looked at the scenery. He was very quiet and did not often speak to me. When we began to climb the crags of Loch-an-uan I thought he would not be able to scramble up, for he was rather lame, and I offered to assist him, but he would not have any help from me. When we got to the top he sat a long time on the edge of the rocks, looking about him, but seldom asked me any question ; and we returned the same way as we went up.

From Invercauld Lord Byron went on a visit to Mar lodge, where he remained some days as the guest of the Earl of Fife, and it is said that he narrowly escaped a serious accident at the Linn of Dee.

Perhaps when Byron crossed the old bridge spanning the Dee below Invercauld he heard how Duncan Calder, the Seer of Glen Lui, foretold that in time to come a thorn bush would grow from a pool of the Dee beneath Craig Cluny. At the time his prophecy seemed fantastic, but in 1752 a bridge was built over the Dee beside this pool, and at the side of one of the arches a thorn bush did indeed grow as Duncan had foretold.

It was a few years after the building of this bridge that the Duke of Atholl obtained some larch seed from abroad and from it raised the first larch trees grown in the Scottish Highlands. Two of these trees are still in full vigour of growth beside the venerable cathedral at Dunkeld. The Duke was Invercauld's brother-in-law, and presented him with several of the original seedlings which he planted near the house of Invercauld. The last of these old larches died, I understand, about fifty years ago.[1]

The rallying-cry of the Farquharsons was Carn-na-Cuimhne (Cairn of Remembrance). In the old *Statistical Account* (1795) the Rev. Charles MacHardy, Minister of Crathie and Commissioner on the Invercauld estates, writes as follows of the Cairn of Remembrance :

On the lands of Monaltry, and on the N. bank of the river Dee, in a narrow pass, where there is not above 60 yards from the river to the foot of a high, steep, rocky hill, stands a cairn, known by the name of Carn-na-cuimhne, or Cairn of remembrance. The military road is carried along the foot of this hill, and through this pass. The tradition of the country is, that, at some period, the country being in danger, the Highland chieftains raised their men, and marching through this pass, caused each man lay down a stone in this place. When they returned, the stones were numbered ; by which means it was known how many men were brought into the field, and what number was lost in action. Since that period, Carn-na-cuimhne has been the watch-word of the country. At that period, every person capable of bearing arms was obliged to have his arms, a bag, with some bannocks in it, and a pair of new mended shoes always in readiness ; and the moment the alarm was given that danger was apprehended, a stake of wood, the one end dipped in blood (the blood of any animal), and the other burnt, as an emblem of fire and sword, was put into the hands of the person nearest to where the alarm was given, who immediately ran with all speed, and gave it to his nearest neighbour, whether man or woman ; that person ran to the next village or cottage (for measures had been previously so conserted that every one knew his route), and so on, till they went through the whole country ; upon which every man instantly laid hold of his arms etc. ; and repaired to Carn-na-cuimhne, where they met their leaders also in arms, and ready to give the necessary orders. The stake of wood was named Croishtarich. At this day, was a fray or squabble to happen at a market, or any public meeting, such influence has this word over the minds

---

[1] In a field beside Abergeldie Castle, lower down the river, is an old larch believed in this district to be one of the Dunkeld seedlings.

of the country people, that the very mention of Carn-na-cuimhne would, in a moment, collect all the people in this country, who happened to be at said meeting, to the assistance of the person assailed.

In the *Records of Invercauld* (p. 188) it is observed that about the time when the old *Statistical Account* was written the County Road passed nearer to the River Dee than the present one, and touched the bank of the river at what was formerly known as the Boat of Carn-na-Cuimhne.

I cannot recall any place-name beginning with " Boat " remaining at the present time on Deeside, but on Speyside, as I have recorded in Chapter XXVIII, Boat of Garten, Blacksboat and other names of this sort show where the ferries or "boats" were stationed in the old days before bridges were built over the river.

It was in the days when the Fiery Cross was carried swiftly through the land that the great pine woods of Mar suffered severely from " Waste and Abuses ". In an old record of 1760 (*Records of Invercauld*, p. 142) it is mentioned that the largest and finest trees were often felled for the most trifling purposes and that another destructive practice, which then universally prevailed, was the cutting-out of the hearts of the finest trees to serve as candle-fir. The pines thus treated died, and the value of their timber was lost. At this time a tenant when he moved from the district was accustomed to pull down his house and carry off the timber with him, and it was necessary therefore to fell trees to build a house for the in-coming tenant. It is clear that at that time more attention was paid to the preserving of the old pine forest than at the present day, for we find it written that as

fir-woods do not spring from the Root, but are propagated by the blowing of the seed in the grounds immediately adjacent to the old woods, or in the openings, where they have freedom of air, these highland fir woods are not fixed to a particular spot but gradually shift their stances ; injunctions are given to present damage being done to the forests.

The MacKenzies of Dalmore, who lived near the site of the present Mar Lodge, are said to have been a branch of the Kintail

MacKenzies. The first Dalmore married a daughter of Fionnlagh Mór. The MacKenzies were in possession of the estate of Dalmore for upwards of 140 years, and before the rising of 1745 sold the property to the Duffs.

They " marched " with Invercauld, and on occasion inter-married with the Invercauld Farquharsons, for as far back as the year 1666 Roderick MacKenzie of Dalmore married the widow of Robert Farquharson of Invercauld. James MacKenzie of Dalmore, as a vassal of the Earl of Mar, had been obliged (what-ever may have been his personal inclination) to come " out " under the Earl in the rising of 1715, and, like most of his neigh-bours, found himself at its close a ruined man. The estates and superiorities of the Earl were forfeited, and his vassals were indeed in unfortunate plight.

In the year 1705 — that is, ten years before the rising — we find (*Records of Invercauld*, p. 117) a record of " Kenneth MacKenzie of Dalmore, fforrester to the sd. Noble Earle (Earl of Mar) his haill woods, parks and forrests within the Earledome of Mar ".

There is a tradition in Mar that the Dalmore MacKenzies were most strenuous assailants of the Lochaber caterans, and it is said that one of the last of the MacKenzies, Seumas na Pluic, James of the Fat Cheek, was slain by the caterans in Gleney in the year 1726 or shortly afterwards. In *Legends of the Braes of Mar* (p. 154) the legend of the slaying of Seumas na Pluic is given in a vivid manner. The Lochaber raiders, it appears, had " lifted " the cattle in Gleney, and Dalmore (Seumas Mór na Pluic) with two of his sons set off up the glen. Dalmore, before going ahead to parley with the chief of the caterans, told his sons to watch his move-ments carefully ; if he should raise his hand to his brow it would be a signal for them to fire at the cattle-lifters. The chief robber on this occasion was the renowned Ceatharnach Dubh, and as MacKenzie of Dalmore endeavoured to persuade him to deliver up the stolen cattle on payment of a certain sum of money he (Dalmore) unconsciously raised his hand to his bonnet. His sons, taking this to be the prearranged signal, fired at and killed the sentinel guarding the bothy door in which the caterans were resting. The Ceatharnach Dubh, not without reason believing that he was betrayed, ran back, seized the fallen sentry's gun, and shot and killed Seumas Mór na Pluic. At the time when the *Legends* were written (1876), a cairn of stones "near the hunting shiel of the Duffs, in the Alltan-Odhar" marked the spot where Dalmore fell. I have not seen the cairn myself, but Mrs. Grant, Pinewood, Inverey, writing to me on the subject in 1940, mentioned that her husband knew the old cairn, which still stands beside the ruined shieling. In the fight that followed the slaying of Seumas Mór both his sons also fell, so the day was an evil one for the House of Dalmore.

It was this same Seumas na Pluic who buried his treasure — taken from the Lochaber raiders — first in Garbh Choire Dhé, then (as I have described in Chapter XXXI) under Craobh an Oir, the Tree of Gold, on the slope of Carn Crom, and finally on Carn Geldie beneath a huge stone. In *Legends of the Braes of Mar* (p. 158) this old story is set down, and it is said that the man who will discover the gold will be one Ruaraidh Ruadh (Red Roderick), a MacKenzie on both his father's and his mother's side, one misty evening while searching for a strayed ox.

The MacKenzies of Dalmore left Mar in sad circumstances. Bad times had come to the district after the '15. The Dalmores saw Glen Lui depopulated, themselves involved in a lawsuit with the Auchendryne Farquharsons, and they had no choice but to sell the estate to the Duffs.

As I have mentioned, the Lochaber raiders were a thorn in the flesh of the people of Mar. Dalmore and Invercauld, Inverey and Balmoral were often raided. In the *Records of Invercauld* (p. 232) a commission concerning the trying of certain caterans is quoted :

COMMISSION BY KING CHARLES

In favour of ROBERT FARQUHARSON of Invercauld, for trying certain caterans.   CHARLES R.

CHARLES by the grace of God King of great Brittane, ffrance and Ireland, defender of the faith, To all and sundrie our lieges and subjects whom it affiers and to whom this our seal shall come, greeting.

Forasmikle as Conell McEantach, Conell McEantach mor, Neil McEantach, Angus McEantach, his brother, Angus McGillavrach, Callum McAngus McAlister, and others, all broken men of the clan Cameron came under cloud and silence of night, sorners and oppressors, into the bounds and Lordship of Mar, being lodden in form of war with hagbuts, firelocks, targets and pistolls, reft and away taken the haill insight plenishing, goods and gair being in the town stent house of FQuharson, some of the said tanants having raised the alarm, and John Gordon in Glenbarnes hearing the same and having followed the said limmers a certain space, they turned upon him and so cruellie pursued him of his life that twa arrested and shot ane hagbut at him and hurt him deadly therewith in the arme, whereupon the crie being risen in the countrie, and sundrie gentlemen of the countrie having risen and followed the said limmers, in end they wer apprehended and delivered to Robt. Farquharson of Invercalde, ane of the bailies of the said Lordship who comitted them to ward in our cousin, the Earl of Mar's house, where they presntlie remain, and whereat the exhibition of the said limmers before our justices to underly there triall and asmithment will be verie fasheous and troublesome to the countrie, and hardlie will ane Assyse be gotten to put upon them at all. Therefore we think it more expedient for the ease of the countrey that they shall be tryed at home wher they committed their sorning. For the qth purpose we have made and constitute, and to the tenor herof make and constitute our Provost of Aberdeen . . . Areskine of Pittoddrie and the said Robt. Farquharson our justices in that pairt to the effect underwritten . . . and we ordane our said justices and commissioners to returne ane formale report in wrett under their hands of ther proceedings in this commission between . . . and the day of . . . next coming. Given under our Signe att Halyrudhouse this first day of November 1638.

Legends of the past — the traditions of stirring times when a man's life depended on his skill with claymore and *sgian dubh* and his aim with his gun — are fast disappearing from Mar. There are few persons living who can now point out on the summit of Morrone — that fine hill which rises steeply from Braemar village and which visitors often climb — the ruins of the dwelling of the Cailleach Bheathrach, she whose milch cows were the hinds of the forest. It would seem that this mythical carlin is the same as Cailleach Bheur, the Hag of Winter, who is still spoken of in many parts of the West Highlands and may be commemorated in Beinn na Cailliche in the Isle of Skye. Her hill of Morrone is well worth climbing : the ascent is easy and the view of the Cairngorm summits is particularly fine. Another expedition still easier to make is to the Gallows Tree, a very old pine on the left-hand side of the main road to the Linn of Dee, a couple of hundred yards west of the entrance to Mar lodge. A gravel-pit was excavated beside this tree. The pine, its roots undermined, fell into the pit and died, but it has again been set upright and now, gaunt and lifeless, is held in position by wire stays. On this tree was hanged in the late fifteenth century Lamont of Inverey, the only son of his widowed mother. When the mother saw that her entreaties for the life of her son were of no avail, she cursed the Farquharsons and predicted their downfall in a Gaelic rhyme of which the following English translation is given in *Legends of the Braes of Mar* (p. 55) :

> This tree will flourish high and broad,
>   Green as it grows to-day,
> When from the banks o' bonnie Dee
>   Clan Fhionnlagh's all away.

The author of *Legends* continues (it must be remembered that he wrote in 1876 when the tree was still vigorous) :

And this prophecy is regarded as now accomplished. Any one will show you the dark doom'd pine ; but where are the Monaltries, flowers of chivalry ; the Invereys, indomitable in war ; the Auchendrynes, stout and true ; the Balmorals, glorious as fleeting ; the Allanquoichs, ever worthy ; and the Tullochcoys, heroes to the last ? All and every one of them are gone. Invercauld became extinct in the male line, and this, it is held, sufficiently fulfils the prophecy. Finzean, as not at all concerned in the transactions of that time, may be fairly held not to come within the scope of the malediction.

And now the old tree has itself died, and with its death one of the few links in Mar of a past age are gone.

A short distance west of the Gallows Tree is a favourite river ford of the red deer. Near the middle of the Dee here is a cranny among the rocks on the river-bed that to my own knowledge has cost two stags their lives. I saw one stag trapped by the rising river here and drowned, and heard of another which met the same fate.

West of the Gallows Tree is Inverey, a small village where most of the inhabitants are either active or retired deer-stalkers. Red deer may here be seen feeding close to the public road and are scarcely less timid than the cows of the district. West of Inverey is the celebrated Linn of Dee where the river flows through a narrow gorge. In times of spate the scene here is awe-inspiring, but spates are short-lived, and when the water is low and clear, salmon can be seen swimming in the " pots " or endeavouring to leap the falls. Salmon in plenty do succeed in forcing this barrier, yet it is curious that almost all the fish which are seen to make the leap fail, and fall back into the foaming tumult beneath them.

The main road ends at the Linn, but there is a public road west to the Bynack, and from the Bynack two rights-of-way lead through the hills — one by way of Glen Tilt to Blair Atholl, the other along the course of the Geldie to Geldie lodge, thence over the watershed to the head of Glen Feshie, and down Glen Feshie — a glen which increases in grandeur and beauty as it broadens — to Glen Feshie lodge and to the Spey valley beyond. Near Glen Feshie lodge the path winds close to a ruined chapel, on the wall of which are to be seen the remains of frescoes by the great artist Landseer.

CHAPTER XXXV

THE COUNTRY OF BALMORAL

BALMORAL, the Highland residence of the King and Queen, stands on the south bank of the River Dee some eight miles east of Braemar.

The lands of Balmoral extend southward to the dark massif of Lochnagar, a hill that was sung of by the poet Byron and is a landmark from near and far — from the distant environs of Aberdeen and from the low ground of Angus away to the south. The words written by Queen Victoria in her *Leaves* when, in September 1848, she and Prince Albert looked for the first time on their future Highland home, were : " All seemed to breathe freedom and peace, and to make one forget the world and its sad turmoils ".

In the year 1564 we find that Balmoral, by the charter of Queen Mary to the Earl of Moray, was part of the Earldom of Mar. In an old valuation dated June 17, 1635, it is recorded that " Balmorall pertains to James Gordon of Balmorall ".[1] Before the end of the seventeenth century Balmurell or Balmurrell (as it was then spelled) came into the possession of Charles Farquharson, grandson of the first Farquharson of Inverey and half-brother of John, the Black Colonel — probably through an intermarriage with one of the Gordons of Abergeldie. Charles was succeeded by his nephew, James Farquharson of Balmurrell, who was " out " in 1715 and 1745 and was severely wounded at the battle of Falkirk in January 1746. On his death and the death of his nephew the estates of Balmoral and Inverey then fell to

[1] *Records of Invercauld*, p. 113.

The Dee, near Balmoral, looking west

Alexander Farquharson of Auchendryne, descended from the first Farquharson of Inverey by the latter's second wife, Agnes Ferguson. Although for many years owners of, and resident at Balmoral, the Auchendryne-Inverey Farquharsons always designated themselves as " Farquharson of Inverey ". James Farquharson sold Inverey, Balmoral and Auchendryne to the second Earl of Fife towards the end of the eighteenth century.

Balmoral was later rented by Sir Robert Gordon, on whose death in 1847 the lease was acquired by the Prince Consort, who bought the freehold five years later, and in our respected and revered Royal Family it has since remained.

The magnificent old pine forest of Ballochbuie is part of the Balmoral estate. Here the trees have changed little since the days when wolves roamed the forest and kite and goshawk had their home here. About the year 1907 I was shown by Charles Macintosh, the King's deer-stalker, a nest of the kite in one of these old pines. The kite had then been extinct in that country — as indeed throughout Scotland — for upwards of forty years, yet the nest, built in the fork of the tree, was even then in a good state of repair.

In very early times the MacGregors of Ballochbuie are legendary figures of fleetness and strength in Mar and Balmoral. In the day of Malcolm Ceann Mór, the King decreed that a great race should be run up a steep, rocky hill, Craig Choinnich,[1] and offered as a prize a splendid claymore and a purse of gold. On the level grassy ground between the base of the hill and the River Dee the King, his nobles and the people of the district assembled on the morning of the great day. Conspicuous among the competitors were the two elder sons of MacGregor of Ballochbuie. The eldest had already achieved fame by pursuing a wild boar from Glen Callater, through Glen Cluny, thence across the Cairngorms and back again to the Dee at Balmoral — all in the course of a single day's hunting — but when the runners were scaling

[1] Craig Choinnich is held locally to have been named after Kenneth II of Scotland.

the rocky slopes of the hill the youngest son of Ballochbuie, who for some reason not recorded had been delayed in his coming, hurried to the King and pleaded that he might be allowed to run. The King good-humouredly told him that he was too late, but since the lad continued to plead earnestly with him he at length gave his consent. Here is a vivid account of that historic race (*Legends of the Braes of Mar*, p. 14) :

The race became more and more exciting. Some of the hindermost had indeed given over ; but all those who were not despairingly far behind, put forth thew and sinew and pressed close after each other, ready to take advantage of every accident. The two M'Gregors had indeed left the others considerably behind, but they might both fail ; now was the critical moment. Young M'Gregor sprang forward with unabated energy, passing the others one after one. They were now hanging on the brow of that steep which stands as a wall to a kind of steppe sloping from the east westwards, and from behind which rises the last elevation seen from the castle plain. The youth was now next to his brothers. They had scaled the steep, but, as the last of them was disappearing behind it, his form rose erect on its edge, then bent forward, and plunged in headlong pursuit after them.

Now close behind them, he cried out—

" Halves, brothers, and I'll stop."

" Gain what you can," replied the hero of the boar hunt, " and keep what you can. I will do the same."

The second was too breathless to speak.

The young lad never halted ; even while he spoke he rushed onwards, and the first, who had taken a breathing-space, saw him pass the second, and bound within a few paces of the place where he himself was. They were now engaged on the last steep, and as they re-appeared to the spectators there were two abreast, both equally ardent, both exerting themselves to the utmost.

" Now, brother," said the youngest again, " halves and I will yield."

" No, never," returned he, " keep what you gain."

They felt their heads dizzy, their eyes dim and painful — the hearts beat louder than the sound of their footsteps — every muscle and sinew was tightened to breaking — the foam in their mouths seemed dried into sand — their bleeding lips, when closed glued themselves together — the sweat pearled on their skin in cold drops — and their feet rose and fell mechanically more than otherwise. Now they come in sight of the goal — now the judges encourage them by their cheers — now they seem renewed again in vigour. The youngest put his whole soul forth ; the oldest summoned up all the strength of his tougher frame. Terribly pressed, he was yet determined to gain, and stretched out his arm to impede the motion of his rival, but felt nothing. They had only four yards to go. He looked to his side, expecting to see him on the ground. At that moment the tartans grazed the skin of his knee. His brother had leaped forward below his outstretched arm. Furious, he bounded on and fell, his hand clutching with iron grasp the kilt of his rival. He was yet two yards from the flag and his strength was exhausted. He could not drag the other's prostrate body one step, and now he saw the hindermost fast approaching, encouraged by this incident. Quick as thought, loostening the belt of his kilt, he resigned it to the hero of the boar-hunt.

" I have yielded everything to you hitherto," quoth he, " and I will that also."

He reached the signal with three feeble springs, seized the staff and threw it into the air ; then, falling down buried his face in the fresh heather and damp earth. A loud shout from the plain told that the spectators had seen someone gain. But the victor and his vanquished brothers heard it not. They lay all three, within a few paces of each other, unable to move arm or limb, but they panted so strongly that their bodies seemed to rise of themselves from the ground. When they rose up, their faces were deadly pale, checkered with livid black lines and spots.

The youngest had reached the top in three minutes.

Thus the origin of the Braemar games is in legend traced back to the days of Malcolm of the Big Head.

The hill of Lochnagar, almost 3,800 feet above sea level, which is the highest ground on the Balmoral deer forest, takes its name from a small loch cradled deep in a corrie immediately beneath the hill-top. Professor W. J. Watson in a letter informs me that the old Gaelic name for the loch is Loch na Gàire, Loch of the Outcry, with reference to violent wind.

Of Lochnagar Byron sang :

> Years have rolled on, Lochnagar, since I left you,
> Years must elapse ere I tread you again ;
> Nature of verdure and flowers has bereft you,
> Yet still are you dearer than Albion's plain.
> England ! thy beauties are tame and domestic
> To one who has roved o'er the mountains afar :
> Oh for the crags that are wild and majestic !
> The steep frowning glories of dark Lochnagar !

In the months of summer a strange bird in fine calm weather may sometimes be seen flying fast on scimitar-like wings backwards and forwards over the precipices of Lochnagar. Eagle and ptarmigan are at home here, but to see the swift is unexpected. And yet swifts on still days of June and July often perform aerial evolutions on this hill, more than 3,500 feet above sea level. They are perhaps attracted from the glens by the insects which

rise on the warm air currents, but one observer has put it on
record that he has seen a swift flying over the Lochnagar precipice with a straw in its bill and it is possible that, like the Alpine
swift, the British swift may at times forsake the steeples and

Corgarff Castle

castles which are usually its home and make its nest in some
cranny of a precipice of the high hills.

In the old *Statistical Account* mention is made that

upon the mountains, Loch-na-garaidh and others connected with them,
there is snow to be found all the year round; and their appearance is
extremely romantic and truly alpine. On them are found pellucid stones,
of the nature of precious stones, equally transparent, beautiful in their
colour; and some of them, particularly the emerald, as hard as any oriental

gem of the same kind. The most common are, the brown, of different shades, and next the topaz. There are also beautiful amethysts and emeralds, though these are rare to be met with, particularly the latter ; and what is remarkable, amethysts only are to be found on Loch-na-garaidh ; emeralds, topazes, and the brown on Binn-na baird ; topazes and the brown kinds only on Binn-na-muick-duidh, and the other mountains in these parishes.

Precious stones are at the present day much more difficult to find on the hills than in the late eighteenth century, when that account was written, for many people since then have searched carefully for them, and the remains of primitive, shallow quarries are often observed by the climber. But, so far as is known, one fine Cairngorm stone still awaits re-discovery in a certain wild corrie. Before a great deer drive, at which the late King Edward VII was one of the rifles, a deer-watcher when crossing near the top of a remote corrie of the Cairngorms as he " moved " the stags saw a splendid quartz crystal showing above the ground. He returned for it at his leisure, but was never able to find it, and it has eluded those who have since that time searched for it.

Crathie church, where their Majesties worship when in residence at Balmoral, stands above the main road, near the gates of Balmoral Castle but on the opposite side of the river. The foundation stone of the present building was laid by Queen Victoria in 1893 ; the earlier church is described in the old *Statistical Account* as " in very bad order and too small ".

The pre-Reformation church of Crathie was dedicated to St. Manirus. The tradition of this saint is recorded in the Aberdeen Breviary, where we are told that in consequence of the difficulty caused by diversity of language among the people (this was during the transition stage between Pictish and Gaelic), Manirus, being " excellently skilled " in both languages — he was perhaps a native Pict trained in Ireland — went to labour at Crathie in Braemar.

Among the grave-stones in the churchyard of Crathie is one which reads :

THIS STONE IS ERECTED
IN AFFECTIONATE
AND GRATEFUL REMEMBRANCE OF

JOHN BROWN

THE DEVOTED AND FAITHFUL
PERSONAL ATTENDANT
AND BELOVED FRIEND OF

QUEEN VICTORIA

IN WHOSE SERVICE HE HAS BEEN FOR 34 YEARS
BORN AT CRATHIENAIRD, 8TH DEC. 1826
DIED AT WINDSOR CASTLE, 27TH MARCH 1883

" That friend on whose fidelity you count, that friend given you by circumstances over which you have no control, was God's own gift."

" Well done, good and faithful servant,
Thou hast been faithful over a few things
I will make thee ruler over many things ;
Enter thou into the joy of thy Lord."

CHAPTER XXXVI

FROM time to time it has been suggested that Braemar and Badenoch should be linked by a road, by way of Glen Geldie and Glen Feshie, but so far money has not been found for this project, and I fear that if ever it were successful much of the charm of beautiful Glen Feshie would be lost.

At present the only through road from Braemar to the south is by way of the Cairnwell and renowned Devil's Elbow into Glen Shee (Gleann Sìth, the Fairy Glen). From Glen Shee the traveller can either continue his journey south by way of Blairgowrie and Perth, or else can branch away to the right, by way of Kirkmichael, and drop down to Pitlochry, whence he may continue the south journey by way of the River Tay to Dunkeld with its cathedral and to Perth, where the tides of the eastern sea bank up the river. It is a lonely road (and in the years before the Great War of 1914–1918 was a narrow one) from Braemar over the Cairnwell and down Glen Shee. The road after leaving Braemar traverses Glen Cluny and at the Cairnwell reaches the watershed between the counties of Aberdeen and Perth : here the road level is 2,200 feet above the sea. No other main road in Scotland reaches this altitude, although the narrow road from Loch Carron to Applecross and the road from Tomintoul to Cockbridge near the headwaters of the Don are both over 2,000 feet at their summits. I have seen ptarmigan at the roadside at the Cairnwell, and I once saw a pair of ptarmigan dozing almost on the road at the watershed between Applecross and Loch Carron, where I have no doubt that they are frequently seen, yet I do not think that any other Highland road except these two lesser roads and the Cairnwell highway reaches the haunts of this bird of the high hills.

At the Cairnwell, in earlier times always spoken of as the Cairn*wall*, the traveller breathes the air of the heights and may well pause in his journey to admire the view. Ahead of him, bearing rather to the left (as he journeys south), is the great hill Glas Maol, which carries a horse-shoe-shaped snow-wreath until well on in the summer.

Above the Cairnwell, but invisible from the road, is Loch Bhrotachan, Loch of Fattening, perhaps named from the fat trout which are found in it. At no great distance from the road, but shut in by hills, are Loch Callater, which the old *Statistical Account* mentions as being celebrated because of its small salmon of about eight pounds weight, and the alpine Loch Kander (Ceanndobhar or High Water).

The battle of the Cairnwell was fought in the year 1644. A body of men from Argyll, known as the Cleansers, ravaged the Highlands of Aberdeenshire that summer, and one night " lifted all the cattle from Glen Shee and Glen Isla ". The men of these glens, discovering their loss, made ready to attack the enemy, and sent a message over the hills to MacKenzie of Dalmore, asking his help. In this fight a certain Braemar worthy known as the Cam Ruadh performed prodigies of valour and skill, shooting the Cleansers one after the other with his arrows with unerring aim and turning what looked like a defeat into a victory. But the Cam Ruadh towards the end of the fight was hit in the posterior by an arrow, and as he returned to Braemar the *cailleachs* at the doors of their houses called out in dismay " Chaim Ruaidh, Chaim Ruaidh ! tha saighead na do thòine ! " (" Cam Ruadh, Cam Ruadh, there is an arrow in your backside ! ") " Tha fios agam fhéin air sin ! " (" I myself know that ! ") was the reply. The story is that when the Cam reached home his wife pulled out the arrow by standing on his back, one foot on either side of the arrow, and exerting all her strength ; and that when the arrow had been removed the Cam celebrated the occasion by eating a large supper of venison !

Another legend of the Cairnwell is the killing of Captain Millar, the commander of the troops stationed in Braemar Castle. A strong man of Mar, known as Domhnall Dubh an t-Ephiteach, who the Braemar garrison had long endeavoured to capture — he on one occasion stripped the sergeant of his clothing and sent him back to the castle without a stitch of covering on him, his hands tied behind his back and his clothes tied round his neck in a bundle — received word that Captain Millar and his wife were to cross the pass. Black Donald awaited his deadly enemy and shot and killed him, then accompanied his widow over the Cairnwell, and according to the legend made himself so agreeable to the lady that before they had reached Glen Shee she asked him to marry her ! The cairn of stones marking where Muckle Millar — as he was called because of his size and strength — fell used to be pointed out, but I doubt whether any person now alive knows where it is.

This event must have been after the time when another Donald, a leading man in Lochaber, came east to raid the cattle of Glen Shee but on his way back, when camping in thick mist, was overtaken and killed by the Glen Shee men in Coire Sìth, the Fairy Corrie.

An interesting account of the old church in Glen Shee, taken, it is said, from an old number of *Chambers's Journal*, may be worth quoting. The date of the *Journal* is not mentioned but presumably is at least eighty to one hundred years ago.

About 30 years ago, I first visited the Spital of Glenshee, and at that time I had never seen a greater curiosity than the place of worship there. It is a chapel of ease belonging to a parish called Kirkmichael, is built with stone and lime, and the roof is flagged with slate. The door was locked, but both the windows were wide open, without either glass or frame so that one stepped as easily in at the windows as at the door. There were no seats, but here and there a big stone placed, and as things of great luxury, there were two or three sticks laid from one of these to another. The floor was literally paved with human bones, and I saw that the dogs had gnawed the ends of many of them by way of amusing themselves in the time of worship. There were also hundreds of human teeth, while in the north-west corner of the Chapel there was an open grave, which had stood so for nearly three months. It had been made in the preceding December for a young man, who had died in the braes of Angus, but it came on such a terrible storm that they could not bring the corpse, so they buried him where he was, and left this grave standing ready for the next. When the service was over, the minister gathered the collection for the poor on the green, in crown of his hat, and neither men nor women thought of dispersing, but stood in clubs about the Chapel, conversing, some of them for upwards of an hour. I have seen many people who appeared to pay more attention to the service, but I never saw any who appeared to enjoy the crack after sermon so much.

After the motorist or cyclist — for few in these days cross the Cairnwell from Braemar to Glen Shee on foot — has reached the watershed he descends abruptly into Glen Beag (the Small Glen) by way of a steep and sharp zigzag known as the Devil's Elbow. The gradient has now been eased and the corners made less abrupt, but in the early days of motoring I remember that one's car had to be pulling well in order to climb the Devil's Elbow from the south. There was a kindly stalker, a friend of mine, who lived at Rhedorrach about two miles down the glen, and he sometimes used to accompany me to the Elbow, if my car was not running too well. At the Devil's Elbow he used to jump out and push me up the steepest parts of the gradient, over a surface that in those days was rough and loose. I have memories of continuing the ascent, not daring to stop, and of looking back and seeing my friend standing exhausted but triumphant, on the road, waving farewell.

In those days it was usual for the Cairnwell to be considered impassable for wheeled traffic during the winter months. The road used to be drifted up, and no attempt made to open it until spring, or even early summer in stormy years. In my boyhood I was much impressed by a photograph showing a gang of men digging through the great snowdrifts and opening the road, and the date on the photograph was about the middle of May. Things are very different now and motorists cross the Cairnwell throughout the year, except for short periods when the road has been drifted up and the roadmen have not had time to clear a passage.

In an old MS. of date *circa* 1683 (MacFarlane's *Geographical Collection*, vol. ii, p. 36) mention is made of the people of Glen Isla (Glenyla) going in summer to

the far-distant Glens which border upon Brae Mar and there live grassing their cattle in litle houses which they build upon ther coming and throwes doun when they come away called sheels, their dyet is only milk and whey and a very little meall and what vennison or wyld foull they can apprehend.

The account goes on to say that " in Glenshie the Minister always preaches in the afternoon in the Irish toungue ". One might indeed have imagined that so far back as this date nothing but Gaelic or, as it was always called, " Irish " would have been spoken in Glen Shee, but the inference from this MS. account is that the morning service was conducted in English.

Where Glen Beag joins Glen Shee is seen the Spital [1] of Glen Shee where motorists often break their journey, both north and south. The country now becomes more fertile, and wooded slopes, and fields of grass and corn, alternate with heathery hillsides.

About eight miles south of the Spital of Glen Shee the road to Kirkmichael branches away to the west, and then, climbing Strath Ardle, crosses a stretch of wild moorland country before descending abruptly to Moulin and Pitlochry.

[1] From the Gaelic Spideal, a hostel.

HINTS ON GAELIC PRONUNCIATION

By Professor W. J. WATSON

THE Gaelic system of spelling has the great merit of being consistent and fairly complete. It has behind it a continuous tradition of over twelve hundred years. Differing greatly from English, it is not hard to master, and once mastered — a matter of a dozen lessons or fewer — it will prove a reliable guide. The hints here given are incomplete, and in any case printed directions require to be supplemented by the living voice.

Stress.—The stress, which is vigorous, falls uniformly on the first syllable. This applies both to uncompounded words and to " strict " compounds, in which the qualifying term comes first ; *e.g.* Conghlais, " hound-stream ". " Loose " compounds, where the qualifying part follows the " generic " term, are stressed on the second part, which should be separated by a hyphen ; *e.g.* Port-righeadh, Portree. One consequence of the vigorous stress is shortening of a long vowel in the unstressed part of a compound ; *e.g.* àird, a cape, with long *a* ; but Dubhaird, " black cape ", with *a* shortened. Another is the extremely light, indefinite quality of final vowels ; *e.g.* coire, a cauldron, corrie, pronounced *kor^e* — two syllables, however.

The letters.—Vowels are sounded much as in Latin (reformed pronunciation) and in German : *i* is always as in Germ. *bin*, Lat. *si* ; (not as in Eng. *sin*) ; *a* stressed is as in Germ. *Bach*, Lat. *an* ; but unstressed *a* is dulled, somewhat like Eng. *u* in *burn* — except when originally long ; *e.g.* clachan, stones, has first *a* open, the second dull ; but clachan, a stone cell, has both vowels open (the *-an* being originally long).

Broad vowels are *a, o, u* ; *slender* vowels are *e, i.* Long vowels are *long* ; they bear, or should bear, an accent.

Some diphthongs, etc.—*ia* : grian, sun : gr(*eea*)n. *ua* : gual, coal : g(*ooa*)l ; both with *a* open. *ao* : gaoth, wind : one vowel sound, like Fr. *cœur*. *aoi* : as *ao* followed by Lat.-Germ. *i*. *eo*, short ; *eò*, long : usually palatalised, like Eng. y*ŏ*, y*ō*. *eoi* : always long, as long *eo* followed by Lat.-Germ. *i*. *eu, é* : one long vowel sound, as in Fr. *dé*. But *è* is as in Eng. *where* lengthened.

Of the consonants, *b, f, m, p* have one uniform sound, except that

413

after a vowel *b* sounds like Eng. *p*, while after a vowel *p* is preceded by a " puff " (somewhat like Eng. *h*) : so, too, are *c* and *t*. The others have two sounds, according as they are in contact with (*a*) a broad vowel, (*b*) a slender vowel.

Broad	*Slender*
c, always hard, as in *cat*.	*c*, always hard, as in *keep*.
g, always hard, as in *got*.	*g*, always hard, as in *get*.
d, no Eng. equivalent ; tip of tongue projects well beyond the upper teeth.	*d*, usually like Eng. *j* in *jewel*.
t, no Eng. equivalent ; tip of tongue pressed firmly against upper teeth.	*t*, like Eng. *tch* in *ditch*.
n is nasal.	*n*, nasal, and usually like Eng. *n* in *knew* ; *i.e.* palatalised.
l, no equivalent Eng. sound.	*l*, like Eng. *l* in *billion* ; *i.e.* palatalised.
s, much as Eng.	*s*, as Eng. *sh*.'
r, no Eng. equivalent.	*r*, much as in Eng. *rest*.

" Aspiration " resulted from a weakening of the consonantal sound when the consonant was originally flanked by vowels ; in Sc. Gaelic it is indicated by *h* after the consonant, except *l*, *n*, *r*.

Broad	*Slender*
ch, as in Germ. *Bach* ; Scots *teuch*. Never as in Eng.	*ch*, as in Germ. *ich* ; Scots *laich*. Never as in Eng.
gh, *dh*, no Eng. equivalent. Like *g* of Germ. *Tag* (*g* soft).	*gh*, *dh*, like Eng. *y* in *yea*, *yet*. Silent after slender vowel.
sh, *th*, as Eng. *h*.	*sh*, *th*, as Eng. *h*.
fh is silent, except in fhuair, " got ", fhathast, " yet ", when it is like Eng. *h*.	*fh*, silent except in fhéin, " self " — sounded as *h*.
bh, *mh*, as Eng. *v* ; *mh* nasal.	*bh*, *mh*, as when broad.
l, somewhat like Eng. *l* in *hull*.	*l*, much as in Eng. *let*, *MacLeod*.
r, much as in Eng. *rash*.	*r*, much as in Eng.

LIST OF GAELIC PLACE-NAMES

415

Beinn Bhàn, Light-coloured Hill, 33
 Bhreac, Speckled Hill, 21
 Bhrodain, 325
 Dhubh, Black Hill, 38
 Lididh, 73
 Mheadhon, Middle Hill, 305
Ben Dòrain, Hill of the Streamlet, 67
 Ime, Butter Hill, 33
 Lui, Calves' Hill, 24
 Mac Dhui, MacDuff's Hill, 281
 More, Big Hill, 68
 Vrackie, Speckled Hill, 152
 Wyvis, High Hill, 358
Blaan Buadach Bretan, Triumphant Blaan of the Britons, 75
Bod an Diabhail, Devil's male organ, 314
Bodach Làmh-dhearg, Red-handed Old Man, 302
Bohuntine, Confluence-town, 180
Boleskine, Town of the Withies, 185
Bonskeid—Bun a sgeoid, Foot of the Corner (of the field), 140
Bovain, 71
Braemar, Uplands of Mar, 384
Brae Lochaber, High Ground of Lochaber, 168
Braeriach, Brindled Hill, 315
Bràghaid Alban, Brae of Alba, 86
Briagach, 182
Bridge of Orchy, old form Glen Urchy, 97
Bynack Mór, 304

Cairngorm, Azure Cairn, 299
Cairntoul, Barn-hill, 352
Cairnwell, formerly Cairnwall, 408
Caisteal a' Chuilein Chursta, Castle of the Cursed Whelp, 154
Cam Ruadh, 409
Caochan na Fala, Streamlet of Blood, 158
Càrie, trap on river or burn for catching fish, 93
Carie Corrie, 93
Carn a' Mhaim, Hill of the Pass, 314
 an Duine Ghointe, Cairn of the Wounded Man, 105
 Elrick, Hill of the Deer-defile, 309

Caslorg Pheallaidh, Foot-mark of Peallaidh, 105
Ceiteirein, Fiends, 14
Ceòl Mór, Big Music, 98
Cill Choinnich, St. Kenneth's Church, 170
 Choireil, St. Cyril's Church, 168
 Mo-Charmaig, Church of my St. Cormac, 96
Cinn Ghiubhsaich, Head of the Fir Wood, 204
Ciste Mhearad, Margaret's Chest, 368
Clach a' Chléirich, Stone of the Priest, 348
 an t-Sandis, Stone of the Whisper, 201
 Bhuaidh, Stone of Virtue, 106
 Dhion, Shelter Stone, 333
 na Gruagaich, Stone of the Gruagach (Fairy), 294
 nam Mèirleach, Robbers' Stone, 242
 nan Ceann, Stone of the Heads, 157
 nan Tàillear, Tailors' Stone, 310
Clachan Aoraidh, The Stones of Worship, 152
Clachnacuddin, Stone of the Tubs, 237
Clais Fhearnaig, Alder Hollow, 345
Coille Bhrochain, Wood of Gruel, 140
Coire an t-Saighdeir, Soldier's Corrie, 352
 Cas, Steep Corrie, 327
 Dhondail, Stirk-dale Corrie, 362
 Domhainn, Deep Corrie, 336
 Éiteachan, 342
 Grogan, Grogan's Corrie, Grogan being probably some man, 39
 nan Uruisgean, Corrie of the Uruisks, 14
 Odhar, Dun-coloured Corrie, 304
 Thearlaich, Charles's Corrie, 223
Coit Ghartain, Boat of Garten, 276
Comgan, 77
Conglais, *River*, Dog Stream, 99
Corrieyaireag, Short Corrie, 184

Innis mo Cholmaig, Isle of my
Colmoc, 3
nan Con, Isle of the Dogs, 6
Invernahavon, Mouth of the River,
194
Iona, believed to have originated
from the misreading of the
word *Ioua*, 62

Kenmore, Great Head, 86
Kilblain, St. Blain's Church, 285
Kinloch Rannoch, Head of Loch
Rannoch, 155

Lag nan Cuimeanach, Hollow of the
Cummings, 295
Lagan a' Bhainne, Hollow of the
Milk, 190
a' Chatha, Hollow of the Battle,
105
Làirig Ghrù, Doubtful, 176
Laoigh, Calf's Pass, 300
Leac nan Cuarain, Flat Rock of the
Sandals, 106
Leannan Sith, Fairy Lover, 211
Lecht, *River*, Hillside, 281
Ledard, Hillside of the Point, 22
Leny, *River*, 73
Leum na Féinne, Leap of the Fin-
galians, 208
Linnhe Fhaolain, St. Fillan's Pool,
78
Loch a' Bhealaich Bheithe, Loch of
the Birch-pass, 166
a' Chait, Loch of the Cat, 95
an Stuirteag, Loch of the Black-
headed Gull, 377
an t-Seilich, Loch of the Willow,
211
Arcleid, Loch of the Difficult
Slope, 27
Bhrotachan, Loch of Fattening,
409
Callater, Hard Water, 409
Duntelchaig, Loch of the Snail-
fort, 255
Eireachd, Loch of the Assembly,
161
Eiseord, 77
Gamhna, Stirk-loch, 290

Loch Iubhair, Loch of the Yew Tree,
78
Kander, White-water Loch, 409
Laidon—Loch nan Lodan, Loch
of the Pools, 70
Lùbnaig—Loch Lubanach, the
Winding Loch (*Lùb*, a bend), 71
Maragan, The Mother Loch, 68
Morar, Big-water Loch, 234
nan Uamh, Loch of the Caves, 145
Pityoulish, 295
Tréig, possibly Loch of Death,
171
Vennachar, Horned Loch, 73
Vrodin, see Legend, 209
Lochan a' Bhainne, Tarn of the
Milk, 301
mhic a' Ghille Chaoil, Loch of the
Son of the Thin Lad, 292
na Bi, Loch of the Pitch-pine, 70
na Mnà, Woman's Loch, 48
nan Cnapan, Loch of the Knolls,
374
Uaine, Green Loch, 304
Lochnagar, Loch of the Outcry, 404
Logierait, 131
Lùban, small loop ; a bow, 101
Lynwilg—Lainn Bhuilg, Field of the
Bag or Bulge, 197

Mam Suim, Rounded Hill of the
Soum—a *soum* was the grazing
of five sheep, 304
Mealfourvonie, Hill of Cold Moor,
255
Meur na Banaraiche, Dairymaid's
Finger, 336
Mòine Bhealaidh, Moss of Broom,
346
Monadh Liath, Grey Hill Range, 193
Morrone, Big Nose, 397
Mórthulaich, Great Ridgy Hill, 302
Moulin—Maoilinn, Brae, Round
Hillock, 92
Moy, Plain (dative), 265
Muckerach, Place of Pigs, 278
Mur-Bhalg, Sea Bag or Bay, 43

Oronsay, an island joined at low
tide to the mainland, 90

INDEX

THE END